The Complexity of Conversion

Studies in Ancient Religion and Culture

Series Editors:

Philip L. Tite, University of Washington

Michael Ng, Seattle University

Studies in Ancient Religion and Culture (SARC) is concerned with religious and cultural aspects of the ancient world, with a special emphasis on studies that utilize social scientific methods of analysis. By "ancient world," the series is not limited to Greco-Roman and ancient Near Eastern cultures, though that is the primary regional focus. The underlying presupposition is that the study of religion in antiquity needs to be located within cultural and social analysis, situating religious traditions within the broader cultural and geopolitical dynamics within which those traditions are located.

This series also encourages cross-disciplinary research in the study of the ancient world. Due to the historical development of various academic disciplines, there has arisen a set of largely isolated and competing fields of study of the ancient world. Often this fragmentation in academia results in outdated or caricatured scholarly products when one discipline does use research from another discipline. A key goal of this series is to help facilitate greater cross- and inter-disciplinary work, bringing together those who study ancient history (especially social history), archaeology (of various methods and geographic focuses, as well as theorists in archaeology), ancient philosophy, biblical studies, early patristics/church history, Second Temple and formative Judaism, and Greek and Roman classics, as well as philologists.

Given the focus on the social and cultural context within which religion functions, the series also publishes studies which explore the various social locations in which real people in antiquity practiced or interacted with their religious traditions. Examples include the domestic cult, food production and consumption, temple worship, funerary practices/monuments, development of social networks, military cult, and ancient medicine.

Finally, the series encourages a broader application of theoretical and methodological tools to the study of the ancient world. While the main perspective is social-scientific (understood broadly), specific analyses from the reservoir of critical theory, narrative theories, economic theory, bio-archaeology, gender analysis, anthropology of religion, and cognitive theory are welcome.

The Complexity of Conversion

Intersectional Perspectives on Religious Change in
Antiquity and Beyond

Edited by
Valérie Nicolet and Marianne Bjelland Kartzow

SHEFFIELD UK   BRISTOL CT

Published by Equinox Publishing Ltd.

UK: Office 415, The Workstation, 15 Paternoster Row, Sheffield, South Yorkshire S1 2BX

USA: ISD, 70 Enterprise Drive, Bristol, CT 06010

www.equinoxpub.com

First published 2021

© Valérie Nicolet, Marianne Bjelland Kartzow and contributors 2021

All rights reserved. No part of this publication may be reproduced or transmitted in any form or by any means, electronic or mechanical, including photocopying, recording or any information storage or retrieval system, without prior permission in writing from the publishers.

British Library Cataloguing-in-Publication Data

A catalogue record for this book is available from the British Library.

ISBN-13   978 1 78179 572 9   (hardback)   978 1 78179 573 6   (paperback)
          978 1 78179 998 7   (ePDF)

Library of Congress Cataloging-in-Publication Data

Names: Nicolet, Valérie, editor. | Kartzow, Marianne Bjelland, 1971- editor.
Title: The complexity of conversion : intersectional perspectives on religious change in antiquity and beyond / edited by Valérie Nicolet and Marianne Bjelland Kartzow.
Description: Sheffield, UK ; Bristol, CT : Equinox Publishing Ltd, 2021. | Series: Studies in ancient religion and culture | Includes bibliographical references and index. | Summary: "The book addresses the complexity of conversion, using a range of cases, texts and theories, and initiates a dialogue between ancient sources and present concepts or practices. Close readings of ancient texts play a central role in the project. Yet, the book also considers how sacred texts and their receptions have influenced the way we generally think about conversion as religious change"-- Provided by publisher.
Identifiers: LCCN 2020005107 (print) | LCCN 2020005108 (ebook) | ISBN 9781781795729 (hardback) | ISBN 9781781795736 (paperback) | ISBN 9781781799987 (epdf)
Subjects: LCSH: Conversion--Comparative studies. | Religions--Relations.
Classification: LCC BL639 .C65 2020 (print) | LCC BL639 (ebook) | DDC 204.2--dc23
LC record available at https://lccn.loc.gov/2020005107
LC ebook record available at https://lccn.loc.gov/2020005108

Typeset by ISB Typesetting, Sheffield, UK

Contents

1. What Is So Complex about "Conversion"?   1
   Marianne Bjelland Kartzow and Valérie Nicolet

2. Shedding Religious Skin:
   An Intersectional Analysis of the Claim That Male
   Circumcision Limits Religious Freedom   21
   Karin B. Neutel

3. Complex Interactions:
   Conversion and Interreligious Dialogue in the Norwegian Context   40
   Anne Hege Grung

4. Conversion in Mystery Religions?
   Theory Meets Mysteries and Conversion   59
   Gerhard van den Heever

5. "Leap, ye lame, for joy":
   The Dynamics of Disability in Conversion   99
   Anna Rebecca Solevåg

6. Reading a Complex Identity in Conversion:
   Interpretations of the Ethiopian Eunuch   123
   Minna Heimola

7. Creating a New Sex: Women Bodies in Conversion   141
   Valérie Nicolet

8. Conversion in/to the Wilderness:
   The Case of the Egyptian Slave Girl Hagar in
   Early Christian and Jewish Texts   162
   Marianne Bjelland Kartzow

9. The Complexity of Aseneth's Transformation   185
   Kirsten Marie Hartvigsen

10. Leaving the Traditions of the Fathers:
    Perspectives on Conversion from a Christianity
    That Did Not Survive   212
    Kristine Toft Rosland

11. Spatial Conversion and Christian Identity in Late Antiquity 235
    Anna Lampadaridi

12. Concluding Remarks 247
    Valérie Nicolet

    Index of References 256
    Index of Modern Authors 258
    Index of Subjects 260

Chapter One

What Is So Complex about "Conversion"?

Marianne Bjelland Kartzow and Valérie Nicolet

[R]eligious conversion entails not merely a change of worldview or ethos, but a change in lifeworld.

Do men and women experience conversion differently?

Conversion occurs in all directions ... [and] is never a neutral act.[1]

Conversion is a contested religious, political, and personal phenomenon. There is more at stake than simply a private question concerning which god, or gods, one wants to recognize and serve. Furthermore, the meaning of conversion changes across time and place. Conversion requires embodiment of new social and religious practices, but also a total change of orientation, a change of worldview, a change in lifeworld. Yet many people are, and were, not in control of their own lives. They find, and found, themselves in a position where they do not have the agency to control their loyalty to a certain religious system. What does conversion mean for them?

This book addresses the complexity of conversion and uses a range of cases, primary sources, and theories, to do so. It also initiates a dialogue between ancient sources and current concepts or practices. The essays in this volume are interested in interdisciplinary, cross-cultural, and cross-historical perspectives. Early Christian and Jewish texts play a central role in this volume, but the volume also discusses how sacred texts and their reception influence the way we think, more broadly, about conversion as religious change.

In many European countries today, the debate on legitimate immigrants and asylum-seekers highlights the complex issues surrounding conversion.[2] An ongoing debate in Norway may serve as an illustration: asylum seekers upon converting to Christianity argue they would now face life-threatening sanctions on account of their new religion, if they were forced to return to

---

1. Eliza F. Kent, "Feminist Approaches to the Study of Religious Conversion," in Lewis R. Rambo and Charles E. Farhadian, eds., *The Oxford Handbook of Religious Conversion* (Oxford: Oxford University Press, 2014), 297–326, here 318–9.

2. See the Introduction to Lewis R. Rambo and Charles E. Farhadian, eds., *The Oxford Handbook of Religious Conversion* (Oxford: Oxford University Press, 2014).

their countries of origin.[3] Public officials, including juridical experts, administration employees, and immigrant authorities, questioned the authenticity and legitimacy of their conversion. Could they prove they were Christians? Did they know central texts of the Bible or core Christian doctrines? Was their conversion sincere or merely an excuse to allow them to stay in the country?[4] The bishops within the Protestant (Lutheran) church in Norway reacted against this scrutinizing of conversion, arguing that baptism constitutes entrance into Christianity. When someone is baptized, he or she becomes a fully accepted member of the Church, regardless of knowledge, way of life, or competence in the Bible. Conversion cannot be precisely measured.[5] The immigration authorities should rather consult bishops and priests, since they are themselves experts when it comes to conversion to Christianity and how it is recognized.[6] This position challenges the immigration procedure, implying that religious leaders could have a veto right in asylum cases. It also exemplifies that conversion can be debated and discussed. Its essence does not simply exist for all to see.

What seems to be at stake in this case is how one decides whether a conversion is real or authentic. Is conversion an inner or outer phenomenon? Furthermore, how do official workers of the government or bishops formulate their ideas about proper conversion? Where do these ideas come from? Who is competent to judge these issues? When religious and political discourses intersect, one needs to decide which perspectives and reasons will be privileged. This is not a new challenge. In relationship with this collection of essays, one of the questions discussed has to do with what we mean by "conversion."

According to Eliza F. Kent in *The Oxford Handbook of Religious Conversion*, entire arenas of social life are transformed by the process of conversion.[7] Whereas she in her article focuses on the impact of gender on conversion using feminist theory, many of the articles in this volume employ intersectional theory, and see gender as one of the categories intersecting with others, such as sexuality, class, age, and race. When reading ancient

---

3. Debate (in Norwegian) reflected in "Une: Strengere asylpraksis ga flere kristne," *Aftenposten* 2013. "Ber prester sjekke at troen er ekte," *Dagen* 10 Feb 2016. "Dåp av asylsøkere," *Norges Kristne Råd* 2016.

4. For related questions in a different context, see David W. Kling, "Conversion to Christianity," in Rambo and Farhadian eds., *Oxford Handbook of Religious Conversion*, 602–3.

5. Janet E. Spittler, "Conversion. I. New Testament. II. Greco-Roman Antiquity," 708–12, here 708–9, in Constance Furey, et al., eds., *Encyclopedia of the Bible and Its Reception Online* (Berlin: De Gruyter, 2012).

6. "Ber prester sjekke at troen er ekte."

7. Kent, "Feminist Approaches."

texts, or looking at the texts' reception, the authors of the volume are not only asking if men and women experience conversion differently, but they are also questioning how ethnicity, social status, or disability, for example, may have influenced individual experiences of conversion. Accordingly, the aim of the volume is to make our notion and understanding of conversion more complex.

Meaning and Impact of Conversion

How is the kind of conversion enmeshed with rights for asylum seekers in contemporary societies related (if at all) with characters encountered in ancient literature? Take, for example, the female protagonist in the ancient novel *Joseph and Aseneth*. She must leave her traditional gods behind to be considered a suitable wife for the (Jewish) patriarch, Joseph. Or slaves and foreigners in ancient Jewish and Christian traditions, who convert or are converted because their master (or their king) converts. What about the prototype of conversion symbolized by the figure of Paul or the Ethiopian eunuch encountered in the book of Acts? Or children and disabled characters in the New Testament? Did they all convert, and if they did, what did their conversion mean? Or young males who want to become better men by changing their way of life and thus convert to Islam?[8] Does conversion always mean the same thing?

The obvious answer is no. This volume attempts to develop and explain this obvious answer, since conversion does not always mean the same thing; yet remains a concept that can cover various phenomena that share similarities. Some articles talk about the *complexity of conversion*, some put "conversion" in quotation marks, others use different terms (like religious hybridity, double belonging) in the hope of being more critical, more nuanced, and more accurate. Evidently, conversion is a term difficult to use, and yet, it is also difficult *not* to use it. Recently, there have been attempts to completely reject the term. We think, though, that a term difficult to use can also help uncover multiple meanings and usages, particularly if one employs it as an analytical tool that delineates an interdisciplinary field, describing similar phenomena with common patterns. Despite its vagueness, the term might highlight common features behind different phenomena. At the same time, the authors are intent on not erasing these differences,

---

8. Michael E. Pregill, "Conversion. V. Islam," in Constance Furey, et al., eds., *Encyclopedia of the Bible and Its Reception Online*, 732–8. For this specific case, see Frode Kinserdal, "Den maskuline konversjonsfortelling: En studie av unge norske menn som har konvertert til Islam" (Det teologiske Menignhetsfakultet, 2010).

Definitions, Rejections, and Clarifications: Making Conversion More Complex

Rejecting the term entirely, Paula Fredriksen proposes a "speedy retirement" for four concepts that routinely appear in scholarship concerned with the centuries marking the beginnings of what would later be known as Christianity. Among them, she places "conversion."[9] According to her, there is a danger in embracing "modern methodologies," such as recent studies of religious conversion, to reconstruct how ancient figures negotiate religious difference and change. It is dangerous because these methods make it too easy and perhaps even desirable to project our own thoughts and values onto ancient people.[10] If conversion is defined as "a deliberate turning … which implies that a great change is involved, that the old was wrong and the new is right" or if a convert is defined as someone "who goes from A to B," this understanding does not adequately describe Paul's orientation toward Jesus, for instance, since Paul was and remained a Jew even after his encounter with Christ. Furthermore, it does not aptly describe the attraction of various individuals to Judaism, at least in the first century.[11] Fredriksen rightly shows the dangers of applying modern categories to the people one encounters in ancient texts, but her approach also indicates the need for a more complex theoretical understanding of conversion. Even for modernity, it is not necessary, for example, to accept the definition of conversion as characterized by "a deliberate turning, a before and an after, a wrong and a right" (see Fredriksen, above). This volume aims to broaden the definition, make it more complex, in a dialogue between modern and ancient worlds, in order to clarify the understanding of both ancient and modern notions of conversion.

In a similar effort aiming to explain conversion, Oxford Press, in 2014, released a volume entitled *The Oxford Handbook of Religious Conversion.*[12] This anthology

---

9. Paula Fredriksen, "Madatory Retirement: Ideas in the Study of Christian Origins Whose Time Has Come to Go," *Studies in Religion* 35.2 (2006): 231–46. These terms, including also nationalism, *religio licita* and monotheism, "obscure more than they clarify" (144).

10. Fredriksen, "Mandatory Retirement," 233, 244.

11. Fredriksen, "Mandatory Retirement," 232–3. She also discusses Paul up and against the "conversion" of Augustine and Luther, see p. 233.

12. Rambo and Farhadian, eds., *Oxford Handbook of Religious Conversion.*

offers a comprehensive exploration of the dynamics of religious conversion, which for centuries has profoundly shaped societies, cultures, and individuals throughout the world. Scholars from a wide array of religions and disciplines interpret both the varieties of conversion experiences and the processes that inform this personal and communal phenomenon. (1)

The volume examines the experiences of individuals and communities who switch religions, but it also considers the cases of those who experience an intensification of their religion of origin, and of those who encounter new religions through colonial intrusion, missionary work, and/or charismatic and revitalization movements. The handbook includes 32 essays and provides overviews of the history of specific religions. It also reflects on studying conversion as an academic discipline, presenting a range of methods and theories deployed in understanding conversion. It finally offers an insight into various forms of de-conversion. As we will see, several themes in the handbook are directly relevant for the analysis found in the present collection of articles: the anthropology or sociology of conversion; the influence of migration on the understanding of conversion; feminist approaches to the study of conversion; legal and political issues surrounding religious conversion; and conversion to Judaism/Christianity/Islam in theological and historical perspectives.

How does the present collection of essays situate itself in this scholarly landscape? Is it still possible to use "conversion" as a productive analytical category or should we leave it behind? On the one hand, "conversion" is too anachronistic and imprecise to be helpful and should be replaced with more nuanced vocabulary. On the other hand, the term still works to help interpreters categorize and study a phenomenon comparatively, even if the phenomenon itself remains difficult to define. What does the volume itself contribute to the construction of the theme "conversion"? When reviewing another similar collection of essays, Mieke Bal rightly observes that one assumption informing the literary genre of the thematic collection of essays is the following: "a theme is a semantic unit, and the recurrence of such a theme can be measured only if one knows with certainty what the theme is."[13] The theme is thus somewhat constructed both by the essays themselves, who offer a particular definition of the theme, and by the authors of the essay who, in turn, bring their own assumptions of what the theme means for them while composing their essays. There is thus no essence of "conversion" that could be found outside of what the essays and their authors themselves construct as they go along.

What can one say then of a collection of essays preoccupied with "complicating conversion," and thus rather outspoken in its desire to deconstruct

---

13. Mieke Bal, "Tricky Thematics," *Semeia* 42 (1988): 133–55, here 133.

what conversion is, and reconstruct it in a more complex, varied, and critical manner? The aim of the essays is precisely to not take the theme of conversion at face value. Rather, the authors are trying to bring to light the "often unconscious assumptions which are taken to be 'natural' certainties"[14] when it comes to conversion. They are delineating the norms and boundaries implied in "conversion," bringing them to the fore and re-inscribing them, while keeping in mind, in particular, the aspects of gender, race, ethnicity, class, and age. There are many "ideological biases" connected to the theme of conversion, and part of the project is to uncover them, and make them apparent. Unconsciously, we all know, or think we know, what one means when one talks about conversion, or, to put it differently, we think we know what is required to qualify something as conversion. Part of the work will be to make these unconscious assumptions explicit, and then to challenge them, and propose different models of conversions.

According to Kling, "[o]ne of the most important and also contentious issues in conversion studies is to define the term 'conversion' itself."[15] All essays in this volume are in one way or the other addressing this challenge, and demonstrate that "[c]onversion in not only a word but a concept, a tool of analysis. It is not only a name but a phenomenon employed by scholars to describe a universal change."[16] This volume meets this challenge in the following way: the authors are hesitant to give one clear cut and static definition of conversion, and rather look for content and cases. Conversion is studied through parameters such as inner/outer phenomenon, individual/collective, and depending whether conversion is by will or by force, although these parameters are seen more as continuums or spectrums than dichotomies. In the following, we are reviewing some suggested models for conceptualizing conversion.

Conceptualizing Conversion

Traditional Understandings of Conversion

When one talks about conversion today, especially in a Christian context, Paul and Augustine are probably the two characters[17] that come most readily

---

14. Bal, "Tricky Thematics," 133.
15. Kling, "Conversion to Christianity," 599. More on definitions and terminology, see Spittler, "Conversion," 708. Also B. Diane Lipsett, *Desiring Conversion: Hermas, Thecla, Aseneth* (Oxford: Oxford University Press, 2011).
16. Kling, "Conversion to Christianity," 599.
17. Here we use "character" voluntarily because both Paul's confession and Augustine's have been so dramatized and theatralized that Paul and Augustine really become "characters" of their own narratives of conversion.

to people's mind. Both are associated with specific images: Paul falling from his horse on the road to Damascus; Augustine under his fig tree, in tears, hearing a voice that tells him "Take, read! Take, read!"[18] It does not matter very much whether these images are historically appropriate. In Christian occidental thought, they appropriately symbolize what a conversion is.[19]

These constructions are so anchored in *occidental* Christian culture that they, for a great part, determine how one understands what a conversion is.[20] If one looks at contemporary sociological approaches, Paul's conversion represents the paradigm of the classical conception of conversion.[21] It does not matter very much that this model does not actually match what one can reconstruct from historical reality. Paul remains the main example for those interested in classical conversion.[22] In this model, conversion is sudden and dramatic. It includes irrational and magical elements, and involves a powerful outside and impersonal motor that leads to negating the former self and affirming a new self. Conversion takes one to a new state that can be qualified as stable. Once conversion is accomplished, this new state remains. The change induced by conversion is usually viewed as positive and is accompanied by a change of beliefs. In this understanding, the individual is the recipient of changes in his or her personality. His or her life is re-orientated. The anthropology associated to this model is centered on the individual and tends to construct the person as passive in the conversion process, the recipient of an experience that he or she cannot completely control but that implies massive changes in his or her life. At the heart of

---

18. Augustine, *Confessions*, Book VIII, chapter 12, 28–30.

19. For recent discussion of conversion, see Ronald D. Witherup, *Conversion in the New Testament* (Collegeville, MN: Liturgical Press, 1994); Walter Homolka, Walter Jacob, and Esther Seidel, *Not by Birth Alone: Conversion to Judaism* (London: Cassell, 1997); Fernando Méndez-Moratalla, *The Paradigm of Conversion in Luke* (London: T&T Clark, 2004); A. Mani, *Religious Conversion: Myths and Reality* (New Delhi: A P H, 2009); Matthew Thiessen, *Contesting Conversion: Genealogy, Circumcision, and Identity in Ancient Judaism and Christianity* (New York: Oxford University Press, 2011).

20. Regarding this understanding, it is interesting to look at the contemporary genre of conversion stories. See for example the video testimony of Brian "Head" Welch, a heavy metal singer who co-founded the band Korn. In this video, he recounts how, after having been heavily addicted to drugs, he decided, partly to become a responsible father, to put his life in Jesus' hands, who saved him and gave him a new life, after having transformed his heart: https://www.youtube.com/watch?v=Rz1L0z1F4ng (last consulted 19 October 2015).

21. See for example Brock Kilbourne and James T. Richardson, "Paradigm Conflict, Types of Conversion, and Conversion Theories," *Sociological Analysis* 50.1(1988): 1–21, and Kling, "Conversion to Christianity," 3.

22. See the description of Kilbourne and Richardson, "Paradigm Conflict," 1–2.

this model, one finds the subjective experiences of the convert. Thus, conversion is understood as an emotional experience, and is explained by psychological categories.[23]

Conversion as Patronage

As Zeba A. Crook notes in his study of ancient conversion, *Reconceptualising Conversion*, it is not simply self-evident that psychology provides the best tools to understand and explain the phenomenon of conversion, and particularly of ancient conversion.[24] However, because this psychological understanding is culturally prescribed, one tends to adopt it easily. As Crook also reminds us, because this model is so easy to adopt, it has dominated New Testament studies of conversion, and particularly studies about Paul's conversion.[25] In particular, William James's work at the beginning of the twentieth century remains one of the main influences on the psychologizing explanations of Paul's conversion. At the heart of James's description, as Crook points out, one finds a divided self, aware of the tension inside of himself or herself and who wishes to resolve this tension. The divided self presupposes an individual aware of the tension at work inside his or her own person, and devoted to introspection. Conversion brings unity to the divided self, and thus also an emotional well-being.

In psychological analyses, emotions are a central category to explain conversion.[26] This psychologizing model has dominated the entire twentieth century. Eventually, Krister Stendahl's article "Paul and the Introspective Conscience of the West" would call into question the many studies of Paul based on this model.[27] As is well known, Stendahl questions the hypothesis that one can properly speak of introspection when it comes to Paul.[28] According to Stendahl, introspection as well as the idea that Paul would have turned to Christianity because of a tortured consciousness are modern concepts that do not correspond to the historical reality of the apostle. Stendahl famously argues that Paul does not experience a conversion to Christianity; rather the letters tell us of an experience of vocation, similar to

---

23. For an overview of the development of scholarship on religious conversion, see Kling, "Conversion to Christianity," 4–9.
24. Zeba A. Crook, *Reconceptualising Conversion: Patronage, Loyalty, and Conversion in the Religions of the Ancient Mediterranean* (Berlin: Walter DeGruyter, 2012).
25. In particular, Crook quotes William James's study, *The Varieties of Religious Experience* (New York: Penguin, 1902).
26. See Crook, *Reconceptualising Conversion*, 22–4.
27. For a list, see Crook, *Reconceptualising Conversion*, 28 n. 45.
28. Krister Stendahl, "Paul and the Introspective Conscience of the West," *Harvard Theological Review* 56 (1963): 199–215.

prophetic calls in the Old Testament. This vocation brings Paul to proclaim the gospel to the nations. In the frame of Stendahl's explanation, Paul does not convert from Judaism to Christianity. He remains inside of Judaism but understands his own role inside Judaism in a new manner.

In addition to Stendahl's arguments, social-scientific approaches to the New Testament have also challenged the idea that one can simply use modern psychological approaches to explain how ancient writers understood themselves.[29] Crook highlights that it is necessary to identify the differences in how ancient and modern individuals perceive the world, before one can appraise the similarities between both worlds. When it comes to explanations of conversion, scholars have neglected the very real differences between the ancient and the modern world. To remedy this situation, Crook offers a different analysis of conversion. He begins with social-scientific approaches and reminds us that in the first century a person was engaged in a much more collective culture than that most westerners experience today. In a collectivistic culture, such as the one in the first-century Mediterranean world, people think mainly in social terms, and depend less on a personal and individualist perspective. In particular, and this is paramount to Crook's explanation of conversion, a person is involved in exchanges and relations of reciprocities embodied in the social institutions of patronage and benefaction.[30]

In Crook's model, the main frame to understand conversion is reciprocity, embodied in the relationships between patron and client in the first century. In the first century, patronage provides a structure for the relationships between persons, but it is also the system through which human beings express their relationship to their gods.[31] Crook is interested particularly in "general reciprocity." He explains that general reciprocity functions between partners that do not have an equal social status. Furthermore, general reciprocity involves the exchange of goods of unequal value. A property of general reciprocity is the demand to be paid back not in nature, but in the form of "homage, loyalty, political support, or information."[32]

---

29. Crook, *Reconceptualising Conversion*, 3.
30. Crook, *Reconceptualising Conversion*, 53
31. Crook, *Reconceptualising Conversion*, 53: "The structure and expectations of general reciprocity, embodied in the social institutions of patronage and benefaction, supply the conceptual and practical framework within which Graeco-Romans, including Hellenised Jews like Philo and Josephus, expressed their understanding and their experience of their interactions with their gods."
32. Crook, *Reconceptualising Conversion*, 57. He quotes Ekkehard W. Stegemann and Wolfgang Stegemann, *The Jesus Movement: A Social History of its First Century* (Minneapolis, MN: Fortress Press, 1999), 36.

Crook notices that the difference between human patronage and divine patronage resides in the fact that gods are immeasurably more generous patrons than human beings.[33] In the clients' responses, however, one observes the same type of behavior whether one is expressing gratitude to a human patron or to a god: the clients articulate their gratitude, present praises and commendation, write these praises down, and spread the good news of the patrons' benefactions at large.[34] The system of patronage provides a relevant hermeneutical frame to understand the relationship between gods and human beings. It also illuminates the notion of conversion. In this context, gods are understood as offering services to human beings, and human beings exhibit the behavior one would expect from a client: they extend loyalty towards their patron.[35] If one admits that, in the first century, relationships between gods and human beings can be understood in terms of patronage conventions, one can explain conversion without relying on psychological categories, difficult to use in the context of the first century.

Even though Crook's presentation of conversion as related to patronage highlights important dimensions of the ancient world, it matters to mention a difficulty related to Crook's approach. Because it relies on social-scientific criticism, Crook's approach inevitably generalizes. While Crook rightly critiques scholars who assume that people in the first century live just "like us" in the twenty-first century, he himself tends to generalize the manner in which people in the twenty-first century understand themselves. For him, occidental persons are individualist, separated from their social context, free and autonomous.[36] To be fair to Crook, he mainly seeks to demonstrate that there is no immediate continuity between the understanding of the self for the modern person, and the understanding of the self for the ancient person. However, it remains true that Crook conceives the "modern human being" in a monolithic fashion, conforming himself to a model that goes back at least to René Descartes[37] when he postulates a sovereign "I," master of his (here, too, the "I" is most often male) destiny.

---

33. Crook, *Reconceptualising Conversion*, 76.
34. See Crook, *Reconceptualising Conversion*, 78.
35. Crook, *Reconceptualising Conversion*, 148–9.
36. See for example Crook, *Reconceptualising Conversion*, 36.
37. As Paul Ricœur indicates: *Oneself as Another* (Chicago, IL: Chicago University Press, 1992), 5: "If this ambition of establishing an ultimate foundation as seen itself radicalized from Descartes to Kant, then from Kant to Fichte, and finally to the Husserl of the *Cartesian Meditations*, it nevertheless seems to me that it is enough to focus on its birthplace, in Descartes himself, whose philosophy confirms that the *crisis* of the cogito is contemporaneous with the *positing* of the cogito."

It would be worthwhile to also account for recent discussions concerning the self, following the work of Michel Foucault, for example.[38] Foucault profoundly challenges the concept of a sovereign subject and demands that one thinks of the subject as being the product of various power relationships, in which the individual inscribes himself or herself more or less harmoniously. In Foucault's thought, the notion of subject disappears, and the self becomes a fluid, changing, flexible notion.[39] For postmodern thinkers, the idea of the autonomy of the self is no longer pertinent. The differences between the ancient understanding of the subject and the modern understanding need to be re-evaluated to account for the reconceptualization and complexification of the notion of the modern subject. And they also need to inform the manner in which we approach conversion for individuals who were not actively involved in the process of conversion, but became something new following the conversion of their master.

An Intersectional Approach

What tools work best to analyze such complex social contexts? At their core, intersectional theories argue that various categories intersect and mutually construct each other in every exchange and negotiation concerned with identity and hierarchy.[40] In recent years, intersectional theories also

---

38. See for example: Michel Foucault, *The Order of Things: An Archaeology of the Human Sciences* (unidentified collective translation; New York: Pantheon Books, 1971; repr. New York: Vintage Books, 1973) which announces the death of man in the second half of the twentieth century: "If those arrangements were to disappear as they appeared, if some event of which we can at the moment do no more than sense the possibility–without knowing either what its form will be or what it promises–were to cause them to crumble, as the ground of Classical thought did, at the end of the eighteenth century, then one can certainly wager that man would be erased, like a face drawn in sand at the edge of the sea" (387). In an interview that took place in 1978, Foucault retraces his reflections on the notion of the subject: "Interview with Michel Foucault," in James D. Faubion, ed., *Power: Essential Works of Foucault* (Paul Rabinow, ed., *Essential Works of Foucault, 1954-1984*, 3 vols.; [New York: The New Press, 1997–2000]), 3: 239–97. See also Michel Foucault, "On the Genealogy of Ethics: An Overview of Work in Progress," in Paul Rabinow, ed., *The Foucault Reader* (New York: Pantheon Books, 1984), 340–72.

39. It is particularly interesting to notice that some trends in postcolonial theory critique this development of the postmodern understanding of the self, that questions the ideal of a fixed self, capable of autonomous decisions, precisely when some ex-colonies are reaching autonomy and the possibility of self-governance. See Kwok Pui-lan, "Elisabeth Schüssler Fiorenza and Postcolonial Studies," *Journal of Feminist Studies in Religion* 25.1 (2009): 191–207.

40. Leslie McCall, "The Complexity of Intersectionality," *Signs: Journal of Women in Culture and Society* 30.3 (2005): 1771–800. Ann Phoenix and Pamela Pattynama,

influenced studies of religion and sacred texts, to a certain degree.[41] Once one takes into account the role of gender, race, ethnicity, age, disability, or social class in conversion stories, one can no longer consider conversion a cognitive or spiritual phenomenon only. Accordingly, instead of focusing solely on the theological dimensions of conversion, intersectionality helps showing that all human phenomena are embodied and embedded in a political, economic, and cultural context, involving a variety of bodies constructed by a set of intersecting structures. For example, when we think about conversion, in ancient texts or in the contemporary debate, it makes a difference what markers of identity are present. What if the newly-converted asylum seeker is also gay? What if the conversion of an entire household in Antiquity meant more freedom for women, but was forced upon slaves? How do intersections of gender, sexuality, social class, and ethnicity construct the conversion of the Ethiopian eunuch mentioned in Acts? How does conversion construct people with disability, if it is linked with healing?

Intersectionality helps us see nuances, and how different parameters of power and hierarchy reinforce and mutually construct each other. In the study of early Jewish and Christian texts, we will build on studies in which attention to gender has been central and which employ intersectional theories.[42]

---

eds., *European Journal of Women's Studies* (*Issue on Intersectionality*) 13 (2006). Jennifer C. Nash, "Re-Thinking Intersectionality," *Feminist Review* 89 (2008): 1–15. Sumi Cho, Kimberlé Williams Crenshaw, and Leslie McCall, "Toward a Field of Intersectional Studies: Theory, Applications, and Praxis," *Signs: Journal of Women in Culture and Society* (*Theme Issue: Intersectionality: Theorizing Power, Empowering Theory*) 38.4 (2013): 785–810.

41. Erica Appelros, "Religion och intersektionalitet," *Kvinnovetenskapelig tidsskrift* 2/3 (2005): 69–80. Elisabeth Schüssler Fiorenza, "Introduction: Exploring the Intersections of Race, Gender, Status, and Ethnicity in Early Christian Studies," in Laura Nasrallah and Elisabeth Schüssler Fiorenza, eds., *Prejudice and Christian Beginnings: Investigating Race, Gender, and Ethnicity in Early Christian Studies* (Minneapolis, MN: Fortress Press, 2009), 1–23. Marianne Bjelland Kartzow, "Intersectional Studies," in Julia M. O'Brien, ed., *The Oxford Encyclopedia of the Bible and Gender Studies* (New York: Oxford University Press, 2014), 364–89.

42. Judith M. Lieu, "The 'Attraction of Women' in/to Early Judaism and Christianity: Gender and the Politics of Conversion," *Journal for the Study of the New Testament* 72 (1998): 5–22; Ross Shepard Kraemer and Mary Rose D'Angelo, *Women & Christian Origins* (New York: Oxford University Press, 1999). Shelly Matthews, *First Converts: Rich Pagan Women and the Rhetoric of Mission in Early Judaism and Christianity* (Stanford University Press: Stanford, 2001). Carolyn Osiek, Margaret Y. MacDonald, and Janet H. Tulloch, *A Woman's Place: House Churches in Earliest Christianity* (Minneapolis, MN: Fortress Press, 2006); Lipsett, *Desiring Conversion*.

Overlapping, Reinforcing, Modifying Conversion

One of the results of approaching conversion with an intersectional perspective is that the concept is inevitably conceived somewhat differently. A modified perspective on conversion allows reflecting on (at least) two important questions about conversion: who can be considered as an agent in conversion, and what does agency mean when it comes to conversion? It also makes apparent how the "other" is constructed in conversion stories. In particular, the interpreter can reflect on who is mentioned by name in conversion stories, who is considered as explicitly converted, and who is merely mentioned as a side product of the main protagonist's conversion. In an intersectional perspective, it becomes apparent that conversion is a contested space and functions differently for different people, depending on their age, gender, status, and race.

Even the notion of "change" is transformed in this reflection. As Ramsey MacMullen puts it, a "convert" cannot help bring certain things into the new "religion" he or she adopts, "involuntarily and unconscious, forgotten in his [or her] pocket so to speak."[43] In such a context, one can wonder how new the "new" religion is, how "new" does it remain, especially with the import of converts. Change affects not only the convert, but perhaps also the religion(s) affected by the import (and desertion) of converts. Perhaps it is the person as much as the religion which is converted. It is also possible to reflect on whether presumed "religious" change can mean different things for different groups. For example, as one article (Anne-Hege Grung's) discusses, conversion to Islam is valued differently when it involves young women converting because they are getting married than when young men convert on their own. Do these different values accorded to conversion also modify what religion might mean?

Re-thinking Religion

Even the ancients disagreed about what constitutes a "religion."[44] What we might today consider as "philosophical schools" also participated in religion for the ancients. The imperial cult in the Roman Empire shows to what degree religion and politics were enmeshed. In fact, as is well known among students of Antiquity, religion was not conceived of as a separate or

---

43. Ramsey MacMullen, "Conversion: A Historian's View," *The Second Century* 5.2 (1985/86): 67–81, here 68.
44. "[O]ne of those differences between the Judeo-Christian and the Greco-Roman lay in the very definition of 'religion'," according to MacMullen, "Conversion: A Historian's View," 71.

private domain to the degree it is today, at least in many Western countries. This, too, influences how we reconstruct and re-imagine the process of conversion. In the Western world, and particularly in secular societies, religion is constructed as having to do with free choice, personal faith and convictions, and a set of ethical practices—this is, for example, very much the position that the French state wants to adopt, as is clear from the many controversies sparked by Muslim women wearing the veil, the burka or, more recently, the burkini, in public.[45] Religion should be restricted to the private sphere. Yet, in the ancient world, we tend to reconstruct religion as belonging to the public sphere and as being connected to social status, gender, ethnicity, or family background, with personal choice playing less of a role in a person's choice of religion (especially if that person is not a free male citizen). Because of these differences, it is truly challenging to talk about religions—and conversion—across history, and it matters to formulate and theorize these differences in the construction of religion. Granted, these are only partially historical objective facts, and they depend very much on the interpreters' perspective. In bringing them to the fore, we are able, once more, to refine the notion of "conversion."

In the ancient world, religious conversion could also mean ethnic change. If ethnicity is also categorized by one's relation to the god(s) one worships, then choosing (or being forced to choose) a new god or new gods often also meant choosing (or being forced to choose) a new ethnic belonging. For example, if one (was) converted to the god of Israel through circumcision, one did not just become a religious devotee of this god; ethnically, one also became a Jew. Religion was thus deeply embedded in other collective entities, such as kinship, ethnic background, and fatherland. As John J. Collins writes, "The practices and beliefs that have traditionally been labelled as 'religion' are seen as constituent parts of the ethnic identity of specific peoples, rather than a free-standing system of thought and practices accessible in principle to anyone."[46] When one looks at conversion, one needs to

---

45. For the interdictions about wearing the burkini on public beaches, see: http://www.lemonde.fr/religions/article/2016/08/17/les-arretes-municipaux-contre-le-burkini-se-multiplient_4983873_1653130.html.

46. John J. Collins, "The Transformation of Aseneth," in Anne Hege Grung, Marianne Bjelland Kartzow, and Anna Rebecca Solevåg, eds., *Bodies, Borders, Believers: Ancient Texts and Present Conversations. Essays in Honor of Turid Karlsen Seim on her 70th Birthday* (Eugene, OR: Pickwick, 2015), 93–108, here 93–4. See also Steve Mason, "Jews, Judeans, Judaizing, Judaism: Problems of Categorization in Ancient History," *Journal for the Study of Judaism* 38.4/5 (2007): 457–512. Anders Runesson, "The Question of Terminology: The Architecture of Contemporary Discussions on Paul," in Mark D. Nanos and Magnus Zetterholm, eds., *Paul within Judaism: Restoring the First-Century Context to the Apostle* (Minneapolis, MN: Fortress Press, 2015), 53–77.

consider all these elements, and not limit conversion to an individual and private, merely spiritual, momentary event.

Complexity, Methodology, Rhetoric

The aim of this collection is not to answer all the questions raised in this first essay. Most of them probably cannot be answered with any acceptable degree of reliability. However, being aware of this difficulty does not preclude from thinking theoretically about these problems. In this volume, many authors initiate a conversation between ancient texts and contemporary discourses. Of course, we are aware that the documents being studied hardly, if ever, discuss the same thing. Yet, we do believe that by using the tools of interdisciplinary studies, trans-religious dialogues, and critical theory, such as intersectionality, we can think more fruitfully about conversion and go beyond the sometimes overheated debates of public media. Hopefully, this framework will contribute to refining our analytical language, in order to benefit from various case studies and literary examples, in constructing a description of a given phenomenon as dense and multifaceted as possible.

Obvious challenges remain when it comes to sources and methodology. Stories of conversion rarely transmit the various voices or experiences of children, disabled persons, slaves, or women. We have few, if any, firsthand records. As Judith Lieu argues: "In practice our evidence makes it difficult to describe the overt motivations for conversions in the ancient world."[47] Yet, at the least, our specific focus emphasizes that the picture is incomplete when one leaves the perspectives and concerns of invisible people out of the frame of analysis. It insists that simply pretending, that what we do not see, does not exist, is not an appropriate response to the evidence. Our task as interpreters is also to theorize the gaps in the sources. We cannot simply equate the sources' silencing of those who suffer from intersectional marginalization with invisibility or inexistence.

To "read against the grain"[48] means that we are aware of how polemical or rhetorical texts work. Our evidence and sources for ancient conversions are overwhelmingly textual, and it is tempting for interpreters to understand the characters and events presented in texts as "real," as if the texts give an accurate account of historical facts. For example, in terms of

---

47. Judith M. Lieu, *Neither Jew nor Greek? Constructing Early Christianity* (London: T&T Clark, 2002), 86.

48. Claudia V. Camp, "Wise and Strange: An Interpretation of the Female Imagery in Proverbs in Light of Trickster Mythology," *Semeia* 42 (1988): 14–36, talks about "undercutting the most obvious message" of the text (33).

gender and conversion, the female body is used to re-inscribe conversion, combined with gendered stereotypes about naïve and feeble new-converts. When 2 Timothy 3.2 constructs "silly little women" as easy targets for false teaching since they change their minds and follow other teachings than the one prescribed by the pastor, gender stereotypes influence ideas about conversion. We cannot take this passage as a source telling us anything about gender and conversion, if we do not approach the gender rhetoric involved in the passage critically. Gender relates to conversion also in other contexts: military campaigns across time and history have used mass conversion to signal victory, combined with rape of surviving women in extreme cases. Both can signify revenge and superiority. In recent terrorism, kidnapping of schoolgirls forced to change their religion has been used as a weapon. Household conversions in Acts hide possible violence and force. Because sources surrounding complex cases are often limited and incomplete, theoretical tools can help the analysis.

Furthermore, this collection's approach also highlights that if one simply accepts the hierarchical structures as they are transmitted by the sources, one might miss the fact that even children, slaves, women, or others who might have been forced to convert could themselves benefit intellectually, or in other ways, from their conversion. In addition, one should not neglect the fact that the forced converts we encounter in ancient texts also contribute to shape, develop, and transform the religious traditions they (willingly or not) joined. Here, for example, a dialogue with some of the slave narratives that transmit the experiences of black slaves on American plantations in the eighteenth and nineteenth centuries highlights the fact that black slaves significantly transformed and shaped the religion (Christianity) imposed on them by their masters.[49]

About This Process and This Volume

The authors of these essays are experts in benefiting from each other's insights, in working across fields and disciplines, and in thinking in a more communal and less individual manner. They know how to challenge recent and accepted conceptualizations within the field of interdisciplinary

---

49. See for example Riggins R. Earl, Jr., "A Critique of Slave Conversion Consciousness: Its Implications for Black Theology and Ethics," *Journal of the I.T.C.* 17.1-2 (1989/90): 1–18 and Clarice J. Martin, "Somebody Done Hoodoo'd the Hoodoo Man: Language, Power, Resistance, and the Effective History of Pauline Texts in American Slavery," in Allen Callahan, Richard Horsley, and Abraham Smith, eds., *Slavery in Text and Interpretation* (Semeia, 83/84; Atlanta, GA: The Society of Biblical Literature, 2000), 203–33.

production of knowledge. Many of the authors are also academically trained in reading texts from Antiquity; they use a set of critical tools and methods on a variety of texts from a variety of genres, in different ancient languages, and from different geographical situations.

The articles collected in this volume are the fruit of an interdisciplinary and communal work around the notion of conversion. The volume opens with two articles using recent situations (the case of a debate around circumcision in Germany and the example of a joint statement concerning conversion made by Muslim and Christian authorities in Norway) to introduce present and past issues around conversion (Karin B. Neutel and Anne-Hege Grung). The third article (Gerhard van den Heever) offers a theoretical bridge to the next articles, reconfiguring understanding of religion and conversion on the basis of mystery cults. The next seven articles use ancient sources (Early Christian and Jewish texts, canonical or not) to reflect upon conversion. The first article discusses the link between disability and conversion in the Gospel of Mark and the theology of John and Charles Wesley (Anna Rebecca Solevåg). Then Minna Heimola takes up the story of the baptism of the Ethiopian eunuch in Acts 8 to highlight the importance of ethnicity and gender for conversion. Valérie Nicolet pursues this focus on gender and analyzes the impact of conversion on the understanding of gender in 1 Corinthians, using tools provided by Judith Butler. In the next chapter, Marianne Bjelland Kartzow traces the destiny of Hagar in Christian, Jewish, and Muslim texts, and demonstrates how Hagar as a character can be read differently when it comes to her faith. With Kirsten Marie Hartvigsen, the volume leaves the canon. Hartvigsen's article pursues issues of gender and ethnicity within the ancient novel *Joseph and Aseneth*. Kristine Toft Rosland explores an apocryphal Coptic text (the *Apocryphon of John*) and shows how it could provide a new sense of belongings for recent converts. Finally, Anna Lampadaridi, using her new translation of *The Life of Porphyri of Gaza*, adds the dimension of geography to the discussion and shows how space could also be transformed—or converted—to accommodate religious change.

Biographical Note

Marianne Bjelland Kartzow is Professor of New Testament Studies at the Faculty of Theology, University of Oslo, Norway. She has published *Gossip and Gender: Othering of Speech in the Pastoral Epistles* (2009), *Destabilizing the Margins: An Intersectional Approach to Early Christian Memory* (2012), and *The Slave Metaphor and Gendered Enslavement in Early Christian Discourse: Double Trouble Embodied* (2018). Her research interests include gender theory, social history, and studies of sacred scriptures.

Since 2013, Valérie Nicolet has been "maîtresse de conférences" at the Institut protestant de théologie (faculté de Paris), where she teaches New Testament and Ancient Greek. In her research, she focuses on the Pauline letters. At the moment, she is working on the rhetorical construction of the law in Galatians. Her scholarship highlights interdisciplinary approaches, more prominently with philosophy, and recently, with queer theory. She has published a book on the construction of the self in Romans, *Constructing the Self: Thinking with Paul and Michel Foucault* (Tübingen: Mohr Siebeck, 2012).

Bibliography

Appelros, Erica. "Religion och intersektionalitet," *Kvinnovetenskapelig tidsskrift* 2/3 (2005): 69–80.

Bal, Mieke. "Tricky Thematics," *Semeia* 42 (1988): 133–55.

Camp, Claudia V. "Wise and Strange: An Interpretation of the Female Imagery in Proverbs in Light of Trickster Mythology," *Semeia* 42 (1988): 14–36.

Cho, Sumi, Kimberlé Williams Crenshaw, and Leslie McCall. "Toward a Field of Intersectional Studies: Theory, Applications, and Praxis," *Signs: Journal of Women in Culture and Society (Theme Issue: Intersectionality: Theorizing Power, Empowering Theory)* 38.4 (2013): 785–810. https://doi.org/10.1086/669608

Collins, John J. "The Transformation of Aseneth," 93–108 in *Bodies, Borders, Believers: Ancient Texts and Present Conversations. Essays in Honor of Turid Karlsen Seim on her 70th Birthday*. Edited by Anne Hege Grung, Marianne Bjelland Kartzow, and Anna Rebecca Solevåg. Eugene, OR: Pickwick, 2015.

Crook, Zeba A. *Reconceptualising Conversion: Patronage, Loyalty, and Conversion in the Religions of the Ancient Mediterranean*. Berlin: De Gruyter, 2012.

Earl Jr., Riggins R. "A Critique of Slave Conversion Consciousness: Its Implications for Black Theology and Ethics," *Journal of the I.T.C.* 17.1/2 (1989–1990): 1–18.

Foucault, Michel. *The Order of Things: An Archaeology of the Human Sciences*. Unidentified collective translation. New York: Pantheon Books, 1971; repr. New York: Vintage Books, 1973.

— "Interview with Michel Foucault," 239–97 in *Power: Essential Works of Foucault*. Vol. 3 of Paul Rabinow, ed., *Essential Works of Foucault, 1954-1984*, 3 vols.). Edited by James D. Faubion. New York: The New Press, 1997–2000.

—"On the Genealogy of Ethics: An Overview of Work in Progress," 340–72 in *The Foucault Reader*. Edited by Paul Rabinow. New York: Pantheon Books, 1984.

Fredriksen, Paula. "Madatory Retirement: Ideas in the Study of Christian Origins Whose Time Has Come to Go," *Studies in Religion* 35.2 (2006): 231–46. https://doi.org/10.1177/000842980603500203

Homolka, Walter, Walter Jacob, and Esther Seidel, *Not by Birth Alone: Conversion to Judaism*. London: Cassell, 1997.

James, William. *The Varieties of Religious Experience*. New York: Penguin, 1902. https://doi.org/10.1037/10004-000

Kartzow, Marianne Bjelland. "Intersectional Studies," 364–89 in *The Oxford Encyclopedia of the Bible and Gender Studies*. Edited by Julia M. O'Brien. New York: Oxford University Press, 2014.

Kent, Eliza F. "Feminist Approaches to the Study of Religious Conversion," 297–326 in Rambo and Farhadian, eds., *Oxford Handbook of Religious Conversion*, 2014.
Kilbourne, Brock, and James T. Richardson. "Paradigm Conflict, Types of Conversion, and Conversion Theories," *Sociological Analysis* 50.1 (1988): 1–21. https://doi.org/10.2307/3710915
Kinserdal, Frode. "Den maskuline konversjonsfortelling: En studie av unge norske menn som har konvertert til Islam," Det teologiske Menignhetsfakultet, 2010.
Kling, David W. "Conversion to Christianity," 602–3 in Rambo and Farhadian, eds., *Oxford Handbook of Religious Conversion*, 2014.
Kraemer, Ross Shepard, and Mary Rose D'Angelo. *Women & Christian Origins*. New York: Oxford University Press, 1999.
Lieu, Judith M. "The 'Attraction of Women' in/to Early Judaism and Christianity: Gender and the Politics of Conversion," *Journal for the Study of the New Testament* 72 (1998): 5–22. https://doi.org/10.1177/0142064X9902107202
—*Neither Jew nor Greek? Constructing Early Christianity*. London: T&T Clark, 2002.
Lipsett, B. Diane. *Desiring Conversion: Hermas, Thecla, Aseneth*. Oxford: Oxford University Press, 2011. https://doi.org/10.1093/acprof:oso/9780199754519.001.0001
MacMullen, Ramsey. "Conversion: A Historian's View," *The Second Century* 5.2 (1985/86): 67–81.
Mani, A. *Religious Conversion: Myths and Reality*. New Delhi: A P H, 2009.
Martin, Clarice J. "Somebody Done Hoodoo'd the Hoodoo Man: Language, Power, Resistance, and the Effective History of Pauline Texts in American Slavery," 203–33 in *Slavery in Text and Interpretation*. Edited by Allen Callahan, Richard Horsley, and Abraham Smith. Semeia, 83/84. Atlanta, GA: The Society of Biblical Literature, 2000.
Mason, Steve. "Jews, Judeans, Judaizing, Judaism: Problems of Categorization in Ancient History," *Journal for the Study of Judaism* 38.4/5 (2007): 457–512. https://doi.org/10.1163/156851507X193108
Matthews, Shelly. *First Converts: Rich Pagan Women and the Rhetoric of Mission in Early Judaism and Christianity*. Standford, CA: Stanford University Press, 2001.
McCall, Leslie. "The Complexity of Intersectionality," *Signs: Journal of Women in Culture and Society* 30.3 (2005): 1771–800. https://doi.org/10.1086/426800
Méndez-Moratalla, Fernando. *The Paradigm of Conversion in Luke*. London: T&T Clark, 2004.
Nash, Jennifer C. "Re-Thinking Intersectionality," *Feminist Review* 89 (2008): 1–15. https://doi.org/10.1057/fr.2008.4
Osiek, Carolyn, Margaret Y. MacDonald, and Janet H. Tulloch. *A Woman's Place: House Churches in Earliest Christianity*. Minneapolis, MN: Fortress Press, 2006.
Phoenix, Ann, and Pamela Pattynama, eds. *European Journal of Women's Studies* (Issue on Intersectionality) 13: 2006. https://doi.org/10.1177/1350506806065751
Pregill, Michael E. "Conversion. V. Islam," 732–8 in Constance Furey, et al., eds., *Encyclopedia of the Bible and Its Reception Online*. Berlin: De Gruyter, 2012. https://www.degruyter.com/document/database/EBR/entry/MainLemma_6352/html
Pui-lan, Kwok. "Elisabeth Schüssler Fiorenza and Postcolonial Studies," *Journal of Feminist Studies in Religion* 25.1 (2009): 191–207. https://doi.org/10.2979/fsr.2009.25.1.191
Rambo, Lewis R., and Charles E. Farhadian, eds. *The Oxford Handbook of Religious Conversion*. Oxford: Oxford University Press, 2014. https://doi.org/10.1093/oxfordhb/9780195338522.001.0001

Ricœur, Paul. *Oneself as Another*. Chicago, IL: Chicago University Press, 1992.
Runesson, Anders. "The Question of Terminology: The Architecture of Contemporary Discussions on Paul," 53–77 in *Paul within Judaism: Restoring the First-Century Context to the Apostle*. Edited by Mark D. Nanos and Magnus Zetterholm. Minneapolis, MN: Fortress Press, 2015. https://doi.org/10.2307/j.ctt9m0vn7.6
Schüssler Fiorenza, Elisabeth. "Introduction: Exploring the Intersections of Race, Gender, Status, and Ethnicity in Early Christian Studies," 1–23 in *Prejudice and Christian Beginnings: Investigating Race, Gender, and Ethnicity in Early Christian Studies*. Edited by Laura Nasrallah and Elisabeth Schüssler Fiorenza. Minneapolis, MN: Fortress Press, 2009.
Spittler, Janet E. "Conversion. I. New Testament. II. Greco-Roman Antiquity," 708–12 in Constance Furey, et al., eds., *Encyclopedia of the Bible and Its Reception Online*. Berlin: De Gruyter, 2012. https://www.degruyter.com/document/database/EBR/entry/MainLemma_6352/html
Stegeman Ekkehard W., and Wolfgang Stegemann. *The Jesus Movement: A Social History of its First Century*. Minneapolis, MN: Fortress Press, 1999.
Stendahl, Krister. "Paul and the Introspective Conscience of the West," *Harvard Theological Review* 56 (1963): 199–215. https://doi.org/10.1017/S0017816000024779
Thiessen, Matthew. *Contesting Conversion: Genealogy, Circumcision, and Identity in Ancient Judaism and Christianity*. New York: Oxford University Press, 2011. https://doi.org/10.1093/acprof:oso/9780199793563.001.0001
Witherup, Ronald D. *Conversion in the New Testament*. Collegeville, MN: Liturgical Press, 1994.

Web Articles

http://www.lemonde.fr/religions/article/2016/08/17/les-arretes-municipaux-contre-le-burkini-se-multiplient_4983873_1653130.html

https://www.youtube.com/watch?v=Rz1L0z1F4ng (last consulted 19 October 2015).

Chapter Two

Shedding Religious Skin:
An Intersectional Analysis of the Claim That
Male Circumcision Limits Religious Freedom

Karin B. Neutel

Male circumcision is an important practice in several religious traditions.[1] Yet the relationship between circumcision and religious belonging, beliefs, and behavior is more complex than is often assumed. While Christianity, for example, is often seen as a non-circumcising religion, many Christian men are in fact circumcised.[2] And even though it is considered a central practice within Judaism, some Jewish parents choose not to circumcise their newborn sons.[3] What circumcision is thought to express and signify varies greatly across cultures and between individuals. This article will focus on one aspect of the complex relationship between circumcision and religion: the idea that male circumcision constitutes an obstacle to religious freedom and to conversion.

The exploration offered here was sparked by a comment in the legal ruling on male circumcision, by the District Court in Cologne, Germany.

---

1. I am grateful to the organizers and participants of the Complexity of Conversion project for an enjoyable and productive collaboration. I would also like to thank Daniel Boyarin, Claudia Bergmann, Hannah Peaceman, Jörg Rüpke, Benedikt Kranemann, and my other colleagues at the Max Weber Centre and the Research Centre "Dynamics of Jewish ritual practices in pluralistic contexts from Antiquity to the Present" for stimulating conversations on the topic of this paper.

2. In some countries that have a predominantly Christian population, such as the United States and the Philippines, male circumcision is widely practiced. See the 2007 report from the World Health Organization "Male Circumcision: Global Trends and Determinants of Prevalence, Safety and Acceptability," 4–5.

3. Although exact numbers are difficult to give, Jewish opposition to circumcision is evident and may be growing, see for example Ephraim Tabory and Sharon Erex, "Circumscribed Circumcision: The Motivations and Identities of Israeli Parents who Choose Not to Circumcise their Sons," in Elizabeth Wyner Mark, ed., *The Covenant of Circumcision: New Perspectives on an Ancient Jewish Rite* (Lebanon: Brandeis University Press 2003), 161–76; http://www.haaretz.com/israel-news/even-in-israel-more-and-more-parents-choose-not-to-circumcise-their-sons-1.436421 (last accessed 7 June 2021).

Among several reasons for objecting to circumcision, the court in Cologne states in its verdict that circumcision hinders a boy's ability to freely decide his own religious affiliation.[4] While this ruling received a great deal of attention in the media, as well as from scholars, the remark about circumcision and religious freedom has remained largely unexamined.[5] Yet from the perspective of the study of religion, this is a statement that raises important questions. Religious affiliation and conversion are generally understood as phenomena which encompass many domains, such as the religious, political, psychological, social, and cultural.[6] Physical aspects, however, are not taken to play a major role, with the exception of neurological and cognitive processes.[7] The purpose of this essay is not to determine the veracity of the claim about the religious consequences of circumcision, but rather to explore the context and perspective from which this claim is made, and the suppositions from which it derives its validity. In this exploration, I will use an intersectional approach. Intersectionality can be deployed as a deconstructive move to challenge often implicit assumptions about sameness and difference in law, politics, and society more generally.[8] In this case, it can shed light on which, and whose, understandings of religion, of conversion, and of circumcision are at play in this type of thought, and how these understandings are related to social difference. I will first examine the Cologne verdict, as well as several later articulations of this same argument by legal scholars, and subsequently focus my analysis on two topics: gender and

---

4.   Landgericht Köln, 151 Ns 169/11 (07-05-2012). For the court's findings, see http://dejure.org/dienste/vernetzung/rechtsprechung?Gericht=LG%20K%F6ln&Datum=07.05.2012&Aktenzeichen=151%20Ns%20169/11 (last accessed 7 June 2021).

5.   An exception is a legal discussion by Tillmann Bartsch. See Tillmann Bartsch, "Anmerkung zu einer Entscheidung des LG Koln, Urteil vom 07.05.2012" (151 Ns 169/11; StV 2012, 603) – Zur religiös motivierten Beschneidung, StV 2012,S. 604–9.

6.   Lewis R. Rambo and Charles E. Farhadian, "Introduction," in Lewis R. Rambo and Charles E. Farhadian, eds., *The Oxford Handbook of Religious Conversion* (Oxford: Oxford University Press, 2014), 1–24, here 2.

7.   So for example, Raymond F. Paloutzian, Erica L. Swenson, and Patrick McNamara, "Religious Conversion, Spiritual Transformation, and the Neurocognition of Meaning Making," in Patrick McNamara, ed., *Where God and Science Meet: How Brain and Evolutionary Studies Alter our Understanding of Religion* (Westport, CN: Praeger Publishers, 2006), 151–69; Kelly Bulkeley, "Religious Conversion and Cognitive Neuroscience," in Rambo and Farhadian, eds., *Oxford Handbook of Religious Conversion*, 240–55.

8.   See Sumi Cho, Kimberlé Williams Crenshaw, and Leslie McCall, "Toward a Field of Intersectionality Studies: Theory, Applications, and Praxis," *Signs: Journal of Women in Culture and Society (Theme Issue: Theorizing Power, Empowering Theory)* 38.4 (2013): 785–810, here 800.

religion. This will show how assumptions about sameness and difference underlie the claims made about circumcision and conversion.

The Cologne Verdict and Similar Perspectives on Religious Freedom

In the spring of 2012, the District Court in Cologne presented a ruling in the case of a doctor who circumcised a four-year old Muslim boy, at the request of his parents. This case ended up in court after the boy was taken to the emergency room because of complications, where it was assumed that the circumcision had not been performed according to medical standards, and authorities were brought in.[9] The doctor, who was accused of causing bodily harm to another person by using a dangerous instrument, was acquitted on the grounds that he could not have known that he was breaking the law by performing non-therapeutic circumcision. The court, however, did declare male circumcision to be a form of bodily harm and therefore a violation of the boy's rights.

In addition to weighing arguments about bodily integrity and autonomy of the child on the one hand, and the religious freedom of the parents on the other, the verdict also mentions the presumed effects that circumcision would have on the boy's freedom of religion. The verdict states on this issue:

> Zudem wird der Körper des Kindes durch die Beschneidung dauerhaft und irreparabel verändert. Diese Veränderung läuft dem Interesse des Kindes später selbst über seine Religionszugehörigkeit entscheiden zu können zuwider. Umgekehrt wird das Erziehungsrecht der Eltern nicht unzumutbar beeinträchtigt, wenn sie gehalten sind abzuwarten, ob sich der Knabe später, wenn er mündig ist, selbst für die Beschneidung als sichtbares Zeichen der Zugehörigkeit zum Islam entscheidet.[10]

> [T]he circumcision changes the child's body permanently and irreparably. This change runs contrary to the interests of the child in deciding his religious affiliation independently later in life. On the other hand, the parental right of education is not unacceptably diminished by requiring them to wait until their son is able to make the decision himself whether to have a circumcision as a visible sign of his affiliation to Islam.[11]

The verdict understands the permanent change to the boy's body as impairing his ability to freely decide his religious affiliation. Although it is not made explicit, the reasoning of the court appears to be that a circumcised

---

9. For details of the case and the verdict, see Jan F. Orth, "Explaining the Cologne Circumcision Decision," *The Journal of Criminal Law* 77/6 (2013): 497–511.
10. Landgericht Köln, III, 7.
11. Translation Orth, "Explaining the Cologne Circumcision Decision," 503.

boy is already bound to a certain religious tradition by the physical "change" that he has undergone. In this way, his religious freedom would be curtailed. This is an intriguing argument, since it assumes that the process of religious affiliation and, by implication, the process of conversion, is different for circumcised men, as compared to other people. While the Cologne court does not further clarify the claim that circumcision impairs religious freedom, similar arguments have occurred in subsequent legal discussions of circumcision. I will here analyze three publications that are part of the debate that followed the Cologne verdict and that make more detailed assumptions about the connections between circumcision, conversion, and religious freedom.

The first is by Dutch philosopher of law Paul Cliteur, who elaborates on this specific argument in a discussion of the Cologne verdict.[12] In a blog post for the Leiden Law Blog entitled "Male circumcision," Paul Cliteur lauds the verdict as "one of the most spectacular rulings of this summer." He describes the verdict as "criminalizing male circumcision." Cliteur agrees with the court that circumcision has a negative impact on the religious freedom of the boy in question:

> The parents can educate their children but not permanently mutilate their bodies to earmark them as belonging to a certain religious community.
>
> The practice of circumcision violates also the right to free choice in matters religious and otherwise. When someone is permanently physically mutilated or earmarked to proclaim his or her adherence to a religious community this violates the freedom of religion as well. According to a human rights regime one has not only the right to choose a religion, but also to abandon or reject a religion. Physically earmarking someone else makes it more difficult for a person to change his opinion about this religion.[13]

Cliteur here expresses a largely similar view on the impact of the physical on the religious, reformulating the point made by the Cologne court and elaborating it somewhat. Where the Cologne court verdict speaks about "deciding his religious affiliation independently," Cliteur refers to "the right to free choice in matters religious" and the ability "to change his opinion about this religion." Cliteur is more disapproving in his description of circumcision; rather than state that it "changes the child's body," Cliteur

---

12. See http://leidenlawblog.nl/articles/male-circumcision#.UCN1E2i3Iyw (last accessed 7 June 2021). Cliteur discusses male circumcision more extensively in a subsequent publication: Paul Cliteur, "Morele en immorele religieus gelegitimeerde praktijken in het gezondheidsrecht," in Govert den Hartogh and Paul Cliteur, eds., *Ethiek en gezondheidsrecht* (Preadvies uitgebracht voor de Vereniging voor Gezondheidsrecht, jaarvergadering 25 April 2014), 91–185.

13. See http://leidenlawblog.nl/articles/male-circumcision#.UCN1E2i3Iyw.

describes a circumcised body as "physically mutilated" and "earmarked to proclaim his or her adherence to a religious community."

The second publication is by German legal scholars Reinhard Merkel and Holm Putzke, who make a similar claim. After the Cologne verdict, in December of 2012, the German parliament explicitly legalized circumcision performed for religious or cultural reasons. In response to this new legislation, Merkel and Putzke describe the Cologne verdict as "a resounding decision" that declared non-therapeutic circumcision "bodily assault." The main object of their paper is to point out the flaws in the current law and to explain "the difficulty that any legal attempt to protect medically irrelevant genital cutting is bound to face."[14] On the conflict between religious freedom and circumcision, Merkel and Putzke state the following:

> Moreover, the imposition of an irreversible mark of a religious membership contradicts the right to self-determination and the child's own (negative) freedom to avoid, or (positive) freedom to adopt, any particular religion. Parents doubtlessly have a constitutional right to initiate their child into a religious community. But this right does not extend beyond the time when the child acquires the ability to decide on such matters for himself. If parents do not have a right to determine their child's religious affiliation for the child's lifetime, why should they have a right to permanently mark their children's bodies with a symbol of that affiliation? It is, in this respect, quite irrelevant that this mark is ambiguous and does not necessarily point to a religious faith: it was engraved onto the child's body for that reason alone.[15]

Merkel and Putzke emphasize the symbolic meaning of circumcision as "an irreversible mark of a religious membership" with which parents "permanently mark their children's bodies" to symbolize affiliation. It is "engraved onto the child's body" for reasons of religious faith, even though they acknowledge that circumcision as such may be ambiguous and may have other meanings. When it comes to religion, Merkel and Putzke mention "the right to self-determination" and the "freedom to avoid," or "to adopt," any particular religion. At some point in time, "the child acquires the ability to decide on such matters for himself."

The final iteration of the claim about circumcision and religion that I want to discuss maintains that "infant circumcision is morally unjustifiable because it violates the child's right to an open future."[16] Eldar Sarajlic

---

14. Reinhard Merkel and Holm Putzke, "After Cologne: Male Circumcision and the Law. Parental Right, Religious Liberty or Criminal Assault?," *Journal of Medical Ethics* 39.7 (2013): 444–9, here 444.

15. Merkel and Putzke, "After Cologne," 447.

16. Eldar Sarajlic, "Can Culture Justify Infant Circumcision?," *Res Publica* 20 (2014): 327–43, here 327.

challenges the view that social and cultural benefits can justify parental authorization of circumcision, and focuses particularly on previous discussions of circumcision by Michael and David Benatar in 2003 and by Joseph Mazor in 2013.[17] Although Sarajlic finds these authors unclear with regard to specifically religious benefits, he infers several claims from their writing, and here I will focus on two of these claims.[18] The first claim is that "circumcision serves the child's metaphysical interests in salvation or fulfilling the covenant with God," which, according to Sarajlic, would be particularly relevant for Jews. For them, it could be claimed that "male children are circumcised to bring the covenant into existence and form a bond between the metaphysical and the physical." The second claim for religious benefits for both Jews and Muslims could be that "circumcision represents an initiation of the infant into the community of faithful."

After reconstructing the possible claims for religious benefits of circumcision in this way, Sarajlic goes on to challenge each of them. He questions the first claim by referring to the possibility of religious change:

> the claim about metaphysical salvation presumes that the child will necessarily share their parents' metaphysical beliefs once it is grown up ... It is plausible to assume that most children end up having the same religious beliefs as their parents, but this is not necessarily so. Individuals often change their beliefs, shed the religious assumptions inherited from parents or adopt new ones. Undergoing an irreversible bodily modification when non-autonomous to provide consent can significantly affect the subsequent development of the individual. It can diminish their sense of selfhood by limiting the degree of self-determination and control over one's life.[19]

Like the other authors examined so far in this paper, Sarajlic thus assumes that undergoing circumcision, here described as "irreversible bodily modification," will affect a boy's subsequent "self-determination and control" with regard to religion.

Concerning the claim to religious belonging through circumcision, Sarajlic objects:

> A plausible valuation of communal membership must be accompanied by the exit option that allows members to opt out freely at any time without grave consequences. When the membership is involuntarily imposed and marked by an irreversible bodily modification, the exit avenues are significantly

---

17. Michael Benatar and David Benatar, "Between Prophylaxis and Child Abuse: The Ethics of Neonatal Male Circumcision," *The American Journal of Bioethics* 3/2 (2003): 35–48; Joseph Mazor, "The Child's Interests and the Case for Permissibility of Male Infant Circumcision," *Journal of Medical Ethics* 39 (2013): 421–8.
18. Sarajlic, "Can Culture Justify Infant Circumcision?," 334.
19. Sarajlic, "Can Culture Justify Infant Circumcision?," 335.

> narrowed. The fact that few men choose to opt out later in life may actually reflect the fact that they have been physically marked as members, rather than the assumption that they do not wish to opt out because they value their community.
>
> However, one may also suggest that opting out from Muslim and Jewish communities has nothing necessarily to do with circumcision: men can freely exit these communities and circumcision does not prevent them in doing so. Furthermore, one may claim that circumcision is a fairly inconspicuous modification of the body, so no necessary stigma is attached to communal disintegration of the individual. True, circumcised men may be free to exit one community and integrate into another without visible marks, but this argument is sustained only against an externalist assumption about identity. One's identity is not necessarily affirmed or altered through a visible (external) change. Inner self-understanding and perception play an important role as well. A bodily modification such as circumcision can significantly diminish the ability of a person to perceive himself as a member of the non-circumcising community.[20]

Sarajlic focuses here specifically on the consequences of circumcision for the possibility to leave a particular religious community. This possibility is significantly limited, he claims, when "membership is involuntarily imposed and marked by an irreversible bodily modification." The fact that few Jewish and Muslim men do so, may, according to Sarajlic, be evidence of this process. He maintains that while circumcision is not a formal hindrance and is in itself inconspicuous, identity is determined not only by what is visible, but also by inner self-understanding. In this way, he argues, circumcision would make it more difficult for "a person to perceive himself as a member of the non-circumcising community."

Having examined some recent publications that make claims about circumcision and religious freedom similar to those of the Cologne verdict, I now turn to an intersectional analysis of these claims by looking at their assumptions about gender and religion.

The Interests of the Child: Gender Assumptions

One remarkable aspect of the discussions outlined above is the virtual absence of any observations on gender. Even though male circumcision is a practice that relates exclusively to male bodies, and more specifically to male genitals, this fact and its implications do not receive any attention in these reflections on circumcision and conversion. Yet if the claim about circumcision and religious freedom is true, it would mean that Jewish and Muslim men are bound to their religion in a way that Jewish and Muslim

---

20. Sarajlic, "Can Culture Justify Infant Circumcision?," 335.

women are not. It would constitute a clear case of religious gender discrimination. I leave aside any possible similar effects of female genital cutting on women's religious freedom, since the sources discussed here do not raise this either.[21] In general, a similar argument about religious freedom appears to be largely absent from the debate on female genital cutting, although the practice certainly can have religious connotations for practitioners.[22]

The silence concerning gender in the discussions on male circumcision stands in strong contrast to other contested practices that specifically relate to women and female bodies, such as head and face coverings, and female genital cutting. In these cases, the debates tend to have a strong focus on the gender implications of these practices. In connection with these issues, religion is often seen as harmful to women and as promoting gender inequality. Similar questions about religious gender constructions could be asked about male circumcision, but are not put forward by the authors under discussion here.

While the claim made in these sources is a direct claim about religious gender discrimination, this is not drawn out by the authors and remains implicit. This is noteworthy also because the presumed gender inequality would offer the possibility to empirically substantiate the claim that circumcised men are less free to convert. If true, studies on religious conversion should be able to see a difference in the rates of religious change in Jewish and Muslim women, compared to those of Jewish and Muslim men. Reliable data on religious change are scarce, much less gender specific rates of conversion, but in theory, such evidence could support or challenge the idea that circumcision strongly affects religious choice. Yet, rather than

---

21. Sarajlic even does so explicitly: "Though making comparison with female circumcision is often made in the literature, I will refrain from making any comparisons and will look exclusively at the male case" (Sarajlic, "Can Culture Justify Infant Circumcision?," 328). Merkel and Putzke do briefly discuss FGM, but do not mention that it might have similar implications for religious freedom ("After Cologne," 446, note v).

22. It is of course difficult to show its absence conclusively, but any mention of religious freedom is absent from arguments listed against FGM in major campaigns such as those by the "End FGM European Network" (see http://www.endfgm.eu/en/ [last accessed 7 June 2021]) or "Stop FGM now" (see http://www.stop-fgm-now.com/why-are-we-having-campaign [last accessed 7 June 2021]). On religion as an important motivator for female genital cutting, see for example Lori Leonard, "Adopting Female 'Circumcision' in Southern Chad: The Experience of Myabé," in Bettina Shell-Duncan and Ylva Hernlund, eds., *Female "Circumcision" in Africa: Culture, Controversy, and Change* (Boulder, CO: Lynne Rienner Publishers, 2000), 167–92, here 168; Mary Nyangweso Wangila, *Female Circumcision: The Interplay of Religion, Culture, and Gender in Kenya* (New York: Orbis Books, 2007), 162; "Eliminating Female Genital Mutilation: An Interagency Statement OHCHR, UNAIDS, UNDP, UNECA, UNESCO, UNFPA, UNHCR, UNICEF, UNIFEM, WHO," World Health Organization (2008).

criticize circumcising religions for a sexist practice, the sources discussed here instead mask any gendered aspects of circumcision.

It is worth noting that in other types of discourse critical of male circumcision, such gender implications are highlighted. To give one example, Miriam Pollack offers criticism from an explicitly Jewish perspective, and states that "Circumcision is a rite of male domination—domination and the entitlement of domination over other men, women, and children, both institutionally and personally. It is the essence of patriarchy."[23] So while it is certainly possible to bring in gender implications of male circumcision, the sources discussed here refrain from doing this.

Gender Language

Not only is there no reflection on gender, but the terminology used by the authors discussed above even tends to hide the fact that male bodies are at stake here. They do so by opting for gender neutral or gender inclusive language, instead of terms that denote male gender or anatomy. While the Cologne verdict does refer specifically to "the boy" ("der Knabe") in three instances, it speaks far more frequently about "the child" ("das Kind"). In stating that circumcision "changes the child's body" (der Körper des Kindes) permanently and irreparably, a change which "runs contrary to the interests of the child (dem Interesse des Kindes)," the verdict chooses language that conceals the gendered aspect of the practice.

This effect is even stronger in Cliteur, who not only writes about "children" and "their bodies," but also uses terms such as "someone" and "a person." While Cliteur does speak of "a person" changing "his opinion" about religion, this appears to be not so much a single attempt at gender specificity, but rather a slip into androcentrism, since he earlier refers to "someone" proclaiming "his or her adherence to a religious community."[24]

Although Merkel and Putzke do frequently use the term "boy" in their article, they do not reflect specifically on male gender. In their discussion of religious freedom, they speak consistently about "the child" or "children," such as when they ask "If parents do not have a right to determine their child's religious affiliation for the child's lifetime, why should they have a right to permanently mark their children's bodies with a symbol of that affiliation?"[25]

Sarajlic is the exception in referring several times to "men," for example, when he observes that "circumcised men may be free to exit one community

---

23. Miriam Pollack, "Circumcision: Identity, Gender, and Power" (https://muse.jhu.edu/article/584975/summary [last accessed 7 June 2021]).
24. See http://leidenlawblog.nl/articles/male-circumcision#.UCN1E2i3Iyw.
25. Merkel and Putzke, "After Cologne," 447.

and integrate into another." Yet he adopts a comparable strategy to that of the other authors in speaking predominantly in inclusive terms such as "the child," "the individual" and "a member" of a community.[26]

These authors thus tend to construct their argument not on the basis of specific gendered repercussions of circumcision, but, perhaps unconsciously, choose instead to broaden the focus to more general considerations and principles, assumed to affect everyone. This reluctance to address the gender aspects of male circumcision may be connected to dominant gender constructions, especially those associated with weakness and physicality. The question of what is appropriate for women in terms of dress, behavior, and sexuality is a recurring social theme, while male bodies are much less of a religious and cultural battleground. Female bodies are more often culturally constructed as vulnerable, and victimhood tends to be seen as feminine.

Marie Fox and Michael Thomson have highlighted the effects of these gender constructions specifically for the debate about male circumcision. Since the focus of their criticism is routine medical circumcision, they discuss gender constructions in a healthcare context, but what they point out applies more generally:

> In health care, as in other legal disciplines, male bodies have functioned as the norm and therefore tended to be less politically contentious than other bodies ... Debates concerning these bodies [of women and fetuses] have often focused on their vulnerability to harm—as is evident in the framing of debates around female circumcision. By contrast, male bodies are typically constructed as safe, bounded and impermeable. We would argue that this construction is problematic in a number of ways ... We would suggest that this may make it more difficult to uncover harms to boys—a contention which seems to be borne out by the tendency of Anglo-American legal commentators to minimise the harms inflicted on boys by circumcision with a concomitant propensity to exacerbate the risks occasioned by less invasive forms of female circumcision. Our suggestion is that within law the role of abuse victim is feminised, so that the discursive construction of victims may produce a greater acknowledgment of harms perpetrated against girls.[27]

If victimhood is feminized, as Fox and Thomson explain, then presenting men as victims constitutes a feminization of men. Moreover, emphasizing harm specifically to men challenges the construction of male bodies as "safe, bounded and impermeable." For Fox and Thomson, this process clarifies a reluctance to critique male circumcision in a medical context.

26. Sarajlic, "Can Culture Justify Infant Circumcision?," 335.
27. Marie Fox and Michael Thomson, "Short Changed? The Law and Ethics of Male Circumcision," *The International Journal of Children's Rights*, 13 (2005): 161–81, here 175–6.

In the sources discussed in this article, which do criticize male circumcision, these underlying gender constructions can help explain the absence of any specific reference to male gender. Presenting male circumcision as a violation of human rights more generally, rather than as a challenge to the bodies and rights of boys and men in particular—much less acknowledging the possibility that they are cut exactly because they are male—preserves and strengthens existing gender constructions that see the male body as the norm, and as inviolable. The approach chosen in the sources discussed here thus falls into a pattern seen more widely in discussions of circumcision. Even in criticizing the practice, the authors steer clear of drawing any implications for men as men, which would question existing constructions of masculinity.

Choosing Belief: Constructions of Religion

We now turn from gender to constructions of religion that underlie the argumentations of the sources. Again, an analysis of the language used is helpful to uncover assumptions. Throughout the sources examined here, there is a consistent understanding of religion and religious affiliation as a matter of conscious decision and opinion. The Cologne verdict speaks about the time when the boy will "be able to make the decision" whether to "have a circumcision as a visible sign of his affiliation to Islam."[28]

While language about community and belonging also occurs in these sources, it is used predominantly in connection with childhood, and has a negative connotation. Cliteur states that parents cannot "permanently mutilate" children "to earmark them as belonging to a certain religious community" and that being "physically mutilated or earmarked to proclaim his or her adherence to a religious community" violates freedom of religion. Religion formulated more positively entails "the right to free choice in matters religious," "the right to choose a religion, but also to abandon or reject a religion" and the ability "for a person to change his opinion about this religion."[29]

Merkel and Putzke similarly oppose the "irreversible mark of a religious membership" and initiation "into a religious community" to "self-determination and the child's own (negative) freedom to avoid, or (positive)

---

28. "Umgekehrt wird das Erziehungsrecht der Eltern nicht unzumutbar beeinträchtigt, wenn sie gehalten sind abzuwarten, ob sich der Knabe später, wenn er mündig ist, selbst für die Beschneidung als sichtbares Zeichen der Zugehörigkeit zum Islam entscheidet," Landgericht Köln, III, 7.

29. See http://leidenlawblog.nl/articles/male-circumcision#.UCN1E2i3Iyw.

freedom to adopt, any particular religion," and the child's ability "to decide on such matters for himself."[30]

Sarajlic is even more specific about this cognitive, belief-focused understanding of religion, in referring to "metaphysical beliefs" about "metaphysical salvation." He notes that "Individuals often change their beliefs, shed the religious assumptions inherited from parents or adopt new ones."[31] Sarajlic differs, however, in using the language of community not only for the bonds created by the parents, but also for the religious affiliations of adult men: "circumcised men may be free to exit one community and integrate into another without visible marks." He even understands those who do not practice circumcision as bound together into a community: "A bodily modification such as circumcision can significantly diminish the ability of a person to perceive himself as a member of the non-circumcising community."[32]

The understanding of religion that underlies these claims about circumcision and conversion is thus focused on conscious decisions, opinions, assumptions, and beliefs of the individual. These conscious beliefs of the individual are opposed to community, which these authors, with the exception of Sarajlic, appear to associate with a lack of control.

This understanding of religion as primarily cognitive and focused on specific beliefs or opinions is characteristic of many contemporary discussions of religion, as will be shown below. Yet despite this focus on religion as an intellectual choice, the argument made by these authors rests on a presumed impact of the physical on religious opinions and religious freedom. Being physically "marked," as these authors describe it, is assumed to have a strong influence on how religious opinion is formed, thereby compromising religious freedom. Exactly how the physical change has this effect is not specified or argued, but the fact that it is significant suggests that even though these authors describe religion as a matter of belief, they do to some extent consider it to be "embodied."

The understanding of religion as primarily a matter of belief and opinion is quite prevalent in a legal context, as well as in contemporary society more broadly. Religion is notoriously difficult to define with any degree of consensus, yet as Jeremy Gunn observes, when the law needs to decide on freedom of religion, it must work with some concept of what religion is, even though explicit legal definitions are rare.[33] Linda Woodhead notes that

30. Merkel and Putzke, "After Cologne," 447.
31. Sarajlic, "Can Culture Justify Infant Circumcision?," 335.
32. Sarajlic, "Can Culture Justify Infant Circumcision?," 335.
33. T. Jeremy Gunn, "The Complexity of Religion and the Definition of 'Religion' in International Law," *Harvard Human Rights Journal* 16 (2003): 189–215, here 190.

"Legal accounts of religion often take a similarly belief-based view of religion, as in the common tendency in the USA to define religion (broadly) in terms of 'sincerely-held religious, moral or ethical beliefs', and (narrowly) as beliefs asserted in an 'authoritative sacred text' and 'classic formulations of doctrine and practice'."[34] The German Federal Administrative Court defines religion as "any specific certainty as regards the whole of the world and the origin and purpose of mankind."[35]

Such an understanding of religion as focused on the beliefs and convictions of individuals is thus prevalent, yet it is not the only possible way to conceptualize religion and in fact excludes certain aspects of religion that can also be significant. In discussing the complexity of religion in relation to law, Gunn distinguishes, in addition to "religion as belief," two other concepts: "religion as identity," and "religion as way of life":[36]

> While religion as belief emphasizes doctrines, religion as identity emphasizes affiliation with a group. In this sense, identity religion is experienced as something akin to family, ethnicity, race, or nationality. Identity religion thus is something into which people believe they are born rather than something to which they convert after a process of study, prayer, or reflection.[37]

The third facet of religion, "religion as a way of life" is described by Gunn as "associated with actions, rituals, customs, and traditions that may distinguish the believer from adherents of other religions."[38] Clearly, the concept of religion prevalent in the sources examined here falls in the first category, that of "religion as belief," and tends to ignore aspects of religion that are significant in the other two categories.

In her analysis of the concept of religion, sociologist Linda Woodhead presents a "taxonomy of five major concepts of religion in social scientific study."[39] Woodhead distinguishes "religion as culture," "religion as identity," "religion as relationship," "religion as practice," and "religion as power." The first concept, "religion as culture," is distinguished into several

---

34. Linda Woodhead, "Five Concepts of Religion," *International Review of Sociology* 21.1 (2011): 121–43, here 123. Woodhead here quotes Winnifred F. Sullivan, *The Impossibility of Religious Freedom* (Princeton, NJ: Princeton University Press, 2005), 147.

35. See Lucy Vickers, "Religion and Belief Discrimination in Employment–the EU law" (2006), a report for the European Commission, accessible at http://ec.europa.eu/social/BlobServlet?docId=1689&langId=en (last accessed 7 June 2021).

36. Gunn, "Complexity of Religion," 200–5.

37. Gunn, "Complexity of Religion," 201.

38. Gunn, "Complexity of Religion," 204.

39. Woodhead, "Five Concepts," 122.

subcategories, of which for us "religion as belief and meaning" is particularly important. As Woodhead states

> One of the most popular conceptions of religion today if one takes as evidence not only academic work but the discourse of politicians, legal professionals, journalists, and everyday talk is of religion as belief. On this account, being religious has to do with believing certain things, where that amounts to subscribing to certain propositions and accepting certain doctrines.[40]

As noted above, Woodhead sees this understanding as dominating legal discourse. Woodhead traces this type of understanding back to the "confessionalization" of religion after the Reformation, which "tended to define and distinguish different forms of religion (particularly Christianity) in terms of distinctive 'confessions of faith'."[41] She points out a further influence in positivism and the sociology of religion, which reinforced this understanding of religion by reducing it to quantifiable aspects such as membership and assent to propositional beliefs. Woodhead concludes:

> Thus the conception of religion as a matter of belief is a distinctively modern one, with a bias towards modern Christian, especially Protestant, forms of religion ... Above all, it seems to be bound up with a scientism and empiricism which assumes that all knowledge is primarily a matter of (testable) propositional belief, and with a shift of attention from the oral and practised to the literate and encoded.[42]

This conception of religion thus underrepresents other significant aspects, such as identity, relationships, and practice. Many scholars of religion share Woodhead's analysis that the concept of religion as belief, widely used today, is closely bound up with Protestant Christianity. The anthropologist Stanley Tambiah connects the concept of religion to developments within Christianity during and after the Reformation:

> The main message, as it issued during the Reformation from the mouths of Zwingli and Calvin, was that men should not put their faith in any external institution, the Church, or in any religious system as embodying the divine. Instead *religio* designated something personal, inner and transcendentally oriented.
>
> It is essentially in the modern period, since the Enlightenment, that a particular conception of religion that emphasizes its cognitive, intellectual, doctrinal and dogmatic aspects, gained prominence.[43]

---

40. Woodhead, "Five Concepts," 123.
41. Woodhead, "Five Concepts," 123.
42. Woodhead, "Five Concepts," 123–4.
43. Stanley J. Tambiah, *Magic, Science and Religion and the Scope of Rationality* (Cambridge: Cambridge University Press, 1990), 4.

In his study *The Western Construction of Religion*, Daniel Dubuisson calls religion "the legitimate daughter of Christianity." He traces the development of the concept of religion back even further within Christianity and observes that:

> Just like the notion itself, the most general questions concerning religion, its nature and definition, its origins and expressions, were born in the West ... The exclusively Western history of questions relative to religion is, of course, inseparable from the intellectual history of the West, since it is from its own history that the West drew a complex of systematic reflections (from philosophy to theology, from anthropology to sociology or psychology) that were to lead to the universalization of a concept born of Christian apologetics dating from the first centuries of our era.[44]

It is thus characteristic for this particular concept of religion as applied here to circumcision and conversion that it limits religion to a matter of individual beliefs and convictions, which excludes many other possible understandings of religion. In addition, this concept of religion is derived from Protestant Christian thought and thus potentially problematic when applied to other religions, for which, unlike Christianity, beliefs may not be central to self-understanding. I would argue that these Protestant Christian roots raise particular problems in connection with circumcision, something which have so far been unexplored in scholarship on religion. Given the fact that the concept of religion as belief is bound up with a long history of Christian reflection and debate on its own nature, it is also bound up with a long history of reflection on, and rejection of, circumcision. Throughout Christian history, circumcision was a target and symbol of what idealized Christianity was not—physical, gendered, embodied—and is therefore closely bound up with Christian self-understanding. Given the scope of this article, I can only offer a brief support of this argument, which I hope to elaborate more fully elsewhere.

New Testament sources clearly show that nascent Christianity, from its earliest witness in the writings of Paul, was involved in a heated debate about male circumcision.[45] As is evident from his letters, Paul strongly rejected the circumcision of non-Jewish men who wanted to convert to his gospel about Christ. Other early Christ-believers, however, argued that these men needed to become circumcised to join the community.[46] While

---

44. Daniel Dubuisson, *The Western Construction of Religion: Myths, Knowledge, and Ideology* (Baltimore, MD: The Johns Hopkins University Press, 2003), 9.

45. See for example Paul's letter to the Galatians, Phil. 3.2-9, Acts 15.1-21.

46. On this dispute see Matthew Thiessen, *Contesting Conversion: Genealogy, Circumcision, and Identity in Ancient Judaism and Christianity* (Oxford: Oxford University Press, 2011); Karin Neutel and Matthew Anderson, "The First Cut is the

some Christ-believers continued to practice circumcision, the Pauline view appears to have become dominant quite early on. Christians subsequently polemicized against circumcision more generally, including all circumcision practiced by Jews, not just by proselytes. These Christians pitted their own religion against this practice, as being superior for relying on internal faith, rather than external practice. An example of this is the second-century apologist Justin Martyr, who writes in his dialogue with the Jew Trypho:

> We also, therefore, because of our belief in God through Christ, even though we are uncircumcised in the flesh, have the salutary circumcision, namely, that of the heart, and we thereby hope to be just and pleasing to God, since already we have obtained his testimony from him through the words of the prophets. (Dial. 92.4)

Several centuries later, Augustine writes that "the symbolism of the circumcision of the flesh has been transferred to a circumcision of the heart."[47] As these examples indicate, circumcision was an important issue in the first centuries and polemics against it were a way of constituting and expressing Christian self-understanding.[48] The Christian adoption and transformation of the originally Jewish notion of circumcision of the heart entailed a fundamental criticism of the practice of circumcision. It was seen as something external and secondary only, while the essence of religious observance was presented as internal and spiritual. Throughout the Middle Ages and Early Modern times, Christian thinkers continued to use male circumcision as a foil against which to argue their own identity, and usually superiority.[49] True circumcision was the circumcision of the heart, which was internal, and private; a matter of conviction, rather than practice, and of the individual, rather than the community. The formation of the concept of religion in tandem with this growing Protestant Christian emphasis on internal, personal belief cannot thus be separated from opposition to circumcision. The

---

Deepest: Masculinity and Circumcision in the First Century," in Peter-Ben Smit and Ovidiu Creanga, eds., *Biblical Masculinities* (Sheffield: Phoenix Press, 2014), 228–44; Karin Neutel, *A Cosmopolitan Ideal: Paul's Declaration "neither Jew nor Greek, neither Slave nor Free, nor Male and Female" in the Context of First-Century Thought* (London: T&T Clark, 2015).

47. Augustine, *Sermon 260* (in Mary Sarah Muldowney, ed., *Sermons on the Liturgical Seasons* [trans. by Mary Sarah Muldowney; Washington, DC: Catholic University of America Press, 1959]).

48. See Andrew S. Jacobs, *Christ Circumcised: A Study in Early Christian History and Difference* (Philadelphia, PA: University of Pennsylvania Press, 2012), esp. 41–71.

49. See for example, Irven Michael Resnick, *Marks of Distinction: Christian Perceptions of Jews in the High Middle Ages* (Washington, DC: The Catholic University of America Press, 2012); Eva Johanna Holmberg, *Jews in the Early Modern English Imagination: A Scattered Nation* (Aldershot: Ashgate, 2012).

application of this concept of religion as belief to the practice of male circumcision thus already carries with it an implicit rejection of this physical, embodied ritual.

Conclusion

My analysis has made it clear that the claim in legal discourse that circumcision limits religious freedom is based on several assumptions associated with cultural majority views. Regarding gender, the absence of any questioning of the implications of circumcision for men as men, serves to confirm conventional gender constructions. By using inclusive terms that are not gender specific, the authors examined here present circumcision as relating not specifically to men, but to human beings in general. A comparison with the gendered discourse on contested practices concerning women shows that this is a strategy that relies on men being presented as the norm and as less physically vulnerable and culturally contentious than women.

With regard to religion, a similar mainstream view can be recognized. By limiting religion to the convictions and beliefs of the individual, the sources privilege an understanding of religion that, while purporting to be secular and neutral, is in fact a Western, Protestant Christian construction. Moreover, this concept of religion has its roots in a rejection of circumcision and projects this rejection back onto contemporary circumcision practices.

When these understandings of gender and religion are exposed as overlapping and intersecting social locations, they highlight the extent to which these sources are invested in socially dominant perspectives, while expressing little awareness of their own situatedness or the many other possible perspectives from which these issues can be approached and experienced. This observation does not, of course, constitute a verdict on the veracity or the relevance of the claim about circumcision and conversion. It does, however, suggest that there will be many other ways in which to understand the implications of male circumcision for religious affiliation.

Biographical Note

Karin Neutel is Associate Professor in New Testament Exegesis at Umeå University in Sweden. Her research focuses on ancient and contemporary attitudes towards male circumcision, and on the use of the Bible in European anti-migration debates. She has published *A Cosmopolitan Ideal: Paul's Declaration "Neither Jew nor Greek, neither Slave nor Free, nor Male and Female" in the Context of First-Century Thought* (T&T Clark, 2015).

Bibliography

Bartsch, Tillman. "Anmerkung zu einer Entscheidung des LG Koln, Urteil vom 07.05.2012" (151 Ns 169/11; StV 2012, 603) – Zur religios motivierten Beschneidung, StV 2012,S. 604–9.

Benatar, Michael, and David Benatar. "Between Prophylaxis and Child Abuse: The Ethics of Neonatal Male Circumcision," *The American Journal of Bioethics* 3/2 (2003): 35–48. https://doi.org/10.1162/152651603766436216

Bulkeley, Kelly. "Religious Conversion and Cognitive Neuroscience," 240–55 in Rambo and Farhadian, eds., *Oxford Handbook of Religious Conversion*, 2014.

Cho, Sumi, Kimberlé Williams Crenshaw, and Leslie McCall. "Toward a Field of Intersectional Studies: Theory, Applications, and Praxis," *Signs: Journal of Women in Culture and Society* (*Theme Issue: Intersectionality: Theorizing Power, Empowering Theory*) 38.4 (2013): 785–810. https://doi.org/10.1086/669608

Cliteur, Paul. "Morele en immorele religieus gelegitimeerde praktijken in het gezondheidsrecht," 91–185 in *Ethiek en gezondheidsrecht*. Edited by Govert den Hartogh and Paul Cliteur. Preadvies uitgebracht voor de Vereniging voor Gezondheidsrecht, jaarvergadering 25 April 2014.

Dubuisson, Daniel. *The Western Construction of Religion: Myths, Knowledge, and Ideology*. Baltimore, MD: The Johns Hopkins University Press, 2003.

Fox, Marie, and Michael Thomson. "Short Changed? The Law and Ethics of Male Circumcision," *The International Journal of Children's Rights*, 13 (2005): 161–81. https://doi.org/10.1163/ej.9789004148949.i-337.84

Gunn, T. Jeremy. "The Complexity of Religion and the Definition of 'Religion' in International Law," *Harvard Human Rights Journal* 16 (2003): 189–215.

Holmberg, Eva Johanna. *Jews in the Early Modern English Imagination: A Scattered Nation*. Aldershot: Ashgate, 2012.

Jacobs, Andrew S. *Christ Circumcised: A Study in Early Christian History and Difference*. Philadelphia. PA: University of Pennsylvania Press, 2012. https://doi.org/10.9783/9780812206517

Leonard, Lori. "Adopting Female 'Circumcision' in Southern Chad: The Experience of Myabé," 167–92 in *Female "Circumcision" in Africa: Culture, Controversy, and Change*. Edited by Bettina Shell-Duncan and Ylva Hernlund. Boulder, CO: Lynne Rienner Publishers, 2000.

Mazor, Joseph. "The Child's Interests and the Case for Permissibility of Male Infant Circumcision," *Journal of Medical Ethics* 39 (2013): 421–8. https://doi.org/10.1136/medethics-2013-101318

Merkel, Reinhard, and Holm Putzke. "After Cologne: Male Circumcision and the Law. Parental Right, Religious Liberty or Criminal Assault?," *Journal of Medical Ethics* 39.7 (2013): 444–9. https://doi.org/10.1136/medethics-2012-101284

Muldowney, Mary Sarah, ed. *Sermons on the Liturgical Seasons*. Translated by Mary Sarah Muldowney. Washington, DC: Catholic University of America Press, 1959.

Neutel, Karin. *A Cosmopolitan Ideal: Paul's Declaration "neither Jew nor Greek, neither Slave nor Free, nor Male and Female" in the Context of First-Century Thought*. London: T&T Clark, 2015.

Neutel, Karin, and Matthew Anderson. "The First Cut is the Deepest: Masculinity and Circumcision in the First Century," 228–44 in *Biblical Masculinities*. Edited by Peter-Ben Smit and Ovidiu Creanga. Sheffield: Phoenix Press, 2014.

Nyangweso Wangila, Mary. *Female Circumcision: The Interplay of Religion, Culture, and Gender in Kenya*. New York: Orbis Books, 2007.

Orth, Jan F. "Explaining the Cologne Circumcision Decision," *The Journal of Criminal Law* 77/6 (2013): 497–511. https://doi.org/10.1350/jcla.2013.77.6.877

Paloutzian, Raymond F., Erica L. Swenson, and Patrick McNamara. "Religious Conversion, Spiritual Transformation, and the Neurocognition of Meaning Making," 151–69 in *Where God and Science Meet: How Brain and Evolutionary Studies Alter our Understanding of Religion*. Edited by Patrick McNamara. Westport, CN: Praeger Publishers, 2006.

Pollack, Miriam. "Circumcision: Identity, Gender, and Power," https://muse.jhu.edu/article/584975/summary (last accessed 7 June 2021).

Rambo, Lewis R., and Charles E. Farhadian. "Introduction," 1–24 in Rambo and Farhardian, eds., *Oxford Handbook of Religious Conversion*, 2014. https://doi.org/10.1093/oxfordhb/9780195338522.013.033

Rambo, Lewis R., and Charles E. Farhadian, eds. *The Oxford Handbook of Religious Conversion*. Oxford: Oxford University Press, 2014. https://doi.org/10.1093/oxfordhb/9780195338522.001.0001

Resnick, Irven Michael. *Marks of Distinction: Christian Perceptions of Jews in the High Middle Ages*. Washington, DC: The Catholic University of America Press, 2012. https://doi.org/10.2307/j.ctt2851pt

Sarajlic, Eldar. "Can Culture Justify Infant Circumcision?," *Res Publica* 20 (2014): 327–43. https://doi.org/10.1007/s11158-014-9254-x

Sullivan, Winnifred F. *The Impossibility of Religious Freedom*. Princeton, NJ: Princeton University Press, 2005.

Tabory, Ephraim, and Sharon Erex. "Circumscribed Circumcision: The Motivations and Identities of Israeli Parents Who Choose Not to Circumcise their Sons," 161–76 in *The Covenant of Circumcision: New Perspectives on an Ancient Jewish Rite*. Edited by Elizabeth Wyner Mark. Lebanon: Brandeis University Press, 2003.

Tambiah, Stanley J. *Magic, Science and Religion and the Scope of Rationality*. Cambridge: Cambridge University Press, 1990.

Thiessen, Matthew. *Contesting Conversion: Genealogy, Circumcision, and Identity in Ancient Judaism and Christianity*. Oxford: Oxford University Press, 2011. https://doi.org/10.1093/acprof:oso/9780199793563.001.0001

Vickers, Lucy. "Religion and Belief Discrimination in Employment–the EU law" (2006). A report for the European Commission, accessible at http://ec.europa.eu/social/BlobServlet?docId=1689&langId=en (last accessed 7 June 2021).

Woodhead, Linda. "Five Concepts of Religion," *International Review of Sociology* 21.1 (2011): 121–43. https://doi.org/10.1080/03906701.2011.544192

Web Articles

http://dejure.org/dienste/vernetzung/rechtsprechung?Gericht=LG%20K%F6ln&Datum=07.05.2012&Aktenzeichen=151%20Ns%20169/11 (last accessed 7 June 2021).

http://www.endfgm.eu/en/ (last accessed 7 June 2021).

http://www.haaretz.com/israel-news/even-in-israel-more-and-more-parents-choose-not-to-circumcise-their-sons-1.436421 (last accessed 7 June 2021).

http://leidenlawblog.nl/articles/male-circumcision#.UCN1E2i3Iyw (last accessed 7 June 2021).

http://www.stop-fgm-now.com/why-are-we-having-campaign (last accessed 7 June 2021).

Chapter Three

Complex Interactions:
Conversion and Interreligious Dialogue in the Norwegian Context

Anne Hege Grung

This article explores the process of creating a text that communicates a joint declaration on the right to conversion. It was put together by a Contact group bringing together the Islamic Council of Norway (ICN) and the Church of Norway (CoN) and released in 2007.[1] As a member of the Contact group, I was involved in the working process for realizing the document. In my analysis of the process, I discuss the status of such a joint statement—a consensus-based text, written in a secular language. I also give a brief overview of the Norwegian context related to religious conversion, specifically conversion from and to the Christian and Islamic traditions. In this context, a question surfaces and highlights the connection between conversion, identity politics, and the discourse on immigration: who has the authority to decide whether a person is a convert or not? Is conversion a religious, legal, or political matter, or all three? Or should we view conversion primarily as a social matter, signaling an altered form of belonging to family and other socially structured groups?

Finally, I discuss how various concepts of conversion may function more broadly in Norway's context of increased religious plurality, interreligious families, and religious hybridity. Due to ongoing transformations within the European populations when it comes to questions of religious belonging, religious identity, and processes of secularization and migration, studies of religious conversion are highly relevant for many different perspectives. In Christian theological traditions, exploring the paths and formation of the converts has often been connected to what used to be perceived as the original conversion, the one of the apostle Paul, who experienced a miraculous calling resulting in his on-the-spot conversion from Judaism to Christianity

---

1. The event was covered at the website of the Church of Norway including a picture of the Secretary General and the leader of the Islamic Council of Norway, and the Secretary General from the CoNs desk for international and ecumenical affairs and the author of this article as a member of the Contact group: http://www.gammel.kirken.no/?event=dolink&famID=17453 (last consulted 16 August 2017).

on the road to Damascus. In our current context, we need to move beyond this prototypical narrative and make an empirical turn in our studies of this phenomenon, whether we work on biblical texts, other texts, discourses, or qualitative material.

Understanding and Exploring Religious Conversion in Different Ways

How one views and analyzes the concept of conversion determines which aspects are deemed most significant, and scholars of religion, theologians, psychologists, social scientists, and scholars of law all have different ways of exploring it. When discussing religious conversion, the traditional explanation or definition of the phenomenon among religious scholars may come close to a quotation used in the introduction of *The Oxford Handbook of Religious Conversion* and presented as an influential and traditional description of the phenomenon. It is taken from Arthur D. Nock's book, *Conversion*, published in 1933:

> By conversion we mean the reorientation of the soul of an individual, his deliberate turning from indifference or from an earlier form of piety to another, a turning which implies a consciousness that a great change is involved, that the old was wrong and the new is right. It is seen at its fullest in the positive response of a man to the choice set before him by the prophetic traditions.[2]

In this understanding, conversion is individual, irreversible, and primarily connected to the "prophetic traditions," meaning Judaism, Christianity, and Islam. With its focus on "piety" and "consciousness" and "turning from indifference," it reflects the religious standards of Protestantism as the criteria for defining religious conversion in general. The description also establishes as a premise that religious traditions are stable and have fixed boundaries, which allow to absolutely determine whether a person is an insider or an outsider. This is connected to a notion of religion and religious traditions as stable, but also as mutually exclusive.

People do seek new traditions because of curiosity or spiritual quest, and in the process, they might find new individual convictions. But the process may not be simple nor straightforward: in her work, Berit Thorbjørnsrud mentions "conversion careers," implying that many people convert more than once.[3] People may convert and then re-convert, or seek refuge for a

---

2. Arthur D. Nock, *Conversion: The Old and the New in Religion from Alexander the Great to Augustine of Hippo* (Oxford: Oxford University Press, 1933), as quoted in Lewis R. Rambo and Charles E. Farhadian, eds., *The Oxford Handbook of Religious Conversion* (Oxford: Oxford University Press, 2014), 5.

3. Berit Thorbjørnsrud, "Who Is a Convert? New Members of the Orthodox Church in Norway," *Temenos* 51.1 (2015): 71–93.

time in a different religious tradition.⁴ In her study of Western and Eastern Europeans converting to Orthodox churches in Norway, she suggests the term "religious pilgrims" to describe these converts, in contrast to the term "religious tourists," which indicates a less stable affiliation to the faith tradition.⁵ Rambo and Farhadian point out that recent studies of religious conversion are more concerned with "constructing new identities."⁶ These studies open up space for social, political, and intercultural dynamics, connected to social mobility such as interaction between groups, and migration.⁷ The *Oxford Handbook of Religious Conversion* dedicates specific chapters to various patterns of conversion connected to different religious traditions, in addition to the overall presentations based on different scholarly perspectives such as psychology and social anthropology. This means that conversion needs to be addressed and studied differently according not only to geopolitical, cultural, and discursive contexts, but also with regard to differences between religious traditions themselves. Thorbjørnsrud's article and the *Oxford Handbook* both view religious conversion mainly from the individual convert's or the religious communities' perspective.

As I have suggested, religious conversion is also a political and legal matter. In these contexts, however, the definition of religious conversion is often simple when it comes to the legal issue surrounding it, at least in Norway: it is simply a matter of official membership in a faith organization. In political life and its connected discourses, there seems to be little interest in how religious conversion is to be understood and investigated on a personal and/or religious group level. Rather, the concern is how to decide where people actually belong, as I will show later in this article. In some cases, religious conversion is a disputed political issue, especially when refugees and asylum seekers convert to a country's majority religion. In other cases, religious conversion is explained in terms of national treason or engagement with anti-establishment militancy if people formerly belonging to the national religious majority convert to religious traditions that are met with suspicion in certain discourses. We find this situation with Islam and Muslim groups in present-day Europe.

---

4. Thorbjørnsrud, "Who Is a Convert?," 73.
5. Thorbjørnsrud, "Who Is a Convert?," 73.
6. Rambo and Farhadian, eds., *Oxford Handbook of Religious Conversion*.
7. Rambo and Farhadian, eds., *Oxford Handbook of Religious Conversion*, 6–7.

The Joint Statement on the Right to Conversion (Proposed by the Contact Group between the Church of Norway and the Islamic Council of Norway)

The contact group between the Church of Norway and the Islamic Council of Norway was established in 1994 and consists of clergy and lay leaders from the Muslim communities and the Church of Norway (Lutheran). The group meets regularly, three to four times a year, and discusses matters of relational and political importance for Muslims and Christians in Norway. Since 1997, the group has published 12 statements or open letters that share a joint view and common reasoning on current, urgent matters. The joint statement on the right to conversion, released in 2007,[8] was such a statement, perhaps the most disputed of all.

Although the right to freedom of religion and beliefs (without any restrictions) has been firmly established in the Norwegian constitution since 1964,[9] religious conversion touches upon many other aspects, in addition to the formal and juridical. For example, religious affiliation as well as conversion (when it is made official as a legal act) may affect religious norms and laws concerning marital status. Religious affiliation, and conversion, might also play a role in processes related to political asylum and to applications for individual residence permits, depending on existing national laws and practice. The 2007 statement does not engage in legal discourses at all, neither secular nor religious. Instead it focuses on how Christian and Islamic communities in Norway should face the possible religious and social consequences of religious conversion among their members. The statement condemns any negative sanctions following conversion, including discrimination and harassment. It also remarks that missionary activity should be performed according to "ethically accepted standards" to ensure that conversion "happens freely."[10] The statement proposes an international perspective—pointing out that conversion should be accepted "in Norway or

---

8. Here is the link to the English covering of the presentation of the joint statement including the English translation of the statement itself: http://www.gammel.kirken.no/english/news.cfm?artid=149142 (last consulted 16 August 2017).

9. Inge Eidsvåg, Tore Lindholm, and Barbro Sveen, "The Emergence of Interfaith Dialogue: The Norwegian Experience," in Tore Lindholm, W. Cole Durham Jr., and Bahia G. Tahzib-Lie, eds., *Facilitating Freedom of Religion and Belief: A Deskbook* (Leiden: Brill/Nijhoff, 2004), 777–89, here 779.

10. In 2009, two years after the statement on the right to conversion, The Oslo Coalition of Religious Freedom and Belief launched a document on missionary activities and human rights. The discussions preceding this document started in 2005 and were thus ongoing at the time of the statement of conversion and some were involved in both processes. This document can be found here: https://www.jus.uio.no/smr/english/about/programmes/oslocoalition/docs/groundrules_english.pdf (last consulted 16 August 2017).

abroad." This dimension of the statement underlines the discursive relatedness of the language of human rights: human rights are universal, not contextual in nature. But it also shows the ambitions of the statement-makers: they expect the statement to be read internationally, and to contribute to the international discourse on conversion.

The statement explicitly says that the practice of religion according to individual choices should be accepted in the public as well as in the private sphere. Finally, it includes a positive comment about the need to welcome converts within their new religious community:[11]

> As religious communities we experience joy within our respective contexts whenever a person wishes to share our faith and join our religious community. Therefore we also respect a person's right to convert to a different religion than our own.[12]

After several meetings and lengthy discussions throughout 2005 and 2006 (it was discussed at all the meetings of the Contact group, four every year), both within the contact group and in the religious communities themselves, including the imam committee of ICN, the statement was adopted. It was addressed to the Christian and the Muslim communities, as well as to the general public. The statement makes at least one indirect but significant theological point when it comes to conversion, namely that conversion is possible and even legitimate for the religious traditions of Islam and Christianity, at least as they are interpreted by the members of the Contact group. The Muslim participants, in particular, in the group understood that, in many Islamic discourses, this is a point of controversy. This might be especially the case in Muslim majority countries, where it could be illegal for a Muslim to convert away from Islam. However, the Muslim participants relied on two elements to argue for their position: their interpretation of Norwegian legislation as valid for everyone living in Norway including themselves, and their reading of Quranic texts, for example Sura 2.257, "There is no compulsion in religion." The latter is connected to the freedom of the individual believer, and at the same time reflects a view of God in Islam as always greater than the human conceptualizing of God. The expression *Allah Akhbar* is always pointing to this; it literally means God is greater. For most Muslims, this entails that humans may not judge individuals on matters of faith and practice. It remains a divine matter.

---

11. http://www.gammel.kirken.no/english/news.cfm?artid=149142 (last consulted 16 August 2017).

12. http://www.gammel.kirken.no/english/news.cfm?artid=149142 (last consulted 16 August 2017).

The statement does not address specific challenges connected to conversion, such as intermarriage between Muslims and Christians, or non-Muslim women's rights to keep the religion of their choice when marrying a Muslim man. Further, the statement does not discuss the religious affiliation of children born in Muslim-Christian marriages. Intermarriage between Muslim and non-Muslims is difficult for many Muslims because of the traditional Islamic legislation which states that a Muslim man may marry a Christian or Jewish woman, yet a Muslim woman should only marry a Muslim man. The question of intermarriage may be difficult for Christians too, for social, cultural, and possibly religious reasons. When working on the text these aspects came up in the discussions. Yet the group decided to keep the message as simple as possible to preserve the consensus, but also to avoid possible discussions that would have obscured what was considered as the most important content. This is also why the statement does not address issues of a more political nature, such as asylum seekers who come from a Muslim background and seek to be baptized in Christian churches (and by this convert to Christianity) in order to apply for political asylum or a residence permit in Norway.

What Authority Does the Joint Statement Carry, and How Is it Interpreted?

If one goes back to the Contact group's joint statement and inquires how the involved parties themselves and the general public criticized, used, and reported on the text, one can present the following observations. As a member of the group and someone involved in these processes, I had access to these reactions from an insider perspective. The declaration is available in Norwegian and in English, and it was diffused internationally through interactions between dialogue participants in Norway and colleagues elsewhere. The text was criticized both for being too vague (not covering problems related to marriage and asylum seekers as mentioned above) and too explicit. The latter critique was mostly directed at Norwegian Muslims by international voices. Because the document addresses an international audience and includes a universal perspective, Muslims speaking from contexts not aligned with the core message of the statement questioned the right of Norwegian Muslims to make such a joint statement with the Church of Norway, especially since many Muslim communities reject the notion of conversion away from Islam.

The statement was also presented as a token for the successful Muslim-Christian dialogue in Norway in international fora such as the World Council of Churches, and as a text representing progress because it fully acknowledges freedom of religion through dialogue. However, later, new members who were representing the Islamic Council of Norway in the Contact group contested the authority of the text. This reflected new Norwegian Muslim leadership who questioned the Islamic Council of Norway about the text. Their primary challenge concerned the statement's authority to establish the right to convert as a global Islamic principle, also applicable to Muslim majority societies or ideal Muslim communities/states. Some Muslim leaders disagreed with the position that the statement should be authoritative beyond the Norwegian context.[13] At a meeting of the Contact group in 2013, some of the new representatives from ICN (new in the Contact group since 2007) indicated that the current leadership of the organization wished to discuss whether the statement was still representative for them. They asked whether they should withdraw from it since the statement no longer represented the view of the current representation of ICN or the Contact group. The statement would then become a historical document with no present authoritative status.

The various challenges to the text show that there are still tensions around the question of conversion, and even around the practice of issuing such joint statements. In addition, with changes in the leadership of religious communities and with the increase of international communication including social media, issues surrounding conversion become more complex. It is however interesting to note that, despite these critics, in October 2015, the secretary general of ICN referred to the 2007 joint statement in a significant Norwegian newspaper, *Aftenposten*, and claimed that the statement was still important and represented the view of most Norwegian Muslims.[14] The secretary general added a remark on the difference between religious and secular laws, and explained that one could find many examples of issues that religious laws condemned but that secular laws considered legal. He also underlined that Muslims have different views and represent a variety of positions. The secretary general's statements can be interpreted as an attempt to avoid criticism from all sides—from Muslims and non-Muslims who are both supporting *and* rejecting the statement. He confirms the stance that he and ICN (and most Norwegian Muslims) support the right to convert religiously, and at the same time indicates that he understands those who may consider that religious conversion is prohibited in Islam according to religious laws. More positively, one can say that he repeats a recognized

---

13. Olav Elgvin, "Secularists, Democratic Islamists and Utopian Dreamers. How Muslim Religious Leaders in Norway Fit Islam into the Norwegian Political System," (Master's thesis in Peace and Conflict Studies; University of Oslo, 2011), 43.

14. *Aftenposten* 17.10.2015 interview with Mehtab Afsar.

distinction between religious and secular laws, and he argues that religious law is only valid for the people who accept it.

In the Church of Norway, people did not reflect on the statement widely when it comes to its content. Two probable reasons explain this lack of reaction: (a) religious freedom as a principle is taken for granted, and (b) the issue of conversion has not really been surfacing within the Church because it has not really concerned substantial numbers of religious converts either way. The Church's focus has rather been on keeping its members from leaving the Church and motivating them to baptize their children. The statement has, however, been used to legitimate the usefulness of Muslim-Christian dialogue and to highlight the willingness of the Church's Muslim dialogue partners to commit to religious freedom as a human right. At the same time, the Church of Norway has been publicly challenged lately for their praxis of receiving Muslim converts. This challenge, however, does not come from Muslim communities, but from Norwegian authorities, as I will show below.

What is the status and influence of such a joint statement within the concerned religious communities and among the general public? What we have is a text established through dialogue, the product of consensus. It is a negotiated text between Christians and Muslims involved in the Contact group at a specific period of time. Where and how does one ground the authority of such a text? Within religious communities, the canonical texts have some kind of authoritative status, even when they are discussed and disputed. Could the joint statement's authority be derived from the authority of the Bible and the Quran?

Faruc Terzic, head of the Norwegian imam committee at the time the joint statement was approved, analyzed all the joint statements from the Contact group in an article entitled "Theological Principles versus Secular Language."[15] He writes that the statements "appear as public declarations, aiming at both local and global audiences."[16] He notes that none of the statements refer to or cite texts from the Bible or the Quran, and classifies the language in these texts as "ecumenical," because intra- or interreligious partners in a dialogue communicate in a shared language.[17] He remarks that the statements are not using specific theological language, that would belong to any of the two traditions, but claims that there are "visible

---

15. Faruk Terzic, "Theological Principles versus Secular Language: An Analysis of Joint Statements of the Council on Ecumenical and International Relations of the Church of Norway and the Islamic Council of Norway," *Norsk Tidsskrift for Misjonsvitenskap* 4 (2013): 233–47.
16. Terzic, "Theological Principles versus Secular Language," 233–47.
17. See Terzic, "Theological Principles versus Secular Language," 238.

traces of traditional theology present in the argumentations."[18] About the 2007 statement in particular, Oddbjørn Leirvik indicates that its style is inspired by human rights language, while it also refers to relevant religious resources within both traditions.[19] Leirvik then suggests that the statement about the right to conversion shows how interreligious textual endeavors may establish a language of common, ethical character, and mark a turn towards "secular" language.[20] He concludes that current interreligious dialogue in modern societies often seems to produce such a common language, thus making religious arguments more accessible to the general public. Two reasons might explain this evolution: the statements need to be understood outside of the communities that produce them, and the persons involved in producing them are familiar with "human rights language."

It seems rather obvious then that the joint statement on religious conversion can only "borrow" limited authority from the canonical scriptures or theology within the two traditions. In the context of interreligious dialogue in Lebanon, Yvonne Y. Haddad and Rahel Fischbach state that the function of joint Muslim-Christian statements during the 1980s was to start a wider discussion within the concerned faith communities, and introduce scholarly discourses on themes of interest to the faith communities.[21] They note that the themes of interest were often different between Christians and Muslims. Thus, the statements probably influence the groups' discourses diversely, depending on themes. In Muslim communities, the statement from the Contact group seems to have functioned as an opener for discussion about conversion; yet, in the Church of Norway, it merely added to the ongoing discourse on Muslim-Christian dialogue.

The statement's authority was also anchored in the Contact group's dialogue itself, as well as in the thorough process involved in producing and deciding on the final text. For this authority to be accepted, the Contact group must be perceived as representative, and the participants in the group must embody their respective faith communities. Jeannine Hill Fletcher calls this kind of dialogue the parliamentary model of dialogue.[22] The

---

18. Terzic, "Theological Principles versus Secular Language," 239.
19. Oddbjørn Leirvik, *Interreligious Studies: A Relational Approach to Religious Activism and the Study of Religion* (London: Bloomsbury, 2014), 49.
20. See Leirvik, *Interreligious Studies*, 50.
21. Yvonne H. Haddad and Rahel Fischbach, "Interfaith Dialogue in Lebanon: Between a Power Balancing Act and Theological Encounters," *Islam and Christian-Muslim Relations* 26.4 (2015): 423–42, here 429.
22. Jeannine Hill Fletcher, "Women in Inter-Religious Dialogue," in Catherine Cornille, ed., *The Wiley-Blackwell Companion to Inter-Religious Dialogue* (Hoboken: Wiley-Blackwell, 2013), 168–83, here 170.

authority of the dialogue is connected to the idea of representation. While the religious communities are being represented, the representatives remain separate individuals, and the significance of the dialogue's outcome will also depend on the interaction and relation between the individual participants.[23] In the case of the 2007 statement, both the Church Council of the Church of Norway and the Imam committee of ICN approved the text negotiated by the Contact group. This provides the text with the formal status of an official policy for the two parties. At the same time, the authority derived from the process, from the Contact group's decisions and from the faith communities, is fluid, and connected to specific individuals who take part in the process and are committed to it through relationships of mutual accountability. When some of the Muslim participants in the Contact group later questioned the statement, as I indicated above, and suggested that it was part of history rather than a relevant, authoritative text for the present, this fluidity, and thus vulnerability, surfaces. However, these views on the statement in their turn also have limited authority, and in fact the secretary general of the ICN later used the statement in Norwegian media to illustrate the ICN's view on conversion as mentioned earlier.

The Background of the Statement and the Surrounding Norwegian Discursive Context on Religious Conversion

A couple of decades ago, most religious conversions in Norway were intra-Christian, in particular between the Church of Norway and the Roman Catholic Church. Today, in the Norwegian context, the most common "conversion" is probably the shift from being religiously affiliated to becoming without any religious belonging, or "secular." This is a shift in individual belief not reflected in the traditional descriptions of religious conversion, where non-religious views or life-stances[24] as categories are not part of the horizon. Currently, when one uses the term "religious conversion," most people in Norway connect it to a change between Christianity and Islam. Yet, the scope of its occurrence is not very well mapped. The contact group's decision to launch a joint statement on conversion was not motivated by the observation of a widespread practice. Rather, it shared the expectation of

---

23. Anne Hege Grung, *Gender Justice in Muslim-Christian Readings: Christian and Muslim Women in Norway Making Meaning of Texts from the Bible, the Koran and the Hadith* (Amsterdam: Brill Rodopi, 2015), 69, 86–7.

24. The notion "life stance" is used for non-religious belief systems in the Norwegian discourse, such as in the name of the "Council for Religious and Life Stance Communities": http://www.trooglivssyn.no/index.cfm?id=136722 (last consulted 16 August 2017).

an increase in the practice. Additionally, there were not many reports about social problems or harassments connected to conversion. This was in 2007; in 2016, there are still only few reports about converts from Islam to Christianity or the reverse. In 2007, Muslim leaders estimated the number of converts to Islam in Norway to be around five hundred. In 2015, Kari Vogt estimates the number of converts to Islam to be around three thousand.[25] Christian leaders have not given out any estimated numbers of converts to the Church of Norway.

In 2016, the real numbers on both sides are still hidden, and there are no statistics available since Norway does not have public records of religious affiliation for its individual citizens. The lack of statistics and the resistance to estimate numbers might reveal that the topic itself is still sensitive, but the lack of numbers is probably also due to the lack of formal registration. Norwegian law prohibits the systematic registration of people according to their religious affiliation. People's religious belief is only registered when they are formally members of a faith (or life stance) community. Conversion is considered a private matter, and faith communities, both Muslim and Christian, seem to keep instances of conversion to themselves. There is no publicity about people having converted to one's faith community from the communities themselves.

The current public discussions about conversion to Islam in Norway have to some extent been connected to discourses of Muslim radicalization and extremism. Consequently, conversion to Islam may be interpreted as a form of political resistance, considered with suspicion by the majority and viewed as dangerous by some. The Norwegian public seem to agree that more young men are converting to Islam than in previous years. These conversions are sometimes explained by a phenomenon called "copain de l'Islam" in French (in Norwegian: "kompis-islam," "Islam-buddy").[26] According to this explanation, young men convert because of their friends' religion, thus embodying the fact that within a post-traditional society, it is now possible to follow the practices of friends rather than of family. It remains to investigate why and whether this affects young men to a larger degree than young women. Presently, the question of non-Muslim women converting because they marry Muslim men is not put forward, even though it used to be the main reason for conversion a decade ago. As people living in Norway will probably increasingly marry across religious lines, it might become a significant reason for

---

25. Kari Vogt cited in an article by Lena Lindgren in *Morgenbladet*, 27.03.2015.
26. *Morgenbladet*, 27.03.2015.

conversion in the future. These marriages will create new challenges for faith communities when it comes to relating to multi-religious families, particularly for life rituals (marriages, births, deaths). The publicity surrounding conversion due to marriage and family issues is different from that about seemingly politically motivated conversion. The former is rarely addressed in public, yet the latter is regularly taken up in the media. It is unclear if one would observe the same difference in publicity when it comes to conversion of men versus conversion of women. Rather, it suggests that family and marriage are located inside the private sphere, and that conversions that occur in this context are also seen as private matters. In contrast, so-called political conversions are enmeshed in broader current discourses about Islam as a political factor in Norway and Europe. As such, they are perceived as more public.

Church staff in the Church of Norway unofficially report that small numbers of Muslims, primarily former Shia Muslims with an Iranian background, have converted to the Church of Norway. As I have already mentioned, conversions from Islam to Christianity are often connected with discourses on immigration and asylum seekers. These conversions are thus colored with political overtones. In several cases, Norwegian authorities have questioned the sincerity of these conversions and suspected that they were motivated by a supposedly easier access to asylum and residence permits upon conversion. There are also cases of reportedly aggressive proselytizing by Christian churches at organized centers where asylum-seekers live until their case is settled. The Islamic Council of Norway protested against this, claiming that this type of proselytizing goes against the recognized principles for ethical mission, where one should exercise caution and restraint when encountering vulnerable individuals and groups. For the Church of Norway, this type of proselytizing is mostly practiced by congregations that do not belong to the official Church of Norway; and the Church of Norway has no authority over these denominations. The Church also insists that freedom of religion must be respected equally, for Christian congregations (pointing out the right to bear witness to one's faith in public, even if this witnessing must be inscribed in agreed ethical standards) and for the asylum seekers, who should be granted the freedom to change their religious affiliation and beliefs if they so desire, like anyone else in Norway.

Persons seeking political asylum or residence permits in Norway who claim they have converted from Islam to Christianity have become a challenging political question in recent years. Indeed, part of the issue depends on who has the right to decide whether an individual's conversion is *pro forma* or authentic? Should ministers/priests/pastors in the churches, or official state employees working on the cases have the last word? Can political authorities dismiss a person's claim to have converted and on what grounds? How do you measure personal faith? And how much does personal faith have to do with religious identity and belonging?[27]

In an interview in the Christian newspaper *Vårt Land* on 4 February, 2015, a retired minister challenged the ongoing practice of official authorities in UNE (*Utledningsnemda*, the Norwegian authorities' committee on applications for asylum and residence permits) which decides, after investigations, whether a Muslim has really converted to Christianity. He refers to a particular case where the convert allegedly was asked to clarify his understanding of the Christian triune God and to explain the difference between the Christian and the Islamic views of sin. The minister commented: "Even myself, I could not have answered the question on the notion of sin."[28] Apparently, UNE's investigations are organized as some kind of doctrinal exam. Questions about an individual's personal faith are not regarded as an interesting way to map a person's actual faith. In addition, the definition of conversion used is narrow, and a broader definition of conversion—a definition that would insist on feelings of affiliation, the establishing of social relations, or friendship—does not seem to be present. The notion of religious pilgrims[29] or the possibility of multiple belonging do not fit the immigration regulations where people are sorted in categories mostly defined by their past, while the person's present or future is less significant.

In the current political climate in Norway, the question of conversion from Islam to Christianity is highly contested when it comes to asylum seekers. One of the challenges is connected to the power of definition: who has the right to decide whether a person is a proper Christian and a sincere convert? And based on which understanding of conversion? From an ecclesial perspective, the Church claims to have the right to define a person's commitment to, and inclusion in, the Church of Norway. If a person is baptized, he or she is legally a member of the Church. If doctrinal knowledge were to be defined as the basis of church membership, then conversion and membership would be understood completely differently. For the Church, doctrinal knowledge is a foreign criterion for becoming a member according to current Lutheran ecclesiology. For UNE, particularly in the context of current discussions about asylum seekers in Norway, the matter is not that simple.

The discussions surrounding the conversions of asylum seekers can help us discern what may be considered as "classic" religious conversions

---

27. See Rambo and Farhadian, *Oxford Handbook of Religious Conversion*, on the traditional view of conversion.

28. http://www.vl.no/troogkirke/unes-konvertitt-intervjuer-får-strykkarakter-1.314635 (last consulted 16 August 2017).

29. See Thorbjørnsrud, "Who Is a Convert?"

to Christianity and Islam in Norway. It should not be something happening due to a person's need for physical or mental refuge, or in order to be included in a certain social group, or to front specific political preferences. UNE is highlighting that actual knowledge about the religious tradition you want to convert into is crucial; the Church of Norway highlights baptism as the ritual inclusion in the Church. Performing the Islamic credo in front of witnesses is universally seen as the act of conversion to Islam. The Christian and Islamic communities are concerned that the converts receive sufficient knowledge about their new affiliation, but this is not a premise for conversion.

In religiously plural societies, people's religious affiliations cannot be taken for granted. Recently, this has also become the case in Norway. Different societies negotiate questions related to religious affiliations in various ways: what does it entail to belong to a religious community? Is it at all possible to change religious belief and affiliation? How is religious identity negotiated? Different societies answer these questions differently at different times. Historically, in Europe, people's religious affiliation first depended on the decisions of the political rulers. There was little or no space for individuals to take their own decisions in this matter. In 1648, the peace treaty of Westphalia, ending the Thirty Years War, relied on the principle dating back to Augsburg in 1555, which declared that individual citizens should hold the same religion as the ruler of each territory. This knitted geopolitical location and religious belonging closely together and underlined the idea of conversion as political treason in the European context. To be a loyal and recognized citizen, one had to uphold the right faith in the right place. To change religion meant that you had changed place of living (or that your ruler had changed his/her religious affiliation). The agreement in Westphalia stated that Christians belonging to other denominations than the ruler of the state had a right to stay and could practice their minority faith according to certain rules. This marks the beginning of a developing freedom of religion as it is known today, although the focus was on the state, not on the individual believer.[30] When one analyzes the present Norwegian context, it is possible to say that freedom of religion is at stake concerning refugees and asylum seekers. It is difficult to combine the process of seeking refuge in Norway and at the same time convert to the Norwegian majority religion. Rather, the attempt to convert to Christianity for originally Muslim asylum seekers has been instrumentalized into an argument

---

30. Malcolm D. Evans, "Historical Analysis of Freedom of Religion or Belief as a Technique for Resolving Religious Conflict," in Lindholm, Durham Jr., and Tahzib-Lie, eds. *Facilitating Freedom of Religion or Belief*, 5.

to keep people out of the Norwegian nation and to construct conversion as a politically messy business.

Even in post-traditional societies, religious belonging remains strongly connected to other belongings and identities regarding family, culture, social groups, and nation. In Norway, being Norwegian and being a member of the Church of Norway and thus a Lutheran Christian used to be the two sides of the same coin. Norwegian public space used to be religiously dominated by the Church of Norway. In addition, the Church of Norway was intertwined with the state authorities and Norwegian laws. The state's monarch was head of the Church. In recent times, even with the establishment of a separation between Church and state in Norway, the Norwegian king decided to uphold the connection between the Church and the monarch and refused to accept freedom of religion for the ruling monarch. Instead, he insisted that the monarch must be a member of the Church of Norway. However, Norwegian public space has gradually become more secularized in the sense that public references to the Church and Christianity have become less significant. In the last decades, it has also become more marked by other religious traditions. In 2014, 76 % of the Norwegian population were still members of the Church of Norway, and 2.6 % of the population were registered in Islamic communities.[31] But the religious demography also varies within the country. Oslo is the most diverse city in terms of the cultural and religious background of its population. In certain parts of the city, some 20% of Oslo's population has a Muslim background. In the entire city, 7% of the population is registered within Islamic faith organizations.[32] Oslo has no less than six purpose-built mosques, three of them in the city center, one purpose-built Buddhist temple, one synagogue and numerous places for worship for Christians of many denominations as well as for Sikhs, Hindus, Baha'i, and others.

Religious pluralization in Norway follows two trends: one is increased secularization related to a decrease of members in the Church of Norway, although Norway still has a solid majority of its inhabitants belonging to the former state Church. The other trend is increased immigration and settlement of people that were brought up in other religious traditions.[33] Religious

---

31. https://www.ssb.no/kultur-og-fritid/artikler-og-publikasjoner/hva-forteller-statistikkene-om-religion-tro-og-livssyn-i-norge (last consulted 16 August 2017).

32. https://www.ssb.no/kultur-og-fritid/artikler-og-publikasjoner/et-mangfold-av-tro-og-livssyn (last consulted 16 August 2017).

33. See Anne Hege Grung, "Die zwei Pluralismen: Positionen und Diskussionen in Norwegen," in Peter L. Berger, Silke Steets, and Wolfram Weisse, eds., *Zwei Pluralismen: Positionen aus Sozialwissenschaft und Theologie zu religiöser Vielfalt und Säkularität* (Münster: Waxmann, 2017), 91–103.

conversions as such have not contributed much to the pluralization of the religious landscape–especially if one does not include conversion to a "secular worldview."

There are social, religious, and legal structures to contain what we may call "traditional pluralism." Such is the case in many Middle Eastern countries, where the population usually resists conversion and refuses marriage across religious and confessional boundaries, out of respect for their own group. This is particularly the case among religious minorities, who fear being assimilated to the majority. In addition, the legal and political structures strongly encourage stability regarding religious affiliation to maintain a certain balance. This mostly means that there are usually no legal structures to acknowledge interreligious marriages for example, and that people's religious belonging is registered and sometimes directly connected to their national citizenship.

In the structures of more recently established pluralism (which often entails acknowledgment of a greater historical pluralism, too), within countries with secular legislation and religious freedom such as Norway and most other European states, religious conversion is legal, and having marriages and families in which individuals have different religious affiliation is legally possible. Why, then, does the issue of conversion remain so sensitive? Cultural pluralism may alter cultural practices and patterns and establish culturally hybrid environments. Religious identity, however, is viewed differently, because religious traditions, unlike cultural traditions, are considered to be mutually exclusive. Even if double religious belonging is claimed by a substantial number of people globally, religious hybridity on an individual level is often met with suspicion. In Norway, it is illegal to belong to more than one religious or life-stance community, because the communities get financial state support *per capita*. This means that full conversion has economic consequences. This system discourages double legal belongings since it could be considered as cheating the system. It is possible to say that a full double belonging or a multiple religious identity being implemented in practice is considered illegal in Norway, not by the religious communities, but by the legal authorities.

The challenges relate to a society obsessed at large with religious identity politics. For many, one also needs to account for a feeling that the past, when religiosity, political, and national belonging were intimately connected, appears as a stable ideal. The present situation, however, demands to view and review religious identity to include new understandings of conversion if we are to grasp, and relate to, the emerging forms of religiously hybrid families, multiple religious belonging, religious pilgrims, and a more fluid religious landscape.

Religious converts may represent a challenge in many ways: they may question stable boundaries between groups; they might challenge identity politics discourses; they might test their own social environment of family and friends, or their former fellow—as well as new—believers. Converts usually expose themselves to experiences that under other conditions are evaluated positively as courageous, adventurous, as characterizing someone who seeks knowledge and establishes new relationships. This may well be how the converts' new religious community views them, but religious conversion is also seen as a suspicious act challenging political and social stability. However, converts who are aware of their past and present can achieve translation skills between religious and also cultural traditions, something also regarded—under most circumstances—as a valuable skill for a community. Kwok Pui-Lan's concepts of "diasporical consciousness" and "dialogical imagination" are useful when exploring the value of such skills.[34] Diasporical consciousness entails that a person moving between different traditions or cultures and knowing them all intimately may be able to convey insights from one tradition/culture to another. Dialogical imagination means that one has a reservoir of varied experiences and insights which enables one to be creative and use many different resources when encountering human challenges as an individual or a group—or a society. In the Norwegian context, there are several examples of converts from the majority religion to minority religions such as Buddhism and Islam who play important roles for bridging gaps between the majority and these minorities. For some, it is challenging to still be regarded as a convert several decades after they made the change of religious affiliation. They nevertheless use their diasporic consciousness as a resource.[35]

Between the human rights-discourse connected to freedom of speech and freedom of religion, and reflected to some degree in the Contact group's statement, and the political discourses connected to conversion, we find the vulnerable individual, or family, who may not be able to find acceptance because of their choice of religion. In a situation where religious identity is becoming a social and political label that may be too explicit or problematic for the individual to carry, people are finding new solutions: they will adopt double belonging, religious hybrid identities, or they will stay completely unmarked in the public and restrict their religious convictions to the private sphere. If one performs religious conversion, what does it really

---

34. Kwok Pui-Lan, *Postcolonial Imagination and Feminist Theology* (London: SCM Press, 2005).
35. To mention only two examples from Norway: Lena Larsen, a convert to Islam, and Egil Lothe, a convert to Buddhism, have played important roles in interreligious dialogues as well as within their "new" religious communities for more than two decades.

mean, and for whom? The interpretative possibilities are numerous, and the consequences vary depending on who decides who one is: oneself, one's friends and family, and/or the concerned faith communities, and, in present Norway, also the state authorities at various levels.

Biographical Note

Anne Hege Grung is Professor in Interreligious Studies at the Faculty of Theology, University of Oslo. She teaches gender and interreligious relations and interfaith chaplaincy, and is presently doing research on the discourse of violence against women among the religious leadership and feminist NGOs in Lebanon. In 2015, she published the book *Gender Justice in Muslim-Christian Readings: Christian and Muslim Women in Norway Making Meaning of Texts from the Bible, the Koran and the Hadith*. The article "Negotiating Gender Justice between State, Religion and NGOs: A Lebanese Case" was published in 2018.

Bibliography

Eidsvåg, Inge, Tore Lindholm, and Barbro Sveen. "The Emergence of Interfaith Dialogue: The Norwegian Experience," 777–89 in Lindholm, Durham, and Tahzib-Lie, eds., *Facilitating Freedom of Religion and Belief*, 2004. https://doi.org/10.1007/978-94-017-5616-7_35

Elgvin, Olav. "Secularists, Democratic Islamists and Utopian Dreamers. How Muslim Religious Leaders in Norway Fit Islam into the Norwegian Political System." Master's thesis in Peace and Conflict Studies. University of Oslo, 2011.

Evans, Malcolm D. "Historical Analysis of Freedom of Religion or Belief as a Technique for Resolving Religious Conflict," 1–17 in Lindholm, Durham, and Tahzib-Lie, eds., *Facilitating Freedom of Religion and Belief*, 2004. https://doi.org/10.1007/978-94-017-5616-7_1

Grung, Anne Hege. *Gender Justice in Muslim-Christian Readings: Christian and Muslim Women in Norway Making Meaning of Texts from the Bible, the Koran and the Hadith*. Amsterdam: Brill Rodopi, 2015. https://doi.org/10.1163/9789004306707

—"Die zwei Pluralismen: Positionen und Diskussionen in Norwegen," 91–103 in *Zwei Pluralismen: Positionen aus Sozialwissenschaft und Theologie zu religiöser Vielfalt und Säkularität*. Edited by Peter L. Berger, Silke Steets, and Wolfram Weisse. Münster: Waxmann, 2017.

Haddad, Yvonne H., and Rahel Fischbach. "Interfaith Dialogue in Lebanon: Between a Power Balancing Act and Theological Encounters," *Islam and Christian-Muslim Relations* 26.4 (2015): 423–42. https://doi.org/10.1080/09596410.2015.1070468

Hill Fletcher, Jeannine. "Women in Inter-Religious Dialogue," 168–83 in *The Wiley-Blackwell Companion to Inter-Religious Dialogue*. Edited by Catherine Cornille. Hoboken: Wiley-Blackwell, 2013. https://doi.org/10.1002/9781118529911.ch11

Leirvik, Oddbjørn. *Interreligious Studies: A Relational Approach to Religious Activism and the Study of Religion*. London: Bloomsbury, 2014.

Lindholm, Tore, W. Cole Durham Jr., and Bahia G. Tahzib-Lie, eds. *Facilitating Freedom of Religion and Belief: A Deskbook*. Leiden: Brill/Nijhoff, 2004. https://doi.org/10.1007/978-94-017-5616-7

Nock, Arthur D. *Conversion. The Old and the New in Religion from Alexander the Great to Augustine of Hippo*. Oxford: Oxford University Press, 1933.

Pui-Lan, Kwok. *Postcolonial Imagination and Feminist Theology*. London: SCM Press, 2005.

Rambo, Lewis R., and Charles E. Farhadian, eds. *The Oxford Handbook of Religious Conversion*. Oxford: Oxford University Press, 2014. https://doi.org/10.1093/oxfordhb/9780195338522.001.0001

Terzic, Faruk. "Theological Principles versus Secular Language: An Analysis of Joint Statements of the Council on Ecumenical and International Relations of the Church of Norway and the Islamic Council of Norway," *Norsk Tidsskrift for Misjonsvitenskap* 4 (2013): 233–47.

Thorbjørnsrud, Berit. "Who Is a Convert? New Members of the Orthodox Church in Norway," *Temenos* 51.1 (2015): 71–93. https://doi.org/10.33356/temenos.49447

Web Articles

http://www.gammel.kirken.no/english/news.cfm?artid=149142 (last consulted 16 August 2017).

http://www.gammel.kirken.no/?event=dolink&famID=17453 (last consulted 16 August 2017).

https://www.jus.uio.no/smr/english/about/programmes/oslocoalition/docs/groundrules_english.pdf (last consulted 16 August 2017).

https://www.ssb.no/kultur-og-fritid/artikler-og-publikasjoner/et-mangfold-av-tro-og-livssyn (last consulted 16 August 2017).

https://www.ssb.no/kultur-og-fritid/artikler-og-publikasjoner/hva-forteller-statistikkene-om-religion-tro-og-livssyn-i-norge (last consulted 16 August 2017).

http://www.trooglivssyn.no/index.cfm?id=136722 (last consulted 16 August 2017).

http://www.vl.no/troogkirke/unes-konvertitt-intervjuer-får-strykkarakter-1.314635 (last consulted 16 August 2017).

Chapter Four

Conversion in Mystery Religions?
Theory Meets Mysteries and Conversion

Gerhard van den Heever

Conversion as a radical, deliberate, and often sudden change of religious orientation and association with particular cults was not a constant or common pattern of religious experience, socialization, or expression in the ancient world. This holds true also for the related phenomena of mission, call, and revival, as well as for the mysteries, even if based on ideas of innocence and redemption.[1]

Conversion in the sense of change of religion or confession on the basis of personal conviction was unknown to Greco-Roman Antiquity before the appearance of Christianity.[2]

Religion is social. However much we might believe religion is about our personal mystical experiences or the stuff we believe, a religious journey is always formed by relationships, communities, world events, and the like. My journey out of evangelicalism is just one of many, but it is a path many, many people share in broad outline.[3]

Introduction: Defining the Field of Investigation

To speak of conversion in Greco-Roman mystery religions is to open the proverbial hornet's nest of stinging questions. This is because, by posing the question, one immediately enters a very complex field of study in which several constitutive departure points are put in question. For instance, in spite of a long history of the study of mystery religions, the very existence of such a category as a separate kind of religion is fundamentally questioned in recent scholarship: can one speak of mystery religions at all, or should one only designate mysteries as options within "normal" religious

---

1. Hubert Cancik, "Conversion. II. Greco-Roman Antiquity," in *Religion Past and Present*. https://doi.org/10.1163/1877-5888_rpp_COM_01673.
2. Wolfgang Bienert, "Conversion. IV. Church History, 1. Early Church," in *Religion Past and Present*. https://doi.org/10.1163/1877-5888_rpp_COM_01673.
3. Greg Carey, "Milestones in My Journey out of Evangelicalism," *Democracy on Fire: Resources for Resistance*, 14 March 2018. http://democracyonfire.blogspot.com/2018/03/milestones-in-my-journey-out-of.html.

formats, that is, do they constitute a separate category of religious phenomena? In addition, the history of research into mystery religions in the past two centuries (to stipulate only the study of the field since the rise of history of religion, *Religionsgeschichte*, as field of focus) has itself contributed to much confusion on the topic such that the conventional categories by means of which to approach and theorize the phenomenon are steadily being redescribed and reconceived.[4] And lastly, given the long shadow cast by Alfred Darby Nock's 1933 classic, *Conversion: The Old and the New in Religion from Alexander the Great to Augustine of Hippo*,[5] on how conversion is still understood, any study of conversion in the Greco-Roman world will necessarily also be inflected by contemporary redescriptive theorizing of religion and religious discourses. This means, in short, that religion is no longer theorized as the inner, private domain of individual emotions and convictions stemming from an irruption into the human world of an otherworldly sacred, but as a social discourse itself, as a subset of those cultural performances by means of which social formations are constructed, maintained, and the boundaries thereof policed. One might say that the topic "conversion in mystery religions" is a paradigmatic site of discourse on which all other constituent sub-discourses flounder and are consequently reconceived. My aim here is, consequently, not to provide final answers and perspectives, but rather to problematize my topic. Ergo, this essay is an exercise in question-raising.

Redescribing Conversion:
Dealing with the Long Shadow of Arthur Darby Nock

The first two cited epigraphs at the beginning of the essay encapsulate very much the more contemporary understanding of conversion in the Greco-Roman world. This is in contrast, for instance, to the influential work of Arthur Darby Nock on conversion in ancient religions on the one hand, and to the work of religio-historical scholars like Richard Reitzenstein, Gustav Anrich, and Martin Dibelius, on the other hand, who in various ways sought to read the apostle Paul's theology and early Christian discourse

---

4. See for instance, overviews of research and statements of the taxonomic problems involved: Gerhard van den Heever, "Making Mysteries: From the Untergang der Mysterien to Imperial Mysteries–Social Discourse in Religion and the Study of Religion," *Religion and Theology* 12.3/4 (2005): 262–307; Tennyson Jacob Wellman, "Ancient *Mystēria* and Modern Mystery Cults," *Religion and Theology* 12.3/4 (2005): 308–48.

5. Arthur Darby Nock, *Conversion: The Old and the New in Religion from Alexander the Great to Augustine of Hippo* (Oxford: Oxford University Press, 1933).

either as continuous with Greco-Roman mystery religions, or in some ways in contrast to these.⁶ With regard to conversion in the Greco-Roman religious world, the world in which Christianity took shape and in which "converts" made the "life-changing decision" to join Christian cult groups, it is the work of Arthur Darby Nock that is the constantly referenced authority for the conventional understanding of conversion as a (rather sudden) total reorientation of life, in both religio-historical as well as in comparative studies in religion.

In his classic book, *Conversion*, Nock defines conversion as follows: "By conversion we mean the reorientation of the soul of an individual, his deliberate turning from indifference or from an earlier form of piety to another, a turning which implies a consciousness that a great change is involved, that the old was wrong and the new is right."⁷ What one should immediately understand is that *Conversion* is not simply a study of conversion, but a wider encompassing study of the religious history of the Mediterranean world into which Christianity took shape and spread, as an account of Christian origins and as an explanation for the eventual success of Christianity. Note the three core orientations in this definition: a focus on "the soul," a focus on "the individual," and the matter of intention (or, to put it in a more redescriptive manner: (a) an individual event sited in deeply held convictions; (b) intense commitment; and (c) moral judgment about the personal past).

While Nock drew much on the work of William James on religious experience,⁸ nevertheless in his discussion of "conversions" in modern Christianity, Nock claims that such comparisons with repentance and inner conversions in enthusiastic revivalist movements (that is, of the late eighteenth through early twentieth centuries) do not constitute an exact parallel case since in these movements an appeal can be made to prior existing Christian commitments, something lacking in the context in which Christianity

---

6. I use the terms "mystery religions," "mystery cults," and "mysteries" as synonyms here as I do not think these are distinct phenomena, as I argue below.

7. Nock, *Conversion*, 7. Note the phrase "turning from indifference." This is, I would contend, a leftover from Nock's study of William James's work, which was a study of religious revival movements in the United States.

8. See for instance his insistence that conversion entails a "consciousness that a great change is involved … seen at its fullest in the positive response of a man to the choice set before him by the prophetic religions. We know this best from the history of modern Christianity …" which Nock then follows with a description drawn from James about the conversions and turnings involved in eighteenth-century revivalist preaching, involving turnings away from a sinful life towards a newly envisioned state of holiness, Nock, *Conversion*, 7–8.

first appeared.⁹ Rather, according to Nock, what is new in Christianity is that it is a *prophetic religion*. By contrast, what characterizes ancient Mediterranean religions is their embeddedness in society and culture, manifesting in myth and ritual (they are what is called *primal religions*, that is, the religion/cult and ethnic formation are coextensive).¹⁰ "Beliefs and worship" in these societies and cult formations, "were as a rule *supplements rather than alternatives* to ancestral piety."¹¹

For Nock, Christianity (and Judaism) played into uncatered-for and deep-seated needs existing within inhabitants of that world; the prophet (whether John the Baptist or Jesus) fuses

> into a white heat combustible material which is there, to express and to appear to meet the half-formed prayers of some at least of his contemporaries ... The message of John the Baptist and of Jesus gave form and substance to the dreams of a kingdom which had haunted many of their compatriots for generations. We cannot understand the success of Christianity outside Judaea without making an effort to determine the elements in the mind of the time to which it appealed.¹²

Christianity introduced something new and alien to the Greco-Roman world. Hence, conversion "is seen at its fullest in the positive response of a man to the choice set before him by the prophetic religions."¹³

What is commonly understood to be denoted by the term "conversion" with reference to religion, first manifests in history, according to conventional understanding, with the rise of Christianity in the Greco-Roman world (and Judaism, to a degree).¹⁴ The kind of argument that Nock makes

---

9. Nock, *Conversion*, 7–9. Therefore, as well, themes of repentance from the Old Testament are also not applicable, since they express calls to return to stricter adherence to purer, unadulterated versions of Israelite religious tradition.

10. See Michael Pye, "Religion and Identity: Clues and Threads," in *Strategies in the Study of Religion. Vol. 2: Exploring Religions in Motion* (Religion and Reason, 52; Berlin: de Gruyter, 2013), 319–26. This definitional distinction between primal and critical religions is significant since the theoretical distinction casts the debate on conversion in a different light.

11. Nock, *Conversion*, 12 (my emphasis).

12. Nock, *Conversion*, 9.

13. Nock, *Conversion*, 7.

14. For conversion in early Judaism, the most prominent case is that of the fictional character, Aseneth, in the pseudepigraphical novel, *Joseph and Aseneth*, cf. Randall D. Chesnutt, *From Death to Life: Conversion in Joseph and Aseneth* (Journal for the Study of the Pseudepigrapha Supplement, 16; Sheffield: Sheffield Academic Press, 1995). As with the case of Lucius in Apuleius's novel, *Metamorposes, or The Golden Ass*, here too a case for the evidence of a real conversion is pleaded from a work of fiction. And similarly, the question of the relation between fictional invention and real events comes into play. See the discussion of, and negative conclusion about, comparisons with

has often been critiqued in recent religio-historical and religio-comparative scholarship in that it assumes the incomparability of Christianity in order to pursue comparison with the aim of demonstrating the difference between Christianity and Greco-Roman religions, in so doing undermining the project of comparison.[15]

It has been argued by a number of scholars in the fields of the general study of religion, theory of religion, and religio-historical study (and I particularly draw here on the work of James C. Hanges, who—with others—has argued this extensively), in consonance with recent scholarship on comparison in the study of religion, that comparison cannot serve to undermine, at worst negate, comparison—as still occurs in much religio-historical scholarship and mainly in historical study that is theological in orientation. I use the phrase "theological in orientation" because this is what Nock's work on conversion essentially is, theology masking as history. The timing of the publication of *Conversion* is also significant. It came still in the heyday of the theological fashion of the day, a time very much determined and shaped by the triumphalist tone of the *Religionsgeschichtliche Schule* that, for all its religio-historical comparative work, assumed the superiority of (liberal) Christianity as the acme of human religious development, and in the context of nascent dialectic theology. In the broad stream of dialectic theology (especially, and famously, associated with the work of the Swiss-German theologian, Karl Barth), Christianity is understood as a faith, a response to being called by Jesus Christ, and not a religion, which is "human work" of rituals and practices. While Nock was by education and profession a classicist who then went on to found a graduate program in history of religion,

---

conversions to and initiations into Greco-Roman mystery religions in Chesnutt, *From Death to Life*, 217–53. James Rives, commenting on Nock's study of conversion, made the point (drawing on the work of Jörg Rüpke) that the possibility of "conversion" in the late ancient world indicated a change in the nature of religion and its position in society, James B. Rives, "Sacrifice and 'Religion': Modeling Religious Change in the Roman Empire" (unpublished paper). Thus, rather than elucidating a specific set of religious experiences and reorientations, what is actually enunciated by the use of the concept of "conversion," is the interplay of positional discourses, *inter alia*, gestured to by the concepts of primal and critical religions.

15. James Constantine Hanges, "Interpreting Glossolalia and the Comparison of Comparisons," in James Constantine Hanges, Thomas A. Idinopulos, and Brian C. Wilson, eds., *Comparing Religions: Possibilities and Perils* (Numen Book Series, 113; Leiden: Brill, 2006), 181–218; James Constantine Hanges, "'Severing the Joints and the Marrow': The Double-Edged Sword of Comparison," *Religion and Theology* 20.3/4 (2014): 331–44. See also the famous statement in this regard in Jonathan Z. Smith, *Drudgery Divine: On the Comparison of Early Christianities and the Religions of Late Antiquity* (Jordan Lectures in Comparative Religion, 14; Chicago, IL: University of Chicago Press, 1990).

the contents of his study on conversion shows him very much at home in the intellectual discourse on religion of his time (a discourse that was theological in orientation). When earlier I drew attention to the core features of Nock's definition of conversion, namely to the issues of "soul," the "individual," and intention, these three core features should be understood in terms of what I have described above as the discourse on religion at the time, namely that the sacred resides outside of human reality and irrupts into it, to which calling the human individual responds.

This "comparison in service of negating comparison" is clearly seen in another work that focuses on Apuleius's "conversion." Slightly more than a decade before Nock, Martin Dibelius published his study on Apuleius's initiation into the cult of Isis.[16] Like Nock, who devotes a whole chapter (chapter nine) to the "conversion" to the cult of Isis of Lucius, the main character of Apuleius's comic fiction, *The Metamorphoses, or The Golden Ass*, Dibelius focuses on the cult of Isis and initiations into the cult as a comparative foil against which to highlight the rise of Christianity. Thus for Dibelius, the cult of Isis becomes paradigmatic of the religious history of the Greco-Roman world.[17] At the end of the book, Dibelius concludes: "Die Überlegenheit

---

16. Martin Dibelius, *Die Isisweie bei Apuleius und verwandte Initiationsriten* (Sitzungsberichte der Heidelberger Akademie der Wissenschaften, Philosophisch-Historische Klasse, Jahrgang 1917, 4. Abhandlung; Heidelberg: C. Winter, 1917). I refer to this as Apuleius's conversion, for the sake of the argument, following convention which sees the novel as autobiographical (Lucius = Apuleius), although there are also some interpretations of the novel that do not assert—with good reason—such a close identification between the authorial voice/actor and the real author.

17. "In der Tat: ein ägyptischer Kult, auf griechischen Boden verpflanzt, in lateinischer Sprache geschildert—die Linie, die von Osten nach Westen führt, scheint deutlich zu sein. Und sodann: eine alte nationale Religion, durch Mystik vergeistigt, durch synkretistischen Universalismus entschränkt—man sieht, wie die grossen Tendenzen des Zeitalters sich begegnen," [Indeed: an Egyptian cult, transplanted on to Greek soil, expressed in the Latin language, the line that leads from East to West is clear. Thus: an old national religion, spiritualized through mysticism, broadened through syncretic universalism—one can see how the big tendencies of the period come together, trans. GvdH], Dibelius, *Isisweie*, 1. It was Richard Reitzenstein, with his study on Hellenistic mystery religions who showed the importance of the cult of Isis for the understanding of not only mysteries but also for the religious history of the period, and argued on the basis of the emotionality involved in the initiation for an understanding of the initiation as conversion. Cf. Richard Reitzenstein, *Die hellenistischen Mysterienreligionen nach ihren Grundgedanken und Wirkungen* (Nachdruck der 3., erweiterten und umgearbeiteten Auflage; Darmstadt: Wissenschaftliche Buchgesellschaft, 1977). Also for Reitzenstein, in spite of a lengthy comparison of Pauline language with that of mystery religions, in the end Paul's message of Christ is unique: "… Seine Religion bleibt trotz der Entlehnung neu und sein eigen … sie ist nie Allgemeingut, sondern mehr oder weniger immer Sonderbesitz," [His (Paul's) religion remains new and unique in spite of

des Christentums dokumentiert sich unserem Blick gewiß vor allem darin, daß es mehr und anderes bot, als Mysterien, Gnosis und synkretistischen Propheten ... ihnen auch überlegen, kraft seines originalen Gehalts und kraft der Tendenz der Ausschließlichkeit, mit der er diesen Gehalt sicherte."[18] Ergo, the most cited example of conversion in Greco-Roman mystery religions, that of the character Lucius in *The Metamorphoses* (as a stand-in for the author, Apuleius) becomes a counterfoil to conversions to Christianity in the early years of the Christ-cult movements, the lesser member of the comparison that serves to highlight the superiority of Christianity.

For all his enduring influence in setting the tone and framework for understanding the emergence of Christianity as a religion premised on a radical break with one's religious past, Nock's legacy in the definition and description of conversion in ancient religions (Greco-Roman, Judaism, and Christianity) has been subjected to critique. For instance, Janet Spittler, in her essay on conversion in the *Encyclopedia of the Bible and its Reception*, critiques Nock for limiting "genuine conversion to the only two ancient religions that required exclusivity, i.e., Christianity and Judaism. [And his emphasis on] internal reorganization of the individual soul largely disregards the communal, social aspects of conversion."[19] In addition, Spittler shows how for the New Testament itself, occurrence of the terms μετανοεῖν/ μετάνοια and ἐπιστρέφειν as well as the realities they evoke, is relatively scarce ("Unsurprisingly, most NT conversions take place in Acts ... Indeed, while the notion of a fundamental change is perhaps implicit, the explicit language of turning, repentance, or even belief is largely absent from the descriptions of Paul's conversion in Acts 9, 22, and 26, as well as from his own letters").[20] According to Spittler, while Nock notes some examples of

---

some borrowing ... it [true religiosity] is not common property but rather to a more or lesser extent always unique, trans. GvdH], Reitzenstein, *Die hellenistischen Mysterienreligionen*, 423.

18. Dibelius, *Die Isisweie*, 53, "The superiority of Christianity becomes evident in our eyes especially therein, that it offered something more and something different than the mysteries, Gnosis, and syncretistic prophets ... it is superior to these by virtue of its original contents and through its tendency to exclusivism by means of which the contents were secured" (trans. GvdH).

19. Janet E. Spittler, "Conversion. I. New Testament. II. Greco-Roman Antiquity," 708, in Constance M. Furey, et al., eds., *Encyclopedia of the Bible and Its Reception Online*.

20. Greg Sterling, "Conversion. III. Judaism. A. Second Temple and Hellenistic Judaism," *Encyclopedia of the Bible and Its Reception Online*, 709–10. For Second Temple Judaism, Greg Sterling makes the case that Nock's definition of conversion does provide a framework for understanding the transition some Gentiles underwent in becoming proselytes or epelytes; and goes on to highlight only a few undisputed

genuine conversion in Greco-Roman religions, they were (for Nock) the exception, while for early Christianity conversions were the rule as regards the formation of early Christian cult groups.[21] The biggest problem, however, resides in the fact that the conception of conversion with which Nock operates has been derived from a particular understanding of what Christianity entails, which then becomes the standard for identifying (or not) similar phenomena in Greco-Roman Antiquity, which is the problem of a circular argument, "modern notions of conversion, however, are so deeply rooted in the very texts under consideration that the resulting analyses verge on tautology."[22]

By contrast, Birgitte Bøgh recently suggested a new framework for conceptualizing conversion in Greco-Roman mysteries in a move beyond Nock, drawing on contemporary studies of conversion to establish a taxonomy of characteristics by means of which one can identify, surmise, or postulate deep conversion in mystery religions.[23] Rightly identifying the

---

portrayals of conversion: Philo's *On Conversion* (*Peri metanoias*), part of the exposition on the laws, *On Virtues*, conversion being the acceptance of the ethical monotheism of Judaism; Josephus's account of the conversion of the royal family of Adiabene (*Antiquities* 20.17-96); and the romance novel *Joseph and Aseneth* narrating the conversion of Aseneth. "There is thus evidence that some pagans turned to the ethical monotheism of Judaism. Conversion typically required more than virtue: it required adherence to Jewish law, most notably circumcision," Sterling, "Conversion," 712.

21. Qua Spittler: "Perhaps the most fundamental critique of Nock's still quite influential argument is that, given the limits of the literary record, *every* conversion account from antiquity should be regarded as exceptional" (712). Apart from Apuleius's *Metamorphoses* chapter 11, that is, the initiation of Lucius, there is also the putative conversion described in the *Cebes Tablet*, an *ekphrasis* on a painting depicting the cycles of life, section 11 which depicts the choices for correct opinions and life paths; and in philosophical literature the exhortations to turn away from wrong opinions to a new mode of life and a new understanding of the universe, Spittler, "Conversion," 711.

22. Spittler, "Conversion," 712.

23. Birgitte Bøgh, "Beyond Nock: From Adhesion to Conversion in the Mystery Cults," *History of Religions* 54.3 (2015): 260–87. Some of the theoretical and comparative work featured in Bøgh's taxonomizing are Lewis Ray Rambo, *Understanding Religious Conversion* (New Haven, CT: Yale University Press, 1993); John Lofland and Norman Skonovd, "Conversion Motifs," *Journal for the Scientific Study of Religion* 20.4 (1981): 373–85; Giuseppe Giordan, ed., *Conversion in the Age of Pluralism* (Religion and the Social Order, 17; Leiden: Brill, 2009); Nancy Shumate, *Crisis and Conversion in Apuleius' Metamorphoses* (Ann Arbor, MI: University of Michigan Press, 1996); H. Newton Malony and Samuel Southard, eds., *Handbook of Religious Conversion* (Birmingham, AL: Religious Education Press, 1992); and, not cited, but also worthwhile consulting, Lewis Ray Rambo and Charles E. Farhadian, eds., *The Oxford Handbook of Religious Conversion* (Oxford: Oxford University Press, 2014). Bøgh's essay is a rich anthology and resource for literature on conversion both in the study of religion in

problem of definition as key to reconceptualizing conversion in mystery religions, Bøgh goes on to state that "[t]he problem with employing a very narrow definition of conversion, on the other hand, is that the standards are set so unrealistically high that only 'Pauline' experiences are acknowledged as conversions. Consequently, a wide range of religious experiences, including those of most ordinary Christians, are in fact excluded from the discussion."[24]

In envisioning this wide range of deep religious experiences Bøgh constructs a polythetic definition of conversion: a change in religious identity (including intensification of belief and commitment), entering a community of collective worship and self-identifying as such (often cast as exclusive membership), changed behavior (including participating in new rituals), and commitment expressed in deep and deepened attachment (which includes highly emotively charged expressions of piety and adherence).[25]

By noticing a far wider variety of re-identifications, a much more nuanced picture is reached regarding initiation and conversions to mystery religions, so Bøgh proposes. Then, drawing on the work of Lofland and Skonovd, Bøgh adds six different conversion motifs:[26] intellectual conversion (a new satisfying cognition of truth), mystical conversion (dramatic event with paranormal experiences, high emotivity and dramatically changed behavior), experimental conversion (exploring different possibilities before settling for a chosen religious formation), affectional conversion (ties of fictive kinship and affirmation leads to choice for new religious group), revivalist conversion (crowd conformity with emotional spikes in group contexts), and coercive conversion (individuals pressurized to join the group).[27] This set of taxonomies for conversions is then enlarged by taxonomies deriving from studies emanating from the field of sociology of religion, and particularly from a study of the sociology of conversion:[28] soft conversions versus hard conversions (process, tentative, and transient, versus permanent

---

general, and with regard to Greco-Roman Antiquity (even if I come to different conclusions than she does).

24. Bøgh, "Beyond Nock," 268.
25. Bøgh, "Beyond Nock," 272–3.
26. Conversion motifs are the thematic elements and key experiences indicated in and emphasized by conversion narratives, David W. Kling, "Conversion to Christianity," in Rambo and Farhadian, eds., *Oxford Handbook of Religious Conversion*, 616–7.
27. Lofland and Skonovd, "Conversion Motifs," 373–85.; cited by Bøgh, "Beyond Nock," 275.
28. Giordan, *Conversion*, see n. 18 above: Bøgh references the essays by Luigi Berzano and Eliana Martoglio, "Conversion as a New Lifestyle: An Exploratory Study of Soka Gakkai in Italy," 213–41; Enzo Pace, "Convert, Revert, Pervert," 189–212; and Kieran Flanagan, "Conversion: Heroes and their Sociological Redemption," 371.

and public);[29] vertical, exclusive type (sudden radical change), processual conversion (gradual transformation), and interactionist/horizontal conversions (through social networks, embodying a lifestyle according to socially accepted behaviors and cultural expressions);[30] and rational-instrumental (based on calculation), rational-value-oriented (adhesion to a belief systems and its values), and traditional-conformist (conforming to the social games enforced by the majority of the society).[31]

Bøgh's 2015 essay sets out in programmatic manner the theoretical framework and scope of the bigger project (in addition to the two cases her article includes) coordinated by researchers at Aarhus University in Denmark, 2012, aimed at "investigating the significance of conversion and initiation for the formation and transformation of religious identity among pagans and Christians from 100–500 CE."[32] Framing the theme like this already suggests that the wider encompassing issue at stake is the complex processes of cultural and discursive changes that, along with shifting demographic changes, resulted in a dominant Christian culture.[33]

I draw attention to the context of thinking about conversion in ancient and late Antique religion as this "rhetoric of inquiry" is of the utmost importance for evaluating the continued utility of the concept of conversion as applied to the study of ancient religious phenomena— does it have explanatory and illuminatory power at all? That is the question.

Redescribing Religion, Ancient Religion (and Mysteries) ... and Conversions

Despite a very worthy attempt to move the debate on conversions in ancient mysteries away from the strict categories of Nock, the essay by Bøgh raises a number of critical issues that, in my view, warrant a redescription of the key terms in the debate. To start with, such a very wide range of phenomena of religious behavior and experiences that are taken to circumscribe the contours of possible conversion experiences also circumscribes practically all possible religious experiences and practices in ancient religious formations to the effect that conversions as such disappear from view (that is, when all of these are included, what is left of something distinctive as

---

29. Flanagan, "Conversion."
30. Berzano and Martoglio, "Conversion as a New Lifestyle."
31. Pace, "Convert, Revert, Pervert."
32. Birgitte Secher Bøgh, ed., *Conversion and Initiation in Antiquity: Shifting Identities—Creating Change* (Frankfurt am Main: Peter Lang, 2014), 9–10.
33. I say "dominant," but well aware that at the level of popular religion "Christianities" intersected deeply with local practices of long-standing tradition.

conversion?). To be sure, Bøgh raises the issue of limits to the conceptual content of "conversion" in her survey of the history of research into conversion, especially the study of conversion in ancient religions, in her "Introduction" to *Conversion and Initiation in Antiquity*: "What areas has conversion have (to have) an effect on (theological ideas, beliefs, behaviour, emotions, worldview, habits, values, social circles, missionary tendencies) if we insist that not all religious change is a conversion?"[34]

Second, the most significant source on which Bøgh draws, *Conversion in the Age of Pluralism*,[35] is not so much a collected volume on conversion but on the *sociology of religion*, and especially the complex contestations that have come to define complex societies characterized by a melting pot of divergent, oppositional, or complementary identity formation projects. I use the term "contestations" here deliberately, since the emergence of interest in conversion within sociology of religion is traced back to the work of Margaret Singer at the University of California, Los Angeles, with her work on "brainwashing" as a model for understanding how and why people were being recruited to new religious movements, as well as the work of Rodney Stark and John Lofland (then both at the start of their academic careers at the University of California, Berkeley) on conversions. The context and the timing of the work of these authors are significant; all three came in the middle of the tumultuous decade of the 1960's which saw massive cultural fracturing and social redefinition occurring in the United States of America, especially with its epicenter in California, a cultural shift that also manifested in the rise of New Religious Movements.[36] This offers a different approach to the topic of "conversion," namely rather to focus not so much on how individuals enter religious formations but rather how religious formations get constituted in the first place in the context of increasing fractious social disaggregations.

Third, the perspective from which the collection of essays in *Conversion in the Age of Pluralism* approaches conversion is that of the individual:

> Although the theme of conversion is not one that has a long history in sociology, it constitutes a privileged observation point to study society, especially the complex framework *linking together the individual and the socio-cultural contexts in which he is included*. Change in the *personal biographic route* and social and cultural change are very closely interwoven when we speak of conversion: values, speech, norms, behaviors, beliefs, lifestyles, relations,

---

34. Bøgh, *Conversion and Initiation in Antiquity*, 10.
35. See n. 22 above.
36. Roberto Cipriani, "Preface: The Sociology of Conversion," in Giordan, ed., *Conversion*, vii–viii. The rise in interest in conversion encodes the Angst pertaining to the identity-disaggregation of society into multiple social formations.

interests—everything becomes open to potential debate when *the individual decides to "convert."* The experience of believing often originates in or is accompanied by the experience of conversion, which is expressed in terms of radical change, a transformation that is almost always described in terms of a "before" and an "after," to the point of leading to a kind of "re-birth" and to the *construction of a new identity*.[37]

Here I would suggest that a meaningful redirection of the questions regarding conversion as set up in Nock's work and his legacy in theological studies takes its cue from contemporary theory of religion, especially those theorists that emphasize—and redescribe, reconceptualize—religion as a social discourse.[38]

What was the concept of conversion meant to explain? Just as there is talk of the "conversion career" illuminating the process of conversion in the religious life cycle of "converts," one can also investigate *the career of the concept of conversion*.

Redescribing Religion

As Martin Gosman states in his preface to *Paradigms, Poetics and Politics of Conversion*:

---

37. Giuseppe Giordan, "Introduction: The Varieties of Conversion Experience," in Giordan, ed., *Conversion*, 1–10.

38. The literature and the debates surrounding this approach have now become extensive and I signal only a bare minimum of orientation points. This new direction of thinking about religion is conventionally identified with the work of Jonathan Z. Smith as the inspiration for this new way of theorizing, but lately it is mostly identified with the work of Russell T. McCutcheon; for an overview of what is called a socio-rhetorical approach in the theory of religion, Steffen Führding, *Jenseits von Religion? Zur sozio-rhetorischen "Wende" in der Religionswissenschaft* (Bielefeld: transcript, 2015). An important programmatic essay is Russell T. McCutcheon, "Redescribing 'Religion' as Social Formation: Toward a Social Theory of Religion," in Thomas A. Idinopulos and Brian Courtney Wilson, eds., *What Is Religion?: Origins, Definitions, and Explanations* (Studies in the History of Religions, 81; Leiden: Brill, 1998), 51–72. The work of Bruce Lincoln has also been foundational, e.g., *Gods and Demons, Priests and Scholars: Critical Explorations in the History of Religions* (Chicago: University of Chicago Press, 2012). See also the essays by Veikko Anttonen on the sacred as a social and spatial performance: Veikko Anttonen, "Rethinking the Sacred: The Notions of 'Human Body' and 'Territory' in Conceptualizing Religion," in Thomas A. Idinopulos and Edward A. Yonan, eds., *The Sacred and Its Scholars: Comparative Methodologies for the Study of Primary Religious Data* (Numen Book Series, 73; Leiden: Brill, 1996), 36–64; Veikko Anttonen, "Sacred," in Willi Braun and Russell T. McCutcheon, eds., *Guide to the Study of Religion* (London: Cassell, 2000), 271–82; Veikko Anttonen, "Space, Body, and the Notion of Boundary: A Category-Theoretical Approach to Religion," *Temenos* 41.2 (2005): 185–201.

In the terms of Durkheimian sociology, conversion is a *fait social*. Although they are rarely treated as a cultural phenomenon, conversions can obviously be interrogated for the norms, values and presuppositions of the cultures in which they take place. In this way conversion can help us to shed light on a particular culture. At the same time, the term evokes a dramatic appeal that suggests a kind of suddenness, although in most cases conversion implies a more gradual process of establishing and defining a new—religious—identity.[39]

The reference to Durkheim frames the study in terms of understanding religion (and the sacred—that with which religion is purportedly concerned) as the social, that is, religion is a social discourse. In addition, the concept conversion refers to—and opens a view on to—normal processes of social formation in a given society, and as cultural fact, encapsulates the idea of identity performances that lies at the heart of culturing in society.[40]

In theorizing religion like this, the concept "religion" is a collective noun for the ensemble of mythmaking, world-making, identity-making, and socially formative projects that make up what we conventionally call a religious tradition.[41] I use the phrase "religion as a social discourse" here, but it should be understood that discourse (as even in the sense of religious

---

39. Martin Gosman, "Preface and Acknowledgements," in Jan N. Bremmer, Wout Jac van Bekkum, and Arie L. Molendijk, eds., *Paradigms, Poetics, and Politics of Conversion* (Groningen Studies in Cultural Change, 19; Leuven: Peeters, 2006), vii.

40. I have often promoted the following working definition of the concept "culture": Culture is the performance of identity, which identity (or "strategic acts of identification"—Jean-François Bayart) circumscribes the imagined belonging to an imagined community, which is continually evoked through acts of social formation and acts of social maintenance (i.e., the establishment and patrolling of boundaries), which manifest in an array of signifying practices as the markers of identification (speech, dialect, patois, and argot; mannerisms and habituated behavior; "distinctions"—tastes in clothing, music, food, and sport, all in accordance with acquired and operationalized social, cultural, and symbolic capital; typical haunts and favored spaces—how we define, arrange, organize, and inhabit spaces, and so on). As such, culture is neither singular nor univocal, in reality it evokes the constant conflict between the various participants in the discursive *agon* of defining identity and, thereby, manufacturing the self (and others) and society. This sociocultural conflict is institutionalized in a symbolic economy, and embodied in inculcated tastes (which range from social and traditional customs, to preference for these or those identity markers, to adherence to seemingly transcendental universals such as religious traditions). Built into the concept of culture are the notions of class identity and social history. This is more than adequately demonstrated by the social exigencies denoted by terms such as mainstream/dominant culture, sub-culture, counterculture, and the like. The study of culture is also the study of the persuasions (hidden and overt) that facilitate or induce participation in strategic acts of identification.

41. Burton L. Mack, *The Christian Myth: Origins, Logic, Legacy* (New York: Continuum, 2001), 83–99, on a social theory of religion (the chapter is titled: "Explaining Religion: A Theory of Social Interests").

discourse) is not just the term for the contents of sets of representations (which range from the spoken word, text, gesture, ritual, environments as arranged space, the rhythms of life as hidden persuasions). "Discourse" includes the social location that forms the originary matrix for the particular invention of the set of representations. "Discourse" also includes the social interests encompassed/encapsulated in and giving rise to the set of representations. Finally, "discourse" includes the logic governing the interrelations between these factors or aspects, as well as the institutionalization of such "domained" representations in canons of tradition, schools of thought, habitus as habituated action, social formations, cultural and socio-political-economic conventions, that is, as discursive formations.[42]

While "discourse" itself appears as nebulous concept, it is actually a *taxon* with which to investigate all the concrete operational sites of a given historical society's sense of self—its self-understandings, its self-representations, and its self-reinscriptions; the way in which these manifest in social and political institutions, the monumentalized built environment, public texts and literary traditions—and the way power (understood as the operation of "force relations"—Foucault's term) is dispersed through all interactional sites of engagement or withdrawal. Instead of viewing power/force relations as the concrete instantiation of power exercised by an individual or a repressive institution, Foucault considers the more pervasive and insidious mechanisms by which power affects the lives of individuals intimately, somatized in shaping bodies, bodily actions, attitudes and dispositions, discourses, cognition of reality and everyday lives. Discourse understood like this has as its complement embodied discipline as habitus, as embodied rule conformance.[43] The implications for reconsidering the phenomenon of conversions

---

42. This is a definition I evolved over the years, but it comes very close to that found in David J. Howarth and Yannis Stavrakakis, "Introducing Discourse Theory and Political Analysis," in David J. Howarth, Aletta J. Norval, and Yannis Stavrakakis, eds., *Discourse Theory and Political Analysis: Identities, Hegemonies and Social Change* (Manchester: Manchester University Press, 2000), 3–4: "We take discourse or discourses to refer to systems of meaningful practices that form the identities of subjects and objects. At this lower level of abstraction, discourses are concrete systems of social relations and practices that are intrinsically political, as their formation is an act of radical institution, which involves the construction of antagonisms and the drawing of political frontiers between 'insiders' and 'outsiders'. In addition, therefore, they always involve the exercise of power, as their constitution involves the exclusion of certain possibilities and a consequent structuring of the relations between different social agents. Moreover, discourses are contingent and historical constructions, which are always vulnerable to those political forces excluded in their production, as well as the dislocatory effects of events beyond their control."

43. The foregoing comes from a statement I made with reference to James Hanges's

to mystery religions lies in resituating the study of conversions in normal processes of social formations that are simultaneously highly affectively charged and go hand in hand with disciplinary procedures to effect rule conformance as new lifestyle. Related to this retheorizing of religion is recent rethinking of what religious experience is.[44] In a constructivist understanding of religious experience, as understood in line with Steven Katz and Wayne Proudfoot, *language, tradition, and culture constitute religious experience* (and *mutatis mutandis*, the experience of being called by a "mystery deity" and hence also the intense experience that goes with such cult entry), which does not refer to some inner experience of divine reality but the *affectively charged interaction with the process of constructing religious discourse*.[45]

This kind of perspective is particularly relevant for understanding complex societies, especially when such complex societies result from imperial histories with their large diasporic ethnic movements and resulting interwoven (and constantly contested) identity formations.[46] The much-discussed spread of so-called oriental cults—and the later mysteries were all exotic imports from the "Orient" or Romanized versions of such originally Near Eastern cults—over the Mediterranean world should be understood in the context of migrations of ethnic groups.[47]

---

study on cult foundations and founder figures in the Greco-Roman world, Gerhard van den Heever, "Introduction: Paul, Founder of Churches. Cult Foundations and the Comparative Study of Cult Origins," *Religion and Theology* 20.3/4 (2014): 265–6.

44. Gerhard van den Heever, "A Multiplicity of Washing Rites and a Multiplicity of Experiences: The Discursive Framing of a Bodily Practice," *Religion and Theology* 21.1/2 (2014): 142–58.

45. Wayne Proudfoot, *Religious Experience* (Berkeley, CA: University of California Press, 1985). See also Ann Taves, *Religious Experience Reconsidered: A Building-Block Approach to the Study of Religion and Other Special Things* (Princeton, NJ: Princeton University Press, 2009); Craig Martin, Russell T. McCutcheon, and Leslie Dorrough Smith, *Religious Experience: A Reader* (Sheffield: Equinox, 2012). See also the important theoretical article on experience as a category for theorizing religion, Robert H. Sharf, "Experience," in Mark C. Taylor, ed., *Critical Terms for Religious Studies* (Chicago, IL: University of Chicago Press, 1998), 94–116 (republished as "The Rhetoric of Experience and the Study of Religion," *Journal of Consciousness Studies* 7.11/12 (2000): 267–87).

46. In his *Encyclopedia Britannica* essay on Hellenistic religions, as well as in other publications, Jonathan Z. Smith makes a cogent case for the varied and multiple manifestations of religious formations and traditions in Antiquity, in that quite a number of religious formations existed in both an original homeland setting (and the shape that goes with it) and a diasporic version (typically a hybrid version that has adapted to its new setting)

47. Which in itself is a shorthand for the multiplicity of contingencies that brought members of the same ethnic groups together in Greco-Roman diaspora settings, whether as families, settlers (forced or voluntary, free persons, or as slaves), as individuals

Jonathan Z. Smith outlined the process as follows in the programmatic statement with which he opened his entry on Hellenistic religions in the *Encyclopedia Britannica*:

> The study of Hellenistic religions is a study of the dynamics of religious persistence and change in this vast and culturally varied area ... Almost every religion in this period occurred in both its homeland and in diasporic centres ... Each of these native religions also had diasporic centres that exhibited marked change during the Hellenistic period.[48]

The interplay between the two versions of each religion and cult resulted in different and differentiating systems of divine mediation with mobile ("utopian") techniques and agencies of divination developing in diaspora settings. This went hand in hand with the weakening of traditional ties between religion and land, weakening of ethnic ties (and hence the rise of the need for "conversion" as entry into elective cult formations, with a concomitant universalism); and a mixture of cult adherents with native representatives constituting the early specialist class with either Greek-speaking second and third generation immigrants or "converts"/newly joined adherents from groups for whom the religion was not native, a phenomenon that led to codification of traditions and precepts and translation of cult mythography, and the reinterpretation of the cult in its new context.[49] The typical form in which these diasporic expressions of migrated religions and cults manifested, was the voluntary association.[50] For the early imperial era, mysteries or mystery cults manifested as a wide variety of elective or voluntary associations.

Redescribing Mysteries

One cannot approach a study of mystery religions in the period under consideration without acknowledging the role played by conventional scholarly

---

(traders, craftsmen, etc.), but who linked up with and joined communities of whichever shape or orientation of fellow ethnic group members. I use the term "oriental cults" here well mindful of the fact that Orient and Roman were mutually implicating terms—not only were originally oriental/Levantine cults adapted to suit Roman tastes and sentiments, but often (and this specifically in the case of the cult of Isis) such cults were made oriental and exoticized to emphasize their sapiential and revelatory superiority, Miguel John Versluys, "Orientalising Roman Gods," in Laurent Bricault and Nicole Bonnett, eds., *Panthée: Religious Transformations in the Graeco-Roman Empire* (Religions in the Graeco-Roman World, 177; Leiden: Brill, 2013), 235–59.

48. Jonathan Z. Smith, "Hellenistic Religions," in *The New Encyclopedia Britannica*, Macropedia Vol. 18 (15th edn.; ed. Philip W. Goetz; Chicago, IL: Encyclopedia Britannica, 1986), 925.

49. Smith, "Hellenistic Religions," 925–6.

50. Smith, "Hellenistic Religions," 927.

discourse on the topic in setting the tone for our understanding of mystery religions (and so predisposing the study for much of the late nineteenth and most of the twentieth century).[51] Typical of the conventional picture of mystery religions in much of twentieth-century scholarship is an understanding of mysteries arising in a context of the decline in *polis* cults and cults of traditional deities; heightened irrationality and emotionality; a search for personal salvation by lost individuals (hence mystery cults are "individualistic"); promotion of personal relationships with the respective deities; alternative societies offering communal worship and communal life. Gustav Anrich in his then groundbreaking work, *Das antike Mysterienwesen*,[52] delineated the "religious meaning" of the mystery cults thus: the goal of the mysteries is the attainment of *sōtēria* guaranteed by the initiation rite, and this *sōtēria* consists of "blessed immortality" in the afterlife, as well as a new life on earth in union with and under the protection of the particular deity; next in importance to immortality is the idea of purification (*Entsühnung/Kathartik*) effected in a wide variety of rituals from water lustrations to blood baptisms like the *taurobolium* and *kriobolium*—initiations that effect a subjective experience of unity with the divine, and the objective attainment of the realities constituting the *sōtēria*, so that the *mystēs* has now received the *character indelebilis* of *sacratus*, *renatus*, and *tauroboliatus*; the benefits accrued from initiation into a mystery do not preclude multiple initiation into other mysteries, the reason being the increasingly magical-superstitious view taken of the mysteries, which prompted the initiands to seek ever more secure guarantees for the *sōtēria* in multiple initiations and purifications.[53]

However, in the context of the redescriptive theorizing of religion suggested above, it is possible to rather understand mysteries as manifestations and installations of "normal" cultural repertoires obtaining in a world

---

51. I discussed this at much greater depth in van den Heever, "Making Mysteries," and Gerhard van den Heever, "'Loose Fictions and Frivolous Fabrications': Ancient Fictions and the Mystery Religions of the Early Imperial Era" (PhD dissertation; University of South Africa, 2005), http://uir.unisa.ac.za/handle/10500/1510. For this overview I referenced Peter Green, *Alexander to Actium: The Historical Evolution of the Hellenistic Age* (Berkeley, CA: University of California Press, 1993), 587–600; F. W. Walbank, *The Hellenistic World* (rev. edn.; Cambridge, MA: Harvard University Press, 1993), 218–21; Antonia Tripolitis, *Religions of the Hellenistic-Roman Age* (Grand Rapids, MI: Eerdmans, 2001), 16–7.

52. Gustav Anrich, *Das antike Mysterienwesen in seinem Einfluss auf das Christentum* (Göttingen: Vandenhoeck & Ruprecht, 1894).

53. A very short overview of the changing understandings of mysteries in scholarship is found in Jan N. Bremmer, *Initiation into the Mysteries of the Ancient World* (Münchner Vorlesungen zu Antiken Welten, 1; Berlin: De Gruyter, 2014), "Preface," vii–xiii.

redolent of performance culture.⁵⁴ Roman culture, especially the early imperial period, was a theatrical culture of drama and mime, of dramatic representation and spectacle-making, of role-playing and identity-making.⁵⁵ Thus Angelos Chaniotis has shown how theatricality and performance was often the way in which to facilitate the epiphany of the gods in religious celebrations (his presentation was focused on the eastern provinces of the Roman Empire).⁵⁶ Chaniotis demonstrates how public performances, processions, and rituals contributed to the emotional response of the audience—devotees in the making of experiences of divine presence— to put it differently: the sacred resulted from a richly staged *son et lumière* pageant.⁵⁷ Looking at mysteries in this context of ancient (religious) theatricality it does not make sense to try to distinguish—for our purposes here—between "civic" mysteries and "sacred" mysteries.⁵⁸ From their origins in the eighth century BCE in Eleusis (the paradigm of all later mysteries) through subsequent foundations of mysteries in Samothrace, Lycosura, and Andania, as well as other local mysteries described by Pausanias; and

---

54. Wellman, "Ancient *Mystēria* and Modern Mystery Cults," 308–48; Harry O. Maier, "Vision, Visualisation, and Politics in the Apostle Paul," *Method and Theory in the Study of Religion* 27.4/5 (2015): 312–32; Angelos Chaniotis, "Staging and Feeling the Presence of God: Emotion and Theatricality in Religious Celebrations in the Roman East," in Bricault and Bonnet, eds., *Panthée*, 169–89.

55. Nicholas Purcell, "Does Caesar Mime?," in Bettina Bergmann and Christine Kondoleon, eds., *The Art of Ancient Spectacle* (New Haven, CT: Yale University Press, 1991), 181–93.

56. Chaniotis, "Staging and Feeling the Presence of God." The point made by Maier, and by implication Chaniotis, is that even in the case of early Christian cult founder figures like Paul, a spectacle-like staging served to elicit strong pathic responses such that one could imagine that "conversions" in Pauline communities consisted of strong emotional responses to these stagings, see for instance the implied performance stagings in Gal. 3.1—"It was before your eyes that Jesus Christ was publicly exhibited as crucified!" "Publicly exhibited" here translates *proegraphē*, which recalls vivid performance as kind of *ekphrasis*, that is, vivid presentation to make absent things present. Similarly, in 1 Cor. 4.9 Paul states, "For I think that God has exhibited us apostles as last of all, as though sentenced to death, because we have become a spectacle to the world, to angels and to mortals." Spectacle here translates *theatron*, again a reference to a very vivid ekphrastic performance presentation with a view to gain the rhetorical advantage of not only making his sufferings real, but to evoke emotions of sympathy in the audience.

57. I made a similar point with regard to mystery religions in the Roman Empire in their intersection with ancient Greek fiction, namely that they all subsisted in a "sea of visual performances," van den Heever, "'Loose Fictions and Frivolous Fabrications'."

58. As Bøgh, "Beyond Nock," 272, does. In fact, in her perspective—and judging from the examples offered of conversion phenomena—only the mystery cults of Isis, Dionysus, and Mithras count as examples of mysteries in which conversions and related phenomena played a role.

later the translocal "entrepreneurial" mobile mysteries of Dionysus, Isis, Cybele, and Mithras, the example of Eleusis provided the blueprint for the foundation of mysteries—cults and performances.[59] When even in the context of emperor cult one could found—and perform—mysteries (as shown so clearly in the inscriptions discussed by H. W. Pleket in "An Aspect of the Emperor Cult: Imperial Mysteries") and that even in combination with mysteries of Demeter and Dionysus, then one can understand that the character of mysteries had changed in the transition from the late Hellenistic to the early Roman period.[60] Outside of the classical circle of deities with mysteries, deities like Isis, Dionysus, Helios-Sun, Mithras, Sabazios, Jupiter Dolichenus, and Heliopolitanus feature large in the mysteries of the imperial era, which in our period now also included imperial mysteries.[61]

The net effect was that in the early Roman imperial period a number of cults had, alongside the "normal" temple-centred cultic institutions and performances, also mystery formats, like Artemis in Ephesus and Hecate in Aegine, to name only two traditional cults not "originally" associated with mysteries. So Phil Harland:

> In fact, the notion of separate "mystery religions" (hence the old scholarly term) is problematic in that one could encounter mysteries as rituals in honour of deities within various contexts, from official civic and imperial cults to unofficial guilds and associations ... Despite secretive dimensions of their rituals, associations of initiates were by no means shy in making their presence known within their hometowns.[62]

---

59. From the very many overviews of mysteries/mystery religions available, I refer only to Fritz Graf, "Mysteries," *Brill's New Pauly*; Michael B. Cosmopoulos, ed., *Greek Mysteries: The Archaeology of Ancient Greek Secret Cults* (London: Routledge, 2003).

60. H. W. Pleket, "An Aspect of the Emperor Cult: Imperial Mysteries," *Harvard Theological Review* 58.4 (1965): 331–47.

61. In the period under consideration the door to the club of classical mystery cults was prised open: the flowering of mysteries of the imperial era should be seen as a sign of the vitality and flowering of "paganism": "In a sizable number of cults well enough documented for us to tell true innovations from features that are simply not earlier known to us, a general refreshing can be seen over the course of the second and third centuries. It affected the rituals associated with Demeter at Pergamon, Artemis at Ephesus, Hecate at Lagina, and the hoax at Abonuteichus [i.e. the cult of Glycon instituted by Alexander, Lucian's 'false prophet'—GvdH]. All these developed their own 'mysteries' because, perhaps, that was the thing to do," Ramsay MacMullen, *Paganism in the Roman Empire* (New Haven, CT: Yale University Press, 1981), 106. On imperial mysteries, see alongside Pleket, "Aspect of the Imperial Cult," also Philip A. Harland, *Associations, Synagogues, and Congregations: Claiming a Place in Ancient Mediterranean Society* (Minneapolis, MN: Augsburg Fortress Press, 2003), 115–60.

62. Philip A. Harland, *Dynamics of Identity in the World of the Early Christians: Associations, Judeans, and Cultural Minorities* (New York: T&T Clark, 2009), 49.

The flowering of mystery cults or mystery religions characterizes the religious world of the early Roman Empire.[63] The flowering of mysteries therefore does not indicate religion in decline, a view that led an earlier generation of historians of Greco-Roman religion to posit a theory of a search for personal religion, mysticism, and salvation religion in Antiquity (the needs that gave rise to Christianity and its "rapid popularity and spread"). In fact, quite the opposite was true: "pagan" religion was alive and well, and flourishing.[64]

The reason why the mysteries proliferated in the early Roman Empire is precisely because they created networks of relationships for the celebration of power and its benefits (given that the mysteries created miniature copies of imperial society), and by doing so, helped to undergird imperial society.[65] And as will be seen in the examples offered at the end of this essay, it was typical of mystery cult groups to have elites and aristocrats take the leading roles (a feature that abounds in inscriptions during our era). As Fritz Graf points out: "Initiation into the mysteries creates special social, often regional connections between initiates (*sýmmystai*, IG XII 8,173, Z. 13; IGUR 3,225) ... The initiates at Samothrace formed themselves in the home cities into cult societies (*samothrakiastaí*)."[66] One can appreciate this when

---

63. Cf. the vexing question raised by Ugo Bianchi regarding the paucity of evidence for mysteries of the "oriental gods" before the imperial era: Ugo Bianchi, "Iside Dea Misterica. Quando?," in *Perennitas: Studi in onore di Angelo Brelich/Promossi dalla cattedra di religioni del mondo classico dell'Università degli Studi di Roma* (Rome: Edizione dell' Ateneo, 1980), 9–36. The rich world of mystery religions is a defining characteristic of the Roman Empire. On the relationship between mystery cults/mysteries and the context of the Roman Empire, see Gerhard van den Heever, "Redescribing Graeco-Roman Antiquity: On Religion and History of Religion," *Religion and Theology* 12.3/4 (2005): 211–38.

64. Cf. Henk S. Versnel, "Religieuze stromingen in het Hellenisme," *Lampas* 21.2 (1988): 121; and Luther H. Martin, "The Anti-Individualistic Ideology of Hellenistic Culture," *Numen* 41.2 (1994): 117–40, for a critique of the conventional portrayal of religious associations as indications of the pathology of late ancient religion—far from demonstrating the decline of Greco-Roman religions with a concomitant alienation and "cosmic and social loneliness" of inhabitants of the Hellenistic and Roman worlds, they demonstrate the vitality of continual socialization and re-socialization in that world.

65. "It was certainly recognized throughout antiquity, at least by people able to look at their world with any detachment, that religion served to strengthen the existing social order," MacMullen, *Paganism*, 57. The practice of multiple initiations into different mysteries just demonstrates the social function of religion even clearer (Hadrian had himself initiated into various mysteries). The fact that so many deities could live peacefully next to each other in the same shrine and sanctuary and even be dressed in exchanged garb surely tells a tale of the construction of an empire out of divergent peoples and their worldviews and myths as social narratives of identity (93–4).

66. Graf, "Mysteries." As an example of others: for Teos, Ionia in Asia Minor, a

one looks at the mysteries from a different vantage point, not from the perspective of the so-called injunction to secrecy, nor from the viewpoint of initiation, nor from the vantage point of the (now lost, if ever they did exist) mystery myths, but from the viewpoint of the mysteries as *drama mystikon*, as performance and mime-pageant, as pointed out above.

As the empire set in, imperial cult (including rites for members of the imperial family) was integrated into other public cults as well as into the cultic life and rituals of various associations.[67] Particularly notable in connection with and illustrative of the imperialization of mystery cults, are the Ephesian inscriptions suggesting imperial imagery and pageantry included in the mysteries of Dionysus.[68] An inscription dating from the time of Commodus indicates that the emperor himself, as "new Dionysus," participated in the processions.[69] Given that these mystery processions included the bearing of imperial images, the showing of imperial images and objects,[70] impersonation of gods and divine enactments,[71] the presence of light effects,[72] performances, processions, theatrical competitions and musical contests and choruses,[73] these performances served both to constitute a

---

locality with a very famous association of stage actors, there is a well-known *thiasos tōn dionysiastōn*, SEG 4,598.

67. Harland, *Associations*, 116–32.

68. Harland, *Associations*, 130–1.

69. Harland, *Associations*, 130, cf. IEph 293.

70. The office of *sebastophant* is attested in numerous inscriptions. The *sebastophant* (revealer of the sacred object, the imperial image) is a parallel office to the *hierophant* known from the classical mysteries.

71. There was already a long history to this: the way the emperor was painted red to resemble the cult statue of Iuppiter Capitolinus and impersonated the statue during Roman triumphs; the way in which both Cleopatra and Mark Antony impersonated Aphrodite and Dionysus during their famous Nile barge-trip; the re-enactments of the god Dionysus's conquests in the advents into Ephesus of Mark Antony as "new Dionysus" in 38 BCE and Hadrian as "new Dionysus" in 129 CE.

72. Similar to other mysteries, cf. Harland, *Associations*, 131. For light effects in other mysteries, see the description in Apuleius's *Metamorphoses, or the Golden Ass*, Bk. XI; for Mithraic mysteries, see Luther H. Martin, "Performativity, Narrativity and Cognition: Demythologizing the Roman Cult of Mithras," in Willi Braun, ed., *Rhetorics and Realities Early Christianities* (Waterloo, ON: Wilfrid Laurier University Press, 2005), as well as Roger Beck, "Four Men, Two Sticks, and a Whip: Images and Doctrine in a Mithraic Ritual," in Harvey Whitehouse and Luther H. Martin, eds., *Theorizing Religions Past: Archaeology, History, and Cognition* (Walnut Creek, CA: AltaMira, 2004), 87–103.

73. Cf. the Gytheum inscription regulating a festival in honour of Tiberius, Robert K. Sherk, ed., *The Roman Empire: Augustus to Hadrian* (Translated Documents of Greece and Rome, 6; Cambridge: Cambridge University Press, 1988), 57–9.

80 The Complexity of Conversion

cosmological order as well as an arrangement and conceptualization of society.[74] Religion, as the presence of divinity, was constituted and constructed by the performance. Considering the overwhelming experiences occasioned by the ever-increasing "over-the-topness" and raucousness of imperial processions and spectacles,[75] which themselves were blown-up and exaggerated versions of the myth of the conquering Dionysus (and compare this to the famous—and historically paradigmatic—Dionysiac procession staged by Ptolemy II Philadelphus in the 270s BCE, recounted by Callixeinos, an account preserved in Athenaeus's *Deipnosophistae* 5, 196a–203b); and considering that the mysteries (even, and especially, the classical mystery of Demeter at Eleusis) were essentially mime-pageants—*son et lumière, tableaux vivants*[76]—one can imagine how a religious experience was created by, and in the sensory overloading performance of, narratives of deities juxtaposed with imperial images and ideology.

Did One Convert to a Mystery Cult? Two Vignettes of Redescription

> In all of this there is and can be nothing monotheistic, nothing of the exclusive. Rather, Isis remains one among an infinite number of gods whose existence she never thinks to doubt, whose demands on human worshippers she never contests … In view, therefore, of the non-exclusive, non-competitive, polytheistic setting in which Isis is placed, Lucius' experience of her cannot in my view properly be classified as a "conversion" comparable to the cases of Christian conversion studied by James.[77]

Mysteries, mystery cults, mystery religions operated on a different logic to late nineteenth- and twentieth-century conceptions of religion. Even though, amid a general drift towards monotheism in the post-classical world, certain

---

74. Harland, *Associations*, 132–6. The work of Catherine Bell on ritual and performance is especially relevant here: Catherine Bell, "Performance," in Mark C. Taylor, ed., *Critical Terms for Religious Studies* (Chicago, IL: University of Chicago Press, 1998), 205–24, and Catherine Bell, *Ritual Theory, Ritual Practice* (New York: Oxford University Press, 1992).

75. Referred to above in the reference to the work of Maier, Chaniotis, and Purcell, nn. 51 and 52.

76. At its zenith in the imperial era the Telestērion at Eleusis could house a few thousand spectators seated on stone pavilions arranged around and focused on the open, flat space in the middle on which stood the Anaktoron, the chamber housing the cult objects and from the hierophant emerged surrounded by the fiery glow, Nancy Evans, "Sanctuaries, Sacrifices, and the Eleusinian Mysteries," *Numen* 49 (2002): 227–54: "the experience was primarily visual," Evans, "Sanctuaries," 245 n. 43, and to this I would add, visual participation in a mimed performance.

77. Keith Bradley, "Contending with Conversion: Reflections on the Reformation of Lucius the Ass," *Phoenix* 52.3/4 (1998): 326.

cults like that of Isis and Dionysus did evoke sentiments of singular attachment (in other words, embodied henotheistic tendencies in their official cult propagation), multiple initiations were not rare.[78]

I want to draw on two examples to question the conventional portrayal of conversion in the context of mystery cults. The first is a reconsideration of the paradigmatic example of conversion, that of Lucius (=Apuleius?) in *The Metamorphoses, or the Golden Ass*, and the second a series of inscriptions celebrating multiple initiations. In between I also raise the question of the meaning of conversion in contexts of cultural "reconstitutions."

Apuleius, Lucius, and The Metamorphoses: *An Example of Conversion?*

It is generally recognized that the ancient novel (which category includes the Greek romance novels of Chariton, Xenophon of Ephesus, Achilles Tatius, Longus, and Heliodorus; the Latin novels of Petronius, Apuleius; and the anonymous *Apollonius, King of Tyre*) provides accurate depictions of social realities of the first two centuries of our era. With regard to Apuleius, two aspects of his depiction of the "conversion" of Lucius stand out: The comparison with Apuleius's *Apologia*, his defense against accusations of using magic to con a wealthy widow out of her fortune, highlight a number of themes that also occur in his bawdy picaresque novel, *Metamorphoses, or The Golden Ass*, a novel about an overly inquisitive Lucius who dabbles in magic and accidentally turns himself into a donkey—the end of which comes when the goddess Isis calls him to devote himself to her and be initiated into her cult, which initiation turns him into a human again. Aspects of his initiation and the costs involved are typical for the period. As well, his depiction of Isis as *myrionyma*, the goddess with many names, encapsulating the persons and names of other female deities, is well attested for our

---

78. On ancient henotheism, see Henk S. Versnel, *Inconsistencies in Greek and Roman Religion. 1. Ter Unus: Isis, Dionysos, Hermes, Three Studies in Henotheism* (Studies in Greek and Roman Religions, 6.1; Leiden: Brill, 1990). Typical for Dionysus was the exclamation, Εἰς Διόνυσος! "Dionysus is one (or: the only one)!" Typical for Isis: te tibi una quae es omnia dea Isis! "you are the one and only, god Isis!", CIL X, 3800; or perhaps better: Dionysus is the one! Or, Isis is the one and all! On the general drift towards monotheism, see Bruce Lincoln, "Epilogue," in Sara Iles Johnston, ed., *Ancient Religions*, (Cambridge, MA: Harvard University Press, 2007), 241–51; Jörg Rüpke, "Patterns of Religious Change in the Roman Empire," in Ian H. Henderson and Gerbern S. Oegema, eds., *The Changing Face of Judaism, Christianity, and Other Greco-Roman Religions in Antiquity* (Studien zu Jüdische Schriften aus hellenistisch-römischer Zeit, 2; Gütersloh: Gütersloher Verlagshaus, 2006), 13–33; Guy G. Stroumsa, *The End of Sacrifice: Religious Transformations in Late Antiquity* (trans. Susan Emanuel; Chicago, IL: University of Chicago Press, 2011).

period.[79] However, it is the very picaresque and burlesque character of the novel that should caution against reading the Lucius story as simple, unambiguous, and transparent access to the religious reality of conversion in a mystery cult. Given the fact that the earlier antecedent Greek versions of the base story are known (the *Onos, The Donkey*, of Loukios of Patrai; and Lucian of Samosata's *The Ass*, a forerunner of the current *Metamorphoses*, Lucian and Apuleius were close contemporaries—the three novels together represent a raucous ribaldry of send-up comedy), and that one should regard Photius's entry in the *Bibliotheka* on Apuleius's *Metamorphoses* as "taking a serious view of magic and superstition" with a good pinch of salt, there is perhaps every reason to discount the *Metamorphoses* as a serious expression of conversion to a mystery cult.[80]

In Keith Bradley's reading of the *Metamorphoses*, the novel abounds with references to other deities apart from Isis: in the celebrated Book 11, Serapis, Osiris, Horus, Anubis, Ma'at, Hathor, Thermuthis—all of these gods whom Lucius encounters in the procession at Cenchreae, and whom he worships during his first initiation. While it is Isis who provides the remedy (the rose to eat) that restores Lucius to human form, at no point is an injunction given to worship Isis alone. In fact, at the end of the novel, Lucius is also initiated into the mysteries of Osiris. Thus, for his final initiation, Lucius acknowledges that he acts according to the will of all the gods. As Bradley puts it:

> In view, therefore, of the non-exclusive, non-competitive polytheistic setting in which Isis is placed, Lucius' experience of her [=Isis] cannot in my view properly be classified as a "conversion" comparable to the cases of Christian conversion studied by James ... There is no rejection of one and an embracing of a radically different system of religious knowledge, no heightened awareness of a single dominant god already familiar to the worshipper, nothing to suggest that Lucius' previous religious knowledge was "wrong" (to

---

79. See Gerald N. Sandy, "Apuleius' *Golden Ass*: From Miletus to Egypt," in Heinz Hofmann, ed., *Latin Fiction: The Latin Novel in Context* (London: Routledge, 1999), 68–86, for problems inherent in the identification of the novel as straightforwardly autobiographical: "The Golden Ass has tempted many readers to make the kinds of links between the author and the protagonist, between the *auctor* and the *actor*, that generally evoke skepticism now" (68). The classic treatment of Apuleius's *Metamorphoses* as religious text portraying conversion and cult initiation is Apuleius of Madauros, *The Isis-Book–Metamorphoses Book 11*, ed. J. Gwyn Griffiths (EPRO, 39; Leiden: Brill, 1997).

80. "Our confidence in Photios' account of the *Metamorphoseis* is not enhanced by the fact that he identified the *narrator* 'Loukios of Patrai' as its author. The Greek narrator Loukios is a believer in magic and other superstition, like Apuleius' Lucius (*Met.* 1.20.3), but this tells us as little about the *author's* attitude and the tone of the work as Lucius' various pronouncements tell us about Apuleius' beliefs or the ultimate purpose of the *Golden Ass*," Sandy, "Apuleius' *Golden Ass*," 88.

use Nock's term), or that he turns away from his past religious life, or that he undergoes a radical and total change of religious allegiance.[81]

From Apuleius's personal history we can reconstruct how he came to know the cult of Isis (and related Egyptian deities). There was a temple of Isis in Sabratha, the Tripolitanian city where Apuleius was tried for magic, while across the forum opposite the basilica where the trial took place was also a temple of Serapis. It is known from archaeological discoveries that the cults of Isis and Serapis were well entrenched along the coastal road through Tripolitania to Alexandria that Apuleius had intended to travel only to find himself detained at Oea. While the cult of Isis was not prominent at Madauros, where Apuleius grew up, dedicatory inscriptions testify to many deities worshiped there, including a number of gods that had mystery cults. At Carthage where he went to school, Isis and Serapis were well worshiped, but it was during his time in Athens that Apuleius encountered a cult of Isis and Serapis that stamped the religious culture of the city. The prevalence of Isis was such that she was even worshiped at Eleusis. Another piece of *Lokalkolorit* that made it into the *Metamorphoses* is the reference to the Altar of Pity (the old Altar of the Twelve Gods, also mentioned by Pausanias) that Lucius is said to have finally reached (*Met.* 11.15). It was while in Greece that Apuleius had himself initiated into a number of mysteries just like Lucius in the novel. It is known from other inscriptional evidence that priests in mystery cults were often initiated into other mysteries as well, such that it is not possible to speak of monotheistic mysteries demanding sole commitment of their adherents.

Thus, for all the knowledge Apuleius had of the Egyptian cults of Isis and Serapis, it is "not enough to prove that he himself was a devotee of Isis, or, most crucially, that he ever experienced a revelation of the goddess that he invented for Lucius ... Nonetheless, to set the description of Lucius' revelation in its cultural context is enough to demonstrate that the notion of an exclusive devotion to a single divinity, the obvious exceptions apart, was a notion that had no real place in Apuleius's religious world."[82] By any measure, the tale of Lucius's restoration to human form in the *Metamorphoses* is not a record of a religious conversion. As it is, we know from Apuleius's *Apologia* that he had been initiated into the mysteries of Dionysus and from the *Florida* (16.38 and 18.38) that he was a priest of Asclepius. That is, his initiation into the cult of Isis barely qualifies as a conversion to a henotheistic deity.

---

81. Bradley, "Contending with Conversion," 326.
82. Bradley, "Contending with Conversion," 331.

Syncretism and Conversion

If conversion implies a life-changing decision, a "total reorientation of the soul," a "turning from one form of piety to another," then the question of *what is being turned to* becomes acute. There exists by now a mountain of evidence that Christianity was not a pure "something completely different" to the philosophical and cultic discourses obtaining at the time of its emergence (in contradistinction to an earlier generation of scholarship premised on the essential difference between nascent Christianity and the surrounding religious world). Every religious formation gestates in a process of cultural bricolage. As Kurt Rudolph puts it so succinctly: "For the history of religions, there has never been a 'pure religion': this would be an ahistorical construct. Indeed, every religion is a syncretistic phenomenon."[83] Popular philosophy, Cynic-Stoic philosophical conceptions and ethics, informed much of the inner make-up of Christian proto-theology and practice, and that right from the beginning.[84] On the level of popular practices, early Christian group—and individual Christians—showed outwardly the same social organization as that of mystery cult groups, and lived in the same world redolent of demons and magic as their non-Christian neighbors.[85] As David Frankfurter argued in *Religion in Roman Egypt* and newly in *Christianizing Egypt*,[86] "conversion" is an inappropriate concept to describe and

---

83. Kurt Rudolph, "Early Christianity as a Religious-Historical Phenomenon," in Birger A. Pearson, ed., *The Future of Early Christianity: FS Helmut Koester* (Minneapolis, MN: Fortress Press, 1991), 17–8.

84. Abraham J. Malherbe, *Moral Exhortation: A Greco-Roman Sourcebook*, Vol. 4 of *Library of Early Christianity* (Philadelphia, PA: Westminster John Knox Press, 1989); Abraham Malherbe, *Paul and the Popular Philosophers* (Minneapolis, MN: Augsburg Fortress Press, 1989); Abraham J. Malherbe, *Light from the Gentiles: Hellenistic Philosophy and Early Christianity. Collected Essays, 1959-2012*, ed. Carl R. Holladay, et al. (*Supplements to Novum Testamentum*, 150; Leiden: Brill, 2014); Tuomas Rasimus, Troels Engberg-Pedersen, and Ismo Dunderberg, eds., *Stoicism in Early Christianity* (Grand Rapids, MI: Baker Academic, 2010); Troels Engberg-Pedersen, *John and Philosophy: A New Reading of the Fourth Gospel* (Oxford: Oxford University Press, 2017).

85. On the form of mystery cult groups, see Philip A. Harland, "Christ-Bearers and Fellow-Initiates: Local Cultural Life and Christian Identity in Ignatius' Letters," *Journal of Early Christian Studies* 11.4 (2003): 481–99; Harland, *Associations, Synagogues, and Congregations*; Harland, *Dynamics of Identity*. On magic: Marvin W. Meyer and Richard Smith, eds., *Ancient Christian Magic: Coptic Texts of Ritual Power* (Princeton, NJ: Princeton University Press, 1999); Clinton E. Arnold, *Power and Magic: The Concept of Power in Ephesians* (Grand Rapids, MI: Baker Academic, 1989); Clinton E. Arnold, *The Colossian Syncretism: The Interface Between Christianity and Folk Belief at Colossae* (Eugene, OR: Wipf & Stock, 2015).

86. David Frankfurter, *Religion in Roman Egypt: Assimilation and Resistance* (Princeton, NJ: Princeton University Press, 2000); David Frankfurter, *Christianizing*

explain the re- and inculturation processes that play out when new symbolic discourses are negotiated as newly-introduced symbolizations interweave with long-established cultural practices, folk customs, and identities.[87]

While the foregoing holds true for religious change in Antiquity, in a broader, contemporary framework the same questions can be raised. If it is true that conversion in Antiquity does not involve a reorientation to a new, coherent, stable set of beliefs and practices, neither is it the case in contemporary "lived religion," as Meredith McGuire argues in *Lived Religion*: Our notion of religion as a "unitary, organizationally defined, and relatively stable set of collective beliefs and practices" is challenged fundamentally by the phenomenon of "extensive religious blending and with-in group religious heterogeneity" that is the norm rather than exception. She continues:

> Our scholarly theories about religious socialization, conversion, and religiously plural societies have long depicted religion at the level of the individual in terms of commitment to the relatively coherent beliefs and practices of a single, received faith tradition (as identified through an organized religion such as Catholicism or Judaism). What if this picture of the historical norm is completely mistaken? We cannot make any assertions about contemporary hybridity as a new phenomenon without seriously considering whether scholars' earlier depiction of individual religious belonging was no more than an artifact of their definitional and methodological assumptions. Furthermore, when we rethink what is religion, we need also to reconsider our conceptions of religious identity and commitment. Perhaps the borders of religious identity and commitment are as contested, shifting, and malleable as the definitional boundaries of religions.[88]

Egypt: Syncretism and Local Worlds in Late Antiquity (Martin Classical Lectures; Princeton, NJ: Princeton University Press, 2017).

87. The following citation is worth repeating in full: "Since well before William James, 'conversion' has usually signified a private shift in spiritual allegiance from one religious identity to another. In this sense the term has carried with it distinct theological overtones inherited from Protestant Christianity, a religion that offers individual salvation from sin and an intimate savior who symbolizes that process, culminating in a decisive shift from darkness to light. The very rupture or decisive shift in religion that we associate with conversion may be historically unusual, the post hoc construction of hagiography or modern psychology. Apart from certain rarefied and idealized testimonies, the shift to Christianity in Antiquity and the Middle Ages, as in early modern Latin America and modern Africa, appears to have involved complex social dynamics, from elite interests in prestige to the public charisma of holy men and the erection of new shrines," Frankfurter, *Christianizing Egypt*, 10. See for instance, for a comparable phenomenon, this time in more contemporary Africa, Sibusiso Masondo, "Indigenous Conceptions of Conversion among African Christians in South Africa," *Journal for the Study of Religion* 28.2 (2015): 87–112.

88. Meredith B. McGuire, *Lived Religion: Faith and Practice in Everyday Life* (Oxford: Oxford University Press, 2008), 186–7.

86   *The Complexity of Conversion*

Perhaps the best analogy and set of *comparanda* to our topic of conversion to mystery religions in Antiquity, is provided by studies of "conversion" to traditional and indigenous religions in contemporary China.[89] Confucianism is woven into the warp and woof of Chinese culture to such an extent that participation in rituals, education in the Confucian canon, moral self-cultivation and participation in Confucian social institutions constitute to a large extent what being Chinese entails—in this sense very comparable to what Hellenism and being a Hellene entailed in the Greco-Roman world.[90] Thus, Confucianism does not stand in opposition to other religious practices and neither does it require renunciation of other religious beliefs. Rather, it is a deepening of community bonds, and a consolidation of multiple religious, social, and cultural identities.[91] With the resurgence of traditional religions in China (as ways of re-asserting traditional culture in the post-Mao era), Chinese religious culture is constituted by a wide variety of religio-cultural trajectories, like Confucianism, Daoism, and Buddhism, each of which is a vehicle for cultural identities, practices, and performances in contemporary China.[92]

Looking at it like this does not even begin to consider the effect of mass conversions such as occurred at various times in Europe, but also in the colonized world such as Africa. In cases like these, "conversion" is rather part of a gradual cultural change effected by the through-set of new political hegemonies.

Multiple Initiations into Mystery Cults

The second example, or properly set of examples, stems from the fourth century and are inscriptions celebrating the memories and achievements of pagan aristocrats in Rome under the Christian Roman Empire of Constantine and his sons. The four inscriptions are from the sanctuary of Cybele/Magna Mater, the Phrygianum, in Rome. The set of inscriptions was found and described during the 1608 construction of the Bramante façade of the St Peter's Basilica in Rome. The inscriptions were part of votive altars set up in the Phrygianum next to the Circus of Nero (on the site of the current St Peter's Basilica) and contain inscriptions self-identifying the dedicants as

---

89. See for instance, Fan Lizhu and Chen Na, "'Conversion' and the Resurgence of Indigenous Religion in China," in Rambo and Farhadian, eds., *Oxford Handbook of Religious Conversion*, 556–78; Anna Sun, "Conversion and Confucianism," in Rambo and Farhadian, eds., *Oxford Handbook of Religious Conversion*, 538–55.

90. Glen Warren Bowersock, *Hellenism in Late Antiquity* (Thomas Spencer Jerome Lectures, 18; Cambridge: Cambridge University Press, 1990).

91. Sun, "Conversion and Confucianism."

92. Lizhu and Na, "Conversion."

holders of priesthoods. The dedicants in question—Ulpius Egnatius Faventinus, Roman aristocrat and "most noble public augur" (CIL 6, 00504), Caelius Hilarianus (CIL 6, 00500), Caius Magius Donatus Severianus (CIL 6, 00507), and Sextilius Agesilaus Aedesius (CIL 6, 00510)—advertised in stone their multiple initiations and priesthoods in a specific stereotypical configuration of cults. Without going into a detailed discussion of the inscriptions and what they represent, I simply want to draw attention to the aspects of the non-exclusive character of the implied initiations.

CIL 06, 00500 13 May 377 CE

> To the Great Idaean Mother of the gods and Attis Men Tyrannus, worshipped by the most illustrious Caelius Hilarianus, duodecimvir of the city of Rome, father of the rites and hieroceryx of Unconquered Mithras, priest of the god Liber, priest of the goddess Hecate, [when] our lord Gratian Augustus and Merobaudes were consuls, on the 3rd day before the Ides of May.

CIL 06, 00504 5 April 383 CE

> To the Great Gods, Ulpius Egnatius Faventinus the most illustrious, public augur of the citizens of Rome, father and hieroceryx of the god Sol Invictus Mithras, archibucolus of the god Liber, hierophant of Hecate, priest of Isis, having undergone the taurobolium and criobolium on the Ides of August, [when] our lords Valens Augustus [for the fifth time] and Valentinian Augustus were consuls, Faventinus gladly renews the vows for another cycle of 20 years [sacrificed] at the gilded bi-horned altar.

CIL 06, 00507 15 April 313 CE

> [When] Our lords Constantine and Maximinus Augustus, [were] consuls for the third time, Caius Magius Donatus Severianus, most illustrious, father of the rites of [Sol] Invictus Mithras, hierophant of Father Liber and Hecate, made the taurobolium, on the 17th day before the Kalends of May

CIL 06, 00510 13 August 376 CE

> To the Great Gods, to the Mother of the gods and to Attis, Sextilius Agesilaus Aedesius, most excellent, barrister in the African court, and barrister in the imperial court, in addition to master of the petitions and master of the imperial inquests, master of letters, master of memoranda, vice-prefect of Spain responsible for sacred rites, father of fathers of Sol Invictus Mithras, hierophant of Hecate, archibucolus of the god Liber, reborn in eternity through the taurobolium and criobolium, sacrificed at the altar [when] our lords Valens for the fifth time and Valentinian Augustus the Younger were consuls, on the Ides of August[93]

---

93. I very gratefully acknowledge the help of my colleague, Dr Adrian Ryan, in the making of these translations. The Latin text of each is added at the end as Appendix. Note: in the case of Sol Invictus Mithras, I took Invictus to mean Sol Invictus although

88 *The Complexity of Conversion*

These inscriptions have conventionally been interpreted as evidence of Christian borrowings from pagan cults—namely, the *taurobolium* and the *criobolium* as precursors for Christian baptism. However, they can be better explained as examples of the effect of the mutual impact of the Christianizing religious context and Christian discourse on traditional religious cult, in which non-Christian (or pagan) aristocrats modeled their cultic practices on that of Christianity, with all the attendant searching for heightened emotional experiences involved in cult initiation.

A remarkable feature of the Phrygianum inscriptions is the stereotypy of the deities mentioned: Magna Mater (Mater Idea) and Attis Men Tyrannus, Sol Invictus/Mithras, Liber Pater (= Dionysus), Hecate, and Isis. Also the stereotypy of the functions listed: *pater* and *hieroceryx* of Sol Invictus/ Mithras (i.e., the highest rank in a Mithraic cult conventicle), archpriest of Dionysus (*archibucolus* of Pater Liber, the Roman version of Dionysus), hierophant of Hecate (Hecate being a deity for magic, but in the time of Julian and in her connection with the *Chaldaean Oracles*, also an oracular deity—in mirroring the inspired speech of charismatic possession in Christianity), priest of Isis, and a *tauroboliatus* and *crioboliatus* of Magna Mater/Cybele. In some discussions of conversion in mystery religions the phrase "taurobolio / criobolioq(ue) in aeter/num Renatus" as found in CIL 06, 00510 has been interpreted as indicative of the experience of conversion: reborn in eternity through taurobolium and criobolium. But the "in aeternam renatus" is probably only an exaggerated, blown-up expression of the interpretation of the experience.

In the long historical trajectory of these cults through the Mediterranean world they have all accrued imperial aspects, if not in fact being the products of imperial discourse, but they also represent deities of mystery cults. Initiation into these mystery cults—as demonstrated by these multiple initiations—is clearly marked as participation in a particular cultural repertoire, namely, cultural performances fitting to the status of the elites being initiated. This raises the vexing question: did these aristocrats convert to these cults? Or did the cults represent vehicles for the maintenance or attainment of social capital, as expressions of venerable tradition?[94] And hence, should they be seen as performances of traditional religion in a world in which imported "oriental cults" with their mysteries had already gained the status of venerable tradition? This specific constellation of cults brilliantly illus-

---

in one instance, for purely stylistic reasons, this was rendered as Unconquered. While the positions occupied by Aedesius are translated, I kept the titles of religious offices as they are in the inscriptions, except for sacerdos which is rendered "priest."

94. But note: none of the cults mentioned was originally a traditionally Roman cult—they were all imports from Asia and Egypt.

trates the political life of religious traditions including the political life of mysteries. While these inscriptions attracted attention in the study of the last phase of Mithraism at the "end of paganism" in Late Antiquity, by virtue of the cults mentioned and the attitudes displayed they open a much wider window on to the discursive foment represented by the long life of mysteries and mystery cults during the millennium of mystery cults since their beginning in Eleusis.

Concluding Remarks

This essay explored the contours within which one can speak of conversion in the context of mystery cults and mysteries. What emerged as *desideratum* is the need to reconceptualize what mysteries are in light of contemporary theory of religion as social discourse. In addition to that is the problem that the only touted example of mystery conversion, that of Lucius in Apuleius's *Metamorphoses*, turns out to be a problematic case. Two final remarks are possible in the light of these foregoing observations: first, that perhaps "conversion" is not an applicable term to use for entry into mystery cult group membership; and second, that perhaps it is best to abandon the term conversion, even for Christianity and Judaism (as well as in the case of other contemporary religious formations). As long as religion is understood as a stable and fixed constellation of doctrines, customs and practices, rituals, and identity formations and discourses, that—taken as a whole—encapsulates, promotes, or stipulates a "complete life orientation" with totalizing demands on morals and lifestyle, it is perhaps possible to maintain the concept of conversion as conventionally understood. However, when religion is understood as the collective noun for complex sets of syncretic, hybridizing cultural practices, identity performances in the context of social formations and re-formations (i.e., the multiple reconstitutions of social aggregates) in which multiple relations to surrounding popular culture are negotiated, then the concept "conversion" loses its conventional meaning in favor of being indicative of normal processes of social formation (which processes of social formation do entail identity boundary drawing, habitus formation as inculcation of rule conformance that goes with the particular social formation).

With reference to the latter remark, I have mentioned earlier that it is worthwhile conceptualizing the position of mysteries vis-à-vis the traditional cults through the terminological matrix of primal versus critical religion.[95] Primal religion describes the situation where religion or institutionalized cult is coextensive with the ethnic formation or with society

---

95. See n. 10 with reference to Pye, "Religion and Identity."

(although this does not mean univocal aggregations; but in the main this describes the city cults or ethno-national pantheons of Antiquity—or as I indicated earlier, any context with a strong residual traditional culture). Critical religion stands in some opposition to these in that adherence is normally elective, and includes formations that promote alternative access to divinity, or alternative philosophico-ethic-moral formations (typically, for Antiquity, the domain for itinerant entrepreneurial cult founders and religious philosophers).[96] While mystery cults in Antiquity normally did not stand in opposition to other public cults, some did: the Christ cult groups of the first two centuries did stand in some critical relationship to both nascent rabbinic Judaism and the surrounding world of Greek and Roman cults, including imperial cult and social contexts strongly determined by imperial cult; similarly Zoroastrianism started as a critical prophetic religion; Buddhism as a critique of the Hinduism of its time. But the distinction primal–critical is not a fixed and stable distinction—the terms indicate fluid positional discourses. Christianity became the primal religion of the Christian Roman Empire, in opposition to critical religions like Montanism; Zoroastrianism became the state religion of the Achaemenid Empire, and later in Arsacid and Sassanian Persia, exercised its hegemonic position in opposition to Christianity, Manichaeism, and the like; and Buddhism became the dominant religion in South East Asia and Sri Lanka to the detriment of other local traditions and religions. Thus, what are indicated are the positional relationships between different discourses and social formations. In the introduction to his monograph *On Roman Religion: Lived Religion and the Individual in Ancient Rome*, Jörg Rüpke cautions that we should not conceive of religion in the Roman world solely in terms of, and with reference to, the main city cults.[97] While he then proceeds to argue for a complementary concentration on lived, "private" religion, the argument applies as well to the many cultic formations simultaneously operating (and in overlap with respect to space and adherents with main civic cults) in the same world. The two terms, primal and critical, describe the various ratios of overlap and intersection that obtain between different religious formations, and thus invite careful conceptualization of the minutiae of the

---

96. Jonathan Z. Smith famously coined the phrase "utopian religion" for this feature of the religious landscape, Jonathan Z. Smith, "The Temple and the Magician," in *Map Is Not Territory: Studies in the History of Religions* (Leiden: Brill, 1978), 172–89. But see also the recent monograph of Heidi Wendt, *At the Temple Gates: The Religion of Freelance Experts in the Roman Empire* (Oxford: Oxford University Press, 2016) for an extensive discussion of such cults.

97. Jorg Rüpke, *On Roman Religion: Lived Religion and the Individual in Ancient Rome* (Ithaca, NY: Cornell University Press, 2016).

complexities of the social aggregation in any given ancient society and local context. Seen like this, the term "conversion" dissolves into a normal process of manufacturing of a social aggregate, with all the implicated affect that accompanies the process.

In his essay, "History and Religious Conversion," Marc David Baer makes the case that "historians of conversion now doubt the totalizing experience of conversion" in favor of a gradual, dynamic, unfolding process through which individual or group beliefs and practices change.[98] Baer lists four categories by which historians conceived of the conversion process, namely acculturation, adhesion or hybridity, syncretism, and transformation. It also entails the conversion of landscape and space. When the various categories of conversion are described: the incorporation of people into a new imperial hegemonic context or socioeconomic system; the fusion of new elements into the pre-existing cultural formation; the bricolage that results in a new complex of religious features; or the transition of tradition, all under the rubric of religious change, then the concept of conversion is hollowed out and one is left with normal processes of fluidity in identity formation, social formation, and cultural constructions and imaginaries.

Biographical Note

Gerhard van den Heever has been a full professor at the University of South Africa since 2012, after a long career as senior lecturer and associate professor, as well as a short stint as minister in a church. He teaches courses in New Testament and Early Christian Studies. His research focuses on the Gospel of John in its Greco-Roman context, Greek and Roman religions—especially the transformations in religious formations from the classical to the Late Antique period, history of religion, and contemporary theory of religion. He is currently editing a collection of essays, *After Religion*, which deals with theorizing historiography of religion in Antiquity. Current projects include an international colloquium on Mapping Transformations towards a Christian Late Antiquity, as well as a publication of essays on Twilights of Greek and Roman Religions.

---

98. Marc David Baer, "History and Religious Conversion," in Rambo and Farhadian, eds., *Oxford Handbook of Religious Conversion*, 25.

Bibliography

Anrich, Gustav. *Das antike Mysterienwesen in seinem Einfluss auf das Christentum.* Göttingen: Vandenhoeck & Ruprecht, 1894.

Anttonen, Veikko. "Rethinking the Sacred: The Notions of 'Human Body' and 'Territory' in Conceptualizing Religion," 36–64 in *The Sacred and Its Scholars: Comparative Methodologies for the Study of Primary Religious Data.* Edited by Thomas A. Idinopulos and Edward A. Yonan. Numen Book Series, 73. Leiden: Brill, 1996. https://doi.org/10.1163/9789004378957_005

—"Sacred," 271–82 in *Guide to the Study of Religion.* Edited by Willi Braun and Russell T. McCutcheon. London: Cassell, 2000.

—"Space, Body, and the Notion of Boundary: A Category-Theoretical Approach to Religion," *Temenos* 41.2 (2005): 185–201. https://doi.org/10.33356/temenos.4779

Apuleius of Madauros. *The Isis-Book-Metamorphoses Book 11.* Edited by J. Gwyn Griffiths. EPRO, 39. Leiden: Brill, 1997.

Arnold, Clinton E. *Power and Magic: The Concept of Power in Ephesians.* Grand Rapids, MI: Baker Academic, 1989

—*The Colossian Syncretism: The Interface between Christianity and Folk Belief at Colossae.* Eugene, OR: Wipf & Stock, 2015.

Baer, Marc David. "History and Religious Conversion," 25–47 in Rambo and Farhadian, eds., *Oxford Handbook of Religious Conversion,* 2014. https://doi.org/10.1093/oxfordhb/9780195338522.013.023

Beck, Roger. "Four Men, Two Sticks, and a Whip: Images and Doctrine in a Mithraic Ritual," 87–103 in Harvey Whitehouse and Luther H. Martin, eds., *Theorizing Religions Past. Archaeology, History, and Cognition.* Walnut Creek, CA: AltaMira, 2004.

Bell, Catherine. *Ritual Theory, Ritual Practice.* New York: Oxford University Press, 1992.

—"Performance," 205–24, in Mark C. Taylor, ed., *Critical Terms for Religious Studies.* Chicago, IL: University of Chicago Press, 1998.

Bianchi, Ugo. "Iside Dea Misterica. Quando?," 9–36 in *Perennitas: Studi in onore di Angelo Brelich/Promossi dalla cattedra di religioni del mondo classico dell'Università degli Studi di Roma.* Rome: Edizione dell' Ateneo, 1980.

Bienert, Wolfgang. "Conversion. IV. Church History, 1. Early Church," in *Religion Past and Present.* http:// dx.doi.org/10.1163/1877-5888_rpp_COM_01673.

Bøgh, Birgitte. "Beyond Nock: From Adhesion to Conversion in the Mystery Cults," *History of Religions* 54.3 (2015): 260–87. https://doi.org/10.1086/678994

—ed. *Conversion and Initiation in Antiquity: Shifting Identities–Creating Change.* Frankfurt am Main: Peter Lang, 2014.

Bowersock, Glen Warren. *Hellenism in Late Antiquity.* Thomas Spencer Jerome Lectures, 18. Cambridge: Cambridge University Press, 1990. https://doi.org/10.3998/mpub.9381

Bradley, Keith. "Contending with Conversion: Reflections on the Reformation of Lucius the Ass," *Phoenix* 52.3/4 (1998): 315–34. https://doi.org/10.2307/1088674

Bremmer, Jan N. *Initiation into the Mysteries of the Ancient World.* Münchner Vorlesungen zu Antiken Welten, 1; Berlin: De Gruyter, 2014. https://doi.org/10.1515/9783110299557

Bremmer, Jan N., Wout Jac van Bekkum, and Arie L. Molendijk, eds. *Paradigms, Poetics, and Politics of Conversion.* Groningen Studies in Cultural Change, 19. Leuven: Peeters, 2006.

Cancik, Hubert. "Conversion. II. Greco-Roman Antiquity," in *Religion Past and Present*. https://doi.org/10.1163/1877-5888_rpp_COM_01673

Carey, Greg. "Milestones in My Journey out of Evangelicalism," *Democracy on Fire: Resources for Resistance*, 14 March 2018. http://democracyonfire.blogspot.com/2018/03/milestones-in-my-journey-out-of.html

Chaniotis, Angelos. "Staging and Feeling the Presence of God: Emotion and Theatricality in Religious Celebrations in the Roman East," 169–89 in *Panthée: Religious Transformations in the Graeco-Roman Empire*. Edited by Laurent Bricault and Nicole Bonnett. Leiden: Brill, 2013. https://doi.org/10.1163/9789004256903_009

Chesnutt, Randall D. *From Death to Life: Conversion in Joseph and Aseneth*. Journal for the Study of the Pseudepigrapha Supplement, 16. Sheffield: Sheffield Academic Press, 1995.

Cipriani, Roberto. "Preface: The Sociology of Conversion," vii–xiii in *Conversion in the Age of Pluralism*. Edited by Giuseppe Giordan. Leiden: Brill, 2009.

Cosmopoulos, Michael B., ed. *Greek Mysteries: The Archaeology of Ancient Greek Secret Cults*. London: Routledge, 2003.

Dibelius, Martin. *Die Isisweie bei Apuleius und verwandte Initiationsriten*. Sitzungsberichte der Heidelberger Akademie der Wissenschaften, Philosophisch-Historische Klasse. Jahrgang 1917, 4. Abhandlung. Heidelberg: C. Winter, 1917.

Engberg-Pedersen, Troels. *John and Philosophy: A New Reading of the Fourth Gospel*. Oxford: Oxford University Press, 2017. https://doi.org/10.1093/acprof:oso/9780198792505.001.0001

Evans, Nancy. "Sanctuaries, Sacrifices, and the Eleusinian Mysteries," *Numen* 49 (2002): 227–54. https://doi.org/10.1163/156852702320263927

Frankfurter, David. *Religion in Roman Egypt: Assimilation and Resistance*. Princeton, NJ: Princeton University Press, 2000.

—*Christianizing Egypt: Syncretism and Local Worlds in Late Antiquity*. Martin Classical Lectures. Princeton, NJ: Princeton University Press, 2017. https://doi.org/10.2307/j.ctt21668cq

Führding, Steffen. *Jenseits von Religion? Zur sozio-rhetorischen "Wende" in der Religionswissenschaft*. Bielefeld: transcript, 2015. https://doi.org/10.14361/9783839431382

Giordan, Giuseppe. "Introduction: The Varieties of Conversion Experience," 1–10 in Giordan, *Conversion*, 2009. https://doi.org/10.1163/ej.9789004178038.i-334.5

—ed. *Conversion in the Age of Pluralism*. Religion and the Social Order, 17. Leiden: Brill, 2009. https://doi.org/10.1163/ej.9789004178038.i-334

Gosman, Martin. "Preface and Acknowledgements," vii–viii in Bremmer, van Bekkum, and Molendijk, eds., *Paradigms*, 2006.

Graf, Fritz. "Mysteries," in *Brill's New Pauly*, edited by Hubert Cancik, Helmuth Schneider, and Christine F. Salazar. https://referenceworks.brillonline.com/entries/brill-s-new-pauly/mysteries-e814910

Green, Peter. *Alexander to Actium: The Historical Evolution of the Hellenistic Age*. Berkeley, CA: University of California Press, 1993.

Hanges, James Constantine. "Interpreting Glossolalia and the Comparison of Comparisons," 181–218 in *Comparing Religions: Possibilities and Perils*. Edited by James Constantine Hanges, Thomas A. Idinopulos, and Brian C. Wilson. Numen Book Series, 113. Leiden: Brill, 2006.

—"'Severing the Joints and the Marrow': The Double-Edged Sword of Comparison,"

Religion and Theology 20.3/4 (2014): 331–44. https://doi.org/10.1163/15743012-12341267

Harland, Philip A. *Associations, Synagogues, and Congregations: Claiming a Place in Ancient Mediterranean Society*. Minneapolis, MN: Augsburg Fortress, 2003.

—"Christ-Bearers and Fellow-Initiates: Local Cultural Life and Christian Identity in Ignatius' Letters," *Journal of Early Christian Studies* 11.4 (2003): 481–99. ttps://doi.org/10.1353/earl.2003.0060

—*Dynamics of Identity in the World of the Early Christians: Associations, Judeans, and Cultural Minorities*. New York: T&T Clark, 2009.

Howarth, David J., and Yannis Stavrakakis. "Introducing Discourse Theory and Political Analysis," 1–23 in *Discourse Theory and Political Analysis: Identities, Hegemonies and Social Change*. Edited by David J. Howarth, Aletta J. Norval, and Yannis Stavrakakis. Manchester: Manchester University Press, 2000.

Kling, David W. "Conversion to Christianity," 598–631 in Rambo and Farhadian, eds., *Oxford Handbook of Religious Conversion*, 2014. https://doi.org/10.1093/oxfordhb/9780195338522.013.026

Lincoln, Bruce. "Epilogue," 241–51 in *Ancient Religions*. Edited by Sara Iles Johnston. Cambridge, MA: Harvard University Press, 2007. https://doi.org/10.4159/9780674039186-027

—*Gods and Demons, Priests and Scholars: Critical Explorations in the History of Religions*. Chicago, IL: University Of Chicago Press, 2012. https://doi.org/10.7208/chicago/9780226035161.001.0001

—*Discourse and the Construction of Society: Comparative Studies of Myth, Ritual, and Classification*. 2nd edn. Oxford: Oxford University Press, 2014. https://doi.org/10.1093/acprof:oso/9780199372362.001.0001

Lizhu, Fan, and Chen Na. "'Conversion' and the Resurgence of Indigenous Religion in China," 556–78 in Rambo and Farhadian, eds., *Oxford Handbook of Religious Conversion*, 2014. https://doi.org/10.1093/oxfordhb/9780195338522.013.024

Lofland, John, and Norman Skonovd. "Conversion Motifs," *Journal for the Scientific Study of Religion* 20.4 (1981): 373–85. https://doi.org/10.2307/1386185

Mack, Burton L. *The Christian Myth: Origins, Logic, Legacy*. New York: Continuum, 2001.

MacMullen, Ramsay. *Paganism in the Roman Empire*. New Haven, CT: Yale University Press, 1981.

Maier, Harry O. "Vision, Visualisation, and Politics in the Apostle Paul," *Method and Theory for the Study of Religion* 27.4/5 (2015): 312–32. https://doi.org/10.1163/15700682-12341356

Malherbe, Abraham J. *Paul and the Popular Philosophers*. Minneapolis, MN: Augsburg Fortress, 1989.

—*Moral Exhortation: A Greco-Roman Sourcebook*. Philadelphia, PA: Westminster John Knox, 1989.

—*Light from the Gentiles: Hellenistic Philosophy and Early Christianity: Collected Essays, 1959-2012*. Edited by Carl R. Holladay, John T. Fitzgerald, James W. Thompson, and Gregory E. Sterling. Supplements to Novum Testamentum, 150. Leiden: Brill, 2014. https://doi.org/10.1163/9789004256521

Malony, H. Newton, and Samuel Southard, eds. *Handbook of Religious Conversion*. Birmingham, AL: Religious Education Press, 1992.

Martin, Craig, Russell T. McCutcheon, and Leslie Dorrough Smith. *Religious Experience: A Reader*. Sheffield: Equinox, 2012.

Martin, Luther H. "The Anti-Individualistic Ideology of Hellenistic Culture," *Numen* 41.2 (1994): 117–40. https://doi.org/10.2307/3270256

—"Performativity, Narrativity and Cognition: Demythologizing the Roman Cult of Mithras," in Willi Braun ed., *Rhetorics and Realities Early Christianities*. Waterloo, ON: Wilfrid Laurier University Press, 2005.

Masondo, Sibusiso. "Indigenous Conceptions of Conversion among African Christians in South Africa," *Journal for the Study of Religion* 28.2 (2015): 87–112.

McCutcheon, Russell. "Redescribing 'Religion' as Social Formation: Toward a Social Theory of Religion," 51–72 in *What Is Religion?: Origins, Definitions, and Explanations*. Edited by Thomas A. Idinopulos and Brian Courtney Wilson. Studies in the History of Religions, 81. Leiden: Brill, 1998. https://doi.org/10.1163/9789004379046_006

McGuire, Meredith B. *Lived Religion: Faith and Practice in Everyday Life*. Oxford: Oxford University Press, 2008. https://doi.org/10.1093/acprof:oso/9780195172621.001.0001

Meyer, Marvin W., and Richard Smith, eds. *Ancient Christian Magic: Coptic Texts of Ritual Power*. Princeton, NJ: Princeton University Press, 1999.

Nock, Arthur Darby. *Conversion: The Old and the New in Religion from Alexander the Great to Augustine of Hippo*. Oxford: Oxford University Press, 1933.

Pleket, Henri Willy. "An Aspect of the Emperor Cult: Imperial Mysteries," *Harvard Theological Review* 58.4 (1965): 331–47. https://doi.org/10.1017/S0017816000002571

Proudfoot, Wayne. *Religious Experience*. Berkeley, CA: University of California Press, 1985.

Purcell, Nicholas. "Does Caesar Mime?," 181–93 in *The Art of Ancient Spectacle*. Edited by Bettina Bergmann and Christine Kondoleon. New Haven, CT: Yale University Press, 1991.

Pye, Michael. "Religion and Identity: Clues and Threads," 314–26 in *Strategies in the Study of Religion. Vol. 2: Exploring Religions in Motion*. Religion and Reason, 52. Berlin: de Gruyter, 2013.

Rambo, Lewis Ray. *Understanding Religious Conversion*. New Haven, CT: Yale University Press, 1993.

Rambo, Lewis Ray, and Charles E. Farhadian, eds. *The Oxford Handbook of Religious Conversion*. Oxford: Oxford University Press, 2014. https://doi.org/10.1093/oxfordhb/9780195338522.001.0001

Rasimus, Tuomas, Troels Engberg-Pedersen, and Ismo Dunderberg, eds. *Stoicism in Early Christianity*. Grand Rapids, MI: Baker Academic, 2010.

Reitzenstein, Richard. *Die hellenistischen Mysterienreligionen nach ihren Grundgedanken und Wirkungen*. Nachdruck der 3. Erweiterten und umgearbeiteten Auflage. Darmstadt: Wissenschaftliche Buchgesellschaft, 1977.

Rudolph, Kurt. "Early Christianity as a Religious-Historical Phenomenon," 9–19 in *The Future of Early Christianity: FS Helmut Koester*. Edited by Birger A. Pearson. Minneapolis, MN: Fortress Press, 1991.

Rüpke, Jörg. "Patterns of Religious Change in the Roman Empire," 13–33 in *The Changing Face of Judaism, Christianity, and Other Greco-Roman Religions in Antiquity*. Edited by Ian H. Henderson and Gerbern S. Oegema. Studien zu Jüdische Schriften aus hellenistisch-römischer Zeit, 2. Gütersloh: Gütersloher Verlagshaus, 2006.

—*On Roman Religion: Lived Religion and the Individual in Ancient Rome*. Ithaca, NY: Cornell University Press, 2016. https://doi.org/10.7591/9781501706264

Sandy, Gerald L. "Apuleius' Golden Ass: From Miletus to Egypt," 68–86 in *Latin Fiction: The Latin Novel in Context*. Edited by Heinz Hofmann. London: Routledge, 1999.

Sharf, Robert H. "Experience," 94–116 in *Critical Terms for Religious Studies*. Edited by Mark C. Taylor. Chicago, IL: University of Chicago Press, 1998.

Sherk, Robert K., ed. *The Roman Empire: Augustus to Hadrian*. Translated Documents of Greece and Rome, 6. Cambridge: Cambridge University Press, 1988. https://doi.org/10.1017/CBO9780511552670

Shumate, Nancy. *Crisis and Conversion in Apuleius' Metamorphoses*. Ann Arbor, MI: University of Michigan Press, 1996. https://doi.org/10.3998/mpub.23280

Smith, Jonathan Z. "The Temple and the Magician," 172–89 in *Map Is Not Territory: Studies in the History of Religions*. Leiden: Brill, 1978.

—"Hellenistic Religions," 925–9 in *The New Encyclopedia Britannica*. Edited by Philip W. Goetz. 15th edn. Vol. 18 of *Macropedia*. Chicago, IL: Encyclopedia Britannica, 1986.

—*Drudgery Divine: On the Comparison of Early Christianities and the Religions of Late Antiquity*. Jordan Lectures in Comparative Religion, 14. Chicago, IL: University of Chicago Press, 1990.

Spittler, Janet E. "Conversion. I. New Testament. II. Greco-Roman Antiquity," 708–12 in Constance Furey, et al., eds., *Encyclopedia of the Bible and Its Reception Online*, 2012. https://www.degruyter.com/document/database/EBR/entry/MainLemma_6352/html

Sterling, Greg. "Conversion. III. Judaism. A. Second Temple and Hellenistic Judaism." 712–13 in Constance Furey, et al., eds., *Encyclopedia of the Bible and Its Reception Online*, 2012. https://www.degruyter.com/document/database/EBR/entry/MainLemma_6352/html

Stroumsa, Guy G. *The End of Sacrifice: Religious Transformations in Late Antiquity*. Translated by Susan Emanuel. Chicago, IL: University of Chicago Press, 2011.

Sun, Anna. "Conversion and Confucianism," 538–55 in Rambo and Farhadian, eds., *Oxford Handbook of Religious Conversion*, 2014. https://doi.org/10.1093/oxfordhb/9780195338522.013.023

Taves, Ann. *Religious Experience Reconsidered: A Building-Block Approach to the Study of Religion and Other Special Things*. Princeton, NJ: Princeton University Press, 2009. https://doi.org/10.1515/9781400830978

Tripolitis, Antonia. *Religions of the Hellenistic-Roman Age*. Grand Rapids, MI: Eerdmans, 2001.

Van den Heever, Gerhard. "'Loose Fictions and Frivolous Fabrications': Ancient Fictions and the Mystery Religions of the Early Imperial Era." PhD Dissertation: University of South Africa, 2005. http://uir.unisa.ac.za/handle/10500/1510

—"Redescribing Graeco-Roman Antiquity: On Religion and History of Religion," *Religion and Theology* 12.3/4 (2005): 211–38. https://doi.org/10.1163/157430106776241213

—"Making Mysteries: From the Untergang der Mysterien to Imperial Mysteries—Social Discourse in Religion and the Study of Religion," *Religion and Theology* 12.3/4 (2005): 262–307. https://doi.org/10.1163/157430106776241150

—A Multiplicity of Washing Rites and a Multiplicity of Experiences: The Discursive Framing of a Bodily Practice," *Religion and Theology* 21.1/2 (2014): 142–58. https://doi.org/10.1163/15743012-02101010

—"Introduction: Paul, Founder of Churches: Cult Foundations and the Comparative Study of Cult Origins," *Religion and Theology* 20.3/4 (2014): 259–83. https://doi.org/10.1163/15743012-12341262
Versluys, Miguel John. "Orientalising Roman Gods," 235–59 in *Panthée: Religious Transformations in the Graeco-Roman Empire*. Edited by Laurent Bricault and Nicole Bonnett. Religions in the Graeco-Roman World, 177. Leiden: Brill, 2013.
Versnel, Henk S. *Inconsistencies in Greek and Roman Religion. 1. Ter Unus: Isis, Dionysos, Hermes, Three Studies in Henotheism*. Studies in Greek and Roman Religions, 6.1. Leiden: Brill, 1990.
—"Religieuze stromingen in het Hellenisme," *Lampas* 21.2 (1988): 111–36.
Walbank, F. W. *The Hellenistic World*. Rev. edn. Cambridge, MA: Harvard University Press, 1993.
Wellman, Tennyson Jacob. "Ancient *Mystēria* and Modern Mystery Cults," *Religion and Theology* 12.3/4 (2005): 308–48. https://doi.org/10.1163/157430106776241141
Wendt, Heidi. *At the Temple Gates: The Religion of Freelance Experts in the Roman Empire*. Oxford: Oxford University Press, 2016. https://doi.org/10.1093/acprof:oso/9780190267148.001.0001

Appendix

CIL 06, 00500 13 May 377 CE
Publication: CIL 06, 00500 (p 3005, 3757) = CIL 06, 30779d = D 04148
Province: Roma
M(atri) d(eum) M(agnae) I(daeae)/ et Attidi Meno/tyranno Conser/vatoribus suis Cae/lius Hilarianus v(ir) c(larissimus) / duodecim<vi=BY>r / urbis Romae / p(ater) s(acrorum) et hieroceryx / I(nvicti) M(ithrae) s(acerdos) d(ei) L(iberi) s(acerdos) d(eae) / Hecate / d(omino) n(ostro) Gratiano Aug(usto) / et Merobaude / conss(ulibus) III Idus / Maias

CIL 06, 00504 5 April 383 CE
Publication: CIL 06, 00504 (p 3005, 3757) = CIL 06, 30779h = CLE 00264 = D 04153 = CIMRM 00514 = SIRIS 00457 = RICIS-02, 00501/0208
Province: Roma
Dis Magnis / Ulpius Egnatius Faventinus / v(ir) c(larissimus) augur pub(licus) p(opuli) R(omani) Q(uiritium) / pater et hieroceryx d(ei) S(olis) I(nvicti) M(ithrae) / archibucolus dei Liberi / hierofanta Hecatae sa/cerdos Isidis percepto / taurobolio crioboliq(ue) / Idibus Augustis dd(ominis) nn(ostris) / Valente Aug(usto) V et Valentinia/no Aug(usto) conss(ulibus) feliciter / vota Faventinus bis deni / suscipit orbis / ut mactet repetens aurata / fronte bicornes

CIL 06, 00507 15 April 313 CE
Publication: CIL 06, 00507 = AE 2004, +00031
Province: Roma
DD(ominis) nn(ostris) Constantino et / Maximino Augg(ustis) III co(n)ss(ulibus) / C(aius) Magius Donatus / Severianus v(ir) c(larissimus) / pater sacrorum / Invicti Mithrae / hierophantes / Liberi Patris et / Hecatarum [t]au/robolium feci(t) / XVII K[a]l(endas) Maias

CIL 06, 00510 13 August 376 CE
Province: Roma
Dis / Magnis / Matri deum et Attidi Se/xtilius Agesilaus Aedesius / v(ir) c(larissimus) causarum non ignobi/lis Africani tribunalis ora/tor et in consistorio / principum item magiste/r libellor(um) et cognition(um) / sacrarum magister epistu/lar(um) magister memoriae / vicarius praefector per / Hispanias vice s(acra) c(onoscens) pa/ter patrum dei Solis Invi/cti Mithrae hierofanta / Hecatar(um) dei Liberi archi/bucolus taurobolio / criobolioq(ue) in aeter/num renatus aram sacra/vit dd(ominis) nn(ostris) Valen/te V et Valentiniano / Iun(iori) Augg(ustis) conss(ulibus) Idib(us) / Augus(tis)

Chapter Five

"Leap, ye lame, for joy": The Dynamics of Disability in Conversion

Anna Rebecca Solevåg

Introduction

In this article, I explore and challenge the dynamics of disability in conversion. Throughout the history of Christianity, miraculous stories of healing have been told to support the truth claims of Christianity and encourage conversion. Healing from disability or illness has also functioned as a metaphor for conversion. Investigating this dynamic reveals interesting aspects of the way conversion has been understood. It also highlights the kind of discourses and practices of which it has been a part.

As an example of this dynamic, I start with the conversion discourse of the early Methodist movement in the eighteenth century. Conversion was a key concept for this early Enlightenment Christian movement. Drawing on New Testament healing narratives, the founders of the movement, the brothers John Wesley (1703–1797) and Charles Wesley (1707–1788), used healing as a metaphor for conversion in their writings. Moreover, the Methodist movement also integrated physical healing in their holistic understanding of salvation, and established systems and institutions to care for adherents with disabilities and ailing health. Conversion, illness, and healing were configured in specific ways, that also demonstrate affinities with Christian positions in the contemporary world.

In the second part, I look at the Gospel of Mark, which contains the earliest Christ-believers' stories about Jesus and his ministry. The Methodists drew on the healing stories of the New Testament in their construction of conversion as healing. But a closer look at some of these texts may reveal a different understanding of conversion, and dynamics between disability and conversion, that differ from what the early Methodists proposed. At this early point in the Jesus movement's history, it is unclear whether one can speak about conversion at all, yet the healing narratives we find in this Gospel are used to persuade the hearers of the Gospel about the truth claims of the "good news," the *euangelion* of Jesus Christ.

I use these examples of the dynamics of disability in conversion to challenge and complicate the term "conversion" as a category for religious change. I also question *for whom* narratives of healing from disability would function and whom they might convince of religious change. Are they aimed at people with disabilities, or at people with bodies that are considered "normal"?

Intersectionality, Disability, and Conversion

Articles in this volume interact with intersectionality as one of the methodological tools used to discuss conversion. This article, too, relies on insights from intersectional theory.[1] However, I use *disability* as a specific lens to frame my research questions. Within disability studies, disability is understood as a cultural or social concept. In this perspective, disability has to do with the limitations a person experiences due to physical hindrances in the environment and with the social barriers that create stigma and prejudice, rather than with the functional limitations of the body and/or mind.[2] In other words, disability is not primarily defined by medicine, and cannot be reduced to a diagnosis that would objectively describes what is "abnormal" with an individual.[3] Rather, disability is connected with social and cultural perceptions about what it means to be "normal" and what it means to be "disabled."[4]

The growing field of disability history starts with the insight that "disability" is not a given across time and space. Rather, disability is part of a historically constructed discourse and depends on shifting ideologies about

---

1. See Elisabeth Schüssler Fiorenza, "Introduction: Exploring the Intersections of Race, Gender, Status, and Ethnicity in Early Christian Studies," in Elisabeth Schüssler Fiorenza and Laura Salah Nasrallah, eds., *Prejudice and Christian Beginnings: Investigating Race, Gender, and Ethnicity in Early Christian Studies* (Minneapolis, MN: Fortress Press, 2009), 1–23.

2. Dan Goodley, *Disability Studies: An Interdisciplinary Introduction* (Los Angeles, CA: Sage, 2011), 8–17.

3. For introductions to Disability Studies and its critique of "the medical model," see for example Gary L. Albrecht, Katherine D. Seelman, and Michael Bury, eds., *Handbook of Disability Studies* (Thousand Oaks, CA: Sage Publications, 2001); Len Barton, Colin Barnes, and Mike Oliver, *Disability Studies Today* (Cambridge: Polity Press, 2002); Lennard J. Davis, *Bending over Backwards: Disability, Dismodernism, and other Difficult Positions* (New York: New York University Press, 2002); Tom Shakespeare, "The Social Model of Disability," in Lennard J. Davis, ed., *The Disability Studies Reader* (New York: Routledge, 2006), 197–204; Tobin Siebers, *Disability Theory* (Ann Arbor, MI: University of Michigan Press, 2008).

4. See Thomson for a discussion on normalcy, deviance, and the contemporary construction of the "normate." Rosemarie Garland Thomson, *Extraordinary Bodies: Figuring Physical Disability in American Culture and Literature* (New York: Columbia University Press, 1997).

the body and health.⁵ In this article, when I refer to "disabled" or "people with disabilities" in various historical contexts, I indicate people or characters designated by various terms of impairment in the sources. I use these terms to name people "who potentially may have faced restrictions on their ability to carry out everyday activities through injury, disease, congenital malformation, aging or chronic illness, or whose appearance made them liable to be characterized by contemporary cultural ideas associated with non-standard bodies."⁶ I use the term "health care system" as a general term for a variety of systems, culturally and historically. The concept is taken from medical anthropology, where health care is understood as a cultural system of "socially organized responses to disease that constitute a special cultural system."⁷

Conversion, as a historical phenomenon, may be defined as "the acquiring of a religious identity not previously held."⁸ Robert Montgomery argues that the spread of religions is not only related to social factors, but also to factors internal to religions themselves. He points to three characteristics of missionary religions like Buddhism, Christianity, and Islam that may explain their spread: a single human mediating figure, their belief and morality systems, their ability to gather and organize people.⁹ In addition, he lists two macro and two micro social causes that may facilitate or preclude conversion: freedom of choice and intersocial relationships (macro); and social relationships and motivations (micro).¹⁰

As Valérie Nicolet and Marianne Bjelland Kartzow argue in the introduction, conversion is not a static phenomenon, unchanging throughout

---

5. See for example Robert Garland, *The Eye of the Beholder: Deformity and Disability in the Graeco-Roman World* (Ithaca, NY: Cornell University Press, 1995); Catherine J. Kudlick, "Disability History: Why We Need Another 'Other'," *The American Historical Review* 108.3 (2003): 763–93; Brian Brock and John Swinton, *Disability in the Christian Tradition: A Reader* (Grand Rapids, MI: Eerdmans, 2012); Sebastian Barsch, Anne Klein, and Pieter Verstraete, eds., *The Imperfect Historian: Disability Histories in Europe* (Frankfurt: Peter Lang, 2013); Allison P. Hobgood and David Houston Wood, eds., *Recovering Disability in Early Modern England* (Columbus, OH: Ohio State University Press, 2013).

6. David M. Turner, *Disability in Eighteenth-Century England: Imagining Physical Impairment* (New York: Routledge, 2012), 11.

7. Arthur Kleinman, *Patients and Healers in the Context of Culture: An Exploration of the Borderland between Anthropology, Medicine, and Psychiatry* (Berkeley, CA: University of California Press, 1980), 24.

8. Robert L. Montgomery, "Conversion and the Historic Spread of Religions," in Lewis R. Rambo and Charles E. Farhadian, eds., *The Oxford Handbook of Religious Conversion* (Oxford: Oxford University Press, 2014), 164-89, here 165.

9. Montgomery, "Conversion and the Historic Spread of Religions," 166–7.

10. Montgomery, "Conversion and the Historic Spread of Religions," 167.

the centuries. They note the tendency to project a modern understanding focused on individual, psychological aspects onto early Christ-believing and Christian texts. This conception of conversion does not necessarily fit the sources from the early Christ-believing movement, since, for example, the ancient Mediterranean culture was less individualistic than contemporary western societies. Moreover, it does not account for questions of agency and power in a hierarchical society where the freedom to choose a new religious affiliation was not open to everyone. The modern concept of conversion tends to emphasize the properly *religious* aspect of change to a degree that can be problematic when looking at ancient texts, especially since our understanding of religion is not the same as in the ancient world. This article introduces disability as a complicating factor in the discussion about (religious) conversion.

"Leap, ye lame"—
Disability and Conversion in the Early Methodist Movement

John and Charles Wesley were both ordained Anglican ministers. After powerful conversion experiences, they devoted the rest of their lives to the Methodist revival movement within the Church of England.[11] Conversion—understood in a very specific way—was an important aspect of the Methodist notion of the Christian life: inside a revival movement, the early Methodist understanding of conversion stresses the idea of a crisis of conscience followed by a renewed faith in the promises of God.[12] Charles Wesley's so-called "Aldersgate experience" became paradigmatic for the early Methodist movement.[13] The narration of one's conversion experience holds a central place within the movement to the point that it develops into a genre, the conversion narrative.[14]

The influence of the Methodist movement has probably shaped how conversion is understood today (see the discussion in the introduction). The Merriam-Webster Dictionary defines conversion as "an experience

---

11. The Methodist movement did not split with the Church of England until after the Wesley brothers had passed away. In the nineteenth century, Methodist denominations were established worldwide.

12. D. Bruce Hindmarsh, "'My chains fell off, my heart was free': Early Methodist Conversion Narrative in England," *Church History: Studies in Christianity and Culture* 68.4 (1999): 910–29, here 917.

13. Deborah Madden, "Introduction. Saving Souls and Saving Lives: John Wesley's 'Inward and Outward Health'," in Deborah Madden, ed., *"Inward and Outward Health": John Wesley's Holistic Concept of Medical Science, the Environment and Holy Living* (Eugene, OR: Wipf & Stock, 2008), 1–13, here 4.

14. Hindmarsh, "'My chains fell off, my heart was free'."

associated with the definite and decisive adoption of a religion."[15] Bruce Hindmarsh has pointed out that the stereotype of climactic conversion is not a universal transhistorical pattern, but is rather typical of the early Methodist tradition. He argues that "a larger pattern of salvation history, sharpened by the Reformation dialectic of law and gospel and an intensely personal sense that salvation is 'for me' (*Christus pro me*), structures these early Methodist narratives."[16] The dictionary definition also points to personal experience as well as to a clear-cut change, both of which are typical of the Methodist understanding of conversion. In other words, the Methodist conversion narratives serve as early examples of the modern understanding that frames conversion as individual and psychological in nature.

Let us now look at how conversion relates to disability, illness, and healing in this tradition. Healing was an important metaphor for salvation in the works of the Wesley brothers, and it becomes central in the Methodist understanding of salvation. In conjunction with this understanding of salvation, the movement also implements new systems of health care as part of their Christian practice.

Healing as a Conversion Metaphor in the Early Methodist Movement

Among the two brothers, John was the preacher and theologian, developing the central tenets of Methodist theology, and Charles was the poet and musician, writing more than six thousand hymns during his life. In the sermons of John as well as in the hymns of Charles, healing functions as a fundamental metaphor for conversion. One can look at the widely-used hymn "O, for a Thousand Tongues to Sing" for an example. The hymn was placed first in John Wesley's *A Collection of Hymns for the People Called Methodists* (published in 1780) and has since then commonly been the first hymn in Methodist hymnals. This is verse six:

> Hear him, ye deaf; his praise, ye dumb,
> Your loosen'd tongues employ;
> Ye blind, behold your Saviour come,
> And leap, ye lame, for joy.[17]

Charles wrote the hymn in 1740 to commemorate his own conversion experience the year before. The imagery of deaf, dumb, blind, and lame is taken

---

15. See the entry: "conversion," https://www.merriam-webster.com/dictionary (accessed 1 February 2017).
16. Hindmarsh, "'My chains fell off, my heart was free'," 911.
17. Lyrics retrieved from Wikipedia. http://en.wikipedia.org/wiki/O_for_a_Thousand_Tongues_to_Sing (accessed 22 January 2015).

from the New Testament healing stories, where these categories of disability are recurring.[18] The metaphorical use of disability in this hymn typifies what disability scholars David Mitchell and Sharon Snyder have called "narrative prosthesis." Mitchell and Snyder argue that *narrative prosthesis* is a common trope in literature throughout the Western tradition, from Sophocles' *Oedipus*, to Shakespeare's *King Lear*, and Melville's *Moby Dick*. Stories featuring disabled characters often "prostheticize"—the story resolves or corrects—deviance because it seems improper in the social context.[19] Categories of disability, like deafness, blindness, and lameness, serve as the marker of difference and deviance, whereas the miraculous healing represents the return to normalcy, "the extermination of the deviant as a purification of the social body."[20]

Another metaphor in the Wesleys' hymns and sermons is the image of Christ as a physician. The biblical background is the Jesus-saying found in Mark: "Those who are well have no need for a physician, but those who are sick; I have come to call not the righteous but sinners" (Mk. 2.17, see also Matt. 9.12). John Wesley refers to both God and Jesus Christ as "physician" at various points in his writings.[21] In Sermon 48, "Self-denial," John Wesley describes Christ as a physician of the soul:

> In all this, we may easily conceive our blessed Lord to act as the Physician of our souls ... If, in searching our wounds, he puts us to pain, it is only in order to heal them. He cuts away what is putrefied or unsound, in order to preserve the sound part. And if we freely choose the loss of a limb, rather than the whole body should perish; how much more should we choose, figuratively, to cut off a right hand, rather than the whole soul should be cast into hell![22]

In the sermon, the physician Jesus becomes something of a surgeon, cutting away putrefied flesh. Wesley here combines the idea of Jesus as physician

---

18. Deafness and muteness are often combined in Greek medical thought, see M. Lynn Rose, "Deaf and Dumb in Ancient Greece," in Davis, ed., *Disability Studies Reader*, 17–32. Lameness, blindness and deafness often occur together in the Bible, and have been called "the biblical trilogy of disability" by Rebecca Raphael. See Rebecca Raphael, *Biblical Corpora: Representations of Disability in Hebrew Biblical Literature* (London: Continuum, 2009).

19. David T. Mitchell and Sharon L. Snyder, *Narrative Prosthesis: Disability and the Dependencies of Discourse* (Ann Arbor, MI: University of Michigan Press, 2001), 53.

20. Mitchell and Snyder, *Narrative Prosthesis*, 54.

21. Randy L. Maddox, *Responsible Grace: John Wesley's Practical Theology* (Nashville, TN: Kingswood Books, 1994), 62–3, 112–3, 121–3.

22. Retrieved from the Wesley Center Online: http://wesley.nnu.edu/john-wesley/the-sermons-of-john-wesley-1872-edition/sermon-48-self-denial/ (accessed 22 January 2015).

of the soul with Matthew 5.30: "if your right hand causes you to sin, cut it off and throw it away; it is better for you to lose one of your members than for your whole body to go into hell." Wesley's imagery connects disability with moral weakness. Putrefaction and the surgical removal of a limb represent the unsound and sinful soul in need of purification. In these examples from the Wesleys' writings, the disabled and wounded seem to be mostly metaphorical. The lame, blind, and deaf represent the sinners in need of spiritual "healing," that is, conversion.

The construction of conversion as spiritual healing in these texts undergirds a certain understanding of the disabled body as inherently sinful and in need of radical change. Disability theologian Nancy Eiesland has critiqued this interpretive move, where "disabled" is conflated with "sinner," and non-normative disabled bodies are discursively deployed to draw out "the powerful alterity assigned to people with disabilities."[23] In the metaphor, disability represents the "before"-state that is clearly labeled as unwanted. In addition, the metaphorical layer projects a theologically unwanted state onto the category of disability since it is associated with sin.

Healing and Conversion in Methodist Theology

However, there are other aspects to the Wesleyan use of disability in conversion that should also be considered. In the following quote, verse three of Charles Wesley's hymn "Come Sinners to the Gospel Feast," the same imagery of the sinner as disabled is invoked. Yet, it remains open whether these sinners, invited to the great feast in the Kingdom of God, are also literally disabled:

> Come, all ye souls by sin oppressed,
> Ye restless wanderers after rest;
> Ye poor, and maimed, and sick, and blind,
> In Christ a hearty welcome find.[24]

The imagery of Christ who welcomes the disabled outcasts to his big feast comes from the parable of the Great Dinner (Lk. 14.15-24). Does the hymn simply conflate "souls by sin oppressed" in the first stanza, with the poor, maimed, sick, and blind, in the third? Or does it include all these categories as deserving Christ's hearty welcome? In the parable, these groups are not healed, but invited to the feast as they are. Although the hymn is unclear, such an inclusive health care practice was concretely put into place within

---

23. Mitchell and Snyder, *Narrative Prosthesis*, 51.
24. United Methodist Hymnal no. 339. Lyrics retrieved from http://www.hymnsite.com/lyrics/umh339.sht (accessed 22 January 2015).

the Methodist movement, as I will show below. But let me first elaborate on the Methodist theology of conversion and salvation.

Wesleyan scholar Randy L. Maddox argues that John Wesley's soteriology focuses on the healing aspects of salvation. In other words, early Methodist soteriology stresses the *therapeutic* aspects of salvation. Such an emphasis is quite different from the more common Protestant stress on the *juridical* aspects of salvation, which insists on notions like guilt and absolution.[25] Maddox argues that this *therapeutic* concern reveals the influence of the early Greek Church Fathers, whom John Wesley prolifically read and frequently quotes.[26] This therapeutic focus results in a holistic understanding of salvation where forgiveness of sins is interwoven with healing from the damages wrought by sin.[27] Illness and pain were at this time commonly understood as part of humankind's post-lapsarian condition, so also for Wesley. However, his emphasis on the healing aspects of salvation was less common. This emphasis did not lead to a one-sided emphasis on divine healing, but resulted in an integrated approach characterized both by faith in miraculous healing and an open attitude towards professional and traditional medical treatments.[28] In other words, Wesley underscored the goodness of the body, even though sinful.[29]

Conversion and the Methodist Health Care System

We should also consider the Wesley brothers' considerable interest in issues of health and folk medicine, which highly influenced the diaconal practice of the Methodist movement. The Wesley brothers lived and wrote in the early days of the British Enlightenment. They believed in progress and science.[30] John Wesley had in fact studied quite a bit of medicine, as was expected of theology students at the time. The rationale behind this requirement lay in the fact that, particularly in a rural parish, the minister might be the most educated person and hence needed to be able to help his parishioners with simpler medical cases.[31] For a period, John served as an Anglican

---

25. Maddox, *Responsible Grace*, 23.
26. Maddox, *Responsible Grace*, 23.
27. Randy L. Maddox, "John Wesley on Holistic Health and Healing," *Methodist History* 46.1 (2007): 4–33, here 7.
28. Maddox, "John Wesley on Holistic Health and Healing," 9–10.
29. Maddox, *Responsible Grace*, 71–2.
30. Maddox, "John Wesley on Holistic Health and Healing," 10–2; Deborah Madden, *"A Cheap, Safe and Natural Medicine": Religion, Medicine and Culture in John Wesley's Primitive Physic* (Amsterdam: Rodopi, 2007), 14–5.
31. Randy L. Maddox, "Reclaiming the Eccentric Patient: Methodist Reception of

minister in the American colony of Georgia, and during his time there he read several medical works.³²

The most popular book that John Wesley published was a little book on folk remedies called *Primitive Physic*.³³ A study of *Primitive Physic* allows to draw out more clearly some of John Wesley's thoughts on disability per se, rather than merely as a metaphor for sinners in need of conversion. The introduction makes clear that Wesley intended the book as an alternative to the consultation of medical doctors for people who could not afford such treatment. In the introduction, he critiques physicians for seeking profit rather than the benefit of humankind.³⁴ Although Wesley viewed pain, sickness, and bodily ailments as part of the human condition after the fall,³⁵ it is clear from his little book of simple remedies that he did not regard miraculous healing through prayer as the only solution. His advice consists of practical, low-cost treatments that anyone could carry out in their homes. To give a sense of what kind of advice and remedies the book contains, some examples:

> The Falling Sickness [epilepsy]. Be electrified: tried. Or, use the cold bath for a month daily: or, take a tea-spoonful of peony-root dried and grated fine, morning and evening for three months: Or, half a spoonful of Valerian-root powdered. —It often cures in twice taking: Or, half a pint of tar-water, morning and evening for three months. [Six more alternative remedies follow].³⁶

> Hypochondriac and Hysteric Disorders. Use cold bathing: Or, take an ounce of quicksilver every morning, and ten drops of Elixir of Vitriol in the afternoon, in a glass of cold water.³⁷

> The Rheumatism. To prevent. Wear washed wool under the feet. To cure. Use the cold bath, with running and sweating: Or, apply warm steams: Or, rub in warm treacle, and apply to the part brown paper smeared therewith: change it in twelve hours: tried. [Nine more alternative remedies follow].³⁸

The remedies suggested by Wesley may seem eccentric, but scholar of Methodist history, Deborah Madden, has shown that he drew on the medical

---

John Wesley's Interest in Medicine," in Madden, ed., *"Inward and Outward Health*, 15-50, here 16.

32. Maddox, "John Wesley on Holistic Health and Healing," 5.
33. Maddox, "John Wesley on Holistic Health and Healing," 3. See John Wesley, *Primitive Physic: Or An Easy and Natural Method of Curing Most Diseases* (Philadelphia, PA: Steuart Andrew, 1791 [1992; 22nd edn.]). Earlier editions held the subtitle: "Or an Easy and Natural Method of Curing Most Diseases."
34. Wesley, *Primitive Physic*, xiii–xv.
35. Wesley, *Primitive Physic*, iii–iv.
36. Wesley, *Primitive Physic*, 78–9.
37. Wesley, *Primitive Physic*, 99.
38. Wesley, *Primitive Physic*, 125–6.

knowledge of the times and was open to new medical insights.[39] For example, several remedies in *Primitive Physic* call for light electric shock. At the time, this was a completely new and progressive treatment, and John had acquired for himself an electro shock apparatus with which he experimented.[40] Electricity was understood by Wesley as a natural remedy—a harnessing of powers from nature that ultimately came from God.[41] The numerous references to "the cold regime," namely cold baths, a cool diet, and so on, also draw on a medical practice that, though ancient in origin, had gained renewed popularity at the time. The idea was to harden the body by exercise and a moderate diet, and to bring it into harmony with its environment, the cold climate of the British Isles.[42]

Another aspect of Wesley's medical thought that clearly bears the stamp of the Enlightenment is his attitude towards madness as a medical category. Rather than following earlier Puritan thought, which generally considered mental disorders as caused by demoniac possession, Wesley saw madness as belonging to the natural sphere. It could therefore be cured by medical treatment.[43] The treatment suggestions concerning epilepsy and hysteric disorders quoted above are examples of this "modern" attitude towards madness.

In addition to *Primitive Physic*'s focus on self-help, the early Methodist movement also inaugurated several new institutions and practices to help disabled and sick people. It started an office of "visitor of the sick" and expected lay traveling preachers to give advice to individuals within the movement who were struggling with ill-health.[44] In 1746, John Wesley opened what may have been the first free dispensary, where people of modest means could gain access to drugs and medical care.[45] These practices, including the distribution of *Primitive Physic*, clearly reflect the holistic notion of salvation and anthropology mentioned above. Moreover, they show a certain "popularization" of medicine and health care. Through pamphlets and holistic pastoral care, not only was health care made available to the underprivileged, but the authority to define and shape the discourse of health and illness was also moved away from the medical elite. Madden

---

39. Madden, *"A Cheap, Safe and Natural Medicine,"* 16–9.
40. Maddox, "John Wesley on Holistic Health and Healing." Several of the remedies in Primitive Physic calls for "electrifying," as in this remedy for blindness: "Or, by electrifying: tried. This cured even a *gutta serena* of twenty-four years standing." Wesley, *Primitive Physic*, 72.
41. Maddox, "John Wesley on Holistic Health and Healing," 24–5.
42. Maddox, "John Wesley on Holistic Health and Healing," 18.
43. Maddox, "John Wesley on Holistic Health and Healing," 12.
44. Maddox, "Reclaiming the Eccentric Patient," 18.
45. Maddox, "Reclaiming the Eccentric Patient," 19.

argues that "this seemingly 'simple' manual contained a hermeneutics of enormous versatility and power."[46] It should also be noted that these practices challenged current gender norms, since women were involved in the distribution of pamphlets and functioned as lay visitors to the sick.[47]

In conclusion, the early Methodist dynamics of disability in conversion is not restricted to the fact that healing is used as a metaphor for conversion. Rather, it also includes ideas about disability, illness, and health ingrained in the Methodist understanding of salvation, and expressed in the diaconal praxis of the movement. If, as I have argued, the early Methodist discourse of conversion has shaped the modern understanding of the term, it is important to look at the healing narratives taken from the New Testament, to see if we may discern a different pattern of disability in conversion.

Mark: Healing and Conversion

I have shown how the early Methodist movement drew on texts from the New Testament as well as on Christian tradition in shaping its ideas about conversion and its relation to disability. Let us now look at the Gospel of Mark, the earliest Gospel in the New Testament, to see how conversion relates to disability there.

There are about 13 healing narratives in Mark. From the very beginning of his ministry, Jesus' healing of illnesses and casting out of demons is an integral part of his proclamation of the good news that "the Kingdom of God has come near" (Mk. 1.15). According to Mark, Jesus' first public action, after his baptism (1.9-11), his temptation in the wilderness (1.12-13) and the call of the first disciples (1.16-20), is to heal a demon-possessed man in the synagogue in Capernaum (1.23-26).[48] This healing story is immediately followed by three more: the private healing of Peter's mother-in-law (1.30-31), who has a fever, the cleansing of a leper (1.40-44) and the healing of a paralyzed man brought in by four helpers (2.1-10). Interspersed among these stories are two summary statements that Jesus healed many sick people and cast out demons (1.34-39). It is clear, then, that in Mark, Jesus' powerful ability to heal spurs his popularity and makes him so famous and sought-out that he needs to hide from the crowds, already by the end of chapter one: "Jesus could no longer go into a town openly, but stayed out in the country; and people came to him from every quarter"

---

46. Madden, "*A Cheap, Safe and Natural Medicine.*"
47. Maddox, "John Wesley on Holistic Health and Healing," 9.
48. In this article, I regard Jesus' exorcisms as healing miracles. Although there are differences in terminology, the same is true of healing of people with leprosy (see for example Mk. 1.40-45). Both can be understood as subcategories of healing stories.

(1.45). The series of healing stories are placed at the beginning of Mark to support Jesus' claim to divinity.[49] However, it is not clear that the stories supply an immediate link between healing and conversion.

If we look more closely at these stories, what exactly is going on? Is anyone converted? What is the relationship between faith and healing? In the very first healing narrative in Mark, the demon-possessed man in the synagogue does not ask Jesus for healing, but screams at him in anger: "What have you to do with us, Jesus of Nazareth? Have you come to destroy us? I know who you are, the Holy one of God" (Mk. 1.24). We do not learn what happens to him after he is healed. It is unclear whether the demon-possessed man was pleased to be exorcised, and whether he became a follower of Jesus. The focus is on Jesus and the crowd, rather than the demon-possessed man. The crowd is amazed (ἐκπλήσσω, Mk. 1.22) at Jesus' authority and starts spreading his fame (1.28). Hence, the narrative functions to build an image of Jesus as powerful and in command of demons who know his identity.

In the next healing story, the disciples bring Peter's mother-in-law to Jesus' attention. She starts to serve Jesus and the disciples as soon as she is healed (Mk. 1.31). This is probably what she used to do before she became sick, too, so no change in attitude towards Jesus can be detected on her behalf. Neither she nor anyone else seem to convert following the healing. In the following story, the leper, in contrast to the man in the synagogue, actively asks to be cleansed, showing his faith in Jesus' healing powers by his words: "if you choose, you can make me clean" (Mk. 1.40). Nevertheless, after he has been healed, he disobeys Jesus' strict orders to remain silent and spreads the word about him (Mk. 1.45).

Going through all the healing stories in Mark, one will find that faith in Jesus on the part of the disabled or sick person seems to be of interest in just a few cases. Jesus remarks upon the faith of only two characters: the woman with the flow of blood (Mk. 5.25-34 and the blind man Bartimeus (Mk. 10.46-52). Jesus says to them: "Your faith has made you well" (ἡ πίστις σου σέσωκέν σε). More often, it is a family member or helper whose faith is being tested (for example, the four helpers of the paralyzed man [2.5], the father Jairus in 5.23-36, the Syrophoenician mother in 7.29, and the father of the demon-possessed boy in 9.17-29). The reaction of the crowd is sometimes mentioned, sometimes not. There is only one healed person in Mark who explicitly becomes a follower of Jesus (10.52), and thus comes close to our notion of a convert. This is the story about Bartimeus, a blind beggar,

---

49. Mary Ann Tolbert, *Sowing the Gospel: Mark's World in Literary-Historical Perspective* (Minneapolis, MN: Fortress Press, 1989); Tat-Siong Benny Liew, *Politics of Parousia: Reading Mark Inter(con)textually* (Leiden: Brill, 1999).

sitting at the roadside outside of Jericho. The story is Mark's last healing narrative, and it takes place as Jesus is on his way to Jerusalem, just before the Easter events. After Jesus has healed Bartimeus, Bartimeus "followed him on the way" (10.52). Somewhat differently, the demon-possessed man in Mark 5.1-20 also wants to follow Jesus, but is turned down by Jesus and encouraged to proclaim to his friends (5.19). In this story, faith is never mentioned, but the witnesses of the exorcism in Decapolis show amazement (πάντες ἐθαύμαζον, 5.20).

In conclusion, in Mark's healing narratives it is Jesus as miracle worker, accomplishing spectacular deeds, who remains the focus of the narratives.[50] The text also pays attention to the crowd and the sick or disabled's family or friends, who are *positively* affected, responding with faith and amazement, and to the Pharisees and/or scribes, whose *negative* reactions are similarly noted (see e.g. 2.6; 3.6; 3.22; 9.14). Mark's narratives display little to no interest in what happens to the disabled characters once healed. The assumption is that they are re-integrated into society. In a sense, then, disability is negated. It is something that needs to be suppressed and erased. Mitchell and Snyder have noted this conundrum when it comes to the representation of disability in narrative: "while stories rely upon the potency of disability as a symbolic figure, they rarely take up disability as an experience of social or political dimensions."[51] In other words, the healing stories, which are often read as presenting symbolic conversion stories in the Christian tradition, do not seem to be about conversion at all, at least not in the Methodist sense. How does this affect our understanding of conversion? And what can we say about religious change in the early Christ-movement?

Conversion—a Contested Term

As noted in the introduction to this volume, Paula Fredriksen argues that the term "conversion" is unhelpful in discussing the religious change that occurs among the first generation of Christ-believers.[52] The term is

---

50. Mark's construction of Jesus as a miracle worker, and focus on Jesus' healing activity differs from other early Christian narratives and texts. I argue elsewhere that there is a wide variety of perspectives and opinions on disability, health, and healing within early Christianity. One example that differs from Mark is the Coptic Act of Peter, which includes a story about unhealing framed as "good." Anna Rebecca Solevåg, *Negotiating the Disabled Body: Representations of Disability in Early Christian Texts* (Atlanta, GA: Society of Biblical Literature Press, 2018), 75–84.

51. Mitchell and Snyder, *Narrative Prosthesis*, 48.

52. See Paula Fredriksen, "Mandatory Retirement: Ideas in the Study of Christian Origins whose Time Has Come to Go," *Studies in Religion* 35.2 (2006): 231–46.

particularly problematic when used about religious change in those who become Christ-believers at a time when the division between Judaism and Christianity into two separate religions has not yet taken place. As Fredriksen puts it: "The term 'converts' entangles us in anachronism, letting in by the back door the idea that 'Christianity' is somehow already a *tertium quid*, something that exists for these people to convert to."[53] To avoid anachronism and confusion, it is better, she asserts, to use the terms that we find in the texts themselves. In Paul's letters, her primary focus, she finds the verb "to turn," ἐπιστρέφω, (away from Greek gods, towards the god of Israel), and the metaphor of adoption.[54] She adds that in Antiquity it is not a matter of "believing in" the gods, but a matter of piety, of respecting the gods, since it is accepted that the gods evidently exist.[55] I agree with Fredriksen that the use of the term "conversion" can cause confusion when speaking about the first generation of Christ-believers, and that it has been used in problematic ways in the past.

What terms do we find in Mark? As already noted, there is *amazement* at Jesus' power and *faith* in his healing ability. Nevertheless, the healing stories in Mark serve the primary function of establishing Jesus' legitimacy, by ascertaining that he has unusual powers. Yet, the kind of amazement and interest that results from seeing or hearing about the miracles is also criticized (Mk. 8.11-12; 9.14-23), and the disciples are chastised for their lack of faith despite the miracles they have seen (Mk. 8.14-21).

The notion of having faith in Jesus does come up, as I have noted, in some healing stories, with terms such as πίστις (2.5; 5.34; 10.52) and πιστεύω (5.36; 9.23-25). This vocabulary seems to differ from Fredriksen's assertion that in Antiquity, one did not *believe* in the Gods, one *revered* them. Yet, πίστις is a term with a broad meaning, that also designates trust, confidence, and piety.[56] Moreover, it is hard to determine whether any of this constitutes "the acquiring of a religious identity not previously held."[57] Only in the case of Bartimeus is there a clear change in position, from sitting on the roadside to following Jesus on the way, but even here it is hard to claim that the change is caused by the healing. Even before Bartimeus is healed, he refers to Jesus as "Son of David" (1.48) and "teacher" (1.51). In other words, it is not clear that any conversion is taking place in Mark's healing stories.

The healing stories at the beginning of Mark have an important function in the narrator's effort to persuade the reader that the claim in Mark

---

53. Fredriksen, "Mandatory Retirement," 234.
54. Fredriksen, "Mandatory Retirement," 237.
55. Fredriksen, "Mandatory Retirement," 239.
56. BDAG and LSJ, s.v., πίστις.
57. Montgomery, "Conversion and the Historic Spread of Religions," 165.

1.1 holds true: Jesus Christ is the son of God. Although there seems to be a development throughout the Gospel, from a faith based on miracles to a faith based on a proper understanding of the cross, it is the series of miracle stories that open up the narrative and lay the foundation for the Gospel's claims about Jesus. Unlike Matthew and Luke, there is no miraculous birth story to carry some of the weight—the Christological claim in 1.1 is unfolded in stories depicting Jesus' power through healing miracles.[58]

Jesus' *logion* "those who are well are in no need of a physician, but those who are sick; I have come to call not the righteous but sinners" (Mk. 2.17// Matt. 9.12//Lk. 5.31) similarly constructs Jesus as healer and even medical doctor. In this saying, Jesus equates sick people with sinners, by using illness as a metaphor for sin. The saying highlights the causal connection between sin and illness also found in some of the healing stories in the Gospel traditions (see e.g. Mk. 2.5; Jn. 5.14; 9.2).

When Mark deploys disabled characters to support his Christological claim, he not only represents Jesus in a specific way—as a powerful healer—but he also constructs and represents disabled characters in a certain way. Mitchell and Snyder's theory of *narrative prosthesis,* noted above in the discussion of the Wesley brothers' metaphorical use of disability, may also shed some light on Mark's use of disabled characters. Mitchell and Snyder argue that disabled figures often represent some form of anomaly or deviance, which is then corrected or resolved, namely "prostheticized," during the course of the story.[59] In the Gospel this "correction" happens through healing, but in other narratives it can take place through punishment, death, or some other eradication of the disabled character from the story. Among Mitchell and Snyder's examples are Hans Christian Andersen's tin soldier, who is thrown into the fire,[60] and Ahab's "apocalyptic fate" in *Moby-Dick.*[61] My analysis shows that the healing narratives in Mark are not conversion stories per se. I have argued that the narratives have little interest in what happens to the disabled character after the healing, and that often the faith of other characters in the story is more important. Mitchell and Snyder's theory of *narrative prosthesis* helps us understand Mark's usage as one example of how literary discourse depends on "the powerful alterity assigned to people with disabilities."[62] Without developed models for analyzing the purpose and function of disability, readers tend

---

58. Gerd Theissen and John Riches, *The Miracle Stories of the Early Christian Tradition* (Edinburgh: Clark, 1983), 213.
59. Mitchell and Snyder, *Narrative Prosthesis*, 53.
60. Mitchell and Snyder, *Narrative Prosthesis*, 56.
61. Mitchell and Snyder, *Narrative Prosthesis*, 136.
62. Mitchell and Snyder, *Narrative Prosthesis*, 51.

to compartmentalize impairment as an isolated and individual condition of existence.[63] On the contrary, these representations of disability are part of a discourse about the body and difference, illness and deformity, with ideological implications.

Challenging the Dynamics of Disability in Conversion

Is it possible to say anything about disabled people and their possible conversion into the early Christ-movement? Did this movement seem like an attractive group to "turn to" for people with disabilities, or individuals who were regarded as having non-normative bodies? Some scholars posit that this was the case.

Hector Avalos claims that the "health care system" proposed by the Christ-movement in the first centuries CE was one of the most attractive characteristics of the new movement and factored heavily in its historical success.[64] He argues that the healing system inaugurated by Jesus exhibited several features that made it attractive in comparison to other healing alternatives. Compared to Jewish and Greco-Roman health care systems, the therapeutic strategies of the Christ movement represented simpler procedures: invoking the name of Jesus and calling for faith rather than pharmaceuticals was all that was required of the patient.[65] Furthermore, Avalos highlights the Christ-believers' reluctance to charge fees from patients as an advantage over against Jewish and Greco-Roman health care systems. It would be particularly opposed to the professional Greek medical tradition (see Mk. 5.26).[66] Geographical and temporal access are other factors mentioned by Avalos. In contrast to Roman military hospitals, *Asklepieia* and/or Jewish ritual baths, healing inside the Christ-movement could happen anywhere and healers were mobile.[67] In addition, unlike Jewish healing which was limited by Sabbath restrictions, healings in the Christ-movement could take place at any time.[68]

Rodney Stark has made a somewhat similar claim. He argues that the superior quality of health care in the Christ-movement compared to

---

63. Mitchell and Snyder, *Narrative Prosthesis*, 51.
64. See Hector Avalos, *Health Care and the Rise of Christianity* (Peabody, MA: Hendrickson, 1999).
    65. Avalos, *Health Care and the Rise of Christianity*, 81–4.
    66. Avalos, *Health Care and the Rise of Christianity*, 91–5.
    67. Avalos, *Health Care and the Rise of Christianity*, 99–107.
    68. Avalos, *Health Care and the Rise of Christianity*, 111–4.

polytheist systems is one important factor behind the rise of Christianity.[69] In particular, Stark underlines how Christians responded to the epidemics of 165 and 251 CE: "When disaster struck, the Christians were better able to cope, and this resulted in *substantially higher rates of survival.*"[70] According to Stark, the Christian religion provided better answers to explain the plague, it offered comfort to those struck *and* it brought better care due to Christianity's social ethical code.[71] Building on this analysis he constructs some highly speculative statistics about the higher mortality rates of polytheists compared to Christians during the plagues, and its contribution to the rise of Christianity.[72]

Avalos's and Stark's hypotheses presuppose that everyone agrees on what constitutes an "attractive health care system" or "better care." An intersectional perspective may paint a more complex picture of what it meant to be disabled in Antiquity. In Antiquity, "the disabled" were not a monolithic group of people; in fact, the term did not even exist yet, to describe a category. What it meant to have a disability in the ancient Mediterranean world varied depending on several factors. First, society did not view all impairments in the same way. To be deaf or hard of hearing had other implications than to be blind or lame. Deafness was often connected with intellectual disabilities, and, in the oral culture of the Roman Empire, a number of offices could not be held by those hard of hearing.[73] To be blind, on the other hand, had cultural connotations to wisdom, particularly the wisdom of old age, as in the Greek tradition of "the blind seer."[74] The cultural significance of leprosy and skin disease in Judaism is another example of culturally constructed restrictions around a particular disability.[75] Illness was sometimes connected with sin or punishment, as reflected in the disciples' question to

---

69. Rodney Stark, *The Rise of Christianity: A Sociologist Reconsiders History* (New York: HarperOne, 1997).

70. Stark, *Rise of Christianity*, 74. Emphasis original.

71. Stark, *Rise of Christianity*, 83–8.

72. Stark, *Rise of Christianity*, 91–4. For a critique of Stark's methodology, particularly pertaining to gender, see Elizabeth A. Castelli, "Gender, Theory, and *The Rise of Christianity*: A Response to Rodney Stark," *Journal of Early Christian Studies* 6.2 (1998): 227–57.

73. Christian Laes, "Silent History? Speech Impairment in Roman Antiquity," in Christian Laes, C. F. Goodey, and M. Lynn Rose, eds., *Disabilities in Roman Antiquity: Disparate Bodies a Capite ad Calcem* (Leiden: Brill, 2013), 145–80; Rose, "Deaf and Dumb in Ancient Greece."

74. Martha L. Rose, *The Staff of Oedipus: Transforming Disability in Ancient Greece* (Ann Arbor, MI: University of Michigan Press, 2003).

75. Joel Baden and Candida Moss, "The Origin and Interpretation of Sara'at in Leviticus 13–14," *Journal of Biblical Literature* 130.4 (2011): 643–62.

Jesus in John 9.2: "Rabbi, who sinned, this man or his parents, that he was born blind?"

Second, there are overlaps between ancient understandings of disability and gender. The Greek term for illness is ἀσθένεια, which literally means "weak." In the Greek medical understanding, weakness is connected with illness, whereas health relates to strength. Women were considered "weak" because of their sex. Hence the category of "woman" comes close to the category of "sick," since both categories have to do with weakness, ἀσθένεια.[76] One can also consider class and economy as factors influencing the construction of sickness and disability. People with economic means could negotiate their impairments very differently from less affluent people, and especially slaves. Whereas well-to-do people with disabilities could rely on slaves for transportation and other menial tasks, poor people were dependent on family or begging. Slaves who no longer held economic value were treated in a manner that reflected this lack of value. In discourse, disability was usually connected with the slavish body and not with the upper-class, free, body—the male body. Hence stigmatization and prejudice may have been worse for upper-class men who deviated from the norms of bodily perfection.

To sum up, some people, whom able-bodied people would characterize as disabled, may not have considered themselves impaired at all, while others may have experienced hardship and stigmatization because of their disability or impairment. In other words, the promise of healing may not be a strong enough motivator towards religious change for a person with what we would perceive to be a disability.

Let us now return to Avalos's and Stark's hypotheses. From an intersectional perspective, one might ask which social groups would find the Christian health care system attractive, and which may not. Another question is which groups were installed as the new system's healers and who was designated as in need of healing. In Acts, only male disciples take over Jesus' healing role, and no children or slaves are healed.

Insights from disability studies may also question these scholars' claims. In particular, one can ask whether a healing miracle, or the prospect of being healed, would have led a disabled person to convert. And further, one could also wonder whether the alleged superior quality of care was sufficient to persuade a person with a non-conforming body of the superiority of the Christ-movement as a religion. For instance, disability theory points out that

---

76. Anna Rebecca Solevåg, "Hysterical Women? Gender and Disability in Early Christian Narrative," in Christian Laes, ed., *Disability in Antiquity* (London: Routledge, 2017), 315–27.

it is an able-bodied assumption to think that a person with a disability would necessarily prefer to be rid of it.[77] Such an "ableist" perspective assumes that to live with a disability is always a misfortune, and projects "difference" and "otherness" onto those with extraordinary bodies.[78] We have few texts, if any, from early Christianity that inform us of how people with disabilities themselves regarded their impairments. However, these views from contemporary disability culture may suggest that also in Antiquity, people with non-conforming bodies could understand their condition and their place in the world in a variety of ways, and sometimes be subversive and defiantly critique ableist views.

Disability theologian Sharon Betcher suggests a fruitful perspective for understanding the miracle stories of the Gospels.[79] She concurs that the tradition of healing narratives are "texts of terror" for people with disabilities. However, she contextualizes the stories as part of a colonial space, in which the bodies of the oppressed, namely slaves, colonial subjects, and so on, were often subjected to disablement as part of colonial politics. In such a space, healing narratives could function as "texts of resistance," protests against oppression.[80] Betcher also notes the possibility that these stories could be told by people who themselves were less than whole.[81]

One might wonder whether people with disabilities also found alternative stories in the New Testament that could have been more attractive and affirming of non-conforming bodies than the healing narratives. In the stories about Zacchaeus, who is short of stature (Lk. 19.1-10), and the Ethiopian eunuch (Acts 8.2-39), people with bodies ridiculed by contemporary society were included into the believing community without being healed or changed in any way. Likewise, Paul's relentless insistence on his broken and in many ways un-manly body (see 2 Cor. 4.7-12; 11.24-28; 12.7-10; Gal. 6.17) and Christ's unhealed post-resurrection body (cf. Jn. 20.24-29) could be part of such a counter-tradition.[82] These texts can be read and interpreted in different ways. I do not claim that Paul intentionally presented himself as an un-manly man or that these narratives were written to challenge ableist ideas about the body. Yet, I argue that these texts hold the

---

77. Siebers, *Disability Theory*, 8.

78. Thomson, *Extraordinary Bodies: Figuring Physical Disability in American Culture and Literature*, 6–9.

79. See Sharon V. Betcher, "Disability and the Terror of the Miracle Tradition," in Stefan Alkier and Annette Weissenrieder, eds., *Miracles Revisited: New Testament Miracle Stories and their Concepts of Reality* (Berlin: De Gruyter, 2013), 161–82.

80. Betcher, "Disability and the Terror of the Miracle Tradition," 175.

81. Betcher, "Disability and the Terror of the Miracle Tradition," 173.

82. Solevåg, *Negotiating the Disabled Body*, 95–116, 133–52.

potential to serve as counter texts to the erasure of difference that happens in the healing narratives.[83] This is of course speculation only, as we have no early Christian texts that directly addresses this issue. If, however, we understand Paul's account of his "thorn in the flesh" as more than a temporary affliction (or even non-bodily temptation, as some interpreters would have it),[84] the earliest Christ-movement texts that we have, the Pauline epistles, are in fact written by a person with a disability.[85]

In her groundbreaking book, *The Disabled God*, Nancy Eiesland argues that the Bible and Christian theology have often been dangerous for persons with disabilities.[86] She highlights three particularly troubling biblical traditions for people with non-normative bodies. These traditions have underpinned "disabling theologies" and helped to shape widespread cultural attitudes regarding disability.[87] The first tradition is the causal relationship that is often, although not consistently, drawn in the Bible between sin and impairment (see Mk. 2.1-10 or Jn. 5.14) and the related connection between holiness and bodily perfection (see Lev. 21.17-23, excluding blind, lame, and blemished people from the Temple). This connection has, among other things, been used to exclude persons with disabilities from ecclesiastical authority.[88] The second is the tradition of virtuous suffering (see, again, Paul's "thorn in the flesh," 2 Cor. 12.7-10), which has engendered passivity and "encouraged persons with disabilities to acquiesce to social barriers as a sign of obedience to God."[89] Finally, the tradition of charitable giving (see Acts 6.1-6) has created a pattern where able-bodied subjects give to help disabled people as if they merely were disabled objects of charity. It

---

83. As I argue in the case of the Ethiopian eunuch in Anna Rebecca Solevåg, "No Nuts? No Problem! Disability, Stigma and the Baptized Eunuch in Acts 8:26-30," *Biblical Interpretation* 24 (2016): 81–99.

84. For interpretations of Paul's "thorn" from a disability perspective, see for example, Martin Albl, "'For Whenever I am Weak, then I am Strong': Disability in Paul's Epistles," in Hector Avalos, Sarah Melcher, and Jeremy Schipper, eds., *This Abled Body. Rethinking Disability in Biblical Studies* (Atlanta, GA: Society of Biblical Literature, 2007), 145–58; Adela Yarbro Collins, "Paul's Disability: The Thorn in His Flesh," in Candida R. Moss and Jeremy Schipper, eds., *Disability Studies and Biblical Literature* (New York: Palgrave Macmillan, 2011), 165–83; Candida R. Moss, "Christly Possession and Weakened Bodies: Reconsideration of the Function of Paul's Thorn in the Flesh (2 Cor 12:7-10)," *Journal of Religion, Disability and Health* 16 (2012): 319–33.

85. Solevåg, *Negotiating the Disabled Body*, 112.

86. Nancy L. Eiesland, *The Disabled God: Toward a Liberatory Theology of Disability* (Nashville, TN: Abingdon Press, 1994), 74.

87. Eiesland, *Disabled God*, 70–1.

88. Eiesland, *Disabled God*, 71–2.

89. Eiesland, *Disabled God*, 73.

also contributed to practices, such as institutionalization, that segregate disabled people.[90]

If we scrutinize the early Methodist movement for these three traits, clearly the metaphorical usage of disability in conversion discourse is such a "disabling theology." However, the holistic understanding of salvation and the diaconal practices of the movement, mentioned above, reflect a rather nuanced attitude towards people with disabilities. As noted, the Methodists stressed the therapeutic rather than the juridical aspects of salvation. This view permitted a positive attitude towards modern medicine rather than a focus on healing only by faith, and emphasized the goodness of the body. Moreover, the innovative diaconal practices gave leadership roles, as well as power to define, to previously excluded groups such as women and the working class. Perhaps we can even glimpse an alternative understanding of conversion in this tradition, in which conversion is not so much healing as it is in-corporation of multiplicity. I have argued that it is unclear whether disability is retained or eradicated in Charles Wesley's hymn "Come sinners to the Gospel Feast," but the wording of the last two stanzas can be interpreted as such a renewed understanding of conversion–conversion as unconditional welcome: "Ye poor, and maimed, and sick, and blind, In Christ a hearty welcome find."

Biographical Note

Anna Rebecca Solevåg is Professor of New Testament Studies at VID Specialized University in Stavanger, Norway, where she is director of the PhD program in Theology and Religion. In her research, she studies the intersections of gender, class, dis/ability, age, and ethnicity, exploring the complexities of identity and negotiations of power taking place at these crossroads. Solevåg is the author of *Negotiating the Disabled Body: Representations of Disability in Early Christian Texts* and *Birthing Salvation: Gender and Class in Early Christian Childbearing Discourse*.

Bibliography

Albl, Martin. "'For Whenever I am Weak, then I am Strong': Disability in Paul's Epistles," 145–58 in *This Abled Body: Rethinking Disability in Biblical Studies*. Edited by Hector Avalos, Sarah Melcher, and Jeremy Schipper. Atlanta, GA: Society of Biblical Literature, 2007.

Albrecht, Gary L., Katherine D. Seelman, and Michael Bury, eds. *Handbook of Disability Studies*. Thousand Oaks, CA: Sage Publications, 2001.

---

90. Eiesland, *Disabled God*, 73–4.

Avalos, Hector. *Health Care and the Rise of Christianity*. Peabody, MA: Hendrickson, 1999.

Baden, Joel, and Candida Moss, "The Origin and Interpretation of Sara'at in Leviticus 13–14," *Journal of Biblical Literature* 130.4 (2011): 643–62. https://doi.org/10.2307/23488272

Barsch, Sebastian, Anne Klein, and Pieter Verstraete, eds., *The Imperfect Historian: Disability Histories in Europe*. Frankfurt: Peter Lang, 2013. https://doi.org/10.3726/978-3-653-03016-7

Barton, Len, Colin Barnes, and Mike Oliver. *Disability Studies Today*. Cambridge: Polity Press, 2002.

Betcher, Sharon V. "Disability and the Terror of the Miracle Tradition," 161–82 in *Miracles Revisited: New Testament Miracle Stories and their Concepts of Reality*. Edited by Stefan Alkier and Annette Weissenrieder. Berlin: De Gruyter, 2013. https://doi.org/10.1515/9783110296372.161

Brock, Brian, and John Swinton, *Disability in the Christian Tradition: A Reader*. Grand Rapids, MI: Eerdmans, 2012.

Castelli, Elizabeth A. "Gender, Theory, and *The Rise of Christianity*: A Response to Rodney Stark," *Journal of Early Christian Studies* 6.2 (1998): 227–57. https://doi.org/10.1353/earl.1998.0034

Collins, Adela Yarbro. "Paul's Disability: The Thorn in His Flesh," 165–83 in *Disability Studies and Biblical Literature*. Edited by Candida R. Moss and Jeremy Schipper. New York: Palgrave Macmillan, 2011. https://doi.org/10.1057/9781137001207_11

Davis, Lennard J. *Bending over Backwards: Disability, Dismodernism, and other Difficult Positions*. New York: New York University Press, 2002.

Davis, Lennard J., ed. *The Disability Studies Reader*. New York: New York University Press, 2006.

Eiesland, Nancy L. *The Disabled God: Toward a Liberatory Theology of Disability*. Nashville, TN: Abingdon Press, 1994.

Fredriksen, Paula. "Mandatory Retirement: Ideas in the Study of Christian Origins whose Time Has Come to Go," *Studies in Religion* 35.2 (2006): 231–46. https://doi.org/10.1177/000842980603500203

Garland, Robert. *The Eye of the Beholder: Deformity and Disability in the Graeco-Roman World*. Ithaca, NY: Cornell University Press, 1995.

Goodley, Dan. *Disability Studies: An Interdisciplinary Introduction*. Los Angeles, CA: Sage, 2011.

Hindmarsh, Bruce D. "'My chains fell off, my heart was free': Early Methodist Conversion Narrative in England," *Church History: Studies in Christianity and Culture* 68.4 (1999): 910–29. https://doi.org/10.2307/3170209

Hobgood, Allison P., and David Houston Wood, eds. *Recovering Disability in Early Modern England*. Columbus, OH: Ohio State University Press, 2013.

Kleinman, Arthur. *Patients and Healers in the Context of Culture: An Exploration of the Borderland between Anthropology, Medicine, and Psychiatry*. Berkeley, CA: University of California Press, 1980. https://doi.org/10.1525/9780520340848

Kudlick, Catherine J. "Disability History: Why We Need Another 'Other'," *The American Historical Review* 108.3 (2003): 763–93. https://doi.org/10.1086/529597

Laes, Christian. "Silent History? Speech Impairment in Roman Antiquity," 145–80 in *Disabilities in Roman Antiquity: Disparate Bodies a Capite ad Calcem*. Edited by Christian Laes, C. F. Goodey, and M. Lynn Rose. Leiden: Brill, 2013. https://doi.org/10.1163/9789004251250_008

Liew, Tat-Siong Benny. *Politics of Parousia: Reading Mark Inter(con)textually*. Leiden: Brill 1999.
Madden, Deborah. *"A Cheap, Safe and Natural Medicine": Religion, Medicine and Culture in John Wesley's Primitive Physic*. Amsterdam: Rodopi, 2007. https://doi.org/10.1163/9789401204958
—"Introduction. Saving Souls and Saving Lives: John Wesley's 'Inward and Outward Health'," 1–13 in *"Inward and Outward Health": John Wesley's Holistic Concept of Medical Science, the Environment and Holy Living*. Edited by Deborah Madden. Eugene, OR: Wipf & Stock, 2008.
Madden, Deborah, ed. *"Inward and Outward Health": John Wesley's Holistic Concept of Medical Science, the Environment and Holy Living*. Eugene, OR: Wipf & Stock, 2008.
Maddox, Randy L. *Responsible Grace: John Wesley's Practical Theology*. Nashville, TN: Kingswood Books, 1994.
—"John Wesley on Holistic Health and Healing," *Methodist History* 46.1 (2007): 4–33.
—"Reclaiming the Eccentric Patient: Methodist Reception of John Wesley's Interest in Medicine," 15–50 in Madden, ed., *"Inward and Outward Health*, 2008.
Mitchell, David T., and Sharon L. Snyder. *Narrative Prosthesis: Disability and the Dependencies of Discourse*. Ann Arbor, MI: University of Michigan Press, 2001. https://doi.org/10.3998/mpub.11523
Montgomery, Robert L. "Conversion and the Historic Spread of Religions," 164–89 in *The Oxford Handbook of Religious Conversion*. Edited by Lewis R. Rambo and Charles E. Farhadian. Oxford: Oxford University Press, 2014.
Moss, Candida R. "Christly Possession and Weakened Bodies: Reconsideration of the Function of Paul's Thorn in the Flesh (2 Cor 12:7-10)," *Journal of Religion, Disability and Health* 16 (2012): 319–33. https://doi.org/10.1080/15228967.2012.731987
Raphael, Rebecca. *Biblical Corpora. Representations of Disability in Hebrew Biblical Literature*. London: Continuum, 2009.
Rose, M. Lynn. "Deaf and Dumb in Ancient Greece," 17–32 in Davis, ed., *Disability Studies Reader*, 2006.
Rose, Martha L. *The Staff of Oedipus: Transforming Disability in Ancient Greece*. Ann Arbor, MI: University of Michigan Press, 2003. https://doi.org/10.3998/mpub.17745
Schüssler Fiorenza, Elisabeth. "Introduction: Exploring the Intersections of Race, Gender, Status, and Ethnicity in Early Christian Studies," 1–23 in *Prejudice and Christian Beginnings: Investigating Race, Gender, and Ethnicity in Early Christian Studies*. Edited by Elisabeth Schüssler Fiorenza and Laura Salah Nasrallah. Minneapolis, MN: Fortress Press, 2009.
Shakespeare, Tom. "The Social Model of Disability," 197–204 in *The Disability Studies Reader*. Edited by Lennard J. Davis. New York: Routledge, 2006.
Siebers, Tobin. *Disability Theory*. Ann Arbor, MI: University of Michigan Press, 2008.
Solevåg, Anna Rebecca. "Hysterical Women? Gender and Disability in Early Christian Narrative," 315–27 in *Disability in Antiquity*. Edited by Christian Laes. London: Routledge, 2017.
—"No Nuts? No Problem! Disability, Stigma and the Baptized Eunuch in Acts 8:26-30," *Biblical Interpretation* 24 (2016): 81–99. https://doi.org/10.1163/15685152-00241p06
—*Negotiating the Disabled Body: Representations of Disability in Early Christian Texts*.

Atlanta, GA: Society of Biblical Literature Press, 2018. https://doi.org/10.2307/j.cdb2hnt1r
Stark, Rodney. *The Rise of Christianity: A Sociologist Reconsiders History*. New York: HarperOne, 1997. https://doi.org/10.1515/9780691214290
Theissen, Gerd, and John Riches. *The Miracle Stories of the Early Christian Tradition*. Edinburgh: Clark, 1983.
Thomson, Rosemarie Garland. *Extraordinary Bodies: Figuring Physical Disability in American Culture and Literature*. New York: Columbia University Press, 1997.
Tolbert, Mary Ann. *Sowing the Gospel: Mark's World in Literary-Historical Perspective*. Minneapolis, MN: Fortress Press, 1989.
Turner, David M. *Disability in Eighteenth-Century England: Imagining Physical Impairment*. New York: Routledge, 2012. https://doi.org/10.4324/9780203117545
Wesley, John. *Primitive Physic: Or An Easy and Natural Method of Curing Most Diseases*. Philadelphia, PA: Steuart Andrew, 1791; 1992, 22nd edn.

Chapter Six

Reading a Complex Identity in Conversion: Interpretations of the Ethiopian Eunuch

Minna Heimola

In Acts, the apostle Philip baptizes an Ethiopian eunuch (Acts 8.23-40). There has been disagreement among scholars whether this story begins the Gentile mission in Acts, whether the eunuch is the first Gentile converted to Christianity, or whether this honor belongs to Cornelius, who will be baptized in chapter ten. The Ethiopian's relationship with Judaism is ambivalent: he has come to Jerusalem on a pilgrimage and owns a scroll of Isaiah, which he is reading, but as a eunuch he remains an outsider; it is commonly assumed that eunuchs could not become proselytes.[1]

It is not only the religious identity of the Ethiopian that is ambivalent in Luke's story. The same is true for his class or position and his gender. The eunuch is in the service of the Ethiopian queen, in a high position. The story makes it obvious that he enjoys a relatively large personal freedom, which makes the pilgrimage to Jerusalem possible. However, a eunuch—possibly castrated regardless of his will—in the service of a queen, was probably a slave, albeit in an influential position. Furthermore, his gender is ambivalent: as a castrate, the character is, so to speak, between genders. One also observes a verbal ambivalence, for the Ethiopian is referred to both as a eunuch (*eunukhos*) and as a man (*anêr*). In part, these ambiguities have precisely enabled very different interpretations of the figure.[2] These ambiguities

---

1. Christopher R. Matthews, *Philip—Apostle and Evangelist: Configurations of a Tradition* (Leiden: Brill, 2002), 77; Charles K. Barrett, *A Critical and Exegetical Commentary on the Acts of the Apostles,* Vol. I (London: T&T Clark, 2004), 421. Scott Shauf, "Locating the Eunuch: Characterization and Narrative Context in Acts 8:26-40," *The Catholic Biblical Quarterly* 71 (2009): 762–75, here 765, does not explicitly comment whether a eunuch could become a proselyte. However, he argues that the word "proselyte" is a technical term in Acts and that it is unlikely that the Ethiopian eunuch would be a proselyte when the term is not mentioned.

2. For a selection of these, see Gitte Buch-Hansen, Marianne Bjelland Kartzow, and Rebecca Solevåg, eds., *Metodemangfold og det nye testamentet: I fotsporene til den etiopiske evnukken* (Oslo: Cappelen Damm, 2013). Already in Antiquity, the identity of the eunuch was constructed in several different ways; for example, among the interpreters of the text in Late Antiquity, he was seen as a Jew by some and as a Gentile by

mark the eunuch as a queer figure, but he is further marginalized as a eunuch, a servant slave and an African. This is reflected in the way he is described only as a eunuch, and not by name. In this article, I analyze this character's identity in conversion, how his identity has been constructed in readings of the text, and finally how his queerness creates a liminal stage in which conversion, understood as recreating identity, is possible.

Occasionally, I will use terminology and methods related to the concept of intersection. Marianne Kartzow and Halvor Moxnes have already employed the idea of intersection in their study of the Ethiopian eunuch.[3] Intersection, or intersectionality, refers to approaches which are now essential in gender and race studies: instead of analyzing the situation of a person by focusing only on gender, intersectional approaches consider several factors and identity markers, which impact the whole: race, class, sexuality, health, and age. The idea of intersection originally emerged to account for the experiences of black women as doubly marginalized. Black women criticized feminism for focusing only on issues that concerned privileged white women and anti-racist activism for emphasizing only the discrimination of black men.[4] Gradually, the category of intersection became broader; it no longer focuses only on race and gender, but also frequently analyzes sexuality and class;[5] sometimes it also includes other social identities like those defined by place of residence, religion, and age group.[6]

I build on the theoretical insights of intersectionality, but I also apply two new theoretical concepts to read the character of the eunuch: from Leslie McCall's, I use intracategorical complexity, an intersectionalist approach in

---

others (for examples, see William Frank Lawrence Jr., *The History of the Interpretation of Acts 8:26-40 by the Church Fathers prior to the Fall of Rome* [Dissertation, Union Theological Seminary, 1984], 83).

3. Marianne Bjelland Kartzow and Halvor Moxnes, "Complex Identities: Ethnicity, Gender and Religion in the Story of the Ethiopian Eunuch (Acts 8:26-40)," *Religion & Theology* 17 (2010): 184–204.

4. Joan Acker, *Class Questions: Feminist Answers.* (Lanham: Bowman & Littlefield, 2006), 35; Kathy Davis, "Intersectionality as Buzzword: A Sociology of Science Perspective on What Makes a Feminist Theory Successful," *Feminist Theory* 9.1 (2008): 67–85, here 68. The concept itself was first used by the legal scholar Kimberle Crenshaw, who analyzed legal cases in the USA from the point of view of the experiences of black women. She demanded that the black community should pay attention to the issues related to gender, and feminists should note also issues related to race. See Kimberle Crenshaw, "Demarginalizing the Intersection of Race and Sex: A Black Feminist Critique of Antidiscrimination Doctrine, Feminist Theory and Antiracist Politics," *The University of Chicago Legal Forum* 140 (1989): 139–67.

5. For class, see particularly Acker, *Class Questions*, 15–44.

6. Leslie McCall, "The Complexity of Intersectionality," *Signs* 30 (2005): 1771–800, here 1781; Davis, "Intersectionality as Buzzword," 68.

which certain individuals are seen as challenging all or several existing categories.[7] A similar idea is found in the concept of "category crisis," developed by Marjorie Garber.[8] These two notions help highlight how the Ethiopian eunuch, with his own identity, challenges identities and categorizations. The Ethiopian eunuch is a particularly fitting example of a character whose identity crosses the boundaries of traditionally constructed groups; his identity is described as ambiguous and "borderline" in several ways. He is in "category crisis" simultaneously when one considers several categories—gender, ethnoreligious identity, and social status. According to Garber, category crisis is "a borderline that comes permeable, that permits of border crossings from one category to another."[9] This category crisis, and the crossing of boundaries attached to it, makes the character particularly suitable for a rich variety of readings.

Being in a state of category crisis which permits border crossings presents an interesting parallel to the act of conversion: the eunuch's queer, permeable identity allows him, as a character, to cross over to the Christ-believer movement. The ambiguous liminality of the conversion story is supported by the queer ambivalence of the language in the Greek text. The story of the eunuch begins with Philip being told by an angel of the Lord to get up and go *kata mesêmbrian* (Acts 8.26). This Greek expression is ambiguous and can refer both to time ("at noon") and place ("towards the south").[10] Sean Burke has suggested that the equivocality of this turn of phrase, together with other ambiguous wordings of the text, creates an ambivalent liminal space

---

7. Leslie McCall has described in her article on the methodology of the intersectionalism different approaches towards categorizations used in intersectionalist studies. She uses the term *intracategorical complexity* of the approach in which the focus is on the "people whose identity crosses the boundaries of traditionally constructed groups" (McCall, "Complexity of Intersectionality," 1774 and 1783).

8. Similar ideas concerning the eunuch have been presented by Sean D. Burke in recent publications, although his focus is more on queer theory than intersection. See Sean D. Burke, "Queering Early Christian Discourse: The Ethiopian Eunuch," in Teresa J. Hornsby and Ken Stone, eds., *Bible Trouble: Queer Reading at the Boundaries of Biblical Scholarship* (Atlanta, GA: Society of Biblical Literature, 2011), 175–89 and *Queering the Ethiopian Eunuch: Strategies of Ambiguity in Acts* (Minneapolis, MN: Fortress Press, 2013).

9. Marjorie Garber, *Vested Interests: Cross-dressing and Cultural Anxiety* (New York: Routledge, 1992), 16–7. Garber's book focuses mostly on cross-dressing as a gender category crisis, but she also mentions other categories: black/white, Jew/Christian, noble/bourgeois, master/slave.

10. Arlo Duba, "Disrupted by Luke–Acts," *Theology Today* 68 (2011): 116–22, here 118.

characteristic of the entire pericope.[11] Apart from that ambiguous expression and the ambivalence related to the figure of the eunuch, there are also other possibly deliberately unclear expressions. For example, in the phrase *hautê estin erêmos* (8.26), *hautê* could refer both to Gaza or the road.[12] There is also a play on words at the beginning of the story: an Ethiopian traveling to Gaza oversees the treasury (in Greek *gaza*) of the Queen.[13] These vague, deliberately ambiguous expressions make it natural to interpret the identity of the eunuch through the categories of intersection and category crisis. Indeed, the readers are at ambiguous crossroads in several ways.

Reading Religious Identity

In scholarly accounts, the eunuch's gender is often considered relevant mostly to evaluate the eunuch's relationship to Judaism. It is obvious that the eunuch has some ties with Judaism: he is committed enough to obtain a scroll containing the book of Isaiah, which he reads while traveling in his chariot (8.28). Reading the scroll emphasizes both the piety and motivation of the eunuch and his status as a wealthy high official.[14] The reference to the Ethiopian's pilgrimage to Jerusalem (8.27) serves a similar function; pilgrimage was an expensive and possibly troublesome endeavor.[15] For Bruce Malina and John Pilch, the Ethiopian eunuch was a "hellenistic Israelite" on pilgrimage.[16]

Despite these evidences, it remains uncertain whether a eunuch could really be a Jew. Deuteronomy clearly places eunuchs outside the Jewish cultic community (Deut. 23.2). Jewish ritual laws reflect strongly negative

---

11. Burke, "Queering Early Christian Discourse," 183; likewise Duba, "Disrupted by Luke–Acts," 118.

12. Barrett, *Commentary on the Acts of the Apostles*, 423. Bruce J. Malina, and John J. Pilch, *Social-Science Commentary on the Book of Acts* (Minneapolis, MN: Fortress Press, 2008), 65 argue instead that the phrase unambiguously refer to the road being in the wilderness. They suggest that baptizing the Ethiopian in the wilderness reflects John the Baptist and his actions in wilderness (Luke 3, 7.24).

13. Malina and Pilch, *Social-Science Commentary on Acts*, 65; see also Matthews, *Philip–Apostle and Evangelist*, 81; Barrett, *Commentary on the Acts of the Apostles*, 425.

14. For example, Malina and Pilch, *Social-Science Commentary on Acts*, 66.

15. Likewise for example James D. G. Dunn, *The Acts of the Apostles* (Peterborough: Epworth, 1996), 114.

16. Malina and Pilch, *Social-Science Commentary on Acts*, 65–6. Likewise, Joseph A. Fitzmyer, *The Acts of the Apostles: A New Translation with Introduction and Commentary* (New York: The Anchor Bible/Doubleday, 1998), 410 argues that he was a Jew or a proselyte.

attitudes towards any mutilation of the body and indicate that those with a deformed body cannot stand before God. The same principle is reflected in the laws prohibiting sacrifice of castrated animals (Lev. 22.24). Josephus, writing in the first century CE, is even more hostile towards eunuchs, comparing them to killers of infants and arguing that they are completely outside salvation (*Ant.* 4.290-291). Philo of Alexandria also describes eunuchs in a negative manner, quoting Deuteronomy (*Spec. Leg.* 2.344). He furthermore elaborates the picture and brings in the Hellenistic stereotypes of the eunuchs as effeminate and vain persons, unable to seek justice and wisdom (*Spec. Leg.* 3.40-42; *Deus Imm.* 111).

And yet, in Isaiah 56, only a few chapters before the passage the Ethiopian reads in our story,[17] there is a promise of salvation for foreigners currently outside the chosen people, and eunuchs are included in this group (Isa. 56.4-5). This was a prophecy for the future, considered as still unfulfilled in the first century, and concerning the eschatological times.[18] Thus scholars usually maintain, based on the Hebrew Bible, Josephus, and Philo, that eunuchs were not accepted inside Judaism and that they could not even enter the synagogues.[19] During the first centuries of the common era, they were clearly outsiders from the Jewish point of view. Scholars frequently argue that eunuchs could not even become proselytes.[20] In that context, the Ethiopian traveling to the Temple could not have entered it.[21] Arlo Duba suggests that the eunuch is aware of his position: when he asks whether he can be baptized (8.36), he seeks reaffirmation, an assertion that he can become a follower of Christ, although he could not become a Jew.[22] In this sense, the Christ movement can be interpreted to fulfill the prophecy of Isaiah (Isa. 56.4-5). Some scholars, like Scott Shauf, have noticed the ambivalence of

---

17   For example, Duba, "Disrupted by Luke–Acts," 119 has noted that Philip would also have discussed this text promising salvation for eunuchs with the Ethiopian.

18.   Dunn, *Acts of the Apostles*, 113.

19.   Walter Stevenson, "Eunuchs and Early Christianity," in Shaun Tougher, ed., *Eunuchs in Antiquity and Beyond* (London: The Classical Press of Wales and Duckworth, 2002), 123–42, here 131.

20.   See n. 1 above.

21.   Dunn, *Acts of the Apostles*, 113; likewise Mona West, "The Story of the Ethiopian Eunuch," in Deryn Guest, Robert E. Goss, Mona West, and Thomas Bohache, eds., *The Queer Bible Commentary* (London: SCM Press, 2006), 572–4, here 572 argues that the eunuch could not be an actual Jew, but was possibly one of the so-called God-fearers. On the contrary Malina and Pilch, *Social-Science Commentary on Acts*, 65–6, who do not see any problem in having a eunuch as a Jew, yet refer to the character as a "hellenistic Israelite."

22.   Duba, "Disrupted by Luke–Acts," 119.

the character's religious identity.[23] This ambivalence can also be traced in ancient commentaries on the story. About half of the early Christian teachers discussing the text view the eunuch as a Jew converting to Christianity while the other half consider him as the first baptized Gentile.[24] Thus, I argue that the religious identity of the character is queer and ambiguous, but it is precisely this vagueness which opens the possibility of conversion.

Gender and Sexual Identity

As stated before, the eunuch is often analyzed in term of his religious identity. Only more recently, the gender of the character has also interested scholars. For instance, Mona West mentions the Ethiopian as an important figure for queer readings of Acts.[25] Apart from the short remark in West, only Burke has noted the potential of the eunuch for queer readings.[26] I will return to these readings later.

In contrast, early Christian readers of the texts were surprisingly interested in the gender of the eunuch. Their readings along the lines of gender reveal and confirm interesting notions of gender in Antiquity. Below I will describe how Bede, Arator, and other writers of Antiquity and Late Antiquity understood the gender of the Ethiopian when commenting on the text.

The text describes the gender of the Ethiopian with some ambiguity: the character is called both a eunuch (*eunoukhos*) and a man (*anêr*). Some of the early readers notice this tension and try to solve it by reading the description

---

23. Shauf, "Locating the Eunuch," 663–765. Likewise also Ernst Haenchen, *The Acts of the Apostles* (trans. Bernard Noble and Gerald Shinn; Oxford: Basil Blackwell, 1982), 314, who described the ambiguous religious identity of the eunuch and sees him as a stepping stone between the mission work focusing exclusively on the Jews and Samaritans and the actual Gentile mission. See also Clarice J. Martin, "A Chamberlain's Journey and the Challenge of Interpretation for Liberation," *Semeia* 47 (1989): 105–35, here 114.

24. For example, Pontius (*Life of Cyprianos* 3), Irenaeus (who says that the Ethiopian already knew God the Father and was only lacking the knowledge about Jesus and baptism; *Adv. Haer.* 4.23.2) and Hieronymus (who refers to the eunuch as a lover of the Law and synagogue frequenter; *Letters* 53.5) view the Ethiopian as a Jew. On the contrary, Eusebius (*Church History* 2.1.13), Ephraem of Syria (according to whom the eunuch is a light to the Gentiles in Ethiopia and all the way to India; *Pearl* 3.2), Chrysostom (who reads the baptism of the eunuch to foresee the conversion of larger groups of Gentiles; *Hom.* 19) and Petrus Chrysologus (although he described the eunuch as a Indian; *Homily* 61) maintained that the Ethiopian was a Gentile. See also Lawrence, *History of the Interpretation of Acts 8:26-40 by the Church Fathers*, 83.

25. West, "Story of the Ethiopian Eunuch," 572.

26. Burke, "Queering Early Christian Discourse"; Burke, *Queering the Ethiopian Eunuch*.

in a metaphorical manner. Bede writes: "he is called a man because of his virtue and integrity of mind, and not undeservedly, for he devoted his study solely to the Scriptures."[27] Thus, Bede notes that while the Ethiopian is *de facto* a eunuch, his mental capacities for and his devotion to the study of biblical texts make him worthy to be called a man.

This reading reflects how Antiquity constructed genders. Men and women were perceived as complete opposites, not only physically, but also psychologically and morally. Men were warm, hard, and resilient, while women were cool and soft; men were virtuous, while women were prone to immorality and petty offences. For example, Lactantius illustrates this connection through etymology: man (*vir* in Latin) is strong (*vis*), and provides the root for virtue (*virtus*), while the word woman (*mulier*) comes from the word *mollitia*, softness.[28] According to Aristotle, women are not only softer than men, but also more impulsive and malicious.[29] At least in some philosophical schools, women were considered incapable of being philosophers,[30] although there were a few notable exceptions.[31] In the context of early Christianity, for example, the Gospel of Thomas states that Mary must be made male in order to progress spiritually.[32] At the same time, women, children, and eunuchs were above all else seen as non-men, persons who had fallen short of the male ideal of Antiquity. They had either lost the status of a man or had not yet (or at all) developed into full manhood. For example, Aristotle compares the body of a woman to the bodies of boys and impotent men.[33] In addition, male and female genitalia were thought to be alike,

---

27. Bede, *Commentary on the Acts of the Apostles* 8.27A.

28. Lactantius, *De opificio Dei* 12.16-17. See also Matthew Kuefler, *The Manly Eunuch: Masculinity, Gender Ambiguity, and Christian Ideology in Late Antiquity* (Chicago, IL: University of Chicago Press, 2001), 20–1.

29. Aristoteles, *Historia Animalium* 9.1: "In all cases, excepting those of the bear and leopard, the female is less spirited than the male; in regard to the two exceptional cases, the superiority in courage rests with the female. With all other animals the female is softer in disposition than the male, is more mischievous, less simple, more impulsive, and more attentive to the nurture of the young: the male, on the other hand, is more spirited than the female, more savage, more simple and less cunning. The traces of these differentiated characteristics are more or less visible everywhere, but they are especially visible where character is the more developed, and most of all in man."

30. For example, Democritus writes that it is dreadful that women would practice argument (fragment 110; see also Prudence R. S. M. Allen, *The Concept of Woman: The Aristotelian Revolution, 750 B.C. – A.D. 1250*, (Grand Rapids, MI: William B. Eerdmans, 1985), 36.

31. For example, Hipporchia of Maroneia, a Cynic philosopher, although she apparently dressed as a man, and Diotima of Mantinea mentioned in Plato's *Symposium*.

32. *Gos. Thom.* 114.

33. Aristoteles, *De Generatione Animalium* 1.20.

with the genitals of men being outside the body while the genitals of women were inside the body and "turned around."[34] Since a woman was a deficient male, with inferior characteristics, it is not surprising that eunuchs, as well as castrated and/or impotent males, were sometimes closely associated with women in thought. For example, Aristotle compares castrated men to women, arguing that castrated males are feminine and vain like women.[35]

Thus, Bede builds his reading of the text on ancient notions of gender: as a eunuch, the Ethiopian is presumably inferior compared to other men. However, his remarkable devotion and integrity (for a eunuch?) makes Bede note that, internally, he is a man rather than a feminine eunuch. In this way, Bede can both maintain traditional ideas of gender and still read the eunuch as an exemplary figure, as an honorary—if not actual—man.

However, not all ancient Christians easily accepted the ancient ideas about gender and masculinity. In Antiquity, maleness was strongly connected with the status of free man and the role of the *pater familias*, the male citizen in a position of power and in charge of his extended household, consisting of wife, children, slaves, freedmen, clients, and others.[36] However, Jesus, as we can reconstruct from the Gospels, certainly did not conform to these expectations, and his death on a cross—a form of execution reserved for slaves—did not help in constructing his maleness in terms that would have been understandable for Antiquity. Mathew Kuefler argues that many early Christians created a new masculine ideal, that of a eunuch or a monk, a celibate, self-controlling male.[37]

In his reading of the Ethiopian eunuch of Acts, Arator seems to reflect this "new," subversive ideal of (Christian) maleness. He writes: "[H]ow rightly is her herald a eunuch! As [faith] proceeds, lust is driven off, and the chaste capture the heavenly kingdoms."[38] In this reading, the eunuch is actually superior to men, because—according to Arator's idealized interpretation—eunuchs are asexual, free of carnal lust. As Marianne Kartzow notes, the eunuch is constructed to be "freed from sexual lust and family responsibilities."[39]

This interpretation of eunuchs was not universally shared—on the contrary, in several sources, eunuchs are described as hypersexual and/or as

---

34. See for example Galen, *De usu partium* 14.II.297.
35. Philo, De *Specialibus Legibus* 3.40-42; *Quod Deus Sit Immutabilis* 111.
36. Jennifer A. Glancy, *Slavery in Early Christianity* (Minneapolis, MN: Fortress Press, 2002), 24–6.
37. Kuefler, *The Manly Eunuch*.
38. Arator, *On the Acts of the Apostles* 1.
39. Marianne Bjelland Kartzow, *Destabilizing the Margins: An Intersectional Approach to Early Christian Memory* (Eugene, OR: Pickwick, 2012), 56.

convenient lovers for both men and women.⁴⁰ However, some early Christians conceived the eunuch's mode of life as something to be appreciated and even actively researched. According to Eusebius, Origen castrated himself.⁴¹ The historical accuracy of this account is uncertain, but what is important is that this was presented as an option available to a Christian man. Justin Martyr also writes about a young Christian man who wanted to castrate himself in order to live a chaste life.⁴² This kind of religiously motivated castration was not only a Christian phenomenon, but there were also self-castrated priests in the cult of Cybele.⁴³

Thus, these two readings of the Ethiopian eunuch reflect a larger debate about gender and masculinity in early Christianity. The early Christian readers of the text want to understand the gender and sexuality of the eunuch in a positive light, although their strategies vary. Some are influenced more by traditional ideas about masculinity, others follow the more radical ideas viewing asexual eunuchs as the male ideal.

Recently, the rise of gender studies and discussions about sexual and gender minorities have again brought the character of the eunuch to the front. This time, his queerness is emphasized, rather than downplayed. In her article in the *Queer Bible Commentary*, West reads the story of the Ethiopian eunuch as a story of liberation for sexual and gender minorities. Like eunuchs in Antiquity, these minorities have been shunned; like the Ethiopian eunuch, they have "struggled to make sense of scripture, to find [their] place in it, when others would use it to condemn [them]."⁴⁴ John McNeill calls the eunuch the patron saint of the queer community and "the first baptized gay Christian."⁴⁵ However, Kartzow has noted that among scholars who emphasize the eunuch's Ethiopian background, his status as eunuch is ignored;⁴⁶ while modern readers focusing on the eunuch as a member of a sexual or gender minority frequently downplay his ethnicity.

---

40. Martial 3.81; see also Shelley Hales, "Looking for Eunuchs: The *galli* and Attis in Roman Art," in Tougher, ed., *Eunuchs in Antiquity and Beyond*, 87–102, here 91.

41. Eusebius, *Church History* VI.8.

42. Justin Martyr, *1 Apology* 29.1-2.

43. John L. Lightfoot, "Sacred Eunuchism in the Cult of the Syrian Goddess," in Tougher, ed., *Eunuchs in Antiquity and Beyond*, 71–86. Motivations varied, though; in Christianity, castration was connected with being free from sexual urges, while in cults of female goddesses, male priests castrated themselves instead in order to resemble the female deity.

44. West, "The Story of the Ethiopian Eunuch," 572–4.

45. John J. McNeill, *Freedom, Glorious Freedom: The Spiritual Journey to the Fullness of Life for Gays, Lesbians, and Everybody Else* (Boston, MA: Beacon Press, 1995), here 143.

46. Kartzow, *Destabilizing the Margins*, 57.

One of the few exceptions to this tendency is Sean D. Burke. His scholarly reading also emphasizes the queerness of the eunuch; however, he argues that the author of Luke/Acts intends to represent the Ethiopian as queer not only in terms of gender and sexuality, but also regarding all categories and identities. According to him, "the ambiguities in the character of the eunuch function rhetorically to destabilize and denaturalize ancient constructions of identity."[47] Arguing for this kind of authorial intention can be problematic, but nevertheless Burke's queering reading highlights the complexity of the character as well as the fact that his identity as a eunuch is a challenge to ancient gender norms. In ancient readings, when the eunuch's "queer" gender identity is brought up, it relates to Christian ideals of chastity and sexual self-control, in contrast with descriptions of eunuch as lustful bisexuals. However, in modern readings, often more open to different sexualities, the eunuch is proudly labeled as a member of a sexual and/or gender minority. These variations in readings reflect different ideals and contexts; but it is the ambiguity of the eunuch/man that allows for all these readings.

It is obvious from the ancient readings of the text that eunuchs were inferior compared to non-castrated males. In this perspective, it is interesting to note that the eunuch is not named and, although he voices questions in the text, his agency in the story is limited. He is the object of a mission that Philip accomplishes, and afterwards, he simply continues his journey (8.39). His identity remains ambiguous, since eunuchs were in ancient thought "thing[s] neither male nor female" (Philo, *Som*. 2.184). Even after conversion, we are facing multiple queerness.

Reading Social Status: Slave or Free?

This marginal position peppered with ambivalence is also apparent when we consider the eunuch's status. In research related to the Ethiopian eunuch, scholars and commentators point out that the eunuch was obviously wealthy, because he had his own carriage as well as the book scroll. He also enjoyed the option to come to Jerusalem on pilgrimage, and his position of power is clear since he manages the treasury of the Queen of Ethiopia.[48] However, it has rarely been noted that his castration, presumably against his will, and his position in service of the Queen imply a status of slave—a managerial and influential slave, but a slave nonetheless.[49] In the ancient world,

47. Burke, *Queering the Ethiopian Eunuch*, esp. 148.
48. For example, Barrett, *Commentary on the Acts of the Apostles*, 425.
49. One of the few studies noting the Ethiopian's contested and complicated social position is Kartzow and Moxnes, "Complex Identities." They note that eunuchs were often slaves, and slaves and eunuchs were both equally "non-men" (197–8).

eunuchs usually were slaves, servants and/or representatives of a high-ranking person or a god (or, more frequently, a goddess).[50] It was precisely their castration which made the eunuchs reliable servants from the point of view of their royal masters: separated from their biological family and infertile due to castration, they could not start a dynasty of their own.[51] Eunuchs were commonly connected to royal women in particular; they could be conveniently used as keepers of the harems and in the service of queens and princesses, because they did not threaten the claim to fatherhood of the male members of the royal household by impregnating their women.[52]

Early Christian readers of the Ethiopian eunuch also rarely point towards his possible status as a royal slave, but rather emphasize his high status, particularly contrasting him with Philip in the story of Acts. John Chrysostom writes that the Ethiopian courtier was of a high status, but he "paid no attention to outward appearance [of Philip]."[53] He wonderingly writes that the Ethiopian, who sat in his chariot, invited "the man of lowly mien, despicable in attire" to join him and to travel together with him.[54] Bede also focuses on the Ethiopian's status, writing how he left the Queen's court behind and travelled far in his search for truth.[55]

This emphasis on the eunuch's position of power might reflect the masculine ideals of Antiquity. As has often been noted, there is a particularly close connection in ancient thinking between gender, sexuality, and status: masculinity was not a right all male persons could gain, but a privilege available to free male citizens, frequently connected to the role of the *pater familias*.[56] Access—or lack thereof—to masculinity implied moral judgment: slaves were considered morally inferior, because they were not in control of their own life. Slaves were often stereotyped as petty thieves and

---

50. Piotr O. Scholz, *Eunuchs and Castrati: A Cultural History* (trans. John A. Broadwin and Shelley L. Frisch; Princeton, NJ: Markus Wiener, 2001), here 68–72. There were also eunuchs in the service of Herod the Great (Josephus *Antiquities* 16.230-233; Glancy, *Slavery in Early Christianity*, 44; Catherine Hezser, *Jewish Slavery in Antiquity* [Oxford: Oxford University Press, 2005], 141). According to Burke, there have been eunuchs in various positions of the courts both in Rome and Byzantium, as well as in India, China and also in Assyria (Burke, "Queering Early Christian Discourse," 179).

51. Vern L. Bullough, "Eunuchs in History and Society," in Tougher, ed., *Eunuchs in Antiquity and Beyond*, 1-17, here 7.

52. Scholz, *Eunuchs and Castrati*, 68–70.

53. John Chrysostom, *Homilies on the Acts of the Apostles* 19.

54. John Chrysostom, *Homilies on Genesis* 35.5.

55. Bede, *Commentary on the Acts of the Apostles* 8.27A.

56. Kartzow, *Destabilizing the Margins*, 48.

liars in Antiquity.⁵⁷ Managerial slaves in charge of large properties had even more options for dishonesty, as depicted in Luke's parable of the dishonest manager (Lk. 16.1-9). Slaves were also often forced into prostitution by their owners and thus they were associated with sexual immorality.⁵⁸

Thus, slaves were connected with various immoralities. Because the early Christian readers wanted to present the Ethiopian eunuch as a sympathetic figure, they downplayed his status as non-free and instead tried to present him as a man (!) of power, emphasizing his high status as an elite male. However, at the same time, these readings present him as a person who is also humble and not ashamed to be taught by someone presumably inferior to him socially. The Ethiopian immediately asks Philip to join him, to teach him, and humbly asks whether he can be baptized. This humility displayed by a figure with a certain status is, however, used as a tool of anti-Jewish polemic in the readings, as has been noted by Kartzow.⁵⁹ The eunuch openly confesses his ignorance and his need to be taught. Athanasius and Bede contrast this to the attitude of Jews, who "persisted in their ignorance."⁶⁰ Bede furthermore criticizes Judaism openly in his reading, when stating that the Ethiopian "found the church's font there in the desert, rather than in the golden temple of the synagogue."⁶¹ This anti-Jewish reading strategy may be another reason for emphasizing the high status of the eunuch and ignoring signs of slavery: as a powerful figure, who still is humble when met by a preacher sent by the Holy Spirit, he is a stronger example of humility before God than someone of lower status.

Obviously, Luke's description of the character with his chariot and book scroll does reflect a person of wealth; nonetheless, the association between eunuchs and slavery was strong in Antiquity and the text could also be interpreted to focus on the eunuch's status as a non-free person. In recent studies and readings, this aspect of the character is newly highlighted. In his book on the Ethiopian eunuch, Burke emphasizes that "one of the constituent elements of ancient constructions of eunuchs was their classing as slaves."⁶² And slaves, even when in influential positions, were still completely dependent on their masters. Male slaves, even when in a high position, were not considered men, a status reserved for free citizens. Slaves could be killed

---

57. David C. Verner, *The Household of God: The Social World of the Pastoral Epistles* (SBL Dissertation Series, 71; Chico, CA: Scholars Press, 1983), 141; Glancy, *Slavery in Early Christianity,* 134–5.
58. Glancy, *Slavery in Early Christianity,* 54–7.
59. Kartzow, *Destabilizing the Margins,* 55–6.
60. Athanasius, *Festal Letter* 19.5.
61. Bede, *Commentary on the Acts of the Apostles,* 8.27A.
62. Burke, *Queering the Ethiopian Eunuch,* 113.

and tortured by their masters.⁶³ Both male and female slaves were also frequently targets of sexual abuse by their masters.⁶⁴

Modern interpretations have brought to the front this marginalized position of the Ethiopian, openly noting these issues. Again, while ancient commentators focus on the powerfulness of the character, modern readers are more likely to pay attention to his status as a non-free person. Yet, even this view of the eunuch as a marginalized figure does sometimes give way to anti-Jewish polemic. The baptism of the eunuch as a marginalized figure is sometimes described as a sign of the radical universalism of Christianity, in contrast to the particularism of Judaism.⁶⁵ Nonetheless, the status of the character as non-free might be relevant when we consider his namelessness—he is described first and foremost through the status of his owner (Acts 8.27). His limited agency in the story is possibly partly related to his position as a slave. Still, we encounter yet again ambivalence—wealth and power regardless of his status as a castrated slave.

Reading Black Skin: Ethnic Identities

The ethnicity of the Ethiopian has played a surprisingly minor role in scholarly explorations of the story, as Clarice J. Martin notes in her article about the Ethiopian chamberlain.⁶⁶ When ethnicity is considered, it is to reflect on how the Ethiopian background of this convert fulfills the prophecy of Psalm 68.31 and how the statement that he is a eunuch realizes the prophecy of Isaiah 56.3-7. In contrast, little interest has been paid to the Ethiopian's ethnographic identity.⁶⁷

Interestingly, the Ethiopian's black skin did inspire early Christian readers and commentators. In many readings, the Ethiopian eunuch is linked with two other notable black biblical characters, the Cushite wife of Moses (Numbers 12) and the black and beautiful woman of the Song of Solomon (1.5-6). For instance, Arator refers to both of these texts when writing about

---

63. Burke, *Queering the Ethiopian Eunuch*, 113–4.
64. Glancy, *Slavery in Early Christianity*, 49–53.
65. Interestingly, when the Finnish Bible translation published in 1992 was made, there was discussion whether Acts 8.26-40 should be titled the "Ethiopian eunuch" or "Ethiopian courtier," and those supporting the former argued that the whole point of the story was that a eunuch could be accepted as a full-fledged member into Christianity, unlike Judaism.
66. Martin, "A Chamberlain's Journey."
67. Martin, "A Chamberlain's Journey," 105.

the Ethiopian of Acts. For him, these texts have already shown that Africans and those with a black skin are accepted by God.[68]

However, as has been noted by Gay L. Byron and others, this acceptance reveals a darker (pun intended) side: the blackness or darkness of the skin is used as a negative symbol for sins, idolatry, and immorality.[69] This was at least partly related to the Old Testament story of Ham, presented as the ancestor of African people. He committed a sin against his father, Noah, and because of this his son Canaan was cursed into slavery by Noah (Gen. 9.18–10.20).[70] Based on this story, commentators associated blackness with sinfulness. These themes appear particularly in readings of the Ethiopian's baptism. Bede writes how "with the water of baptism he made white the blackness of our guilty connection."[71] Here, Bede speaks of all Christians, but, about the Ethiopian of Acts in particularly, he describes how he became white in baptism and here "an Ethiopian changed his skin" (Jer. 13.23).[72] These interpretations appear also in the works of other early Christian commentators. Jerome writes that Christians before salvation are dark like Ethiopians, but become white.[73] Along a similar vein, Ephraem of Syria indicates that the Ethiopian eunuch returned to his country of origin, and "made black men white" when teaching and baptizing them.[74] For early Christian literature, black skin is interpreted as relating to a sinful past, not only in connection to the Ethiopian eunuch but also in readings of the Cushite wife of Moses and the dark-skinned woman of Songs of Solomon. In some early Christian monastic texts, demons appear in the form of an Ethiopian (i.e., black) person.[75]

In modern readings, particularly those by African or African-American theologians, the black skin of the Ethiopian is celebrated and he is considered as one example of the important role of Africans in the Bible, an importance frequently overlooked in European readings and scholarship.[76] The Ethiopian Orthodox Church presents the Ethiopian eunuch as their spiritual ancestor, the first baptized Ethiopian, and as the person who brought Christianity

---

68. Arator, *On the Acts of the Apostles* 1.

69. Gay L. Byron, *Symbolic Blackness and Ethnic Difference in Early Christian Literature* (London: Routledge, 2002), 55–103.

70. Peter Frost, "Attitudes towards Blacks in the Early Christian Era," *The Second Century: A Journal of Early Christian Studies* 8.1 (Spring 1991): 1–11, here 3.

71. Bede, *Commentary on the Acts of the Apostles* 8.26b.

72. See also Frost, "Attitudes towards Blacks in the Early Christian Era," 4.

73. Jerome, *Homily 18 on Psalm* 86.

74. Ephraem, *The Pearl* 3.2-3.

75. Frost, "Attitudes towards Blacks in the Early Christian Era," 4–5.

76. See for example David Tuesday Adamo, *Africa and Africans in the New Testament* (Lanham, MD: University Press of America, 2006), esp. 3, 89–94.

to Ethiopia.⁷⁷ Other African theologians and writers proudly raise the character as an example of the early arrival of Christian faith in Africa, made possible by an African person.⁷⁸ This is related to a larger project, critically analyzing the Eurocentric view of ancient history, and emphasizing instead the influences between African and Asian cultures and the European Mediterranean already early in Antiquity.⁷⁹

However, in some of these readings, when the African identity of the character is emphasized, other aspects of the Ethiopian's identity are downplayed and sometimes even deliberately denied.⁸⁰ Particularly, some African writers avoid the word "eunuch" to describe the Ethiopian, calling him an African officer or court official instead.⁸¹ For example, David Tuesday Adamo actively argues that the character should not be considered a eunuch; the Greek *eunokhos* does not necessarily mean castration but can be translated simply as "officer."⁸² However, as Mikeal Parsons has noted, this reading of the text is historically and linguistically unlikely.⁸³ The gender of the African official is not problematic for all African and African-American readers; for example Martin accepts his status as a eunuch, although she also emphasizes his African origin.⁸⁴ Nevertheless, it seems that some African readers want to present the figure as representing an ideal masculine powerful black male, and thus downplay his ambivalent gender.

It has been a subject of debate whether one can talk of racism in Antiquity. Leaving this discussion aside, it seems safe to say that early Christianity frequently perceived the Ethiopian's black skin as a negative symbol. In Antiquity, Ethiopian descent was also frequently associated with slavery and low social status, possibly because most Ethiopians met by Greeks and Romans were foreign slaves.⁸⁵ Perhaps more importantly, as an African

77. For example, the official home page of the Ethiopian Orthodox Church: http://www.ethiopianorthodox.org/english/ethiopian/Antiquity.html (last consulted 17 August 2017).

78. Paul Mumo Kisau, "The Acts of the Apostles," in Tokunboh Adeyemo, ed., *Africa Bible Commentary* (Nairobi: WordAlive, 2006), 1297–348, here 1342.

79. Possibly most famously by Martin Bernal, *Black Athena: The Afroasiatic Roots of Classical Civilization*. Vol. 1: *The Fabrication of Ancient Greece 1785-1985* (London: Vintage, 1987); see also Martin, "A Chamberlain's Journey," 122.

80. Likewise Kartzow, *Destabilizing the Margins*, 57.

81. Adamo, *Africa and Africans*, 89–92; Yohannes K. Mekonnen, ed., *Ethiopia: The Land, Its People, History and Culture* (Dar es Salaam: New Africa Press, 2013), 216.

82. Adamo, *African and Africans*, 89.

83. Mikeal C. Parsons, *Body and Character in Luke and Acts: The Subversion of Physiognomy in Early Christianity* (Grand Rapids, MI: Baker Academic, 2006), 133–4.

84. Martin, "A Chamberlain's Journey."

85. Frost, "Attitudes towards Blacks in the Early Christian Era," 7.

character going beyond the "no longer Jew or Greek" dichotomy (Gal. 3.28), the Ethiopian eunuch once again challenges and queers categories of ethnicity and race.

Conclusion

My analysis, and the history of interpretation, has shown that the Ethiopian eunuch of Acts is a complicated figure. Both his gender and his status are somehow ambivalent. His ethnic identity as a black African should be obvious enough; nevertheless, in research, it has been ignored. In early Christian readings, problematic aspects of the eunuch's identity have been ignored. His masculinity, understood as a kind of honorary maleness, and his high status have been strongly emphasized, although some readings instead present the character as a model for an alternative masculinity—asexual, eunuch, free from sexual vices. Attitudes towards the eunuch's African ethnicity are more ambivalent in the early readings: while readers frequently refer to biblical black characters, presenting them as positive examples, the black skin of the Ethiopian is a negative symbol associated with sins and idolatry. In their readings, the Ethiopian becomes "an honorary white man" through the cleansing water of baptism. Because of his baptism, these readings transform both his actual gender and skin, making him more like a white male. In contrast, in modern readings, the marginalized nature of the character is frequently emphasized. He is described as a person whose identity is problematic and does not fit ideals of Antiquity. His role can contribute to the empowerment of marginalized persons today.

In Acts, the Ethiopian is not named, which reveals some degree of marginalization. Further, his agency is limited, for he is largely described only as an object of Philip's missionary work. Only in later Christian tradition does his agency become more apparent, when he is made into a mission worker himself, preaching to his fellow Ethiopians. However, the main feature of the eunuch remains his constant ambiguity, his state of being in a category crisis. He is on the borders, or in liminal space. He is actually also literally in liminal space, for he is traveling, and is between two places. This liminal space makes it possible for him to convert and embrace change.

Biographical Note

Minna Heimola has a PhD in the History of Christianity from the University of Helsinki. Her dissertation was on "Christian Identity in the Gospel of Philip" (2010). She has published *Raamattu ja rasismi* (*Bible and Racism*) in 2016, focusing on the issues of identity, gender, and race. Currently, she is studying to become a social worker.

Bibliography

Acker, Joan. *Class Questions: Feminist Answers*. Lanham: Bowman & Littlefield, 2006.
Adamo, David Tuesday. *Africa and Africans in the New Testament*. Lanham, MD: University Press of America, 2006.
Allen, Prudence R. S. M. *The Concept of Woman: The Aristotelian Revolution, 750 B.C. – A.D. 1250*. Grand Rapids, MI: William B. Eerdmans, 1985.
Barrett, Charles K. *A Critical and Exegetical Commentary on the Acts of the Apostles*. Vol. 1. London: T&T Clark, 2004.
Bernal, Martin. *Black Athena: The Afroasiatic Roots of Classical Civilization*. Vol. 1: *The Fabrication of Ancient Greece 1785-1985*. London: Vintage, 1987.
Buch-Hansen, Gitte, Marianne Bjelland Kartzow, and Rebecca Solevåg, eds. *Metodemangfold og det nye testamentet: I fotsporene til den etiopiske evnukken*. Oslo: Cappelen Damm, 2013.
Bullough, Vern L. "Eunuchs in History and Society," 1–17 in Tougher, ed., *Eunuchs in Antiquity and Beyond*, 2002. https://doi.org/10.2307/j.ctv1n35846.5
Burke, Sean D. "Queering Early Christian Discourse: The Ethiopian Eunuch," 175–89 in *Bible Trouble: Queer Reading at the Boundaries of Biblical Scholarship*. Edited by Teresa J. Hornsby and Ken Stone. Atlanta, GA: Society of Biblical Literature, 2011.
—*Queering the Ethiopian Eunuch: Strategies of Ambiguity in Acts*. Minneapolis, MN: Fortress Press, 2013.
Byron, Gay L. *Symbolic Blackness and Ethnic Difference in Early Christian Literature*. London: Routledge, 2002. https://doi.org/10.4324/9780203471470
Crenshaw, Kimberle. "Demarginalizing the Intersection of Race and Sex: A Black Feminist Critique of Antidiscrimination Doctrine, Feminist Theory and Antiracist Politics," *The University of Chicago Legal Forum* 140 (1989): 139–67.
Davis, Kathy. "Intersectionality as Buzzword: A Sociology of Science Perspective on What Makes a Feminist Theory Successful," *Feminist Theory* 9.1 (2008): 67–85. https://doi.org/10.1177/1464700108086364
Duba, Arlo. "Disrupted by Luke–Acts," *Theology Today* 68 (2011): 116–22. https://doi.org/10.1177/0040573611405882
Dunn, James D. G. *The Acts of the Apostles*. Peterborough: Epworth, 1996.
Fitzmyer, Joseph A. *The Acts of the Apostles: A New Translation with Introduction and Commentary*. New York: The Anchor Bible/Doubleday, 1998.
Frost, Peter. "Attitudes towards Blacks in the Early Christian Era," *The Second Century: A Journal of Early Christian Studies* 8.1 (Spring 1991): 1–11.
Garber, Marjorie Garber. *Vested Interests: Cross-dressing and Cultural Anxiety*. New York: Routledge, 1992.
Glancy, Jennifer A. *Slavery in Early Christianity*. Minneapolis, MN: Fortress Press, 2002. https://doi.org/10.1093/0195136098.001.0001
Haenchen, Ernst. *The Acts of the Apostles*. Translated by Bernard Noble and Gerald Shinn. Oxford: Basil Blackwell, 1982.
Hales, Shelley. "Looking for Eunuchs: The *galli* and Attis in Roman Art," 87–102 in

Tougher, ed., *Eunuchs in Antiquity and Beyond*, 2002. https://doi.org/10.2307/j.ctv1n35846.9

Hezser, Catherine. *Jewish Slavery in Antiquity*. Oxford: Oxford University Press, 2005. https://doi.org/10.1093/acprof:oso/9780199280865.001.0001

Kartzow, Marianne Bjelland. *Destabilizing the Margins: An Intersectional Approach to Early Christian Memory*. Eugene, OR: Pickwick, 2012.

Kartzow, Marianne Bjelland, and Halvor Moxnes. "Complex Identities: Ethnicity, Gender and Religion in the Story of the Ethiopian Eunuch (Acts 8:26-40)," *Religion & Theology* 17 (2010): 184–204. https://doi.org/10.1163/157430110X597827

Kuefler, Matthew. *The Manly Eunuch: Masculinity, Gender Ambiguity, and Christian Ideology in Late Antiquity*. Chicago, IL: University of Chicago Press, 2001.

Lawrence Jr., William Frank. *The History of the Interpretation of Acts 8:26-40 by the Church Fathers prior to the Fall of Rome*. Dissertation, Union Theological Seminary, 1984.

Lightfoot, John L. "Sacred Eunuchism in the Cult of the Syrian Goddess," 71–86 in Tougher, ed., *Eunuchs in Antiquity and Beyond*, 2002. https://doi.org/10.2307/j.ctv1n35846.8

Malina, Bruce J., and John J. Pilch. *Social-Science Commentary on the Book of Acts*. Minneapolis, MN: Fortress Press, 2008. https://doi.org/10.2307/j.ctv19cwbg8

Martin, Clarice J. "A Chamberlain's Journey and the Challenge of Interpretation for Liberation," *Semeia* 47 (1989): 105–35.

Matthews, Christopher R. *Philip—Apostle and Evangelist: Configurations of a Tradition*. Leiden: Brill, 2002. https://doi.org/10.1163/9789047400837

McCall, Leslie. "The Complexity of Intersectionality," *Signs* 30 (2005): 1771–800. https://doi.org/10.1086/426800

McNeill, John J. *Freedom, Glorious Freedom: The Spiritual Journey to the Fullness of Life for Gays, Lesbians, and Everybody Else*. Boston, MA: Beacon Press, 1995.

Mekonnen, Yohannes K., ed. *Ethiopia: The Land, Its People, History and Culture*. Dar es Salaam: New Africa Press, 2013.

Mumo Kisau, Paul. "The Acts of the Apostles," 1297–348 in *Africa Bible Commentary*. Edited by Tokunboh Adeyemo. Nairobi: WordAlive, 2006.

Parsons, Mikeal C. *Body and Character in Luke and Acts: The Subversion of Physiognomy in Early Christianity*. Grand Rapids, MI: Baker Academic, 2006.

Scholz, Piotr O. *Eunuchs and Castrati: A Cultural History*. Translated by John A. Broadwin and Shelley L. Frisch. Princeton, NJ: Markus Wiener, 2001.

Shauf, Scott. "Locating the Eunuch: Characterization and Narrative Context in Acts 8:26-40," *The Catholic Biblical Quarterly* 71 (2009): 762–75.

Stevenson, Walter. "Eunuchs and Early Christianity," 123–42 in *Eunuchs in Antiquity and Beyond*. Edited by Shaun Tougher. London: The Classical Press of Wales and Duckworth, 2002. https://doi.org/10.2307/j.ctv1n35846.11

Tougher, Shaun ed., *Eunuchs in Antiquity and Beyond*. London: The Classical Press of Wales and Duckworth, 2002.

Verner, David C. *The Household of God: The Social World of the Pastoral Epistles*. SBL Dissertation Series, 71. Chico, CA: Scholars Press, 1983.

West, Mona. "The Story of the Ethiopian Eunuch," 572–4 in *The Queer Bible Commentary*. Edited by Deryn Guest, Robert E. Goss, Mona West, and Thomas Bohache. London: SCM Press, 2006.

Chapter Seven

Creating a New Sex: Women Bodies in Conversion

Valérie Nicolet

In the book of Acts, one finds conversions of individuals, in the sense defined by William James at the beginning of the twentieth century. These personal conversions are sometimes coupled with the baptism of the household surrounding each single individual. Relying on reflections on the body inspired by Judith Butler, I am imagining how conversion could impact on the silent, invisible, and nameless bodies mentioned in stories of household conversion. To do this, I am looking at the way conversion affects gender and how conversion can inform a theoretical reflection on agency, subjectivity, and power.

Conversion inside the Household

In Acts 16, Lydia, probably a wealthy woman, is the recipient of Paul's personal teaching. She is herself already interested in the god of the Jews, since the author of Acts describes her as σεβομένη τὸν θεόν, "honoring god," or "fearing god," a technical term to designate non-Jews interested in worshiping the god of the Jews. The same is true for the jailor mentioned a bit later (16.27). After a series of paranormal phenomena taking place in the prison he guards, the jailor asks Paul what he should do to be saved. Paul and Silas answer that he needs to trust the Lord Jesus, and thus he will be saved, along with his house (16.31). In the same manner that Lydia's trust is enough to grant access to baptism for all the members of her household, the jailor's trust allows for his salvation and for his household's salvation as well. However, the members of the household are presented as having no say in these conversions.

These two stories present responses to the intervention of some Christ-believer missionaries that correspond to a psychologizing understanding of conversion. For both Lydia and the jailor, at least that is how the stories report it, a change occurs. In Lydia's story, the author of Luke/Acts indicates that "the Lord opened her heart so that she would follow" (Acts 16.14), and the jailor explicitly asks to be saved (Acts 16.30). In both cases, Lydia and the jailor receive teaching from the missionaries and seem to take a decision (or perhaps, to be acted upon by a divine force) in favor of a change in their life. What is less clear from the point of view of a model based on a psychologizing understanding of conversion is what happens to the households connected to Lydia and the jailor.

Household conversions are problematic for a model affirming the necessity of a personal and individual awareness of one's need for conversion. It seems unlikely that children and slaves, and most women of the household, would have the necessary autonomy to individually decide that their master's change of loyalty has a personal significance for each of them. We have, for example, the evidence of Jewish households where the male slaves were circumcised, particularly if they had to handle food for purity reasons.[1] Clearly, here, the conversion makes sense to the master or the head of family, if not to the slave. Shaye Cohen even argues that "These slaves, even if they assented to their conversion (as the Talmud requires them to do), cannot have been motivated by a deep sincere love for the god of Abraham."[2] Non-Jews also became Jews for the sake of marriage. Here too the reasons were often political and led to conversions of convenience that did not always have a lasting impact in time.[3] In this model, conversion is imposed from the outside by the master; it contributes to the advantage of the master, and the subordinates (children, women, male or female slaves) are not allowed to express an opinion concerning this change.

Inside conceptual models that understand conversion in a psychologizing manner, one is forced to present the conversion of slaves and children as an example of what Riggins R. Earl Jr. defines as the "depersonalized mode of conversion."[4] Earl works with the context of slavery in the United States between 1800 and 1860, but his observations can be helpful to understand the context of the first century, even if American slavery is not simply the equivalent of Greco-Roman slavery.[5] However, in both cases, we have

---

1. See Shaye J. D. Cohen, "Crossing the Boundary and Becoming a Jew," *The Harvard Theological Review* 82.1 (1989): 13–33, here 24.

2. Cohen, "Crossing the Boundary and Becoming a Jew," 24–5.

3. Cohen also provides two examples of conversion through marriage, both found in Josephus's *Jewish Antiquities*: Azizus, king of Emesa, is circumcised to marry Drusilla (*Jewish Antiquities* 20.7.1 § 139) and Polemo, king of Cicilia to marry Berenice (*Jewish Antiquities* 20.7.3. §§ 145-146). In the context of this volume, one can also think of the changes that Aseneth traverses to marry Joseph, and of the status of Hagar, as Abraham's concubine.

4. Riggins R. Earl, Jr., "A Critique of Slave Conversion Consciousness: Its Implications for Black Theology and Ethics," *Journal of the I.T.C.* 17.1/2 (1989–1990): 1–18, here 5.

5. American slavery, as is often noted, has a racial dimension not present in

situations in which slavery is the system on which society relies to function, and we encounter contexts in which masters decide, at least externally, the religious orientations of their slaves. According to Earl, the depersonalized mode of conversion corresponds to a situation where it is advantageous for the master that slaves integrate some of the theological teachings contained in the Bible. The plantation owners use the biblical teachings to justify not only the white masters' superiority, but also to describe the ideal Christian slave, hardworking and obedient to his/her master. Docility becomes the criterion according to which one recognizes a converted slave. Disobedient slaves are not only described as rebellious, but also as sinners. They violate the divine organization of the world. Biblical texts, such as 1 Timothy 6.1-2, are used to perpetuate the exploitation of slaves.

With the sources at one's disposal for the first century, it is difficult to evaluate how invisible converts, these bodies without voices and without names that sometimes appear in biblical texts, and are simply converted without ceremony, understand their conversion. Indeed, it seems logical initially to understand these conversions as examples of what Earl calls depersonalized conversion, where the individuals converted have little to no personal implications in the conversion process. In the cases of full household conversion, as Cohen wrote, "we may be sure that the involuntary members of the household (*oikia*) had substantially less enthusiasm, at least at first, for the new religion than did the chieftain who initiated the conversion, but all alike became members of the new community."[6] I propose to think about these converts while focusing on two dimensions: the body, and the re-organization of power relations. I approach both using some theoretical notions developed by Judith Butler and I engage in what others have called a hermeneutic of imagination, building on Elisabeth Schüssler Fiorenza's and Davina Lopez's work, among others.[7] However, even in this

---

the same way in ancient slavery (although it is often captured people who are used as slaves). Both however consists in the enslavement of millions of people to support an empire-like project. On slavery see, among others, Orlando Patterson, *Slavery and Social Death: A Comparative Study* (Cambridge, MA: Harvard University Press, 1982); Dale B. Martin, *Slavery as Salvation: The Metaphor of Slavery in Pauline Christianity* (New Haven, CT: Yale University Press, 1990); Keith R. Bradley, *Slavery and Society at Rome* (Cambridge: Cambridge University Press, 1994); J. Albert Harrill, *The Manumission of Slaves in Early Christianity* (Tübingen: Mohr Siebeck, 1995). and Richard A. Horsley, "The Slave Systems of Classical Antiquity and Their Reluctant Recognition by Modern Scholars," *Semeia* 83/84 (1998): 19–66.

6. Cohen, "Crossing the Boundary and Becoming a Jew," 24.
7. See Elisabeth Schüssler Fiorenza, *Wisdom Ways: Introducing Feminist Biblical Interpretation* (Maryknoll, NY: Orbis, 2001), and Davina Lopez, *Apostle to the Conquered: Reimagining Paul's Mission* (Minneapolis, MN: Fortress Press, 2010). Also,

imaginative enterprise, I am not aiming to reconstruct what life could have been like for those converted in such a manner.

This is the type of work that Antoinette Clark Wire does in her study of 1 Corinthians, reconstructing the theology of the women prophets, who use Paul's message to criticize him and, to use a popular contemporary concept, empower themselves.[8] Wire aims at a historically plausible reconstruction, which dominant interpretation has erased. While I find this type of work necessary (and I will dialogue with Wire's reading of 1 Corinthians), especially in the interpretation of New Testament texts which have long been read as detached from the more problematic cultural aspects of their historical milieu of production (slavery, patriarchy, to name the most obvious), my aim is different. I do not intend to reconstruct the historical response(s) of those unceremoniously converted in the New Testament. Rather, I aim to imaginatively think about what these conversions can teach about gender and gender embodiment.

Imagining Different Bodies and Power-Relationships

In his analysis of slave conversion, Earl describes, among others, the trickster mode. One finds the figure of the trickster in African-American slave narratives as the figure of Br'er Rabbit. It can also be used to describe Dionysus, an ambiguous figure that reaches his goals through his intelligence and his sense of cunning. In the trickster mode, conversion allows slaves to present stories in which the weakest character survives the abuses of his/her

---

what Brigitte Kahl says of her methodology in *Galatians Re-imagined: Reading with the Eyes of the Vanquished* (Minneapolis, MN: Fortress Press, 2010), 4: "Is there a new way to read and hear Paul as we have not read or heard him before? Can we re-imagine a 'liberating (of) Paul', in contrast to his prevailing representation as a misogynistic, homophobic advocate of a disembodied social conservatism and anti-Judaism–a representation firmly rooted in two millennia of Christian-occidental interpretation? Are we at a moment in history when we need to turn 'scripture' against 'tradition' again, holding the text over against its normative received reading? ... *Critical re-imagination* seeks to recover the precious seeds of an alternative meaning that never took root within the dominant history of occidental Pauline interpretation, especially after the emperor Constantine set in motion a history that would convert the Roman Empire to Christianity and conform Christianity to the empire." One can also think of Antoinette Clark Wire's work with 1 Corinthians: *The Corinthian Women Prophets: A Reconstruction through Paul's Rhetoric* (Eugene, OR: Wipf & Stock, 2003 [Minneapolis, MN: Fortress Press, 1990]) and Joseph A. Marchal, "Slaves as Wo/men and Unmen: Reflecting upon Euodia, Syntyche, and Epaphroditus in Philippi," in Marchal, ed., *The People beside Paul: The Philippian Assembly and History from Below* (Atlanta, GA: Society of Biblical Literature Press, 2015), 141–76.

8. See Wire, *Corinthian Women Prophets*.

master through his smartness and his tricks. The trickster does not hesitate to use deception and deceit—values perceived as contravening to the values of the master, and that are in tension with the ethical codes that the masters are trying to impose through their use of the Bible—to survive in a hostile environment. Thus, slaves have the possibility to introduce ambiguity in the dualist system imposed by the plantation masters. In the trickster mode, one cannot simply think of reality in terms of good and evil, with the Whites standing as Good and the Blacks representing Evil. As Earl indicates, the trickster mode "demanded that slaves blur the ethical and theological limits to force a re-organization of reality."[9]

For the invisible bodies in the household, with no voice, and little or no control over their bodies, what Paul presents in Romans 6 for example, where he exhorts the new Christ-believers to no longer bring fruits to their old patron, sin, but to re-direct their loyalty towards the god of Israel, can seem unpractical and as not really directed towards them. For someone (male or female, but particularly female) whose body remains an object at the disposal of one's master, it might seem absurd to hear that one's body should now be used for a new master. However, if one thinks of this in terms of the trickster, these new injunctions allow precisely questioning of the master's domination of the slave's body. If the master and the slave now share the same ultimate master, the conversion of the trickster might at least theoretically challenge the legitimacy of having one's body submitted to an individual who is not the true master of the slave. Conversion might allow re-evaluation of how each individual constructs his or her body. To trace this resistance, one can look at the masters' disciplinary responses. The disciplinary responses indicate points of resistance, spaces where bodies and relationships are proposing alternatives to the dominant system. They are points of agency and subjectivity. In the New Testament, we might have access to these points of friction through the disciplinary texts that respond to them. In Paul, and in the Pauline legacy even more strongly, we find traces of the struggles at play to discipline bodies, for example, in texts such as 1 Corinthians 11.3-16, 14.34-35; Ephesians 6.1-9; Colossians 3.18–4.1; 1 Timothy 2.8–3.1, 6.1-2; Titus 2.1-10.

Here, I do not want to evaluate whether the various scholarly reconstructions of the response to Paul's (or Pauline) disciplinary texts are plausible or if there were really women whose social status could have allowed the

---

9. Earl, "Critique of Slave Conversion Consciousness," 10. A good narrative illustration of trickster techniques is found in Sue Monk Kidd, *The Invention of Wings* (New York: Viking, 2014). See also on the figure of the trickster, Claudia V. Camp, "Wise and Strange: An Interpretation of the Female Imagery in Proverbs in Light of Trickster Mythology," *Semeia* 42 (1988): 14–36.

changes that scholars sometimes presuppose. Rather, I am thinking about the way conversion can be analyzed as impacting the body, and religious practices, in imagining what types of changes can be emerge when one thinks theoretically about conversion of women in particular. In analyzing this change, I focus less on a set of beliefs and on theological commitments, the usual *loci* where conversion is discussed, but more on practices. I follow here a recent pattern in religious studies, that Constance M. Furey also identifies, in concentrating more on the body and religious practices.[10] These studies insist on the body as a site of resistance, presenting physicality as "resistant to social conditioning."[11] One can imagine the possible responses of these other bodies affected by their own conversion or by the conversion of their husbands, heads of household, masters. We can also reflect on how agency is understood in those conversions involving other bodies. One can look at agency, as Furey suggests when she summarizes anthropologist Mary Keller's work, as not dependent on individual subjectivities, but as relying on "interrelationships of bodies and systems of power."[12] Looking particularly at 1 Corinthians, I am exploring how scholars have seen this control take place and I am presenting how scholars reconstruct women's responses to this control. Then, using Judith Butler's work in *Bodies That Matter*, I reflect on the relationship between body and power and how one can today imagine alternative embodying of genders.

Women in Conversion

In her work on 1 Corinthians, Wire reconstructs the response of the Corinthian women to Paul and insists that these women understand Christ as being mediated through their own practices, be it prophecy or glossolalia. For them, Christ offers a "dynamic life," which they express in their own bodies and practices.[13] This understanding of Christ and the women's assurance that they contribute to mediating Christ to the communities grant them an agency and a freedom which Paul, according to Wire, has a hard time accepting and that he brings under control on several occasions. For Wire, the women in Corinth are not keen on accepting Paul's plea for unity and to care for the weaker member. Indeed, their conversion, willing or not,

---

10. See Constance M. Furey, "Body, Society, and Subjectivity in Religious Studies," *Journal of the American Academy of Religion* 80.1 (2012): 7–33
11. See Furey, "Body, Society and Subjectivity," 13.
12. See Furey, "Body, Society and Subjectivity," 19. See Mary Keller's work on possessed women in Zimbabwe and Malaysia: *The Hammer and the Flute: Women, Power, and Spirit Possession* (Baltimore, MD: The John Hopkins University Press, 2002).
13. See Wire, *Corinthian Women Prophets*, 38.

improves their position in society, an advantage they might not be eager to give up. Wire writes that in Corinth, the woman prophet "experienced a surge of status in wisdom, power, and honor."[14] This in turn "reshaped her ethnic identity, caste, and gender in ways that give her more scope."[15] With this surge in status comes also an increase in agency for women, allowing them more control over their bodies, for example. For Wire, this can be reconstructed from the way women in Corinth abstain from sexual relationships, but it can also be seen in the freedom women in Corinth have towards speech. Wire argues that the women in Corinth understand themselves as set apart for communion with God, and sexual abstinence might have been part of their preparations for prayer and prophecy.[16] Women, and slave women particularly, would have gained a control over their bodies previously unavailable to them. This change would have been particularly perceptible for non-Jewish slave women in Corinth, whose status would have risen with their inclusion in the community.[17] Wire concludes: "the women of Corinth appear to have claimed what they lacked, authority over their own bodies (7:4)."[18]

Another example which analyzes the social consequences of cults marked by spiritual experiences, such as prophecy, possession, glossolalia, or ecstasy, is an older study of Dionysiac cults in ancient Greece.[19] In her analysis, Ross Shepard Kraemer reaches the conclusion that the cult of Dionysus, like other ecstatic religious phenomena, participates in compensating for the low social status of women in classical Greece. She uses the work of anthropologist Ioan M. Lewis to indicate that possession cults, here in Africa and the Caribbean, "are fundamentally mechanisms for the expression of aggression and hostility by the powerless against the powerful, combined with some measure of at least temporary redress, confined within the limits of socially nondestructive activities."[20] In her perspective, the Dionysiac cult functions as a regulatory mechanism for social injustices:

14. Wire, *Corinthian Women Prophets*, 65
15. Wire, *Corinthian Women Prophets*, 65.
16. See Wire, *Corinthian Women Prophets*, 83.
17. See Wire, *Corinthian Women Prophets*, 67.
18. Wire, *Corinthian Women Prophets,* 93.
19. Ross Shepard Kraemer, "Ecstasy and Possession: The Attraction of Women to the Cult of Dionysus," *Harvard Theological Review* 72.1/2 (1979): 55–80. See also on the discussion of the attraction of women to various cults, the article by Judith M. Lieu, "The 'Attraction of Women' in/to Early Judaism and Christianity: Gender and the Politics of Conversion," *Journal for the Study of the New Testament* 72 (1998): 5–22.
20. Kraemer, "Ecstasy and Possession," 75. She bases her observations on Ioan M. Lewis, *Ecstatic Religion: An Anthropological Study of Spirit Possession and Shamanism* (Harmondsworth: Penguin, 1971).

"possession thus appears to neutralize the potentially destructive emotions felt by oppressed individuals of a society by permitting them to be vented through highly institutionalized, regulated forms."[21] The women involved in Dionysiac rites are able to temporarily leave the home, and their obligations inside the home. According to Kraemer, women's involvement in the cult of Dionysus might even have served, in the long term, to bring some "social prestige and manipulatory powers,"[22] making it a desirable alternative to "normative male-dominated worship."[23] However, the improvements for Greek women were temporary and functioned mostly as an outlet for their frustrations and deprivations.

Finally, in an analysis of glossolalic women in twentieth-century Appalachian churches, Mary McClintock Fulkerson comes to a similar conclusion concerning the position of women involved in glossolalic experiences: their status improves during worship, but their position at home remains subordinated.[24] In her article on tongue-speaking women in Corinth, Lee A. Johnson uses McClintock Fulkerson's study to discuss the "prominent role of women in the Pauline communities." In a striking parallel to what Kraemer writes about ancient Greek women, Johnson notes that, in Pentecostal Appalachian churches, the practice of tongue-speaking affords some space for women to experience their body and social role differently:

> Those women adept at tongues-speaking in Pentecostal Appalachian churches enjoy advanced social standing because of their spiritual gift. Most of these women have little education, but with the ability to speak in tongues comes the self-confidence that they are instruments of God … In addition, the usual somatic boundaries that are especially rigid for women in conservative, patriarchal groups are often transgressed during a glossolalic service … Therefore, within these tongues-speaking communities, women have limited circumstances within which the normal gender restrictions are relaxed.[25]

Johnson points out that the body becomes a site of freedom in glossolalic experiences for the women of the Pentecostal Appalachian churches. However, this freedom is carefully limited to "inspired speech moments."[26] Outside of worship, "dominant patriarchal ethic regains its pre-eminence."[27]

---

21. Kraemer, "Ecstasy and Possession," 77.
22. Kraemer, "Ecstasy and Possession," 79.
23. Kraemer, "Ecstasy and Possession," 79.
24. See Mary McClintock Fulkerson, *Changing the Subject: Women's Discourses and Feminist Theology* (Minneapolis, MN: Fortress Press, 1994), as quoted by Lee A. Johnson, "Women and Glossolalia in Pauline Communities: The Relationship between Pneumatic Gifts and Authority," *Biblical Interpretation* 21.2 (2013): 196–214.
25. Johnson, "Women and Glossolalia in Pauline Communities," 204.
26. Johnson, "Women and Glossolalia in Pauline Communities," 207.
27. Johnson, "Women and Glossolalia in Pauline Communities," 207.

This detour through the observations of actual practices in Appalachian churches allows Johnson to ask whether Paul also restricts "the non-traditional activities of women to the worship setting."[28] She argues that Paul in fact seeks strict control over somatic displays of the spirit in worship. In relationship to Paul's instructions in 1 Corinthians 11, she writes: "the strictures that Paul describes are more physically confining than the commonplace activity in Pentecostal Appalachian churches, where woman [sic] describe disheveled dress and hair during their worship experience."[29] In agreement with Wire, she affirms that Paul seeks to discipline the Corinthian women, to limit their participation in worship and to make it subordinate to male authority.[30]

For the three works that I have briefly surveyed, ecstasy, possession, glossolalia, and prophecy all have the potential to function as subversive tools to empower members of the lower social classes to take control of their bodies and regain some agency. Wire indicates, and Johnson's reference to glossolalic women in Appalachian Pentecostal churches seems to support this, that it might precisely have been their lower education and their simplicity that contributed to these women being perceived as channels for the divine message.[31] Their link to the divinity advantaged them in the community. Notwithstanding whether these reconstructions are appropriate readings of the material or not, I am interested in seeing how these readings construct a certain female body, and how this female body can then be involved in various relationships of power.

---

28. Johnson, "Women and Glossolalia in Pauline Communities," 208.
29. Johnson, "Women and Glossolalia in Pauline Communities," 209.
30. Anders Eriksson, "'Women Tongue Speakers, Be Silent': A Reconstruction through Paul's Rhetoric," *Biblical Interpretation* 6.1 (1998): 80–104, here 93–4 agrees with this analysis of Paul's restrictions on women's speech. In addition, one can also think of Jorunn Økland, *Women in Their Place: Paul and the Corinthian Discourse of Gender and Sanctuary* (London: T&T Clark, 2005), which focuses more specifically on the way space is gendered in Antiquity. Økland also reflects on the way gender is constructed in Antiquity.
31. See Wire, *Corinthian Women Prophets*, 95, in particular about the virgins mentioned in ch. 7. She refers to a quote by Plutarch explaining the origins of the young virgin dedicated to the Delphic oracle: "Having been brought up in the home of poor peasants, she brings nothing as the result of technical skill or of any other expertness or faculty, as she goes down into the shrine" (Plutarch, *The Oracles at Delphi*). It is another question entirely whether the Pythian prophet at the Delphic oracle perceived herself as elevated in her own status, and gained more independence in the community. Yet another question is to discuss how the perception of women as passive recipients of the spirit can function as an emancipatory tool.

Body/Power

Based on Wire's reading and its interactions with other studies, conversion to, or membership in, groups that have mystical tendencies is presented as meaning greater freedom and greater control over the female body. For example, Wire reconstructs women's withdrawal from sexual relationships in 1 Corinthians 7 as allowing certain women to gain more control over their own bodies, a control Paul is eager to regain or to give back to the husbands. Dialoguing with Judith Butler, I want to analyze the dynamics involved in the creation or, as Butler would say, the materialization[32] and disciplining of various kinds of bodies.

If one keeps Butler in mind, one can reflect upon the norms, repeated and disrupted, to produce various bodies, and materialize sex. It might not, of course, historically correspond to the bodies of converted women in the Corinthian communities, but it might provide tools to reclaim texts about women in the New Testament, texts that have, for a part, negative effects on women, not only in the Corinthian communities, but later as well.[33] Because of that concern in materializing sex, I am particularly interested in Butler's *Bodies That Matter*. Here, Butler aims to work out more carefully her understanding of gender and sex. In particular, as she indicates at the beginning of *Bodies That Matter*, she explains that she had been reproached for neglecting the materiality of the body, because she insisted that "bodies were in some way *constructed.*"[34] At the same time, after the publication of *Gender Trouble*, she was criticized for constructing gender as something that one can just put on every morning and take off at night.[35] What is implied in this critique is the suspicion that Butler reintroduces a willful subject "at the center of a

---

32. See Judith Butler, *Bodies That Matter: On the Discursive Limits of Sex* (London: Routledge, 1993).

33. The texts that I have already quoted earlier (1 Cor. 11.3-16, 14.34-35; Eph. 6.1-9; Col. 3.18–4.1; 1 Tim. 2.8–3.1, 6.1-2; Tit. 2.1-10) come to mind of course. I am also thinking of texts like 1 Pet. 3.1 or Eph. 5.22 sometimes used to force women to stay in abusive relationships (Rosinah Mmannana Gabaitse made this point at a presentation at the 2016 SBL meeting in San Antonio: "Pentecostal Hermeneutic and Violence against Women within Marriage"). Margaret Atwood's *The Handmaid's Tale* (1985) is a powerful fictional representation of the violence that can be done to women on the basis of the Bible, in a so-called Christian world.

34. Butler, *Bodies That Matter*, ix.

35. See Butler, *Bodies That Matter*, ix: "… if I were to argue that genders are performative, that could mean that I thought that one woke in the morning, perused the closet or some more open space for the gender of choice, donned that gender for the day, and then restored the garment to its place."

project whose emphasis on construction seems to be quite opposed to such a notion."[36]

In *Bodies That Matter*, Butler thus sets out to complicate her analysis of the construction or materialization of sex and the body, but she also develops questions of agency and autonomy more carefully. She asks the following questions: "… how are we to understand the constitutive and compelling status of gender norms without falling into the trap of cultural determinism? How precisely are we to understand the ritualized repetition by which such norms produce and stabilize not only the effects of gender but the materiality of sex?" I cannot answer these questions for the Corinthian women, of course. But I want to think with Butler about the repetitions that scholars see these women practice in the community. I also want to see how these reconstructed practices can challenge gender norms and materialize a new sex, or a new understanding of gender. Finally, in the relationships of power that these behaviors call into question, and in particular in the disciplining that occurs in the Pauline tradition, I aim to theoretically reconstruct the outside space created by Paul's letters when he tries to normalize the women's practices. If one keeps in mind what Butler says about the production of abject spaces as corollary to the production of various subjects, it should in principle exist.[37] Here, regardless of whether it was occupied or not, I want to reclaim this space for thinking about gender today.

As Butler writes in *Bodies That Matter*, "'sex' is an ideal construct which is forcibly materialized through time. It is not a simple fact or static condition of a body, but a process whereby regulatory norms materialize 'sex' and achieve this materialization through a forcible reiteration of those norms."[38] In first-century Corinth, what is at stake, from this perspective, is a power struggle over which norms should produce which type of sexed body. Paul is ready to challenge some ways in which women can be involved inside the community of Christ-believers. One sees from the list of his co-workers that some women played an important role in Paul's mission. In 1 Corinthians,

---

36. Butler, *Bodies That Matter*, ix.
37. See Butler, *Bodies That Matter*, xiii: "[The] exclusionary matrix by which subjects are formed thus requires the simultaneous production of a domain of abject beings, those who are not yet 'subjects', but who form the constitutive outside to the domain of the subject. The abject designates here precisely those 'unlivable' and 'uninhabitable' zones of social life which are nevertheless densely populated by those who do not enjoy the status of the subject, but whose living under the sign of the 'unlivable' is required to circumscribe the domain of the subject. This zone of uninhabitability will constitute the defining limit of the subject's domain; it will constitute that site of dreaded identification against which—and by virtue of which—the domain of the subject will circumscribe its own claim to autonomy and to life."
38. Butler, *Bodies That Matter*, xii.

he talks about Chloe (1.11) and presents her as able to send him emissaries (maybe slaves)[39]; he also mentions Prisca (16.19, and one also finds her in Rom. 16.3), who with Aquila helped him in his missions and took care of him. They too held an assembly in their house. Finally, there is Phoebe, mentioned in Romans 16.1-2, presented as a *diakonos* of the church and a benefactor or patron (*prostasis*). However, when confronted with concrete behaviors in Corinth, Paul asserts that the regulatory norms that control the production of women's body in the first century need to remain in place. In the first century, the feminine sex would have been equated with a series of norms that contributed to the materialization of a certain type of bodies.[40] These norms include "the hierarchical pattern of the family, in which the male was always superior to the female."[41] In the community of Corinth, as Paul would like to have it, these bodies were limited to the home, asked to be silent in public and to cover their hair. Passages like 1 Corinthians 11.2-16 or 14.34-36 reveal as much.

In 1 Corinthians 11, Paul recognizes the presence of praying and prophesying women in Corinth but disciplines them in asking them to remain veiled in the assembly. What did it mean for these women to prophesy with their heads uncovered?[42] What concerns me here is that the veiling of the head, or the wearing of one's hair in a bound fashion, and not loosely, is a matter of authority for Paul, and proper hierarchical structure. The way women wear their hair in Corinth challenged Paul's authority and the organization of a community centered around men. One can see from portraits and statues of noble women from the first century that, in everyday life, their hair, even though it was not veiled, was not worn in a loose fashion but in elaborate hairdos that contained it tightly. When they are represented involved in religious rituals, the same women are portrayed with their heads covered with a veil.[43] The Corinthian women in contrast were involved in

---

39. See Gerd Theissen, "La stratification sociale de la communauté corinthienne," in Theissen, *Histoire sociale du christianisme primitif: Jésus-Paul-Jean* (Geneva: Labor et Fides, 1996), 91–138, here 119.

40. See Butler, *Bodies That Matter*, xii.

41. Wayne A. Meeks, *The First Urban Christians: The Social World of the Apostle Paul* (2nd edn.; New Haven, CT: Yale University Press, 2003 [1983]), 23.

42. Wire sees analogies to this behavior in women of Jewish and Christian literature such as "Aseneth or Thecla, who put aside women's dress or head covering when taking on new religious responsibility," but for her, the debate with Paul lies in interpreting the creation account in Genesis, in particular Gen. 1.27 ("So God created humankind in his image, in the image of God he created them; male and female he created them").

43. See for example, two heads of Livia, Augustus' second wife, traditionally represented as a model of virtue, dating from the first century. For all the representations, see: Catalogue from the Augustus exhibit at the Grand Palais, Paris (19 March–13 July

public religious rituals with uncovered heads. In this physical manifestation, they contribute to the manifestation of a new body. This body does not match the physical incarnation of piety by upper-class women in Roman rituals. It proposes other ways of performing female involvement in religion. Attached to the representation of the body of the pious woman in Greco-Roman society were also ideals of virtue, modesty, and decency.[44] Controlled hair, covered head, incarnated feminine virtue, modesty, and decency.

2014): *Auguste. Rome, Scuderie del Quirinale 18 octobre 2013–9 février 2014; Paris, Grand Palais, Galeries Nationales 19 mars–13 juillet 2014* (Paris: Réunion des musées nationaux, 2014). One, in white marble, was found in Béziers in 1844, and dates from the end of the first century BCE or the beginning of the first century CE, and represents Livia with her hair carefully parted in the middle, and bound in the back, in imitation of classical models from Greece. The other was found in Egypt in 1892 and is made from greywacke. It is dated to 20 CE and represents Livia wearing a thin net over her hair, the *reticulatum*. Her hairdo is called *nodus* hairdo, with a broad puffing lock of hair brought back over the forehead (39. Tête de Livie and 40. Tête de Livie, p. 94. Number 40 can be consulted here: http://cartelfr.louvre.fr/cartelfr/visite?srv=car_not_frame&idNotice=2782&langue=fr accessed on 18 March 2016). The same hairdo adorns another head of Livia found in Glanum, and dating to 4–14 CE, as well as another head of an unknown woman, also found in Glanum (246. portrait de Livie and 247. Portrait d'une inconnue, p. 271). In statues where Livia is portrayed as accomplishing a religious ritual, or portrayed as a goddess, she can be represented with a veil over her head. See, e.g., a monumental statue (height 2,20 m) of Livia as Ceres or Fortuna, dating to the second quarter of the first century CE where Livia is represented with a *himation* held with a diadem over her head (137. Livia en Cérès ou Fortuna, p. 191). See also a statue of Livia depicted as praying. It was found in 1778–1779 in Otricoli and dates from the Tiberian era. In this white marble statue, Livia is represented with a large coat that surrounds her and covers her head (264. Livie en orante, p. 289 and 290). This statue has emulated copies which are usually larger than life, and represent the imperial spouses or princesses as priestesses of the imperial cult. In contrast, on the décors of homes, probably in the private space, that represent for example scenes of the Dyonisiac rites, the maenads are represented with flowing hair. See for example, the "Plaque Campana," which dates to the first century BCE, and represents Dionysiac rites, with two satyrs and a maenad (141. Plaque Campana avec satyres et ménades, p. 206, which can also be found here http://cartelfr.louvre.fr/cartelfr/visite?srv=car_not_frame&idNotice=2717&langue=fr consulted on 18 March 2016). For Livia, see: Elizabeth Bartman, *Portraits of Livia: Imaging the Imperial Woman in Augustan Rome* (Cambridge University Press: Cambridge, 1999). See also L. Eurnee-van Zwet, "Fashion in Women's Hairdress in the First Century of the Roman Empire," *Bulletin Antieke Beschaving*, 31 (1957): 1–22.

44. Here too Livia is a good example. She is presented as a model of virtue in Augustus' propaganda in favor of marriage. See for example, the identification of Livia with Ceres: "The identification of Livia with Ceres was very useful in that the goddess seemed to represent a variety of symbols. Not only was the connection with fertility—καρπόφορος—peace and prosperity, but the ancient myth of Ceres and Proserpina (Demeter and Kore) represented the virtues of chastity and motherhood. Ceres was the ideal symbol for the Augustan program and Livia as the grand mother played the role perfectly." See Fred

From my point of view, reading with Butler, the women in Corinth, when they challenge the norms, repeatedly, or embody deviant behaviors, are creating a new sex. It is of course impossible, and perhaps not particularly interesting, to know today whether these women consciously materialized this new sex. However, the disturbances their behaviors occasion suggests that, as Butler writes, we can think of sex in Paul's time as "not simply what one has, or a static description of what one is."[45] Rather, thinking with Butler allows us to understand something about the sex and gender of the women in Corinth and to complexify the categories, to move away from the binary man/woman towards a spectrum where one could be more, or less, male. Joseph Marchal identifies similar concerns when discussing the roles of three characters in Paul's epistle to the Philippians (Euodia, Syntyche, and Epaphroditus). In reconstructing ancient conceptions of gender, he uses the terms wo/men and unmen, "to understand the specific ways in which people like the enslaved and manumitted were placed in terms of gendered status."[46] Wo/men, a term coined by Elisabeth Schüssler Fiorenza, complicates an essentializing understanding of "woman," and allows the inclusion of women in the generic "people."[47] Wo/men and unmen can describe "non-persons" who "likely included the enslaved and manumitted in the ancient world"[48] and at least some women. Wo/men can include male that were not men as well as women, as we will see.

Butler writes: sex "will be one of the norms by which the 'one' becomes viable at all, that which qualifies a body for life within the domain of cultural intelligibility."[49] Sex and the body are thus sites for a contestation of power,

---

Strickert, "The First Woman to be Portrayed on a Jewish Coin: Julia Sebaste," *Journal for the Study of Judaism in the Persian, Hellenistic and Roman Period* 33.1 (2002): 65–91, here 79–80.

45. Butler, *Bodies That Matter*, xii. On gender in Antiquity see, e.g., Jonathan Walters, "'No More than a Boy': The Shifting Construction of Masculinity from Ancient Greece to the Middle Ages," *Gender and History* 5 (1991): 20–33. Also, Jonathan Walters, "Invading the Roman Body: Manliness and Impenetrability in Roman Thought," in Judith P. Hallett and Marilyn B. Skinner, eds., *Roman Sexualities* (Princeton, NJ: Princeton University Press, 1997), 29–43. Quoted here in Marchal, "Slaves as Wo/men and Unmen."

46. Marchal, "Slaves as Wo/men and Unmen," 151.

47. See Marchal, "Slaves as Wo/men and Unmen," 152. As Marchal notes, the spelling first appears in Elisabeth Schüssler Fiorenza, *Jesus: Miriam's Child, Sophia's Prophet; Critical Issues in Feminist Christology* (New York: Continuum, 1994). Marchal points out that it is defined in Schüssler Fiorenza, *Rhetoric and Ethic: The Politics of Biblical Studies* (Minneapolis, MN: Fortress Press, 1999), ix and Schüssler Fiorenza, *Wisdom Ways*, 57–9, 107–9 and 216.

48. Marchal, "Slaves as Wo/men and Unmen," 153.

49. Butler, *Bodies That Matter*, xii.

as well as a sign of intelligibility in the world. Something is understood about the person through its body. If the body is constructed through a ritualized repetition of norms,[50] the challenging of these norms, the practices of deviant bodily behaviors modifies the conception one would have of bodies, and women's bodies in particular. For the Greco-Roman world, women's bodies were only women's bodies if they were at the disposition of the males surrounding them, to be penetrated, but also to insure various tasks in the house. If these bodies become highly visible and loud bodies, in prophesying publicly for example, they no longer fit the traditional description of women. They escape their status as nonpersons. In their challenge of the norms, they are, as Butler writes, no longer qualified for "life within the domain of cultural intelligibility." They need to be disciplined, to fit what is culturally acceptable and comprehensible at the time, to be understood, again, as women. Otherwise, they are a liminal category that the ancient world cannot grasp: neither male, nor female. Or rather, they do not fit in the ancient understanding of gender, where one was either man, or not-man. As Marchal notes, "only certain kinds of males are 'men'—elite, educated, freeborn propertied, imperial, and typically from particular racial/ethnic groups —who rule all who might be wo/men—females but also non-elite, uneducated, enslaved, subaltern, and/or often racially or ethnically dominated groups of males."[51] The behavior of the Corinthian women could call this into question, and thus construct them as male.[52] A group who by definition belongs to the "unmen" category moves to the "male" category, but retains its biologically female characteristics. In Paul's case, the norms for sex and genders are too tightly drawn to allow for an embodying of

50. Butler, *Bodies That Matter*, ix.
51. Marchal, "Slaves as Wo/men and Unmen," 154. Marchal also refers Stephen D. Moore, "Que(e)rying Paul: Preliminary Questions," in David J. A. Clines and Stephen D. Moore, eds., *Auguries: The Jubilee Volume of the Sheffield Department of Biblical Studies* (Sheffield: Sheffield Academic Press, 1998), 249–74.
52. There are other cases in ancient literature of women made male. One can think of Mary at the end of *The Gospel of Thomas*, but it is also present in stories about martyrs (Perpetua, for example) and in the apocryphal story about Thecla, in *Acts of Thecla*. In *Joseph and Aseneth*, Aseneth is also presented as having the face of a young man at the end of the process of her transformation. All these examples are discussed by Elizabeth Castelli, "'I Will Make Mary Male': Pieties of the Body and Gender Transformation of Early Christian Women in Late Antiquity," in Julia Epstein and Kristina Straub, eds., *Bodyguards: The Cultural Contexts of Gender Ambiguity* (New York: Routledge, 1991), 29–49. See for an analysis of similar themes but in discussion with the myth of the primal androgyne, Daniel Boyarin, *Galatians and Gender Trouble: Primal Androgyny and the First-Century Origins of a Feminist Dilemma. Protocol of the Colloquy of the Center for Hermeneutical Studies, 5 April 1992*, ed. Christopher Ocker (Berkeley, CA: Center for Hermeneutical Studies, 1995).

an in-between gender, that would perform some of the prerogatives of the male sex while biologically being female. For Paul, these women who are not materializing their sex in the correct manner need to be put back in the proper category. In his world, this happens by veiling and silencing them. Thus, as Johnson also remarks, Paul can be read through Butler as aiming at "a traditional somatic control for the Corinthian women in worship."[53]

This confusion over sex-materialization might also explain why Paul does not mention the pair "male/female" in 1 Corinthians 12.13, when he uses the (probably) baptismal creed also mentioned in Galatians 3.28. In 1 Corinthians 12.13, he says "For in the one Spirit we were all baptized into one body—Jews or Greeks, slaves or free—and we were all made to drink of one Spirit." He might refrain from suppressing the difference between male and female, because in the Corinthian community, it matters to him very much to distinguish between women and men.

In a Butlerian reading, the space produced by these women in Corinth corresponds to the "abject space" created by the formation of legitimate male and female bodies. Butler helps to delineate that one can think about bodies in terms of proper space. The legitimate male and female bodies know their proper place: legitimate female bodies belong inside the house, they are subordinated to the head of the household, they are limited in their public speech; legitimate male bodies are the ones who can speak publicly, they control worship, and they are entitled to their sexual desire if they are unable to refrain from it. As Butler writes, the formation of legitimate subjects produces a "domain of abject beings, those who are not yet 'subjects' but who form the constitutive outside to the domain of the subject."[54] This zone of the abject functions as a necessary pendant for the subject's domain. As Paul, and the history of interpretation with him, creates a community made of male, disciplined, bodies, which he views as acceptable, a space for what one might perceive as "abject beings" is produced, people (male or female) who do not perform their sex as they should. These people, wo/men, unmen, "will constitute that site of dreaded identification against which—and by virtue of which—the domain of the subject will circumscribe its own claim to autonomy and to life."[55] From the perspective of the Butlerian interpreter, Paul's founding gesture as father of a specific community that should materialize docile bodies also produces an abject outside that the indocile bodies of those who are not male in the way ancient people thought of as male (namely free, elite, and male) can employ—then

---

53. Johnson, "Women and Glossolalia in Pauline Communities," 209.
54. Butler, *Bodies That Matter*, xiii.
55. Butler, *Bodies That Matter*, xiii.

and today—as "a critical resource"[56] to redefine what counts as a legitimate and intelligible experience of Christ and of the spirit. This abject space can precisely be the space where they are produced as subjects.

Key to their construction of this abject space as something that unmen and wo/men can use to their advantage might precisely be Paul's preaching reported in 1 Corinthians 12.13, that affirms that the Christ-believers are baptized in one body, the body of Christ. Paul sometimes exhorts his addressees, for example in Galatians 3.27— right before the baptismal formula also used in 1 Corinthians—and in Romans 13.14, to be clothed in Christ Jesus, to wear Christ as clothing. (The same verb *enduomai* is used, see Rom. 13.14: "Instead, put on the Lord Jesus Christ, and make no provision for the flesh, to gratify its desires"; Gal. 3.27: "As many of you as were baptized into Christ have clothed yourselves with Christ.") We are free to imagine (and indeed we can only imagine, because we have no direct access to these women and how they might have understood their conversion) that, for women who were limited in their agency and constrained in their movements because of the dominant patriarchal ideologies of the ancient world, putting on the body of the male Christ might have suggested or allowed transgressive behaviors, that challenged the way sex was usually performed. We can see these women as queering the expectations related to their sex and using a Pauline doctrine to their own advantage. We can read them as being empowered to do so because the donning of a male body allowed them to perform their own female body in new ways. I would refrain from saying that they gain agency because they can now perform like males in a world that recognized agency as the privilege of free, male adults. But they can perform their female sex in a different way, one that challenges what Paul (and perhaps others around him) has learned to expect from women.

It might be possible to say that they now "pass" as males, to use another notion developed by Butler in *Bodies That Matter*.[57] The problem with "passing," however, as Butler notes, is that it might hide precisely what needs to be exposed and challenged. Daniel Boyarin remarks for example that it would not have been particularly destabilizing to cease being

---

56. Butler, *Bodies That Matter*, xiii.
57. For "passing" in Butler, see *Bodies That Matter*, 122–38. This calls to mind the idea of "camping" developed by Susan Sontag in particular (see Susan Sontag, "Notes on 'Camp'," in *Against Interpretation and Other Essays* [New York: Picador, 1990], 275–92. The essay itself dates to 1964). I do not have the time or the space to develop this here, but it seems that figures of female martyrs passing as male (for example, Thecla) would provide good material for such an analysis.

a woman by remaining a virgin or by renouncing sexuality.[58] However, a woman, who was not a virgin or chaste, but might have still embodied some of the practices reserved to men, could embody womanhood in a new way, that escaped patriarchal categories. Butler suggests that third way, in the abject space. With the notion of "abject beings," Butler helps define a field that is neither male nor female, but that can be occupied by people neglected by the usual subject-making strategies of power. It might also be the space where norms around sex and gender are challenged, the spaces that allow the concept of gender not as binary, but as a cursor on a line which, for Antiquity, goes from unman to man. In the field of "abject-beings," Christ-believers can embody behaviors and practices that incarnate their conversion in ways that let them find forms of activity inside the patriarchal structures of Antiquity and of our contemporary world.

It invites us to rethink the notion of agency in conversion and the way conversion can be embodied. This conversion to a new space is not so much a conversion from an "old" religion to a new one, from Judaism to Christianity for example. Rather it is the new use of the cultural norms put in place by what Schüssler Fiorenza identifies as kyriarchy[59] to create space for agency and resistance. Conversion here happens to be related to transgressing norms. It is a change from one set of norms to another. In the case of Paul, it is inside religious norms, but it could also happen outside of religion. In my analysis of the way women use their bodies to incarnate their conversion, agency is not constructed in terms of "individual subjectivities, but in interrelationships of bodies and systems of power."[60] In these interrelationships of bodies and systems of power, women gain the status of agents. Thinking of conversion in terms of body and power means thinking about these women not as "freely volitional subject,"[61] a self that can make his or her own decisions about religious choice. It is more about "activity" and "constraint" than about freedom or lack of freedom.[62]

In the household conversions I presented at the beginning of this chapter, one can imagine that the decision of the master of the household (female in

---

58. Boyarin, *Galatians and Gender Trouble*, 31. Boyarin indicates that virginity allowed to erase gender and to become androgynous.

59. Schüssler Fiorenza, *Wisdom Ways*, 211 defines the term in the following manner: "Kyriarchy is a socio-political system of domination in which elite educated propertied men hold over wo/men and other men. Kyriarchy is best theorized as a complex pyramidal system of intersecting multiplicative social structures of superordination and subordination, or ruling and oppression." As quoted in Marchal, "Slaves as Wo/men and Unmen," 155.

60. Furey, "Body, Society and Subjectivity," 19

61. Furey, "Body, Society, and Subjectivity," 9.

62. See Furey, "Body, Society, and Subjectivity," 9.

the case of Lydia, male in the case of the jailor) affected various members of the household in different ways. Some might have found themselves at the margins of the subject space delineated by the new Christ-believers. In this abject space, some might have found the path of the trickster, using norms to their advantages, blurring the boundaries between decency and indecency, between good and evil, to delineate their own space for agency and resistance. Butler's analysis of the normalization of gender and sex pushes us to think that this agency and resistance might have materialized itself bodily, in various practices that had the potential to reflect the household's own perception of the new piety of the master. The anonymity of household conversions reminds us that conversion should not be reduced to the explicit expression of beliefs and theological doctrines. We might not have traces of explicit confessions for members of the household, yet in the practices which the members of the household embody, in the way they wear their hair, and participate in worship, these members might gain agency in the new religion that was developing, and experience a conversion concerning their agency and their power over constraints. In the process, they push the boundaries of acceptable behaviors, embracing and occupying the space of the abject as the one where they are free to materialize their sex and their piety in their own ways. They also redefine what conversion might cover: not a confessional change, but a changed look at traditional norms.

Biographical Note

Since 2013, Valérie Nicolet has been "maîtresse de conférences" at the Institut protestant de théologie (faculté de Paris), where she teaches New Testament and Ancient Greek. In her research, she focuses on the Pauline letters. At the moment, she is working on the rhetorical construction of the law in Galatians. Her scholarship highlights interdisciplinary approaches, more prominently with philosophy, and recently, with queer theory. She has published a book on the construction of the self in Romans, *Constructing the Self: Thinking with Paul and Michel Foucault* (Tübingen: Mohr Siebeck, 2012).

Bibliography

Auguste. Rome, Scuderie del Quirinale 18 octobre 2013–9 février 2014; Paris, Grand Palais, Galeries Nationales 19 mars–13 juillet 2014. Paris: Réunion des musées nationaux, 2014.

Bartman, Elizabeth. *Portraits of Livia: Imaging the Imperial Woman in Augustan Rome*. Cambridge University Press: Cambridge, 1999.

Boyarin, Daniel. *Galatians and Gender Trouble: Primal Androgyny and the First-Century*

Origins of a Feminist Dilemma. Protocol of the Colloquy of the Center for Hermeneutical Studies, 5 April 1992. Edited by Christopher Ocker. Berkeley, CA: Center for Hermeneutical Studies, 1995.

Bradley, Keith R. *Slavery and Society at Rome*. Cambridge: Cambridge University Press, 1994. https://doi.org/10.1017/CBO9780511815386

Butler, Judith. *Bodies That Matter: On the Discursive Limits of Sex*. London: Routledge, 1993.

Camp, Claudia V. "Wise and Strange: An Interpretation of the Female Imagery in Proverbs in Light of Trickster Mythology," *Semeia* 42 (1988): 14–36.

Castelli, Elizabeth. "'I Will Make Mary Male': Pieties of the Body and Gender Transformation of Early Christian Women in Late Antiquity," 29–49 in *Bodyguards: The Cultural Contexts of Gender Ambiguity*. Edited by Julia Epstein and Kristina Straub. New York: Routledge, 1991.

Cohen, Shaye J. D. "Crossing the Boundary and Becoming a Jew," *The Harvard Theological Review* 82.1 (1989): 13–33. https://doi.org/10.1017/S001781600001600X

Earl, Riggins R, Jr. "A Critique of Slave Conversion Consciousness: Its Implications for Black Theology and Ethics," *Journal of the I.T.C.* 17.1/2 (1989–1990): 1–18.

Eriksson, Anders. "'Women Tongue Speakers, Be Silent': A Reconstruction through Paul's Rhetoric," *Biblical Interpretation* 6.1 (1998): 80–104. https://doi.org/10.1163/156851598X00237

Eurnee-van Zwet, L. "Fashion in Women's Hairdress in the First Century of the Roman Empire," *Bulletin Antieke Beschaving* 31 (1957): 1–22.

Furey, Constance M. "Body, Society, and Subjectivity in Religious Studies," *Journal of the American Academy of Religion* 80.1 (2012): 7–33. https://doi.org/10.1093/jaarel/lfr088

Harrill, J. Albert. *The Manumission of Slaves in Early Christianity*. Tübingen: Mohr Siebeck, 1995.

Horsley, Richard A. "The Slave Systems of Classical Antiquity and Their Reluctant Recognition by Modern Scholars," *Semeia* 83/84 (1998): 19–66.

Johnson, Lee A. "Women and Glossolalia in Pauline Communities: The Relationship between Pneumatic Gifts and Authority," *Biblical Interpretation* 21.2 (2013): 196–214. https://doi.org/10.1163/15685152-0017A0003

Kahl, Brigitte. *Galatians Re-imagined: Reading with the Eyes of the Vanquished*. Minneapolis, MN: Fortress Press, 2010. https://doi.org/10.2307/j.ctv19cwb7n

Keller, Mary. *The Hammer and the Flute: Women, Power, and Spirit Possession*. Baltimore, MD: The John Hopkins University Press, 2002.

Kidd, Sue Monk. *The Invention of Wings*. New York: Viking, 2014.

Kraemer, Ross Shepard. "Ecstasy and Possession: The Attraction of Women to the Cult of Dionysus," *Harvard Theological Review* 72.1/2 (1979): 55–80. https://doi.org/10.1017/S0017816000029783

Lewis, Ioan M. *Ecstatic Religion: An Anthropological Study of Spirit Possession and Shamanism*. Harmondsworth: Penguin, 1971.

Lieu, Judith M. "The 'Attraction of Women' in/to Early Judaism and Christianity: Gender and the Politics of Conversion," *Journal for the Study of the New Testament* 72 (1998): 5–22. https://doi.org/10.1177/0142064X9902107202

Lopez, Davina. *Apostle to the Conquered: Reimagining Paul's Mission*. Minneapolis, MN: Fortress Press, 2010.

Marchal, Joseph A. "Slaves as Wo/men and Unmen: Reflecting upon Euodia, Syntyche, and Epaphroditus in Philippi," 141–76 in *The People beside Paul: The Philippian*

Assembly and History from Below. Edited by Joseph A. Marchal. Atlanta, GA: Society of Biblical Literature Press, 2015. https://doi.org/10.2307/j.ctt189tt2d.11

Martin, Dale B. *Slavery as Salvation: The Metaphor of Slavery in Pauline Christianity*. New Haven, CT: Yale University Press, 1990. https://doi.org/10.2307/j.ctt1xp3tkh

McClintock Fulkerson, Mary. *Changing the Subject: Women's Discourses and Feminist Theology*. Minneapolis, MN: Fortress Press, 1994.

Meeks, Wayne A. *The First Urban Christians: The Social World of the Apostle Paul*. 2nd edn. New Haven, CT: Yale University Press, 2003 (1983). https://doi.org/10.1017/S0360966900024130

Moore, Stephen D. "Que(e)reying Paul: Preliminary Questions," 249–74 in *Auguries: The Jubilee Volume of the Sheffield Department of Biblical Studies*. Edited by David J. A. Clines and Stephen D. Moore. Sheffield: Sheffield Academic Press, 1998.

Økland, Jorunn. *Women in Their Place: Paul and the Corinthian Discourse of Gender and Sanctuary*. London: T&T Clark, 2005.

Patterson, Orlando. *Slavery and Social Death: A Comparative Study*. Cambridge, MA: Harvard University Press, 1982.

Schüssler Fiorenza, Elisabeth. *Jesus: Miriam's Child, Sophia's Prophet; Critical Issues in Feminist Christology*. New York: Continuum, 1994.

—*Rhetoric and Ethic: The Politics of Biblical Studies*. Minneapolis, MN: Fortress Press, 1999.

—*Wisdom Ways: Introducing Feminist Biblical Interpretation*. Maryknoll, NY: Orbis, 2001.

Sontag, Susan. "Notes on 'Camp'," 275–92 in Susan Sontag, *Against Interpretation and Other Essays*. New York: Picador, 1990.

Strickert, Fred. "The First Woman to be Portrayed on a Jewish Coin: Julia Sebaste," *Journal for the Study of Judaism in the Persian, Hellenistic and Roman Period* 33.1 (2002): 65–91. https://doi.org/10.1163/15700630252947603

Theissen, Gerd. "La stratification sociale de la communauté corinthienne," 91–138 in Gerd Theissen, *Histoire sociale du christianisme primitif: Jésus-Paul-Jean*. Geneva: Labor et Fides, 1996.

Walters, Jonathan. "'No More than a Boy': The Shifting Construction of Masculinity from Ancient Greece to the Middle Ages," *Gender and History* 5 (1991): 20–33. https://doi.org/10.1111/j.1468-0424.1993.tb00161.x

—"Invading the Roman Body: Manliness and Impenetrability in Roman Thought," 29–43 in *Roman Sexualities*. Edited by Judith P. Hallett and Marilyn B. Skinner. Princeton, NJ: Princeton University Press, 1997. https://doi.org/10.1515/9780691219547-003

Wire, Antoinette Clark. *The Corinthian Women Prophets: A Reconstruction through Paul's Rhetoric*. Minneapolis, MN: Fortress Press, 1990. Repr. Eugene, OR: Wipf & Stock, 2003.

Chapter Eight

Conversion in/to the Wilderness: The Case of the Egyptian Slave Girl Hagar in Early Christian and Jewish Texts

Marianne Bjelland Kartzow

Introduction

The biblical character Hagar and the various stories about her invite interpreters to rethink conventional ideas about conversion. It prompts one to ask questions: Who is an insider? What does it mean to change religion? What role do gender, class, and race play in conversion? Conversion is complex to various degrees; it is always negotiated, and it is often a question of life and death, as discussed in the introduction to this book.[1] It involves bodies, power, and can generate conflict, dialogue, or revitalization of traditions. There are significant links between recent debates about conversion and ancient texts. In this article, I focus on one specific character, the Egyptian slave girl Hagar, and how she is constructed in various texts, as stranger, convert, or insider.

Over the years, several studies have been devoted to conversion, also within the field of New Testament Studies. One can note two abundantly discussed themes: the practice of circumcision as a rite of conversion and Onesimus's case in Paul's letter to Philemon. These two rather different topics strongly emphasize male discourse; they are related to the body or to social structures. In contrast, women, girls, or female slaves remain neglected, sometimes by the texts, sometimes by the interpreters, and sometimes by both. I will reflect further on this massive interest in circumcision and Philemon in conversion studies, and seek out potential blind spots in the history of interpretation.

As a case study, I use a character who could not submit to male circumcision, and was not included in the Jesus movement, even though she is mentioned in the New Testament. According to Jewish tradition, Hagar solves Sarah and Abraham's problem of childlessness and infertility, and becomes the first literary character to name God. She is an ambiguous character when

---

1. See Chapter 1, What Is So Complex about Conversion?

it comes to status and belonging: for example, is she an insider or an outsider? Although she quietly leaves the Genesis story in the Hebrew Bible after wandering around in the wilderness with her son, she left some significant traces in ancient literature. I will look at some sources that have something to say about her standing and belonging and her role in relationship to conversion. When one introduces Hagar in discussion about conversion, it becomes necessary to rethink our conceptualization of conversion as limited to *religious change* only.

Scholarly Blind Spots

Hagar appears as a complex and ambiguous character when it comes to status and belonging; still she is almost overlooked in research literature on conversion. Since this study has New Testament scholarship as the point of departure, I will first try to conceptualize Hagar within that research framework. Studies of circumcision in the New Testament are often careful in presenting various contradictory voices in the ancient material—the Hebrew Bible, the Jewish historians Josephus and Philo as well as Rabbinic literature. Over the years, scholars have discussed whether it was common, accepted, or encouraged, that males who were not born Jewish would become insiders through the rite of circumcision, with a variety of conclusions.[2] Surprisingly often, the gender challenge created by this male ritual is reduced to a brief comment and some references.[3] For example, in the recent (otherwise very well argued) book by Matthew Thiessen, *Contesting Conversion*, the author writes that "circumcision was a nonnegotiable criterion for Jewishness (for males)" at a certain period and in a particular context in Antiquity.[4] He refers to a couple of articles on Judaism and female circumcision in a footnote. Such studies risk being blind to the particularity of their conclusions, and tend to generalize the consequences of a male ritual to the entire population.

---

2. See a recent update: Matthew Thiessen, *Contesting Conversion: Genealogy, Circumcision, and Identity in Ancient Judaism and Christianity* (New York: Oxford University Press, 2011).

3. This elephant was already present in the room in the dialogue between Trypho the Jew and Justin Martyr, as discussed in Judith M. Lieu, *Neither Jew nor Greek? Constructing Early Christianity* (London: T&T Clark, 2002), 101–2. See also Judith M. Lieu, "The 'Attraction of Women' in/to Early Judaism and Christianity: Gender and the Politics of Conversion," *Journal for the Study of the New Testament* 72 (1998): 5–22. Shaye J. D. Cohen, "Why Aren't Jewish Women Circumcised?" *Gender & History* 9.3 (1997): 560–78.

4. Thiessen, *Contesting Conversion*, 5.

Whether women, as wives or mothers, could, symbolically speaking, be counted among the circumcised is seldom discussed at any length,[5] and less privileged women, such as female slaves, seem to play no role in the discussion whatsoever. In addition, male slaves are rarely discussed when it comes to circumcision,[6] although, already for Abraham's household, biblical texts indicate clearly that all slaves, those born in the house or bought for money, need to be circumcised (Gen. 17.11-13). Is it possible to say anything relevant about conversion or identity in the context of Second Temple Judaism, if the most central topic discussed only concerns half the population, and if one excludes male slaves from this half?[7]

The other favorite theme, Onesimus's conversion, reveals yet another blind spot in the scholarly production of knowledge. One study's title is rather telling: "Onesimus: A Case Study of Slave Conversion in Early Christianity."[8] In what way can Onesimus's case be anything else or anything more than a model for the conversion of *male* slaves ? How can we at all talk about Christianity at the time of the letter mentioning Onesimus? It is also an open question whether Onesimus did or did not go through a conversion, on the basis of the short text we have at our disposal. What challenges would a female slave have faced? How different would they have been from those of Onesimus, in this triangular drama between prison, household, and the two free men, Paul and Philemon? How would a female slave's gendered vulnerability and sexual availibility influence her potential conversion?[9] It is perhaps symptomatic of gender bias when the same article states that "Onesimus is unique in being the only slave identified by name and status in the New Testament,"[10] as if the slave girl Rhoda in Acts (Acts 12.13-16) or Hagar (Gal. 4.21-31) were not identified by name.[11]

---

5. But see Lawrence A. Hoffman, *Covenant of Blood: Circumcision and Gender in Rabbinic Judaism* (Chicago, IL: University of Chicago Press, 1996).

6. But see Shaye Cohen, who does discuss the case of male slaves circumcised upon their inclusion in a Jewish household: Shaye J. D. Cohen, "Crossing the Boundary and Becoming a Jew," *The Harvard Theological Review* 82.1 (1989): 13–33.

7. Some interpreters discuss whether women are included among "the circumcised." They are never called un-circumcised, a category used of (male) outsiders only, see Lieu, *Neither Jew nor Greek?*, 103–7. See also Hoffman, *Covenant of Blood*.

8. Nicholas H. Taylor, "Onesimus: A Case Study of Slave Conversion in Early Christianity," *Religion and Theology* 3.3 (1996): 259–81.

9. And for that sake: How would *a male slave's* sexual vulnerability and availibility influence *his* potential conversion, a question not discussed in Taylor's article but adressed in Joseph A. Marchal, "The Usefulness of Onesimus: The Sexual Use of Slaves and Paul's Letter to Philemon," *Journal of Biblical Literature* 130.4 (2011): 749–70.

10. Taylor, "Onesimus," 262.

11. More on Rhoda, see J. Albert Harrill, "The Dramatic Function of the Running

Onesimus, however, is unique in some other ways: he is the only *male* slave identified by name and he is the only slave whose destiny is the object of an entire (albeit brief) New Testament letter. But again, how can general conclusions about conversion be drawn when one reflects only on a small selection of the population or group under consideration? Gender and status need to be taken into consideration in discussions of conversion.

Although not concerned about gender, the article previously mentioned nevertheless asks some crucial questions about slave conversion: "[H]ow do we, how does Paul, and how did the owner, define whether, by what means, and at what point, the slave was converted to Christianity?"[12] Here I would add: how would a person like Onesimus define whether, how and when, s/he became a convert? And in connection to a female character such as Hagar: would she have defined herself as a convert? Of course, we have no clear evidences for answering these questions. It creates some methodological difficulties, but theorizing these gaps will at least highlight what we do not know.

Thus, my contribution is to look at a character whose potential conversion is ignored in many of the discussions about conversion. Hagar is a woman and she is a slave. Further, the traveling memory associated to her can be an additional case study which highlights the complexity of conversion in Antiquity and beyond.

Theoretical Framework for Discussing Conversion

Since this article is interested in combining a discussion of hierarchical systems with different traditional and textual perspectives on conversion, the theoretical framework is best constructed using models born from an interdisciplinary conversation.

The Intersectional Turn

First and foremost, I find insights from the ongoing discussion of intersectionality to be particularly useful to theorize the complexity of conversion. We cannot talk about conversion as if it concerns only one category, for example religion, and not consider how gender, class, race, age intersect

---

Slave Rhoda (Acts 12:13-16): A Piece of Greco-Roman Comedy," *New Testament Studies* 46 (2000): 150–7. For another named female slave in early Christian literature, one can think of Blandina, discussed in Marianne Bjelland Kartzow, *Destabilizing the Margins: An Intersectional Approach to Early Christian Memory* (Eugene, OR: Wipf &Stock, 2012), ch. 10.

12. Taylor, "Onesimus," 260.

and mutually construct how religion is perceived, practiced and conceptualized.[13] Biblical scholarship has only very recently begun to apply intersectionality as a theoretical concept,[14] although African feminists, African American scholars, and womanist biblical interpreters in particular have articulated the basic ideas and concerns for some years now.[15] Intersectionality has become essential within recent race and gender theory:[16] two of the leading journals in gender studies have recently published separate thematic issues on intersectionality.[17] Some scholars even talk about "the

---

13. Note also, as discussed in the introduction to this volume and in Gerhard van den Heever's article, that the term "religion" is contested as a relevant category when reading ancient texts, since it did not exist in isolation, but was interconnected to ethnicity, kinship, culture, nation, and geography. I use it as a critical analytical category in this article. See Paula Fredriksen, "Madatory Retirement: Ideas in the Study of Christian Origins Whose Time Has Come to Go," *Studies in Religion* 35.2 (2006): 231–46; Anders Runesson, "The Question of Terminology: The Architecture of Contemporary Discussions on Paul," in Mark D. Nanos and Magnus Zetterholm, eds., *Paul within Judaism: Restoring the First-Century Context to the Apostle* (Minneapolis, MN: Fortress Press, 2015), 53–77; Steve Mason, "Jews, Judeans, Judaizing, Judaism: Problems of Categorization in Ancient History," *Journal for the Study of Judaism* 38.4/5 (2007): 457–512.

14. Elisabeth Schüssler Fiorenza, "Introduction: Exploring the Intersections of Race, Gender, Status, and Ethnicity in Early Christian Studies," in Laura Nasrallah and Elisabeth Schüssler Fiorenza, eds., *Prejudice and Christian Beginnings: Investigating Race, Gender, and Ethnicity in Early Christian Studies* (Minneapolis, MN: Fortress Press, 2009), 1–23; Marianne Bjelland Kartzow, "'Asking the Other Question': An Intersectional Approach to Galatians 3:28 and the Colossian Household Codes," *Biblical Interpretation* 18.4/5 (2010): 364–89. See also Marianne Bjelland Kartzow, "Intersectionality," in Julia M., ed., *The Oxford Encyclopedia of the Bible and Gender* (Oxford: Oxford University Press, 2014), 1.364–89.

15. See various articles in Brian K. Blount, et al., eds., *True to Our Native Land: An African American New Testament Commentary* (Minneapolis, MN: Fortress Press, 2007). See also numerous works by Schüssler Fiorenza and for example Kwok Pui-lan, "Finding a Home for Ruth: Gender, Sexuality, and the Politics of Otherness," in Robert M. Fowler, Edith L. Blumhofer, and Fernando F. Segovia, eds., *New Paradigms for Bible Study: The Bible in the Third Millennium* (New York: T&T Clark, 2004), 135–54.

16. See for example Kathy Davis, "Intersectionality as Buzzword: A Sociology of Science Perspective on What Makes a Feminist Theory Successful," *Feminist Theory* 9 (2008): 67–83; Gudrun-Axeli Knapp, "Race, Class, Gender: Reclaiming Baggage in Fast Travelling Theories," *European Journal of Women's Studies* 12.3 (2005): 249–65.

17. Ann Phoenix and Pamela Pattynama, eds., *European Journal of Women's Studies (Issue on Intersectionality)* 13 (2006). Sumi Cho, Kimberle Williams Crenshaw, and Leslie McCall, "Toward a Field of Intersectional Studies: Theory, Applications, and Praxis," *Signs (Theme Issue: Intersectionality: Theorizing Power, Empowering Theory* 38.4 (2013): 785–810.

intersectional turn," an indication that we can no longer do gender studies without taking intersectionality seriously.[18]

The core idea is as follows: instead of examining gender, race, class, sexuality, age, and religion as separate categories for understanding identity or hierarchy, intersectionality explores how these categories overlap and mutually modify and reinforce each other.[19] Each person belongs to more than one category. When one faces marginalization, it might be difficult to articulate which specific correlative system of oppression is at work. Intersectionality offers a language to talk about cultural complexity. Although intersectionality has its weak points and pitfalls, it may equip interpreters with tools that help ask new questions of ancient texts and contexts.[20] For our specific purpose: When we are looking for models to talk about conversion, we need to take into consideration the impact of gender, social status, ethnicity, disability, or age on religious conversions.[21]

Intersectional Approaches to Slavery

The obvious analytical category to understand slavery is that of social status or class. What defines a slave is that he or she is owned by someone else, and finds himself or herself at the bottom of the social hierarchy.[22] This

---

18. Katarina Mattsson, "Genua och vithet i den intersektionella vändingen," *Tidsskrift för genusvetenskap* 1/2 (2010): 7–22.

19. Patricia Hill Collins, "It's All in the Family: Intersections of Gender, Race, and Nation," *Hypatia* 13.3 (1998): 62–82, here 63.

20. See Kartzow, "'Asking the Other Question'." Note that intersectional theories, although embraced, have also generated critique, for example when the use of intersectionality is "motivated by an ethical-political 'will to empower' underprivileged groups," discussed in Randi Gressgård, "Mind the Gap: Intersectionality, Complexity and 'the Event'," *Theory and Science* 10.1 (2008): 1–15. Some point at the "analytical confusion" that has followed from use of intersectionality, although some of these issues already have "been tackled by feminist scholars"; see Nira Yuval-Davis, "Intersectionality and Feminist Politics," *European Journal of Women's Studies* 13.3 (2006): 193–209, here 206. "[T]o assume an unquestioned similarities of inequalities," where all differences (in class, race/ethnicity, sexual orientation, and gender) incorrectly are considered equal, has been one way of facing multiple discrimination. To employ a "one size fits all" approach confronted with inequality represents a misuse of intersectionality. See Mieke Verloo, "Multiple Inequalities, Intersectionality and the European Union," *European Journal of Women's Studies* 13.3 (2006): 211–28, here 211.

21. See Shuddhabrata Sengupta, "I/Me/Mine—Intersectional Identities as Negotiated Minefields," *Signs: Journal of Women in Culture and Society* 31.3 (2006): 629–39. Erica Burman, "From Difference to Intersectionality: Challenges and Resources," *European Journal of Psychoterapy and Counselling* 6.4 (2003): 293–308, here 294.

22. J. Albert Harrill, *Slaves in the New Testament: Literary, Social, and Moral Dimensions* (Minneapolis, MN: Fortress Press, 2006).

basic reality, however, influences a whole set of other power systems. Several recent studies of religious texts point this out.[23]

Slaves were bodies removed from various forms of connections. Because they were removed from their ancestral kinship relations, they were always outsiders.[24] Enslavement means a total uprooting from one's family, religion, and society of origin, and erases one's identity.[25] Female slaves often represented otherness according to a whole range of parameters: social status and often ethnic origin; in addition, their gender made them particularly vulnerable.[26]

Keeping in mind this intersecting marginality, is it even possible to imagine that slaves could convert at all? Or could they only "be converted" without any say in the decision? Because female slaves were often without any choices and/or power over their own bodies or lives and without any acknowledged family ties, history, tradition, or religion, is it meaningful to talk about conversion in the case of female slaves? Is not the question of female slaves' conversion hopelessly anachronistic? This seems to be the case. Yet, we do have some ambiguous sources from the ancient world inviting us to rephrase the question. As Gert Lüderitz and Joyce M. Reynolds have documented, some inscriptions from Antiquity mention female slave converts to Judaism.[27] In addition, as this article will develop, some ancient texts consider the Egyptian slave girl Hagar, a convert. This is where the conversation between our conceptions and ancient texts provides an interesting and complex dialogue.

---

23. Several works on slavery in early Christian studies have employed intersectional thinking, for example Jennifer A. Glancy, *Slavery in Early Christianity* (Oxford: Oxford University Press, 2002); Catherine Hezser, *Jewish Slavery in Antiquity* (New York: Oxford University Press, 2005); Bernadette J. Brooten (with the assistance of Jacqueline L. Hazelton), ed., *Beyond Slavery: Overcoming Its Religious and Sexual Legacies* (New York: Palgrave, MacMillan, 2010).

24. Marchal, "The Usefulness of Onesimus," 758.

25. Hezser, *Jewish Slavery in Antiquity*, 21–2. Catherine Hezser, "Part Whore, Part Wife: Slave Women in the Palestinian Rabbinic Tradition," in Ute E. Eisen and Christine Gerber, eds., *Doing Gender—Doing Religion: Fallstudien zur Intersektionalitat im Fruhen Judentum, Christentum und Islam* (Tübingen: Mohr Siebeck, 2013), 303–23, here 318

26. Hezser, "Part Whore, Part Wife," 304.

27. Some inscription evidences may point to the possibility that some slave women could become Jewish by adoption. Gert Lüderitz and Joyce M. Reynolds, *Corpus Jüdischer Zeugnisse aus der Cyrenaika* (Wiesbaden: Ludwig Reichert Verlag, 1983). Lieu, *Neither Jew nor Greek?*, 108.

Intersectional Conversion

The concept of conversion needs to be challenged or re-imagined through intersectional theories and through the broad scholarly discussion of slavery in Antiquity. A lot has been said on conversion recently, including in a handbook published by Oxford University Press.[28] Clearly, if one sees conversion as an open and momentary personal and voluntarily move from A to B, as discussed in the introduction to this volume (a move through which the old is considered wrong and is left behind to embrace the new as right—as in the psychologizing understanding of conversion), slaves—and perhaps most persons of the ancient world—were not able to convert. However, we can conceptualize religious change differently, in ways more adequate to a discussion of slavery and conversion.

For example, if we consider that conversion happens *in the heart*, vertically, between one person and god/gods and does not need to be confirmed horizontally in a community or through any rite, any slave at any point in history can convert as much as he or she wants.[29] Such potential conversions, of course, would also be related to a person's social relations. Our problem with this type of conversion, obviously, is that, in the case of the first Jesus followers, we do not have the sources that would provide access to such events, as we have for example for Augustine some hundred years later.[30] Nevertheless, when we think about the roles of slaves, we need to allow for the possibility of such conversions.

Another way to think about slaves' role in conversion is to look at slaves as part of converted households. In the Bible, we find, for example, Abraham's slaves in Genesis or potential slaves of Lydia, the dealer in purple cloth mentioned in Acts (16.11-16). Additionally, there were slaves sold to new owners and integrated into households that belonged to another religious tradition than their former owner. In both cases—as member of converted households or sold into new households belonging to another tradition—slaves were probably not asked whether they wanted to convert. They were required to do so, as part of the loyalty required of slaves.[31] If they refused to be converted, one could imagine that they were threatened with violence or perhaps punished. This is indeed a type of change of

---

28. See Charles E. Farhadian and Lewis R. Rambo, eds., *The Oxford Handbook of Religious Conversion* (Oxford: Oxford University Press, 2014).
29. See the Epilogue in Brooten, *Beyond Slavery*.
30. See Chapter 1, What Is So Complex about Conversion?
31. See Shaye J. D. Cohen, *The Jewish Family in Antiquity* (Missoula, MT: Scholars Press, 1993).

religion, but we need to employ intersectional tools to make sense of such conversions.

As a combination of these two types of conversion, we can also consider the possibility that household slaves, who were initially forced to change their religious practice, could subsequently experience personal change "in their heart" or have religious experiences with the new tradition that could modify their lives or values. Regardless of this change, they nevertheless probably had to continue their lives as owned bodies in the gendered slave system of Antiquity.[32] Together with other rhetorical caricatures and stereotypes used in ancient texts, slaves are accused of being false-converts. Sometimes, they are blamed because their conversion appears insufficiently real or sincere.[33]

Another important aspect in understanding the potential conversion of slaves is how moving, change, and geographic mobility could be part of a slave's life story. For example, as some wives changed religion/ethnicity through marrying and moving to their husband's household—the case that the ancient novel *Joseph and Aseneth* narrates—a similar process could be necessary when a new slave was sold and bought: a new owner could mean a new religious tradition. If a god belonged to a certain place, moving could mean conversion for entire households, including slaves and children. Accordingly, we may say that a slave converted every time he or she was sold or given away to a new and different household, or when he or she was manumitted. When it comes to Jewish households selling slaves, some would argue that such shift or switching would be easier for female slaves than for males, since the latter might have been circumcised upon their first arrival.[34]

Theoretical concepts such as multiple switching of religion or re-conversion may be adequate when trying to understand the change(s) of religion affecting slaves.[35] The concept of "religious switching" might be softer than conversion, and refers to shifts within religious traditions or changes of a less permanent quality. As I have tried to show, a range of different meanings can be re-imagined when conversion of female slaves is discussed.

32. Margaret Y. MacDonald, "Slavery, Sexuality and House Churches: A Reassessment of Colossians 3.18–4.1 in Light of New Research on the Roman Family," *New Testament Studies* 53 (2008): 94–113.

33. Taylor, "Onesimus," 260.

34. Note, however, the critical comments made in Lieu, "The 'Attraction of Women' in/to Early Judaism and Christianity."

35. Wade Clark Roof, "Multiple Religious Switching: A Reserach Note," *Journal for the Scientific Study of Religion* 28.4 (1989): 530–5. Frank Newport, "The Religious Switcher in the United States," *American Sociological Review* 44.4 (1979): 528–52.

The Complexity of Comparing

In searching for Hagar and her potential role when it comes to conversion, I read snapshots of texts where she is mentioned, texts that come from different contexts. Can these texts illuminate each other, and can they provide some tools to interpret New Testament texts about this female slave? As a tool of much academic work, comparing in broad strokes can be a helpful technique, especially in contrast to biblical scholarship which often prefers going in depth when reading one specific text, chapter, or verse. The purpose of comparing, however, is not always given. The social anthropologist Marit Melhuus argues that, instead of comparing objects, the names, or essence of things, we might gain more from comparing meanings, ways of constructing relations between objects or persons, situations, and events.[36] Her aim is to discuss cross-cultural comparison, but her critical approach is relevant when comparing ancient texts. It is also possible to compare a set of analytical questions, as I will do here, by using intersectional theories to comparatively read texts about Hagar. Hopefully, the various groups of texts will contribute to an overall perspective, even though they come from rather different contexts and backgrounds.[37]

Hagar as Case Study: The Texts

Within this theoretical framework, I will discuss four cases in which Hagar's potential conversion is confirmed or rejected, explicitly or implicitly. I start with the story found in Genesis, since all later reflections of Hagar refer to this story in one way or another. Then I will look at how Josephus talks about Hagar in a slightly different way than Genesis. With the rabbinic texts, I briefly present the very different roles given to Hagar in relationship to the specific issue of conversion. These roles range from seeing her as a prominent female convert, to blaming her for returning to the pagan idols the moment she leaves Abraham's house. At the end, I discuss how the Pauline letters treat Hagar, not as an illustration of how ethnicity, class, or gender are erased in Christ, but as a slavish female, who produces offspring according to nature, outside of God's promise.

---

36. Marit Melhuus, "Issues of Relevance: Anthropology and the Challenges of Cross-Cultural Comparison," in Andre Gingrich and Richard Fox, eds., *Anthropology, by Comparison* (London: Routledge, 2002), 70–92.

37. See also Marianne Bjelland Kartzow, "The Complexity of Pairing: Reading Acts 16 with Plutarch's Parallel Lives," in Ruben R. Dupertuis and Todd Penner, eds., *Engaging Early Christian History: Reading Acts in the Second Century* (Durham: Acumen, 2013), 123–39, here in particular the paragraph "Comparing Comparisons," 124–6.

How do various ancient authors describe the character of Hagar? Is she a converted insider or does she remain a stranger? How do the various texts emphasize the different aspects of her character, her religion, gender, ethnicity, and social status? I think her character represents an excellent case study to expose how complex ancient ideas and concepts of conversion were.

Genesis

The textual point of departure is the narrative in Genesis about the childless couple Sarai and Abram, who use the slave girl Hagar from Egypt to give them a son (Genesis 16 and 21). Before this story was included in the pages of Genesis, it probably circulated as oral stories, later merged into this narrative. Hagar becomes Abram's second wife/concubine (Gen. 16.3) and gives birth to Ishmael (Gen. 16.15). Later, as promised early in the narrative, Sarai finds herself pregnant through God's intervention, and her son Isaac is born (Gen. 21.2). Between the births of these two sons, something happens that influences the fate and destiny of these five people, giving them all very distinctive roles in relationship to God, according to gender, age, and status.[38]

As part of God's covenant with Abraham, all males born in the house, sons or slaves, and even those bought for money, are to be circumcised (on the eighth day; see Gen. 17.9-14).[39] Abram is circumcised himself, and so is his son Ishmael, and all the male slaves (Gen. 17.23-27). When Isaac is born, later, he is the first one to be engendered from a circumcised father, and the first one to be circumcised when he is eight days old. In addition to the sign of male circumcision, new names are given to Abram and Sarai, now called Abraham and Sarah (Gen. 17.5 and 17.15).[40]

For one of these characters, the new covenant with God represents neither a ritualization nor a specific sign on the body or re-naming: Abraham is both circumcised and re-named and Sarai is re-named "Sarah" as a sign of the new relation with God. Ishmael is circumcised, although God states

---

38. See also Marianne Bjelland Kartzow, "Navigating the Womb: Surrogacy, Slavery, Fertility–and Biblical Discourses," *Journal of Early Christian History* 2.1 (2012): 38–54. Marianne Bjelland Kartzow, "Reproductive Capital and Slave Surrogacy: Thinking about/with/Bbeyond Hagar," in Anne Hege Grung, Marianne Bjelland Kartzow, and Anna Rebecca Solevåg, eds., *Bodies, Borders, Believers: Ancient Texts and Present Conversations. Essays in Honor of Turid Karlsen Seim on Her 70th Birthday* (Eugene, OR: Pickwick, 2015), 396–409.

39. For a discussion of the manuscript situation related to this eighth day remark, see Thiessen, *Contesting Conversion*, 18–30.

40. On naming and conversion, also including inscription and papyri among the sources material, see G. H. R. Horsley, "Name Change as an Indication of Religious Conversion in Antiquity," *Numen* 34.1 (1987): 1–17, here 7.

in the story that he is not the son with whom God will establish God's covenant (Gen. 17.20-21). Isaac is the first one to be circumcised when eight days old. But what about Hagar? Since she is neither male nor a free woman or the mother of the elected son, what is her role in this drama? In the rather brief information about Hagar in Genesis, her Egyptian origin is mentioned four times and her slave status seven times, as if to emphasize her strangeness.[41] She is ambiguous and complex indeed: both wife and slave, and the mother of a boy who is firstborn and circumcised, but not the heir.

In relationship to the Genesis story, two things are worth mentioning about Hagar. First, some reflections on the potential historical realities employed to construct the narrative universe: since Hagar lives in Sarah and Abraham's house and is entrusted with the role of bearing their firstborn son as a surrogate mother, Hagar is to a certain degree a privileged slave. She belongs to the household's intimate zone, at least sexually, and maybe also emotionally or mentally.[42] What kind of purity regulation would a female slave like her need to follow?[43] Was her ethnicity or social status in any way problematic, since she is presented as qualified to give a Jewish couple their first son? As a mother in the house, what role would be expected of her in relation to the education and upbringing of Abraham's firstborn? Would motherhood construct her as a converted insider, or would her slave status and Egyptian origin leave her an outsider? We do not have access to historical data, but we know that the story was at least considered plausible.

Second, when Hagar is thrown out of Abraham's house and wanders in the wilderness, first as a pregnant woman and then as a mother with her child, she speaks to an angel of God, and is the first one to give the Jewish god a name, *El-roi* (Gen. 16.13). How does this exclusive naming scene contribute to construct her religious status in Genesis and later receptions?[44]

The Jewish Historian Josephus

One very insightful source about Hagar is the Jewish historian Flavius Josephus, in his retelling of biblical stories. In Josephus' narrative, one should pay attention to the details not recognizable from the Genesis story. According to Josephus, Ishmael is still a small child when Hagar flees into the

---

41. Thiessen, *Contesting Conversion*, 39.
42. On the role of female slaves as intimate and sexual partners, see Hezser, "Part Whore, Part Wife," 305 and 310.
43. Hezser, "Part Whore, Part Wife," 316–8.
44. Marianne Bjelland Kartzow, "On Naming and Blaming: Hagar's God-Talk in Jewish and Early Christian Sources," in John T. Greene and Mishael M. Caspi, eds., *In the Arms of Biblical Women* (Piscataway, NJ: Gorgias Press, 2013), 97–119.

desert for the second time, while in Genesis he must be around 13 years, if we respect the age description given for Abraham. Josephus does not mention the scene where Ishmael is circumcised with his father and their slaves, making Ishmael and Hagar even more alien in Abraham's house. In line with this tendency of Josephus, after meeting God's angel for the second time, Hagar stays in the wilderness with her son. Here, they meet some shepherds, who take care of them so they can be safe (*Ant.* 1.215-9). Thus, both Hagar and Ishmael are written out of the story; they find someone else with whom to remain and their days in Abraham's household are short and insignificant. Accordingly, none of them play any role in the new relation between God and Abraham and the rest of his family and slaves.

In Genesis, the story is told differently. We hear of no helpful shepherds in the wilderness. Instead, it seems like Hagar and Ishmael end up in Abraham's household although their return is never described. Towards the end of Abraham's story, we hear the striking detail that after Abraham dies, Isaac and Ishmael bury their father (Gen. 25.9). They are mentioned in that order, namely the youngest first, and the firstborn last, the son of the slave girl. Interestingly, it is not the elected son and heir Isaac alone, or the six sons Abraham has with his third wife Keturah, who bury the patriarch. This seems to indicate that Ishmael, and maybe his mother too, continue to live in the house, in contrast to what Josephus describes.

These two versions concerning the place Hagar and Ishmael reach at the conclusion of the story are, of course, central in order to conceptualize Hagar's role when it comes to the intersections of religion, social position, gender, and ethnicity. If the parameter is insiders versus outsiders, Josephus places Hagar firmly outside Abraham's household and thereby outside God's realm. Without surprise, Josephus does not mention the scene from Genesis where Hagar talks to an angel and gives God a name.[45]

Rabbinic Texts

Rabbinic literature exists in the landscape between biblical commentary and original creative composition, often focusing on one specific verse or even parts of a verse. Most rabbinic texts that pay attention to Hagar belong to the material classified as *midrash haggadah*, namely comments on the non-legal sections of the biblical texts. The oral character of these texts, and their intended polysemy—the belief that the text is subject to multiple interpretations and therefore cannot be reduced to one single "correct" meaning—make rabbinic texts both complex and rich sources for transmission

---

45. Kartzow, "On Naming and Blaming," 104.

processes and identity-making strategies.⁴⁶ Thus, rabbinic texts, rather than providing clear answers, give insights into ongoing discussions. Although some of these texts are written down at a later stage, even centuries after the biblical texts, many interpreters assume they were known as oral traditions earlier and can therefore be relevant as comparative material.⁴⁷ For rabbinic texts, slaves are devoid of relatives and ancestry. Without parents and ancestors, their claim to Jewishness can hardly be maintained.⁴⁸ The category of "female slave" was a vulnerable and ambiguous one.⁴⁹ When it comes to Hagar, her slave status and her Egyptian origin are the object of particular attention in discussions where religious reasoning intersects with ethnicity, gender, and social status.⁵⁰

Hagar as Pharaoh's privileged daughter: one way of explaining the role of Hagar as a slave with Egyptian origins includes her father's admiration for the Jewish tradition. *Genesis Rabbah* (second half of the fifth century CE) develops it best. It presents Hagar as the Pharaoh's daughter. She could have married any prince, but her father chooses to give her to Abraham, due to his remarkable status and superiority, in recognition of God's powerful intervention.⁵¹ "Better let my daughter be a handmaid in this house than a mistress in another house," as her father argues (*Gen. Rab.* 45.1). Accordingly, she is not really Sarah's slave. She does not have the status of a slave, sold from Egypt. Rather, a privileged friend of Abraham perceives that Abraham can provide the best possible life for his daughter. For Hagar, the elite daughter from Egypt, even to be a maid in Abraham's house is better than being a wife in another house.

---

46. Adele Reinhartz and Miriam-Simma Walfish, "Conflict and Coexistence in Jewish Interpretation," in Phyllis Trible and Letty M. Russell, eds., *Hagar, Sarah, and Their Children: Jewish, Christian, and Muslim Perspectives* (Louisville, KY: Westminster John Knox Press, 2006), 101–25, here 105.

47. See for example Miriam B. Peskowitz, *Spinning Fantasies: Rabbis, Gender, and History* (Berkeley, CA: University of California Press, 1997).

48. Hezser, *Jewish Slavery in Antiquity*, 21–2.

49. See discussion in Diane Kriger (with Tirzah Meacham leBeit Yoreh), *Sex Rewarded, Sex Punished: A Study of the Status "Female Slave" in Early Jewish Law* (Boston, MA: Academic Studies Press, 2011).

50. For a broader and more detailed discussion of these rabbinic texts, including more references, see Reinhartz and Walfish, "Conflict and Coexistence," 105–7. See also Dina Stein, "A Maidservant and Her Master's Voice: Discourse, Identity, and Eros in Rabbinic Texts," *Journal of the History of Sexuality* 10.3/4 (2001): 375–97.

51. Note how this striking narrative element of an Egyptian privileged father who chooses a Hebrew man and one of the patriarchs is paralleled in the ancient novel *Joseph and Aseneth*. See Kirsten Marie Hartvigsen's article in this volume.

Hagar as convert: Hagar's Egyptian background or slave status is not an issue when Hagar is called a convert. In *Yalkut Shimoni*, a compilation of midrashim (composed in the twelfth to thirteenth centuries CE), Hagar is listed first among nine righteous female *converts* (Hebr. *ger*).[52] Among those listed, we also find Zipporah (Moses' wife), Rahab, Ruth, and Yael, several of them with Egyptian origins. Hagar is the only woman mentioned who is also called a slave in the Hebrew Bible.[53] Here, her image as a strange female slave from Egypt is negotiated and reformulated, since she is counted among such prominent women of the Jewish tradition. What the idea of conversion indicates in her case, however, is hard to tell. As is often the case in rabbinic texts when it comes to Jewish women, it may have to do with ritual purity;[54] —or maybe her motherhood, or her role in naming God and talking to an angel.

Hagar as unreformed idolater: however, other texts challenge this way of constructing Hagar as prominent and privileged. According to *Pirqe d'Rabbi Eliezer* (an eighteenth- or nineteenth-century CE compilation), Hagar seems to have been rather flexible when it comes to religious worship. The text argues that she may have worshiped the God of Israel when she was in the house of Abraham, but returned to her idolatrous state as soon as she was outside of Abraham's sphere of influence. When she was wandering around in the desert, she started worshiping the idols of her father's home (*Pirqe R. El.*, "Horeb," 29).[55] Whether her worship switching was due to strategy or necessity, the sources do not tell. Obviously, for that text, her "conversion" is only temporary, and she does not delay in returning to the idols as soon as she leaves the house of Abraham. Here, she is constructed as a suspicious religious switcher, whose conversion is merely fake.

Hagar's Egyptian sexuality runs wild: her Egyptian origin also explains why she, in contrast to Sarah, is fertile, according to *Aggadat Bereshit*. Because Hagar comes from a sexually promiscuous people, she can produce

---

52. *Ger* as referring to "resident aliens" with equal rights as native born, see Thiessen, *Contesting Conversion*, 6. See also Mark Glanville, "The *Ger* (Stranger) in Deuteronomy: Family for the Displaced," *Journal of Biblical Literature* 137.3 (2018): 599–623. He concludes in his Hebrew Bible study that the *ger* is a special stranger, who has become an insider.

53. In rabbinic texts *ger* most often means convert, see Reinhartz and Walfish, "Conflict and Coexistence," 106 and nn. 26–28. Full text: "There are righteous *giyorot*: Hagar, Osnat, Zipporah, Shifra, Puah, the daughter of Pharao, Rahab, Ruth and Yael the wife of Heber the Kenite." *Yalkut Shimoni, Remez* 9.

54. Hezser, "Part Whore, Part Wife," 316.

55. Reinhartz and Walfish, "Conflict and Coexistence."

offspring. It is not because she found divine favor.[56] For Sarah, on the other hand, to be able to give birth to her son Isaac is the result of God's grace and intervention. She is a righteous woman, and such women are always mothers. Hagar's pregnancy, in contrast, is a result of her ethnic background, not connected to the will of God but to her people's habit of sexual promiscuity.

Hagar meets the angel so her slave-status can be re-inscribed: it is not only Hagar's Egyptian background that is used to devaluate her. Her slave status also comes to play a central role when *Genesis Rabbah* (45.7) explains why she meets an angel in the wilderness. She needs to be told to go back to her owners' house and show obedience.

These rabbinic texts display variety in their treatment of Hagar: she is the daughter of a man who valued the Jewish God, she is listed among female converts, she is blamed for switching religion as soon as she has the chance, her fertility is connected to her ethnically defined sexuality, and she meets an angel who tells her to remain a slave. The complexity of Hagar's conversion (or lack thereof) appears to be an ongoing conversation in rabbinic sources. At times, Hagar's background and status give her an insider position. At times, her ethnicity, gender, sexuality, and slave status are emphasized to construct her as the worst and lowest character, especially in relationship to experiences that in other contexts and for other women can mean blessing and righteousness: fertility, worship, and divine revelation.

Hagar's Status in Pauline Letters (Gal. 4.21-31; Rom. 9.6-10) and Early Receptions

In many of Paul's letters, familiar characters from the Jewish tradition and the Hebrew Bible function as explanative models for community building and theological reasoning. In two of Paul's most central letters, the forefather Abraham and the two mothers of his first two sons are used as rhetorical tools to describe how not all those who claim they belong to God are real children of Abraham. The story from Genesis 16 and 21, where Abraham and Sarah are presented as childless, must have been familiar to the readers and hearers.[57] Yet, the Hagar we meet in these stories is different than the one found in the texts already mentioned.

According to Genesis, Hagar flees into the wilderness twice, and disappears from the story, while Sarah, Abraham, and their son Isaac are

---

56. Reinhartz and Walfish, "Conflict and Coexistence."
57. See Kartzow, "On Naming and Blaming."

presented as the founding family of the Jewish covenant.[58] The most stable factor in the story is that Abraham is the father of the two boys. He is also said to name both (Gen. 16.15 and 21.3), indicating that on some level, he acknowledges both as sons. When it comes to circumcision, only Isaac submits to this rite at the age of eight days, as required (Gen. 21.4). When the story of Hagar and Sarah and their children is used in Pauline allegories, something happens to the different mothers and their sons, and ethnicity seems to be downplayed. Paul operates with two different concepts of motherhood when it comes to Ishmael and Isaac: Abraham has two sons, but one of them, namely, the son he has with the slave woman Hagar, is "born according to the flesh" (κατὰ σάρκα γεγέννηται), while Isaac whom he has with Sarah is "from the free one, through the promise" (ἐκ τῆς ἐλευθέρας δι' ἐπαγγελίας, see Gal. 4.23). Sarah seems to have no role in the firstborn son's history, although in Genesis, she is the one who intends for her slave to give her a son. Hagar is reduced to flesh only, and her son is reduced to being a slave: "[I]t is not the children of the flesh who are the children of God, but the children of the promise are counted as the descendants" (Rom. 9.8); "Drive out the slave and her child; for the child of the slave will not share the inheritance with the child of the free woman" (Gal. 4.30). The slave woman's son is only born according to the flesh, not an heir, not a real son, not a Jewish boy. Hagar accordingly has no role in the community, and can be used as a symbol of the ultimate outsider. What is even more interesting in that passage, is that the symbol of the ultimate outsider implicitly becomes a metaphor for Israel, or at least those who want to circumcise.[59]

Paul argues in particular with the intersection of slave status and motherhood here. The slave status of Ishmael's mother determines a marginal position for both her and her son. Ishmael did not go through circumcision when he was eight days old and is not the elected son. Paul chooses to use Hagar and her son to argue against those who require that new believers in Christ must be circumcised. Although compared to Mount Sinai and Jerusalem, terms loaded with (ethnic?) insider associations in the Jewish tradition, Paul does not see Hagar as an insider. Although a mother, she is neither Jew, nor Greek, but slave and female, that is an outsider (but see Gal. 3.28).[60]

Hagar's evaluation in early Christian texts outside of the New Testament follows the same tendency: according to the Church Fathers, Hagar and Sarah are codes for synagogue and church. Elisabeth Clark confirms

---

58. Cohen, *Jewish Family in Antiquity*.
59. See for a similar reading of Hagar as the Other, Valérie Nicolet, "Monstrous Bodies in Paul's Letter to the Galatians," in Joseph A. Marchal, ed., *Bodies on the Verge: Queering Pauline Epistles* (Atlanta, GA: Society of Biblical Literature, 2019), 115–41.
60. See Kartzow, "'Asking the Other Question'."

this in her reading of a variety of Church Fathers, in search of Hagar.[61] She finds a very flexible figure: Hagar is not only an outsider to the community as in some Jewish texts. Rather, her role is modified and turned upside down: she also becomes a model for misunderstood Jewish theology, seen from the Christian side. In addition to being a useful figure in Christian anti-Jewish polemic, Hagar is also used as a metaphor for false or wrong teaching, in debates over marriage and asceticism.[62] She becomes a figure guilty of "unchristian" sexual behavior, because of her carnal implication with Abraham.[63]

Hagar cannot be called a convert in any of these early Christian sources. She becomes a very flexible symbol for a whole set of vices and evils; her intersecting marginality is maintained, and she is never considered an insider, or even a sympathetic figure.[64] In these texts, Hagar never converts to Christianity.

Conclusion

As we have seen, Hagar's role is much debated among and between Jewish and Christian authors. If texts such as the apocrypha, martyrdom accounts, and texts from the Nag Hammadi library had been included, perhaps we could have drawn an even more colorful picture. The brief snapshot comparison in this article shows that Hagar does not have a fixed or stable role, and that the Pauline texts represent both continuity and innovation compared to other texts. Theses texts employ Hagar to think with, and at times, she becomes a useful character to address issues of inclusion and exclusion. What is problematic about her is also varying: in some texts her ethnic origin seems to be most problematic, in others it is her slave status, sexuality, or gender that need some negotiation. Seen through the lens of intersectionality, it becomes clear that it is difficult to discuss Hagar's role vis-à-vis conversion as involving only *religious matters*. Her religious position or conversion cannot be understood if one does not consider the intersection of her gender, sexuality, class, and ethnicity. She is a foreign slave, a potential female seducer, but her character is not completely limited by these marginal positions. Her role as the mother of Abraham's firstborn son gives her a privileged position, at least until Sarah becomes pregnant herself. Ishmael is circumcised by his father, and Hagar, as his mother, could potentially be

---

61. Elizabeth A. Clark, "Interpretive Fate amid the Church Fathers," in Trible and Russell, eds., *Hagar, Sarah, and Their Children*, 127–47, here 129.
62. Clark, "Interpretive Fate amid the Church Fathers," 129–31.
63. Clark, "Interpretive Fate amid the Church Fathers," 143.
64. Clark, "Interpretive Fate amid the Church Fathers."

considered an insider, although she herself never goes through any ritual nor is she given a new name. It is obvious that her position in this household is unclear and therefore becomes contested and negotiable in later Jewish and Christian interpretations. In the various sources discussing her, she is presented as a stranger and outsider based on her gender, sexuality, or ethnic origin, as a religious switcher, but also as a true insider, a daughter of Pharaoh, or a convert. Her character, being both suspicious and prominent, negotiates gender and social status, crosses borders between insider and outsider, emphasizing how complex it is to talk about conversion.

When one reads these different texts about Hagar with the lens of intersectionality, it stands to reason that the language of conversion needs to be more nuanced. The story of Genesis is ambiguous and invites creative and contrasting receptions. Hagar talks to an angel and is the first to name the god of the Hebrews. She is used to help the first childless patriarch and his wife. But yet she does not go through any conversion ritual, nor is she re-named. Her reproductive capital is useful for a while, but religiously she is for the most part insignificant. For a foreign female slave like Hagar, it was hard, perhaps even impossible, to become a real insider.

However, the figure of Hagar does not stay in the wilderness of Genesis or in Galatians. She also does not end her days as a symbol of whatever evil could be found in the world, even if the Church Fathers present her in that way. Hagar's role in Islam highlights a specific set of features of the story. Although not mentioned by name, she is introduced as the wife of Abraham/Ibrahim and mother of Ishmael, and she represents the starting point of God's special intervention in history, according to the Qur'an and the Hadith.[65] Presented as a prominent wife and mother, her name and message are part of Islam's sacred history and rituals.[66] In Islamic tradition, Hagar is not left alone in the wilderness, but Ibrahim keeps on visiting her and her son.[67] According to Riffat Hassan

> The dramatic story of Hagar's life shows that class or color is not a deterrent to any person who has faith in God and is resolutely righteous in action. So Hagar does not see herself as a victim of Abraham and Sarah, or of a patriarchal, class- and race-conscious culture.[68]

---

65. For references, see Riffat Hassan, "Islamic Hagar and Her Family," in Trible and Russell, eds., *Hagar, Sarah, and Their Children*, 149–67, here 152–3.

66. Hibba Abugideiri, "Hagar: A Historical Model for 'Gender Jihad'," in Yvonne Yazbeck Haddad and John L. Esposito, eds., *Daughters of Abraham: Feminist Thought in Judaism, Christianity, and Islam* (Gainesville, FL: University Press of Florida, 2001), 81–107, here 87.

67. Hassan, "Islamic Hagar and Her Family," 155–6.

68. Hassan, "Islamic Hagar and Her Family," 155.

The way Islam describes Hagar is of great interest, as Jennifer Glancy also notices when discussing slavery and early Christianity.[69] Her slave status and foreign origin are not part of the Islamic tradition. The outsider of one religious tradition becomes the insider of another. Is she still Hagar? Has she converted? Is it when she becomes Muslim that Hagar gains a real identity? The travelling memory of Hagar illustrates for us that conversion and change can create the most unexpected transformations, of traditions, of religious concepts, of social order, and of individuals.[70] Starting her textual life as a slave girl from Egypt, being the mother of Abraham's firstborn son, but having a contested connection to Abraham's new covenant with God, Hagar nevertheless survives and travels into new landscapes. She does not end her life in the wilderness.[71]

Biographical Note

Marianne Bjelland Kartzow is Professor of New Testament Studies at the Faculty of Theology, University of Oslo, Norway. She has published *Gossip and Gender: Othering of Speech in the Pastoral Epistles* (2009), *Destabilizing the Margins: An Intersectional Approach to Early Christian Memory* (2012), and *The Slave Metaphor and Gendered Enslavement in Early Christian Discourse: Double Trouble Embodied* (2018). Her research interests include gender theory, social history, and studies of sacred scriptures.

Bibliography

Abugideiri, Hibba. "Hagar: A Historical Model for 'Gender Jihad'," 81–107 in *Daughters of Abraham: Feminist Thought in Judaism, Christianity, and Islam*. Edited by Yvonne Yazbeck Haddad and John L. Esposito. Gainesville, FL: University Press of Florida, 2001.

Blount, Brian K., gen. ed., Cain Hope Felder, Clarice J. Martin, and Emerson B. Powery, assoc. eds. *True to Our Native Land: An African American New Testament Commentary*. Minneapolis, MN: Fortress Press, 2007.

Brooten, Bernadette J., (with the assistance of Jacqueline L. Hazelton), ed. *Beyond Slavery: Overcoming Its Religious and Sexual Legacies*. New York: Palgrave–MacMillan, 2010.

Burman, Erica. "From Difference to Intersectionality: Challenges and Resources," *European Journal of Psychoterapy and Counselling* 6.4 (2003): 293–308. https://doi.org/10.1080/3642530410001665904

---

69. Jennifer A. Glancy, "Early Christianity, Slavery, and Women's Bodies," in Brooten, ed., *Beyond Slavery*, 143–58, here 156–7.

70. Trible and Russell, eds., *Hagar, Sarah, and Their Children*.

71. Delores S. Williams, *Sisters in the Wilderness: The Challenge of Womanist God-Talk* (New York: Orbis Books, 1993).

Cho, Sumi, Kimberle Williams Crenshaw, and Leslie McCall. "Toward a Field of Intersectional Studies: Theory, Applications, and Praxis," *Signs (Theme Issue: Intersectionality: Theorizing Power, Empowering Theory* 38.4 (2013): 785–810. https://doi.org/10.1086/669608

Clark, Elizabeth A. "Interpretive Fate amid the Church Fathers," 127–47 in Trible and Russell, eds., *Hagar, Sarah, and Their Children*, 2006.

Clark Roof, Wade. "Multiple Religious Switching: A Reserach Note," *Journal for the Scientific Study of Religion* 28.4 (1989): 530–5. https://doi.org/10.2307/1386582

Cohen, Shaye J. D. "Crossing the Boundary and Becoming a Jew," *The Harvard Theological Review* 82.1 (1989): 13–33. https://doi.org/10.1017/S001781600001600X

—*The Jewish Family in Antiquity*. Missoula, MT: Scholars Press, 1993.

—"Why Aren't Jewish Women Circumcised?" *Gender & History* 9.3 (1997): 560–78. https://doi.org/10.1111/1468-0424.00076

Davis, Kathy. "Intersectionality as Buzzword: A Sociology of Science Perspective on What Makes a Feminist Theory Successful," *Feminist Theory* 9 (2008): 67–83. https://doi.org/10.1177/1464700108086364

Farhadian, Charles E., and Lewis R. Rambo, eds. *The Oxford Handbook of Religious Conversion*. Oxford: Oxford University Press, 2014.

Fredriksen, Paula. "Madatory Retirement: Ideas in the Study of Christian Origins Whose Time Has Come to Go," *Studies in Religion* 35.2 (2006): 231–46. https://doi.org/10.1177/000842980603500203

Glancy, Jennifer A. *Slavery in Early Christianity*. Oxford: Oxford University Press, 2002. https://doi.org/10.1093/0195136098.001.0001

—"Early Christianity, Slavery, and Women's Bodies," 143–58 in Brooten, ed., *Beyond Slavery*, 2010. https://doi.org/10.1057/9780230113893_9

Glanville, Mark. "The *Ger* (Stranger) in Deutronomy: Family for the Displaced," *Journal of Biblical Literature* 137.3 (2018): 599–623. https://doi.org/10.1353/jbl.2018.0032

Gressgård, Randi. "Mind the Gap: Intersectionality, Complexity and 'the Event'," *Theory and Science* 10.1 (2008): 1–15.

Harrill, J. Albert. "The Dramatic Function of the Running Slave Rhoda (Acts 12:13-16): A Piece of Greco-Roman Comedy," *New Testament Studies* 46 (2000): 150–7. https://doi.org/10.1017/S0028688500000096

—*Slaves in the New Testament: Literary, Social, and Moral Dimensions*. Minneapolis, MN: Fortress Press, 2006.

Hassan, Riffat. "Islamic Hagar and Her Family," 149–67 in Trible and Russell, eds., *Hagar, Sarah, and Their Children*, 2006.

Hezser, Catherine. *Jewish Slavery in Antiquity*. New York: Oxford University Press, 2005. https://doi.org/10.1093/acprof:oso/9780199280865.001.0001

—"Part Whore, Part Wife: Slave Women in the Palestinian Rabbinic Tradition," 303–23 in *Doing Gender—Doing Religion: Fallstudien zur Intersektionalitat im Fruhen Judentum, Christentum und Islam*. Edited by Ute E. Eisen and Christine Gerber. Tübingen: Mohr Siebeck, 2013.

Hill Collins, Patricia. "It's All in the Family: Intersections of Gender, Race, and Nation," *Hypatia* 13.3 (1998): 62–82. https://doi.org/10.1111/j.1527-2001.1998.tb01370.x

Hoffman, Lawrence A. *Covenant of Blood: Circumcision and Gender in Rabbinic Judaism*. Chicago, IL: University of Chicago Press, 1996.

Horsley, G. H. R. "Name Change as an Indication of Religious Conversion in Antiquity," *Numen* 34.1 (1987): 1–17. https://doi.org/10.1163/156852787X00119

Kartzow, Marianne Bjelland. "'Asking the Other Question': An Intersectional Approach to Galatians 3:28 and the Colossian Household Codes," *Biblical Interpretation* 18.4/5 (2010): 364–89. https://doi.org/10.1163/156851510X517591
—*Destabilizing the Margins: An Intersectional Approach to Early Christian Memory*. Eugene, OR: Wipf & Stock, 2012.
—"Navigating the Womb: Surrogacy, Slavery, Fertility—and Biblical Discourses," *Journal of Early Christian History* 2.1(2012): 38–54. https://doi.org/10.1080/2222582X.2012.11877257
— "On Naming and Blaming: Hagar's God-Talk in Jewish and Early Christian Sources," 97–119 in *In the Arms of Biblical Women*. Edited by John T. Greene and Mishael M. Caspi. Piscataway, NJ: Gorgias Press, 2013. https://doi.org/10.31826/9781463235611-006
—"The Complexity of Pairing: Reading Acts 16 with Plutarch's Parallel Lives," 123–39 in *Engaging Early Christian History: Reading Acts in the Second Century*. Edited by Ruben R. Dupertuis and Todd Penner. Durham: Acumen, 2013.
—"Intersectionality," 364–89 in *The Oxford Encyclopedia of the Bible and Gender,* Vol. 1. Edited by Julia M. O'Brien. Oxford: Oxford University Press, 2014.
—"Reproductive Capital and Slave Surrogacy: Thinking about/with/beyond Hagar," 396–409 in *Bodies, Borders, Believers: Ancient Texts and Present Conversations. Essays in Honor of Turid Karlsen Seim on Her 70th Birthday*. Edited by Anne Hege Grung, Marianne Bjelland Kartzow, and Anna Rebecca Solevåg. Eugene, OR: Pickwick, 2015. https://doi.org/10.2307/j.ctt1c999nc.25
Knapp, Gudrun-Axeli. "Race, Class, Gender: Reclaiming Baggage in Fast Travelling Theories," *European Journal of Women's Studies* 12.3 (2005): 249–65. https://doi.org/10.1177/1350506805054267
Kriger, Diane, (with Tirzah Meacham leBeit Yoreh). *Sex Rewarded, Sex Punished: A Study of the Status "Female Slave" in Early Jewish Law*. Boston, MA: Academic Studies Press, 2011.
Lieu, Judith M. "The 'Attraction of Women' in/to Early Judaism and Christianity: Gender and the Politics of Conversion," *Journal for the Study of the New Testament* 72 (1998): 5–22. https://doi.org/10.1177/0142064X9902107202
—*Neither Jew nor Greek? Constructing Early Christianity*. London: T&T Clark, 2002.
Lüderitz, Gert, and Joyce M. Reynolds. *Corpus Jüdischer Zeugnisse aus der Cyrenaika*. Wiesbaden: Ludwig Reichert Verlag, 1983.
MacDonald, Margaret Y. "Slavery, Sexuality and House Churches: A Reassessment of Colossians 3.18–4.1 in Light of New Research on the Roman Family," *New Testament Studies* 53 (2008): 94–113. https://doi.org/10.1017/S0028688507000069
Marchal, Joseph A. "The Usefulness of Onesimus: The Sexual Use of Slaves and Paul's Letter to Philemon," *Journal of Biblical Literature* 130.4 (2011): 749–70. https://doi.org/10.2307/23488277
Mason, Steve. "Jews, Judeans, Judaizing, Judaism: Problems of Categorization in Ancient History," *Journal for the Study of Judaism* 38.4/5 (2007): 457–512. https://doi.org/10.1163/156851507X193108
Mattsson, Katarina. "Genua och vithet i den intersektionella vändingen," *Tidsskrift för genusvetenskap* 1/2 (2010): 7–22.
Melhuus, Marit. "Issues of Relevance: Anthropology and the Challenges of Cross-Cultural Comparison," 70–92 in *Anthropology, by Comparison*. Edited by Andre Gingrich and Richard Fox. London: Routledge, 2002. https://doi.org/10.4324/9780203463901_chapter_3

Newport, Frank. "The Religious Switcher in the United States," *American Sociological Review* 44.4 (1979): 528–52. https://doi.org/10.2307/2094586

Nicolet, Valérie. "Monstrous Bodies in Paul's Letter to the Galatians," 115–41 in *Bodies on the Verge: Queering Pauline Epistles*. Edited by Joseph A. Marchal. Atlanta, GA: Society of Biblical Literature, 2019. https://doi.org/10.2307/j.ctvh4zh7m.8

Peskowitz, Miriam B. *Spinning Fantasies: Rabbis, Gender, and History*. Berkeley, CA: University of California Press, 1997. https://doi.org/10.1525/9780520919495

Phoenix, Ann, and Pamela Pattynama, eds. *European Journal of Women's Studies (Issue on Intersectionality)* 13 (2006). https://doi.org/10.1177/1350506806065751

Pui-lan, Kwok. "Finding a Home for Ruth: Gender, Sexuality, and the Politics of Otherness," 135–54 in *New Paradigms for Bible Study: The Bible in the Third Millennium*. Edited by Robert M. Fowler, Edith L. Blumhofer, and Fernando F. Segovia. New York: T&T Clark, 2004.

Reinhartz, Adele, and Miriam-Simma Walfish. "Conflict and Coexistence in Jewish Interpretation," 101–25 in Trible and Russell, eds., *Hagar, Sarah, and Their Children*, 2006.

Runesson, Anders. "The Question of Terminology: The Architecture of Contemporary Discussions on Paul," 53–77 in *Paul within Judaism: Restoring the First-Century Context to the Apostle*. Edited by Mark D. Nanos and Magnus Zetterholm. Minneapolis, MN: Fortress Press, 2015. https://doi.org/10.2307/j.ctt9m0vn7.6

Schüssler Fiorenza, Elisabeth. "Introduction: Exploring the Intersections of Race, Gender, Status, and Ethnicity in Early Christian Studies," 1–23 in *Prejudice and Christian Beginnings: Investigating Race, Gender, and Ethnicity in Early Christian Studies*. Edited by Laura Nasrallah and Elisabeth Schüssler Fiorenza. Minneapolis, MN: Fortress Press, 2009.

Sengupta, Shuddhabrata. "I/Me/Mine—Intersectional Identities as Negotiated Minefields," *Signs: Journal of Women in Culture and Society* 31.3 (2006): 629–39. https://doi.org/10.1086/499318

Stein, Dina. "A Maidservant and Her Master's Voice: Discourse, Identity, and Eros in Rabbinic Texts," *Journal of the History of Sexuality* 10.3/4 (2001): 375–97. https://doi.org/10.1353/sex.2001.0076

Taylor, Nicholas H. "Onesimus: A Case Study of Slave Conversion in Early Christianity," *Religion and Theology* 3.3 (1996): 259–81. https://doi.org/10.1163/157430196X00239

Thiessen, Matthew. *Contesting Conversion: Genealogy, Circumcision, and Identity in Ancient Judaism and Christianity*. New York: Oxford University Press, 2011. https://doi.org/10.1093/acprof:oso/9780199793563.001.0001

Trible, Phyllis, and Letty M. Russell, eds. *Hagar, Sarah, and Their Children: Jewish, Christian, and Muslim Perspectives*. Louisville, KY: Westminster John Knox Press, 2006.

Verloo, Mieke. "Multiple Inequalities, Intersectionality and the European Union," *European Journal of Women's Studies* 13.3 (2006): 211–28. https://doi.org/10.1177/1350506806065753

Williams, Delores S. *Sisters in the Wilderness: The Challenge of Womanist God-Talk*. New York: Orbis Books, 1993.

Yuval-Davis, Nira. "Intersectionality and Feminist Politics," *European Journal of Women's Studies* 13.3 (2006): 193–209. https://doi.org/10.1177/1350506806065752

Chapter Nine

The Complexity of Aseneth's Transformation[1]

Kirsten Marie Hartvigsen

Joseph and Aseneth relates a love story that shares several characteristics with Hellenistic novels or romances.[2] In ancient novels, the beautiful protagonists must overcome a variety of initial obstacles before they are reunited.[3] In *Joseph and Aseneth*, the primary hindrance to the marriage of the protagonists is the fact that Joseph and Aseneth belong to different ethnic groups, each with their distinctive cults. These contrasts, which underlie the plot of the first part of the narrative (1–21), become evident in the initial encounter of the protagonists. Joseph refuses to let Aseneth kiss him because of their divergent religious practices, which in the novel, are intertwined with their membership in different clans and families (8.4-7). To become a woman who can be intimate with Joseph and marry him, Aseneth must undergo a profound transformation that involves several aspects of her being.

The focus on problems caused by the incompatible ethnicities and religious adherences of the protagonists in *Joseph and Aseneth* was probably inspired by Genesis 41.45, 41.50, and 46.20. These are the only verses that mention Aseneth in the Hebrew Bible. In these verses, Aseneth is presented as the daughter of Potiphera, the priest of On. Genesis thus indicates that Aseneth belongs to a different *ethnos* and religion than Joseph, the Hebrew patriarch. Despite their apparent differences, Pharaoh gives Aseneth to Joseph as his wife, and she becomes the mother of his two sons, Manasseh and Ephraim. The idea that the Hebrew patriarch married and had children

---

1. See also Kirsten Marie Hartvigsen, *Aseneth's Transformation* (Berlin: de Gruyter, 2018).
2. Stephen L. West, "*Joseph and Asenath*: A Neglected Greek Romance," *The Classical Quarterly* 24.1 (1974): 70–81; Richard I. Pervo, "Joseph and Aseneth and the Greek Novel," in George MacRae, ed., *Society of Biblical Literature Seminar Papers* 1976 (Missoula, MT: Scholars Press, 1976), 171–81; Howard C. Kee, "The Socio-Cultural Setting of Joseph and Asenath," *New Testament Studies* 29 (1983): 394–413; Sara Raup Johnson, *Historical Fictions and Hellenistic Jewish Identity: Third Maccabees in Its Cultural Context* (Berkeley, CA: University of California Press, 2004), 108–20.
3. Tomas Hägg, *The Novel in Antiquity* (Oxford: Blackwell, 1983). West, "Joseph and Asenath," 77–8.

with the daughter of an Egyptian polytheistic priest, despite the biblical prohibition against intermarriages,[4] apparently puzzled the audiences who later heard or read Genesis, and different justifications were proposed.[5] The most comprehensive explanation of this conundrum was offered in the novel *Joseph and Aseneth*.[6] However, the novel also addresses many issues that are not mentioned in Genesis.

The Different Versions of Joseph and Aseneth

Joseph and Aseneth survives in 16 Greek manuscripts, and has been translated into Syriac, Armenian, Latin, Rumanian, Serbo-Slavonic, Modern Greek, and Ethiopic. The various manuscripts have traditionally been sorted into four families, but Christoph Burchard has recently proposed a more complicated model.[7] Scholars have focused mainly on two recensions; a short version and a long version of the text. With some exceptions,[8] most scholars

---

4. Ross Shepard Kraemer, "The Book of Aseneth," in Elisabeth Schüssler Fiorenza, ed. *Searching the Scriptures* (New York: Crossroad, 1993), 859–88, here 859. John J. Collins, "The Transformation of Aseneth," in Anne Hege Grung, Marianne Bjelland Kartzow, and Anna Rebecca Solevåg, eds., *Bodies, Borders, Believers: Ancient Texts and Present Conversations; Essays in Honor of Turid Karlsen Seim on Her 70th Birthday* (Eugene, OR: Pickwick, 2015), 93–108, here 96.

5. Victor Aptowitzer, "Asenath, the Wife of Joseph: A Haggadic Literary-Historical Study," *Hebrew Union College Annual* 1 (1924): 239–306; Christoph Burchard, "Joseph and Aseneth (First Century B.C.–Second Century A.D.): A New Translation and Introduction," in James H. Charlesworth, ed., *The Old Testament Pseudepigrapha: Expansions of the "Old Testament" and Legends, Wisdom and Philosophical Literature, Prayers, Psalms, and Odes, Fragments of Lost Judeo-Hellenistic Works* (New Haven, CT : Yale University Press, 2010), 177–247, here 177. In his article on the legends of Aseneth, Aptowitzer suggests that three types of accounts were given of Aseneth's background and why she could become Joseph's wife and the mother of his children: (1) Aseneth was actually a member of Jacob's tribe and family, (2) She "was the deliverer of Joseph," (3) She was pious and upright. Early on, the emphasis on Aseneth's descent was combined with a focus on her piety and *Joseph and Aseneth* seemingly constitutes a version of this combination. Aptowitzer, "Asenath," 243–60. Although *Joseph and Aseneth* focuses on Aseneth's piety, elements that may indicate her descent are also present (1.5).

6. On *Joseph and Aseneth* as rewritten Bible, see Susan Docherty, "*Joseph and Aseneth*: Rewritten Bible or Narrative Expansion?," *Journal for the Study of Judaism* 35.1 (2004): 27–48.

7. Uta Barbara Fink, "Textkritische Situation," in Eckart Reinmuth, ed., *Joseph und Aseneth* (Tübingen: Mohr Siebeck, 2009), 33–44; Christoph Burchard, *Joseph und Aseneth: Kritisch herausgegeben mit Unterstützung von Carsten Burfeind und Uta Barbara Fink* (Leiden: Brill, 2003), 9–34.

8. Angela Standhartinger, *Das Frauenbild im Judentum der hellenistischen Zeit*:

argue that the long version of *Joseph and Aseneth* is closer to the original narrative than the other versions. Although the short and the long versions of *Joseph and Aseneth* share the main elements of the story,[9] there are some variations regarding the portrayal of Aseneth and her transformation process,[10] in particular pertaining to Aseneth's attitudes and behavior. In this article, I am using the long version edited by Burchard and Uta B. Fink,[11] with quotations from Burchard's English translation of *Joseph and Aseneth*.[12]

Introduction to the Plot of Joseph and Aseneth

In the novel, Aseneth is presented as the daughter of Pentephres,[13] an Egyptian polytheistic priest. She initially despises all men, including Joseph, but when she sees him enter her family's residence in all his beauty, she falls in love with the Hebrew patriarch. From the perspective of both the male protagonist and the extradiegetic narrator of the novel, Aseneth is a high-status virgin, but also a foreign polyheist who cannot marry Joseph and be intimate with him unless she is transformed into an insider and becomes Joseph's female counterpart, namely a noble Hebrew virgin who worships the living God. Having met Joseph and received his blessing, Aseneth withdraws to her chamber and undergoes a thorough transformation process, involving multiple aspects of her identity.

Aseneth's transformation from a beautiful and boastful Egyptian woman who blesses "dead and dumb" Egyptian gods, into an angelic, humble Hebrew woman who worships the living God comprises the plot of the first part of the novel (1–21). Her transformation thus involves aspects of her ethnicity, which in the novel are intertwined with her religious affiliation. Moreover, her transformation expresses an altered mindset that involves the embodiment of a new feminine ideal. In the novel, Aseneth's altered religious practices and acceptance of the gendered hierarchy transform her from

---

Ein Beitrag anhand von "Joseph und Aseneth" (Leiden: Brill, 1995). Ross Shepard Kraemer, "When Aseneth Met Joseph: A Postscript," in Randal A. Argall, et al., eds., *For a Later Generation: The Transformation of Tradition in Israel, Early Judaism, and Early Christianity* (Harrisburg, PA: Trinity Press International, 2000), 128–35.

9. Collins, "The Transformation of Aseneth," 95.

10. On the views of women underlying the short and the long versions of *Joseph and Aseneth*, see Standhartinger, *Das Frauenbild im Judentum*.

11. Burchard, *Joseph und Aseneth: Kritisch herausgegeben*; Uta Barbara Fink, *Joseph und Aseneth: Revision des griechischen Textes und Edition der zweiten lateinischen Übersetzung* (Berlin: de Gruyter, 2008).

12. Burchard, "Joseph and Aseneth," 202–47.

13. There are some variations between the novel and the Genesis tradition, such as the name of Aseneth's father.

an ignorant woman to a wise woman. The second part of the novel (22–29) focuses on the result of Aseneth's transformation process and relates the way in which Joseph's family receives and incorporates Aseneth. This article focuses on the first part of *Joseph and Aseneth*.

The Text-External and Text-Internal Contexts of **Joseph and Aseneth**

The characters, events, and settings portrayed in the various versions of *Joseph and Aseneth* may reflect the religious interests and circumstances experienced by specific audiences in the text-external world, but the religious concerns and contexts of such text-external audiences are difficult to reconstruct and are thus continuously disputed. If *Joseph and Aseneth* constitutes an important literary source for thinking about female conversion in Antiquity, identification of the original, text-external audience for which the novel was intended could elucidate Aseneth's transformation process. However, several elements make it difficult to classify and interpret the novel in the light of the context of its intended audience: its fictive character, its symbolic features, and the lack of explicit text-external references. As a result, Aseneth's transformation has been interpreted against the backdrop of different ancient contexts.

The answers to the following questions have been particularly important for discussion of the possible text-external contexts of the novel: Should emphasis be put on the context in which the oldest manuscripts were found, namely sixth-century Syria?[14] Or should the text-external context be reconstructed based on the characters, events, and settings depicted in the novel, namely Hebrews living in Egypt? These questions are interrelated with the question of whether *Joseph and Aseneth* should be interpreted literally or allegorically.[15] A literal interpretation of the text-internal context would indicate that the Egyptian Aseneth exchanges worship of Egyptian gods for worship of YHWH. In such a context, Aseneth becomes a model convert and a matriarch similar to Sarah, Rebecca, and Rachel (1.5). Scholars who choose this approach tend to date the text between the mid-second century BCE and the early-second century CE. If the evidence of the sixth-century Syrian

---

14. Davila argues that scholars should prioritize the physical manuscript evidence. He claims that regarding *Joseph and Aseneth* as a Christian work of late antiquity "involves the least extrapolation from the earliest physical evidence for the document and perhaps should be our working hypothesis for the present ..." see James R. Davila, *The Provenance of the Pseudepigrapha: Jewish, Christian, or Other?* (Leiden: Brill, 2005), 195.

15. On the allegorical interpretation of the novel, see Randall D. Chesnutt, *From Death to Life: Conversion in Joseph and Aseneth* (Sheffield: Sheffield Academic, 1995), 72–73.

manuscripts is given priority, the novel is interpreted allegorically in a Christian context. Consequently, Aseneth converts to Christianity, and the marriage between Joseph and Aseneth symbolizes the marriage between Christ and the Church.[16]

These aspects offer some indications as to why scholars have traditionally asked whether *Joseph and Aseneth* is "Jewish or Christian."[17] Early on, scholars such as Pierre Batiffol and Ernest W. Brooks presented *Joseph and Aseneth* as a Christian text inspired by a Jewish legend.[18] This view was, with some exceptions,[19] common until the middle of the twentieth century.[20] Since then, a new scholarly consensus has taken shape, based on the notion that the novel was Jewish.[21] Lately, the Jewish origin of the novel has been challenged by several scholars. Ross Shepard Kraemer suggests that the author could be Jewish, Christian, "theosebic," or Samaritan,[22] but she argues that "a strong case can be made for Christian composition and redaction," and she proposes that Syria could be the area in which it was composed.[23] Based on a different approach to ancient manuscripts, James R. Davila reaches a similar conclusion.[24] Recently, Rivka Nir argues that

---

16. Rivka Nir, *Joseph and Aseneth: A Christian Book* (Sheffield: Sheffield Phoenix Press, 2012), 177.

17. John J. Collins, "Joseph and Aseneth: Jewish or Christian?," *Journal for the Study of the Pseudepigrapha* 14.2 (2005): 97–112.

18. Pierre Batiffol, *Le Livre de la Prière d'Asenath* (Paris: Leroux, 1889), 30–37. Ernest W. Brooks, *Joseph and Asenath: The Confession and Prayer of Asenath Daughter of Pentephres the Priest* (London: SPCK, 1918), xi–xiii.

19. Aptowitzer, "Asenath."

20. Standhartinger, *Das Frauenbild im Judentum*, 5.

21. Burchard, "Joseph and Aseneth," 187. Edith McEwan Humphrey, *The Ladies and the Cities: Transformation and Apocalyptic Identity in Joseph and Aseneth, 4 Ezra, the Apocalypse and The Shepherd of Hermas* (Sheffield: Sheffield Academic Press, 1995), 32. Chesnutt, *From Death to Life*, 71–6. Randall D. Chesnutt, "Bread of Life in Joseph and Aseneth and in John 6," in James E. Priest, ed., *Johannine Studies: Essays in Honor of Frank Pack* (Malibu, LA: Pepperdine University Press, 1989), 1–16, here 2–3. Randall D. Chesnutt, "*Joseph and Aseneth*: Food as an Identity Marker," in Amy-Jill Levine. et al., eds., *The Historical Jesus in Context* (Princeton, NJ: Princeton University Press, 2006), 357–65, here 357. See also Standhartinger, *Das Frauenbild im Judentum*, 5–20; Gideon Bohak, *Joseph and Aseneth and the Jewish Temple in Heliopolis* (Atlanta: Scholars Press, 1996), xiii; Anthea E. Portier-Young, "Sweet Mercy Metropolis: Interpreting Aseneth's Honeycomb," *Journal for the Study of the Pseudepigrapha* 14.2 (2005): 133–57, here 134–5.

22. Ross Shepard Kraemer, *When Aseneth Met Joseph: A Late Antique Tale of the Biblical Patriarch and His Egyptian Wife, Reconsidered* (New York: Oxford University Press, 1998), 273–4.

23. Kraemer, *When Aseneth Met Joseph*, ix.

24. Davila, *Provenance*, 190–5.

"*Joseph and Aseneth* is a Christian work, composed by Christians for Christian purposes."[25] Nir also situates the work in Syria.[26] However, the majority position is still that the novel was composed between the mid-second century BCE and the early-second century CE in Egypt.[27] I suggest that *Joseph and Aseneth* defies clear classification as "Jewish, Christian, or other."[28] In this article, emphasis is put on Aseneth's transformation as it occurs within the narrative world depicted in the novel. Consequently, possible text-external religious contexts of the text will not be explored.

This article focuses on characters, events, and settings that constitute the narrative world, bearing in mind that fiction often mimics aspects of the real world. Through their involvement with different characters and events in the narrative world, the audience may simulate events and their outcomes vicariously.[29] If they identify with Aseneth, they may, for instance, simulate how Aseneth's transformation alters many aspects of her identity to make her a suitable wife for Joseph. Among other things, they experience how Aseneth's transformation process alters her embodiment of female ideals. If *Joseph and Aseneth* was intended for a female readership, as many ancient novels probably were,[30] this simulation could explore both the transformation process involved in moving from one *ethnos* to another and the long-lasting effects of this process on the female identity of the person undergoing such a transformation. Moreover, it would illuminate the female identity of those who already belonged to this *ethnos*. In this respect, the novel presents a female ideal that probably influenced how its female readership interpreted and shaped their role in the community.

Can Aseneth's Transformation Be Classified as Conversion?

From a modern perspective, the religious elements associated with Aseneth's transformation indicate that an analysis of *Joseph and Aseneth* might elucidate important aspects of female religious conversion in Antiquity; she

---

25. Nir, *Joseph and Aseneth*, 4.
26. Nir, *Joseph and Aseneth*, 16–7.
27. Manuel Vogel, "Einführung in die Schrift," in Reinmuth, ed., *Joseph und Aseneth*, 3–31, here 13. On the Egyptian setting, see János Bolyki, "Egypt as the Setting for *Joseph and Aseneth*: Accidental or Deliberate?," in Anthony Hilhorst and George H. van Kooten, eds., *The Wisdom of Egypt: Jewish, Early Christian, and Gnostic Essays in Honour of Gerard P. Luttikhuizen* (Leiden: Brill, 2005), 81–96.
28. Davila, *Provenance*.
29. Kirsten Marie Hartvigsen, *Prepare the Way of the Lord: Towards a Cognitive Poetic Analysis of Audience Involvement with Characters and Events in the Markan World* (Berlin: de Gruyter, 2012), 53–71, 87–90.
30. Hägg, *Novel in Antiquity*, 95–6.

destroys her Egyptian gods, confesses her sins, and starts praying to the Hebrew God. However, research on categorization in ancient history has drawn attention to the anachronistic ways that scholars have employed many categories when they analyze ancient texts and concepts, including the term "conversion."[31] The perspective from which Aseneth's gradual transformation is viewed, that is, whether ancient or modern, and how conversion is defined may thus decide whether this process can be interpreted as a religious conversion or not. In the introduction to *The Oxford Handbook of Religious Conversion*, Lewis R. Rambo and Charles E. Farhadian argue: "While particular definitions may be appropriate to a certain religion at a specific time and place, there is no universal definition that we believe captures all aspects of religious conversion."[32] Definitions of conversion must therefore be constructed to elucidate specific contexts.

According to recent research on religion in the ancient world, the modern definition of conversion with its focus on individual processes, belief, and intent[33] would not make much sense from an emic perspective. In his article "Jews, Judaeans, Judaizing, Judaism: Problems of Categorization in Ancient History," Steve Mason argues that "there was no category of 'Judaism' in the Graeco-Roman world, no 'religion' too, and that the *Ioudaioi* were understood until late antiquity as an ethnic group comparable to other ethnic groups, with their distinctive laws, traditions, customs, and God."[34] In this context, conversion would be understood as

> a movement from one ethnos to another, a kind of change in citizenship .... There was no "religion" to which one might convert, even if one had wished to do so: taking on the Judaeans' laws and customs was different from, and more than, being initiated in the cult of Cybele or joining a philosophical

---

31. When labels such as conversion, class, marriage, nation, etc. are employed to refer to concepts that did not exist in the same form in Antiquity as today, the phenomena presented in the ancient texts are made intelligible to a present-day audience, but the words also veil the differences between the notions portrayed in the texts and modern ideas. See for instance Steve Mason, "Jews, Judaeans, Judaizing, Judaism: Problems of Categorization in Ancient History," *Journal for the Study of Judaism* 38 (2007): 457–512; Ken Stone, "Marriage and Sexual Relations in the World of the Hebrew Bible," in Adrian Thatcher, ed., *The Oxford Handbook of Theology, Sexuality, and Gender* (Oxford: Oxford University Press, 2014), 173–88, here 173–7. Denise Kimber Buell, *Why This New Race: Ethnic Reasoning in Early Christianity* (New York: Columbia University Press, 2005).

32. Lewis R. Rambo and Charles E. Farhadian, "Introduction," in Lewis R. Rambo and Charles E. Farhadian, eds., *The Oxford Handbook of Religious Conversion* (Oxford: Oxford University Press, 2014), 1–22, here 10.

33. Buell, *Why This New Race*, 158–60.

34. Mason, "Jews, Judaeans," 457. See also Collins, "The Transformation of Aseneth," 93–4.

school, notwithstanding parallels to both. It was a change of ethnic-ancestral culture, the joining of another people, as it had been already in the biblical paradigm, Ruth (1:16): "your people shall be my people."[35]

Denise Kimber Buell's study of ethnic reasoning in early Christianity sheds further light on the differences between ancient and modern conceptions of race, ethnicity, religion, and conversion. Buell points out that in interpretations of early Christianity, race and ethnicity are often regarded as a "fixed or given facet of identity, while religion is primarily viewed as voluntary."[36] She suggests, however, that both ethnicity and religion can be associated with fixity and fluidity.[37] Buell also draws attention to four roles religion may play in ethnoracial discourse: "to assert the fixity of ethnoracial differences between groups, to accomplish ethnoracial fluidity (as a means by which one can change membership), to make links between two or more distinctive ethnoracial groups, and to make differentiations within a group."[38] *Joseph and Aseneth* may illustrate all these functions, but in this context, emphasis is on the first two. The plot of the first part of the novel is based on the initial ethnic and religious differences between the two protagonists. Whereas the description in 8.5 suggests that ethnicity and religious adherence are fixed, Joseph's blessing (8.9) and Aseneth's subsequent destruction of her Egyptian gods, adherence to the Hebrew God, and incorporation into the family of the Hebrew patriarch suggest that a change of cultic practices and beliefs is intertwined with a change of ethnoracial affiliation (fluidity). Similar to Mason's study, Buell thus enables us to regard "conversion as a social process that entails the crossing of social boundaries. These boundaries may be understood as religious but also as ethnic and racial."[39]

In *On the Virtues*, Philo provides an emic perspective on the movement of an individual from another *ethnos* to the *Ioudaioi*: "abandoning their kinsfolk by blood, their country, their customs and the temples and images of their gods, and the tributes and honours paid to them, they have taken the journey to a better home, from idle fables to the clear vision of truth and the worship of the one and truly existing God."[40] This passage suggests that aspects which currently are associated with religious conversion, such as the substitution of one cult and god for another, were also involved when a person moved from one *ethnos* to another in the ancient world, but because

35. Mason, "Jews, Judaeans," 491.
36. Buell, *Why This New Race*, 6.
37. Buell, *Why This New Race*, 6–10.
38. Buell, *Why This New Race*, 36.
39. Buell, *Why This New Race*, 158.
40. Philo, *On the Virtues*, 102. Mason, "Jews, Judaeans," 491.

worship was associated with ethnic identity, this was primarily a joining of another *ethnos*.[41] In the words of Buell, "what we might conceive of as a religious process, conversion, could be simultaneously imagined as a process of ethnic transformation."[42]

One can illustrate other differences between an ancient and a more modern approach to conversion by comparing Mason's ideas with the definition proposed in the introduction to *The Oxford Handbook of Religious Conversion*. This definition was earlier presented by Marc Baer and employed in the context of Sunni Islam during the Ottoman Empire:

> [C]onversion is a decision or experience followed by a gradually unfolding, dynamic process through which an individual embarks on religious transformation. This can entail an intensification of belief and practice of one's own religion, moving from one level of observation to another, or exchanging the beliefs and practices in which one was raised for those of another religious tradition. In both cases, a person becomes someone else because his or her internal mind-set and/or external actions are transformed ... Whereas some scholars still posit an artificial distinction between "exterior" and "interior" conversion, I argue that conversion has an internal component entailing belief and an external component involving behavior, leading to the creation of a new self-identity and a new way of life.[43]

In contrast to Mason's and Buell's emphasis on the social context of conversion, which highlights ethnic transformation, Baer's definition focuses on conversion as religious transformation, emphasizing the alteration of the internal mindset or belief, and external actions. Conversion is thus regarded as a personal process. Some of the aspects mentioned in Baer's definition seem to occur in *Joseph and Aseneth*. In particular, Aseneth's mindset and actions are profoundly transformed.

In addition to the facets mentioned in Baer's definition, Aseneth's transformation process seemingly corresponds to other important themes explored by contemporary scholars of conversion, such as points of continuity and discontinuity between the past and the present, the agency of converts, the significance of the human body, rituals, and so on.[44] For instance, in *Joseph and Aseneth*, the agency of Aseneth is evident throughout 9–18, and both continuity and discontinuity of religious practices and bodily

---

41. Shaye J. D. Cohen argues that there was a shift after the Maccabean revolt. From this point on, the term *Ioudaios* was associated with an ethno-religious identity; see Shaye J. D. Cohen, *The Beginnings of Jewishness: Boundaries, Varieties, Uncertainties* (Berkeley, CA: University of California Press, 1999), 137. See also Mason, "Jews, Judaeans," 494–5. Collins, "The Transformation of Aseneth," 94.

42. Buell, *Why This New Race*, 139.

43. Rambo and Farhadian, "Introduction," 11.

44. Rambo and Farhadian, "Introduction," 7–8.

features are important. In this manner, many aspects involved in Aseneth's change of ethnic belonging correspond to those investigated in contemporary research on conversion. It is probably these features of the narrative that have prompted scholars to regard the novel as a story of female religious conversion in Antiquity.[45]

Whether *Joseph and Aseneth* portrays rituals or not is a complicated question. In his early research on the novel, Dieter Sänger used the novel to reconstruct a ritual for the admission of proselytes,[46] but he has recently changed his mind, claiming that the novel cannot be utilized to reconstruct such rituals.[47] According to Randall D. Chesnutt, "[t]here is little if any evidence that Aseneth's story preserves a fixed ritual of initiation … Since Aseneth's experiences are narrated to address certain concerns relating to the sociological dimension of conversion to Judaism, it should not be assumed that her actions reflect rites of initiation regularly practiced in the author's community."[48] In my own research, I argue that the author of the novel probably drew on aspects of genuine rituals, but altered them to suit the requirements of the plot. These rituals were utilized in the novel to elucidate the profound transformation which Aseneth must undergo to become a suitable bride for Joseph. They should not be compared to text-external rituals or used to reconstruct them. Because fiction imitates reality, the novel can draw on the functions of rituals in the real world, namely, to facilitate processes of change. The functions of the ritual components in *Joseph and Aseneth* are complex and are referred to only in passing in this article.[49]

---

45. On conversion in the novel, see Collins, "Transformation of Aseneth," 96. Some scholars argue that Aseneth's transformation process cannot be compared to other ancient conversions because of her outstanding position and of the role she plays in the second part of the novel. Collins, " Transformation of Aseneth," 97 and 102.

46. Dieter Sänger, *Antikes Judentum und die Mysterien* (Tübingen: J. C. B. Mohr, 1980), 174–87.

47. Dieter Sänger, "'Brot des Lebens, Kelch der Unsterblichkeit': Vom Nutzen des Essens in 'Joseph und Aseneth'," in David Hellholm and Dieter Sänger, eds., *The Eucharist—Its Origins and Contexts: Sacred Meal, Communal Meal, Table Fellowship in Late Antiquity, Early Judaism, and Early Christianity. Vol. 1: Old Testament, Early Judaism, New Testament* (Tübingen: Mohr Siebeck, 2017), 206–10. Collins likewise argues that the novel does not refer to rituals. Collins, "The Transformation of Aseneth," 97.

48. Chesnutt, *From Death to Life*, 255.

49. These themes are treated thoroughly in Kirsten Marie Hartvigsen, "The Meal Formula, the Honeycomb, and Aseneth's Transformation," in Hellholm and Sänger, eds., *The Eucharist—Its Origins and Contexts*, 1.223–51; Hartvigsen, *Aseneth's Transformation*.

An Intersectional Approach to Aseneth's Transformation

Baer's definition of conversion and the emic perspective of joining a new *ethnos* both suggest processes that involve the creation of a new self-identity. The novel can therefore be analyzed to define new aspects of Aseneth's identity. The construction of Aseneth's new identity as a Hebrew woman and Joseph's wife is complex; it involves both continuity and discontinuity with features of Aseneth's previous identity as an Egyptian woman. It also involves multiple aspects. To differentiate between and elucidate various facets of Aseneth's identity, how they are interrelated, and how they are preserved, transformed, or replaced in the narrative, I will draw on the theory of intersectionality.

Intersectionality can be regarded as an analytical strategy that elucidates human life and behavior derived from the experiences of marginalized people.[50] The working definition proposed in the article on intersectionality in *The Oxford Handbook of Gender and Politics* suggests the following:

> Intersectionality consists of an assemblage of ideas and practices that maintain that gender, race, class, sexuality, age, ethnicity, ability, and similar phenomena cannot be analytically understood in isolation from one another; instead, these constructs signal an intersecting constellation of power relationships that produce unequal material realities and distinctive social experiences for individuals and groups positioned within them.[51]

Elisabeth Schüssler Fiorenza emphasizes that the theory of intersectionality may also "illuminate how identity is constructed at the intersections of race, gender, class, sexuality, and imperialism."[52] The subsequent analysis of Aseneth's identity and of its transformation focuses on phenomena such as Aseneth's ethnicity, religious adherence, gender, social position, age, and physical ability.[53] The analysis is conducted primarily from a text-internal perspective, but at certain points, text-external, critical perspectives are pointed out. The goal is to elucidate those aspects of Aseneth's identity that

---

50. Patricia Hill Collins and Valerie Chepp, "Intersectionality," in Georgina Waylen. et al., eds., *The Oxford Handbook of Gender and Politics* (Oxford: Oxford University Press, 2013), 58–92, here 58.

51. Collins and Chepp, "Intersectionality," 58–9.

52. Elisabeth Schüssler Fiorenza, "Introduction: Exploring the Intersections of Race, Gender, Status, and Ethnicity in Early Christian Studies," in Laura Nasrallah and Elisabeth Schüssler Fiorenza, eds., *Prejudice and Christian Beginnings: Investigating Race, Gender, and Ethnicity in Early Christian Studies* (Minneapolis, MN: Fortress Press, 2009), 1–23, here 6.

53. Issues of sexuality, in particular virginity, have already been discussed in Marianne Bjelland Kartzow, *Destabilizing the Margins: An Intersectional Approach to Early Christian Memory* (Eugene, OR: Pickwick, 2012), 59–69.

initially make her a candidate for the role as Joseph's spouse and the facets that prevent her from playing this part. The article also presents an analysis of how these aspects are transformed in 1–21, and how Aseneth adopts a different feminine ideal when she becomes a Hebrew woman and Joseph's wife. Some of these characteristics are evaluated similarly by Egyptian and Hebrew characters in the narrative world and by the (Hebrew) extradiegetic narrator, while others are evaluated differently. In many instances, a critical reading of the novel from a contemporary text-external perspective provides additional assessments of the phenomena in question.

The approach of intersectionality must be employed with care. As I have indicated in the previous subdivision, some of the categories listed in the working definition of intersectionality may be employed differently, or may even be missing, in the ancient context. This caution is particularly important pertaining to the concepts of ethnicity and religion. Because of the limited format of the article, I can only provide sketches of the various dimensions of Aseneth's transformation.

The Initial Portrayal of Aseneth: Intricate Intersections of Age, Physical Ability, Ethnicity, Sexuality, and Social Position

The protagonists of the ancient novels "come from the upper levels of society" and their beauty and purity are underscored.[54] Similarly, Aseneth is introduced as the attractive, 18-year-old virgin daughter of Pentephres,[55] the priest of Heliopolis and the chief of the satraps and noblemen of Pharaoh. Intersections of criteria such as Aseneth's age (appropriate for marriage), physical ability (exceptional beauty),[56] sexuality (virginity), and social position (the daughter of the chief of the satraps) make her a desirable wife for any young and powerful man in the Egyptian society. The novel indeed indicates that all the sons of the noblemen, satraps, and kings, and even the firstborn son of Pharaoh, want to marry her (1.6-8). In *Joseph and Aseneth*, the female protagonist is thus presented as an attractive woman, herself aware of her position in Egyptian society (4.9-11). Aseneth lives in seclusion and resents all men, except perhaps the firstborn son of Pharaoh, whom she wants to wed (4.11).

According to the extradiegetic narrator, the physical features associated with Aseneth's beauty do not relate her to other Egyptian women, but

---

54. West, "Joseph and Asenath," 71–3, here 71. On the beauty of the protagonists, see also Hägg, *The Novel in Antiquity*, 6–7.
55. In Genesis, Aseneth's father is called Potiphera.
56. In the novel, the function of the extraordinary beauty of the protagonists may extend our conception of the term physical ability.

rather to significant Hebrew women. "[S]he was tall as Sarah and handsome as Rebecca and beautiful as Rachel" (1.5). In the novel, Aseneth's physical resemblance to the Hebrew matriarchs may constitute an instance of ethnic reasoning. By focusing on the physical attributes that Aseneth has in common with these matriarchs, the extradiegetic narrator suggests that her Egyptian ethnicity is not clear-cut. The fact that Aseneth resembles these matriarchs suggests her fictive descent from these women, a strategy that may function in a similar manner to a forged genealogical claim.[57] Because important aspects of Aseneth's initial physical ability anticipate her later status as Joseph's Hebrew wife, her subsequent entry into God's chosen people (8.9) is facilitated.[58]

In the novel, Aseneth is a privileged woman, but she is restrained to a tower and has limited interaction with other people, probably to secure her sexual purity (2.1, 7-9; 15.14). From a text-internal point of view, Aseneth's uncontested virginity constitutes a prerequisite for joining God's chosen people and becoming Joseph's wife.[59] Accordingly, Aseneth's seclusion is a positive feature. Yet from a text-external, critical point of view, it constitutes a negative element; that is, Aseneth's freedom is restricted despite her beauty, power, and social position.[60] This constraint is underscored by the fact that Aseneth is the possession of men throughout the novel. At the beginning of the novel, she is controlled by her father (4.6) and, after her transformation, by Joseph (20.4). When Joseph first visits the family, Aseneth's father thus informs Aseneth that he wants to *give* her over to Joseph (4.8), and later he states that Joseph will *take* Aseneth as his wife (20.8). However, Joseph proposes that Pharaoh should *give* Aseneth to him (20.9; 21.2-8).[61] Aseneth's marriage thus becomes a transaction between important men who surround her; they are the subjects, whereas she is the object of the transaction. At one point, which is discussed below, Aseneth attempts to influence her father and become a subject in this transaction.

---

57. According to Buell, genealogical claims "imbue ethnoracial identities with a sense of stability, essence, and longevity" even when the genealogies are fabricated. On the function of genealogical claims, see Buell, *Why This New Race*, 40.

58. On the permeable boundaries between Hebrews and Egyptians at the beginning of the novel, see B. Diane Lipsett, *Desiring Conversion: Hermas, Thecla, Aseneth* (Oxford: Oxford University Press, 2011), 95.

59. Kartzow, *Destabilizing the Margins*, 68–9.

60. See Kartzow, *Destabilizing the Margins*, 63–5.

61. On "marriage" in the Hebrew Bible, see Stone, "Marriage," 174–6.

Aseneth's Personality and Female Gender Roles

The portrayal of Aseneth's personality reveals how she exemplifies feminine ideals. Initially, she is characterized as a person who "was despising and scorning every man, and she was boastful and arrogant with everyone" (2.1),[62] but to some extent she also recognizes her father's lordship over her (4.6). The characterization of Aseneth in 2.1 is developed further in the scene where Pentephres suggests that Aseneth should marry Joseph (4.7-12). Aseneth becomes furious and speaks of Joseph in a belittling manner and answers her father "daringly and with boastfulness and anger" (4.12). In 2.1 and 4.12, Aseneth's behavior breaks with traditional feminine ideals, which suggest that a man is a woman's master or lord.[63] Because Aseneth's behavior transgresses the bounds of propriety, Pentephres becomes ashamed.

From a text-external, critical perspective, the scene where Aseneth refuses to be handed over to Joseph to become his wife (4.9-12) represents Aseneth's attempt to free herself from her role as one of her father's possessions. She wants to marry the king's firstborn son, not the Hebrew patriarch. In order to do so, she argues that her father treats her like a captive and she criticizes Joseph's descent, morals, and behavior. Through this behavior, Aseneth attempts to become a subject of the marriage transaction, but she does not succeed. From a text-external perspective, Aseneth's attempt to free herself from her father's governance can be evaluated positively, but from a text-internal perspective, the evaluation is rather negative. In the scene depicted in 4.5-12, the evaluative perspective of Aseneth's Egyptian father corresponds to and merges with the perspective of the Hebrew extradiegetic narrator. As a result, Aseneth's behavior as a young woman who defies her father's suggestion about her future husband is condemned from both an Egyptian and a Hebrew male point of view.[64]

Soon after, when Aseneth sees Joseph and falls in love with him, she realizes that she has been ignorant (6.7), and she wants her father to hand her over to Joseph. The portrayal of Aseneth's personality thus evolves as the plot develops. At this point, Aseneth's wish aligns her evaluative point of view with that of her father and of the extradiegetic narrator. Her subsequent focus on how to become Joseph's slave and serve him (6.8) suggests that she accepts the embodiment of a subservient female gender role. In the narrative world, Aseneth's new mindset apparently constitutes a prerequisite for the transformation process. From a text-internal perspective, this

---

62. Burchard, "Joseph and Aseneth," 203.
63. Stone, "Marriage," 176.
64. The extradiegetic narrator seemingly represents a Hebrew, male point of view in the narrative.

development is thus positive, but from a text-external, critical perspective, Aseneth continues to be governed by the men who surround her.

Introduction of the Conflict that Constitutes the Plot: The Ethnicities and Religious Practices of the Protagonists

Aseneth and Joseph have the following characteristics in common: high social status, exceptional beauty, virginity, and aversion towards members of the opposite sex (8.1), but their ethnicity and the corresponding religious practices differ. The ethnic backgrounds and religious adherence of the protagonists constitute the starting point of the plot of 1–21, a plot which aims at removing these obstacles through a radical transformation of the female protagonist.

The initial contrast between Joseph and Aseneth is emphasized in the scene where Aseneth is introduced to Joseph. Pentephres encourages Aseneth to kiss Joseph, but he refuses because of their divergent religious adherences and practices. Instead, he provides the following explanation:

> It is not fitting for a man who worships God, who will bless with his mouth the living God and eat blessed bread of life and drink a blessed cup of immortality and anoint himself with blessed ointment of incorruptibility to kiss a strange woman who will bless with her mouth dead and dumb idols and eat from their table bread of strangulation and drink from their libation a cup of insidiousness and anoint herself with ointment of destruction. But a man who worships God will kiss his mother and the sister (who is born) of his mother and the sister (who is born) of his clan and family and the wife who shares his bed, (all of) who(m) bless with their mouths the living God. (8.5)[65]

In the novel, Aseneth is portrayed as the daughter of the priest of Heliopolis who worships and sacrifices to Egyptian gods (2.2-3; 3.6). From Joseph's perspective, Aseneth's consumption of staples utilized in the Egyptian cult associates her with death and destruction. Conversely, his own consumption of staples associated with worship of the living God links him with life, immortality, and incorruptibility.[66] Joseph's refusal to kiss Aseneth can be interpreted as a way of marking the boundary between Egyptians and Hebrews and their respective cults.[67] Even though Aseneth resembles the Hebrew matriarchs physically, she is not (yet) a Hebrew.

---

65. Burchard, "Joseph and Aseneth," 211–2.
66. For detailed analyses of the consequences of consuming bread, cup, and ointment in *Joseph and Aseneth*, see Hartvigsen, "The Meal Formula"; Hartvigsen, *Aseneth's Transformation*.
67. According to Lipsett, these staples may function as boundary markers that signal ethnic and religious belonging. Lipsett, *Desiring Conversion*, 104. On oil, food, and

Joseph's utterance suggests that he can only kiss members of his own clan and family who worship the same deity. If Aseneth wants to kiss him, she must thus first join his *ethnos* and worship his God. According to Mason, conversion could be understood as "a movement from one ethnos to another, a kind of change in citizenship." However, Buell suggests that religion could constitute a means to change membership from one ethnic group to another (ethnoracial fluidity).[68] In *Joseph and Aseneth*, the portrayal of Aseneth's transformation process in all probability draws on aspects of genuine rituals that were altered to suit the plot. Aseneth thus employs new cultic elements prior to her actual incorporation into Joseph's family through her wedding and her subsequent meeting with her father-in-law. For instance, her heavenly visitor states that she has eaten the staples according to the Hebrew fashion, albeit symbolically (16.16). The novel may thus suggest that cultic elements constitute a factor of the transformation process that precedes Aseneth's incorporation into God's chosen people. Below, Aseneth's transformation is analyzed in more detail as a process constituted by three phases.

First Phase of the Transformation:
Emphasis on Aseneth's Mindset and Female Gender Role

In the novel, Aseneth's mindset changes prior to her ethnicity, religious practices, and bodily features. As soon as she sees Joseph, she realizes that her former attitude towards him was "foolish and daring" (6.3), and she states: "let my father give me to Joseph for a maidservant and slave, and I will serve him for ever (and) ever" (6.8).[69] Thus, the noblewoman of the beginning of the narrative, who was attended by seven maidens and other members of the staff in her father's house, wants to become Joseph's slave. When Aseneth later confesses her sins, she describes her former proud and arrogant self (12.5), claims that she spoke of Joseph in ignorance, and repeats her desire to become his slave (13.12-14). Aseneth's wish is soon fulfilled. When Joseph returns and does not recognize Aseneth because

---

drink as markers of Jewish identity, see also Randall D. Chesnutt, "Perceptions of Oil in Early Judaism and the Meal Formula in *Joseph and Aseneth*," *Journal for the Study of the Pseudepigrapha* 14.2 (2005): 113–32. Chesnutt, "*Joseph and Aseneth*." On the kiss as a boundary marker, see Christoph Burchard, "Küssen in *Joseph und Aseneth*," *Journal for the Study of Judaism* 36.3 (2005): 316–23, here 319. For a more elaborate interpretation of this scene in the light of the cognitive theory of rituals, see Hartvigsen, "The Meal Formula"; Hartvigsen, *Aseneth's Transformation*.

68. Buell, *Why This New Race*, 161.
69. Burchard, "Joseph and Aseneth," 210. See the entire scene.

of her new, supernatural beauty, she introduces herself as his maidservant (19.5), and she offers to wash Joseph's feet. Aseneth's utterance suggests that she regards him as her lord, reflecting a gendered hierarchy.

In Aseneth's psalm, which concludes the first plot (21.11-21), Aseneth again revisits the familiar themes of her boastful and arrogant attitude, her trust in her beauty, and her contempt for men. Towards the end of the psalm, she states that her encounter with Joseph made her humble. The transformation process depicted in the novel is thus associated with a meek female ideal. In the novel, meekness also characterizes male Hebrew characters, such as Joseph and Levi (8.8, 23.10).[70] Meekness could thus be a feature associated with a female ideal and with being a proper Hebrew. However, Aseneth's father, Pentephres, is also characterized as a gentle man (1.3). This feature could thus suggest that Aseneth has become more aligned with the male ideals presented in the novel.

Aseneth's revision of her former mindset also involves a development from ignorance to wisdom,[71] a theme which in the novel involves a revised attitude and knowledge about the living God, her former religious practices, her attitude and behavior towards men, and her opinion of Joseph (12–13, in particular 13.11-13).[72] As I pointed out above, Aseneth's evaluations of her former self constitute important clues to the construction of the female gender role and ideology of the novel, which are communicated to the text-external female readers through their vicarious simulation of the plot. Aseneth's initial change of mindset probably explains her willingness to become a member of God's chosen people and perform the appropriate religious rituals that facilitate her entry into the Hebrew *ethnos* and her subsequent supernatural physical transformation (religion as a means to accomplish ethnoracial fluidity).[73]

Second Phase of the Transformation: Profound Transformation of Aseneth's Ethnicity and Religious Practices

After his initial refusal to kiss Aseneth, Joseph blesses her and asks God *inter alia* to "renew her," "form her anew," "make her alive again," let her eat the bread of life and drink a cup of blessing, and number her among

---

70. Humphrey, *The Ladies and the Cities*, 74–5.
71. See also Eugene V. Gallagher, "Conversion and Community in Late Antiquity," *The Journal of Religion* 73.1 (1993): 1–15, here 9–10. On Aseneth as Wisdom, see Ross Shepard Kraemer, "Aseneth as Wisdom," in Athalya Brenner and Carole Fontaine, eds., *Wisdom and Psalms* (Sheffield: Sheffield Academic Press, 1998), 218–39.
72. On ignorance, wisdom, and gender, see Kraemer, "Aseneth as Wisdom," 238–9.
73. Buell, *Why This New Race*, 36.

God's people (8.9). After his blessing, Aseneth withdraws to her chamber and repents by removing and throwing away her extravagant garments and ornaments engraved with Egyptian gods, replacing them with a black tunic, a rope, and sackcloth. She also destroys the images of her Egyptian gods and throws them through the window together with the food and drink that constitute their sacrifices. In this manner, Aseneth distances herself from her customs, sacred rites, and Egyptian gods.[74] She sprinkles ashes on her head and for a period of seven days, she weeps, sighs, and screams, without ingesting food or drink. On the eighth day, she addresses the God of the Hebrews, confesses her sins, and prays for acceptance (11.3–13.14).

Through the actions that take place in 9–13, which can be interpreted as rituals of grief and purification, Aseneth separates herself from the cult of the Egyptian gods and acknowledges the superiority of the cult of the Hebrew living God. Like her altered opinion of Joseph, her newfound wisdom also makes her realize that the Egyptian gods which she used to worship are "dead and dumb idols," and that she had worshipped them in ignorance (13.11). Aseneth's actions and confessions prepare not only her chamber but also her body for the arrival of a heavenly visitor, Joseph's heavenly counterpart, in Aseneth's first chamber (14.1–17.10).

After the rites of separation, Aseneth's heavenly visitor tells her to go into her second room and put off her garments of mourning and dress in an untouched linen robe and a twin girdle of virginity.[75] Moreover, she removes the ashes and washes her hands and face with living water, which probably should be interpreted as a ritual of purification. When she returns, the visitor states: "you will be renewed and formed anew and made alive again, and you will eat blessed bread of life, and drink a blessed cup of immortality, and anoint yourself with blessed ointment of incorruptibility" (15.5).[76] Through this utterance, the heavenly visitor reminds Aseneth of Joseph's blessing. Furthermore, his status as a supernatural being indicates that she will in fact be able to participate in Hebrew religious practices in the future. He also promises her that she will become Joseph's wife, and gives her a new name and function, that is, City of Refuge. Finally, he tells her to dress as a bride.

The appearance of the heavenly being, his statement that her acts of humiliation and confession of her sins have been seen and heard (15.2-3), and his promises to Aseneth (15.5-6), corroborate the information according

---

74. See Philo, *On the Virtues*, 102.
75. According to Kartzow, Aseneth's virginity could be a premise for Aseneth's conversion. Kartzow, *Destabilizing the Margins*, 68–9.
76. Burchard, "Joseph and Aseneth," 226.

to which her name has been entered into the "book of the living in heaven" (15.4). By mentioning the entry of her name in the heavenly register of citizenship, the heavenly being confirms her membership with God's chosen people.

Aseneth's transformation involved distancing herself from her family, customs, sacred rites, and images of the gods (9.1–13.14).[77] Instead, she becomes a member of a new *ethnos* and can practice its customs and rites. Moreover, she was promised to marry Joseph and thus become a member of his family. As Joseph's wife and a member of God's chosen people, she will function as a City of Refuge, a function that to some extent depersonalizes Aseneth by relating her to the cities that performed this function. In the second part of the novel (22–29), this name and function constitute an important part of the plot.[78]

When Aseneth subsequently invites her heavenly visitor for a meal of bread and wine, he insists that she should also bring him a honeycomb, but she does not have one in her storeroom (15.14–16.7). The heavenly visitor then, through a speech-act, produces a heavenly honeycomb made "from the dew of the roses of life" in paradise, and the heavenly man and Aseneth both eat a portion of the comb of life. Subsequently, the heavenly visitor interprets this event in the following manner: "Behold, you have eaten bread of life, and drunk a cup of immortality, and been anointed with ointment of incorruptibility" and he states that her body will be renewed (16.16).[79] Through her consumption of the heavenly honeycomb of life, Aseneth has apparently ingested the food of angels and taken part in religious practices equivalent to those earlier mentioned by Joseph (8.5). Moreover, by ingesting the angelic food of life, she becomes associated with the living God in a manner that prepares her for eternal life.[80] This event thus realizes Joseph's blessing and the promises of the heavenly visitor in the narrative world.

By ingesting a piece of the honeycomb of life, Aseneth becomes connected with the living God and the religious practices of the Hebrews. This confirms that she has become a full member of God's chosen people, which in turn suggests that religion may constitute a means to accomplish

---

77. See Philo, *On the Virtues*, 102.
78. See Hartvigsen, *Aseneth's Transformation*.
79. Burchard, "Joseph and Aseneth," 229.
80. For similar insights, see Collins, "The Transformation of Aseneth," 100. According to Andrea Lieber, Aseneth's consumption of angels' food transforms her into an angel; Andrea Lieber, "I Set a Table before You: The Jewish Eschatological Character of Aseneth's Conversion Meal," *Journal for the Study of Pseudepigrapha* 14.1 (2004): 63–77, here 65.

ethnoracial fluidity.[81] Because the ethnicity of both protagonists from this moment on is Hebrew, the main obstacle preventing the two protagonists from getting married is removed, and they are permitted to kiss.[82] Aseneth's membership in the Hebrew *ethnos* and her consumption of the honeycomb of life prepare her for the transformation of her body.

Third Phase of the Transformation: Enhancement of Aseneth's Physical Ability

Since Aseneth already looks like an ethnic Hebrew woman, becoming a member of the Hebrew *ethnos* should not require supernatural physical transformation. However, the narrative portrays a significant change regarding Aseneth's bodily features. When Aseneth dresses as a bride (18.5-11), her innate beauty is transformed, and she looks like an angelic being. In this manner, Aseneth's initial physical ability, that is, her renowned beauty, is enhanced beyond human measure. In the novel, supernatural physical ability is a feature that the transformed Aseneth shares with male and female Hebrew characters.[83] The fact that Aseneth's transformation into an angelic being occurs when she dresses as a bride may suggest that the main public ritual that marks her transition to the Hebrew *ethnos* is the wedding.[84]

In the novel, Aseneth is gradually transformed. The first aspect of Aseneth's physical transformation occurs when she changes from the black robe into the new, untouched linen robe. Having removed the ashes and washed her hands and face with living water, she puts on a linen veil. Her heavenly visitor tells her to remove the veil "[f]or you are a chaste virgin today, and your head is like that of a young man" (15.1).[85] In this manner, Aseneth's transformation process seemingly enables her to transcend traditional gender divisions,[86] at least during the liminal phase constituted by the heavenly visit. Aseneth's resemblance to a young man may underscore the fact that at this point, she has become more aligned with the noble ideals associated with the male characters and the (male) extradiegetic narrator of the novel.

As I indicated above, Aseneth's ingestion of a piece of the heavenly honeycomb initiates the process which alters her body into something her

---

81. On this function of religion, see Buell, *Why This New Race*, 36.
82. For a more thorough analysis of this scene, see Hartvigsen, *Aseneth's Transformation*. Hartvigsen, "The Meal Formula."
83. See below.
84. On this function of the wedding, see Collins, "The Transformation of Aseneth," 101.
85. Burchard, "Joseph and Aseneth," 225–6.
86. Burchard, "Joseph and Aseneth," 226.

heavenly visitor can only compare to nature in its paradisiac state. "Behold, from today your flesh (will) flourish like flowers of life from the ground of the Most High, and your bones will grow strong like the cedars of the paradise of delight of God, and untiring powers will embrace you, and your youth will not see old age, and your beauty will not fail forever" (16.16). Ingesting a piece of the honeycomb of life gives her eternal life. However, Aseneth's physical appearance does not explicitly change until she dresses as Joseph's bride in a robe "like lightning in appearance" (18.5-11).[87] In this scene, Aseneth discovers her supernatural beauty:

> And Aseneth leaned (over) to wash her face and saw her face in the water. And it was like the sun and her eyes (were) like a rising morning star, and her cheeks like fields of the Most High, and on her cheeks (there was) red (color) like a son of man's blood, and her lips (were) like a rose of life coming out of its foliage, and her teeth like fighting men lined up for a fight, and the hair of her head (was) like a vine in the paradise of God prospering in its fruits, and her neck like an all-variegated cypress, and her breasts (were) like the mountains of the Most High God. (18.9)[88]

Aseneth's supernatural physical transformation underscores her incorporation into God's chosen people. Like the main Hebrew characters in the novel, she is depicted as an angelomorphic being.[89] The portrayals of the Hebrew matriarchs, Joseph, Jacob, Levi, and Benjamin indicate that they all possess extraordinary physical features; in some cases, their attractiveness borders on heavenly beauty, in other cases, they have superior intellectual and physical capacities (see 1.5; 5.4-7; 22.7-8, 13; 23.2, 8-15; 26.6; 27.1-6; 28.9; 28.17). Some aspects of the supernatural appearance of Aseneth and of other Hebrew characters are reminiscent of characters in apocalyptic literature who are transformed into angelic beings.

The portrayals of Aseneth in 16.16 and 18.9 are complex and may evoke different intertextual contexts which are thematically interrelated. The comparisons of Aseneth's bodily features to plants may evoke depictions of the Garden of Eden/Paradise and motifs in the Song of Songs. The Garden of Eden/Paradise is also evoked by the description of the garden surrounding

---

87. On how light and shining signifies correspondence with divinity in Hellenistic romances, see Meredith J. C. Warren, "A Robe Like Lightning: Clothing Changes and Identification in Joseph and Aseneth," in Kristi Upson-Saia, et al., eds., *Dressing Judeans and Christians in Antiquity* (Farnham: Ashgate Publishing, 2014), 137–53.

88. Burchard, "Joseph and Aseneth," 232. According to Humphrey, Aseneth "has taken on the vastness of a strong and protected land of God: fields, vegetation, fighting men, protective mountains (18.8)." Humphrey, *The Ladies and the Cities*, 101.

89. George J. Brooke, "Men and Women as Angels in *Joseph and Aseneth*," *Journal for the Study of Pseudepigrapha* 14.2 (2005): 159–77.

Aseneth's abode (2.11-12). Aseneth's garden functions as a safe haven for some of the bees mentioned in 16.22-23. This feature is reminiscent of Aseneth's new name and function in the second part of the novel, namely City of Refuge (15.7). However, the comparison to plants is a device also employed to portray the personified, female Wisdom in Sirach 24.13-17. These portrayals of Aseneth may therefore also underscore her newfound wisdom.[90]

After the transformation of Aseneth's personality, her inclusion in the book of the living in heaven, her consumption of the honeycomb, and her preparation for her future wedding—all confirming her position as a Hebrew woman—Aseneth's new status becomes visible through the supernatural enhancement of her physical ability. Whether the exceptional physical abilities of the Hebrew characters in the novel pertain to Hebrews in general, or just to prominent members of Joseph's immediate family, is difficult to ascertain. In the novel, the Hebrew characters are all members of Joseph's family. The depiction of Joseph's half-brothers (27.7–28.8) and the scene with the two types of bees (16.17-23) may, however, indicate that supernatural physical ability is not a characteristic of all Hebrews.

In the novel, supernatural abilities are not only associated with the Hebrew characters. Pentephres, the Egyptian priest, counselor of Pharaoh, and Aseneth's father, also possesses superior intellectual ability (1.3). In 4.7-8, his knowledge of the merits of the living God[91] and the virtues of Joseph lead him to suggest a wedding between his daughter and the Hebrew patriarch. Although Aseneth is a stranger who must be transformed into a supernatural member of God's chosen people, the position and insights of her father make her a suitable candidate for the role as one of the Hebrew matriarchs.

Summary

This article has analyzed Aseneth's transformation using insights from current research on conversion and the theory of intersectionality. Intersections between Aseneth's ethnicity, religious adherence, gender, social position, age, and physical ability were emphasized. Some of these aspects, such as her social position and physical ability, made Aseneth an attractive wife for most men, including Joseph, whereas others made her unfit to be Joseph's wife.

---

90. See also Hartvigsen, *Aseneth's Transformation*, 67–137.
91. According to Lipsett, Egyptian characters, including Aseneth's parents, speak of a singular God. Lipsett, *Desiring Conversion*, 99.

In the novel, *Joseph and Aseneth,* Aseneth is presented as a privileged, female member of a wealthy, Egyptian family, and her father is an influential satrap and a polytheistic priest. Moreover, she possesses an extraordinary physical ability, namely her astonishing beauty. From a Hebrew point of view, however, Aseneth's admirable social position and physical ability were not sufficient to allow her to become Joseph's bride. To marry him, she must distance herself from her Egyptian customs, sacred rites, and gods,[92] and join the Hebrew *ethnos* that worships the living god. Certain elements of Aseneth's physical ability, such as her resemblance to the Hebrew matriarchs, as well as her father's recognition of the Hebrew god, facilitate this development of the plot.

In *Joseph and Aseneth*, ritual elements are employed to depict Aseneth's separation from her Egyptian *ethnos* and her subsequent incorporation into the Hebrew *ethnos*. Aseneth's efforts to become part of the Hebrew *ethnos* are acknowledged since her name is written in the book of the living in heaven. Moreover, she is allowed to eat the heavenly honeycomb of life, which corresponds to the blessed bread of life, blessed cup of immortality, and the blessed ointment of incorruptibility that are consumed by those who bless the living God (8.5; 16.16). As a proper Hebrew woman, she constitutes a suitable wife for Joseph and a worthy matriarch. When Aseneth dresses as a bride, her novel status as a Hebrew woman is confirmed by the angelomorphic transformation of her body.

In sum, Aseneth's comprehensive transformation alters her mindset, ethnicity, religious adherence, and physical appearance, and she becomes a humble and wise angelomorphic Hebrew woman who worships the living God. Studies of categorization in ancient history and ethnic reasoning in early Christianity enable us to view Aseneth's conversion process as a social process, that is, the joining of a new *ethnos*.

Aseneth's behavior as a woman develops in the narrative. In an initial dispute with her father over whom she should marry, Aseneth challenges Pentephres's role as her lord. Through this act, Aseneth dissociates herself from the feminine ideals which Egyptian and Hebrew women are expected to embody. As soon as she sees Joseph, however, Aseneth herself begins to conform to the evaluative points of view and feminine ideals held by the extradiegetic narrator and important male characters in the narrative. Through her gradual transformation, Aseneth thus learns and accepts how proper (Hebrew) women should behave. From a text-internal perspective, Aseneth's acceptance of her position in the gendered hierarchy is regarded as a positive development; and through vicarious simulation of the plot, the

---

92. See Philo, *On the Virtues*, 102.

female values and ideals embraced by Aseneth are conveyed to the addressees of the novel, who were probably also women.

Biographical Note

Since 2019, Kirsten Marie Hartvigsen has been Associate Professor at the Department of Teacher Education and School Research (University of Oslo) where she teaches Religious Education. In her research, she has focused on the Gospel of Mark and the novel *Joseph and Aseneth*. At present, she is working on how the Bible is taught in Norwegian public schools. She has published two monographs that highlight interdisciplinary approaches, *Prepare the Way of the Lord: Towards a Cognitive Poetic Analysis of Audience Involvement with Characters and Events in the Markan World* and *Aseneth's Transformation*.

Bibliography

Aptowitzer, Victor. "Asenath, the Wife of Joseph: A Haggadic Literary-Historical Study," *Hebrew Union College Annual* 1 (1924): 239–306.

Batiffol, Pierre. *Le Livre de la Prière d'Asenath*. Paris: Leroux, 1889.

Bohak, Gideon. *Joseph and Aseneth and the Jewish Temple in Heliopolis*. Atlanta, GA: Scholars Press, 1996.

Bolyki, János. "Egypt as the Setting for *Joseph and Aseneth*: Accidental or Deliberate?," 81–96 in *The Wisdom of Egypt: Jewish, Early Christian, and Gnostic Essays in Honour of Gerard P. Luttikhuizen*. Edited by Anthony Hilhorst and George H. van Kooten. Leiden: Brill, 2005. https://doi.org/10.1163/9789004331013_006

Brooke, George J. "Men and Women as Angels in *Joseph and Aseneth*," *Journal for the Study of Pseudepigrapha* 14.2 (2005): 159–77. https://doi.org/10.1177/0951820705051957

Brooks, Ernest W. *Joseph and Asenath: The Confession and Prayer of Asenath Daughter of Pentephres the Priest*. London: SPCK, 1918.

Burchard, Christoph. *Joseph und Aseneth: Kritisch herausgegeben mit Unterstützung von Carsten Burfeind und Uta Barbara Fink*. Leiden: Brill, 2003.

—"Küssen in *Joseph und Aseneth*," *Journal for the Study of Judaism* 36.3 (2005): 316–23. https://doi.org/10.1163/1570063054377688

—"Joseph and Aseneth (First Century B.C.–Second Century A.D.): A New Translation and Introduction," 177–247 in *The Old Testament Pseudepigrapha: Expansions of the "Old Testament" and Legends, Wisdom and Philosophical Literature, Prayers, Psalms, and Odes, Fragments of Lost Judeo-Hellenistic Works*. Edited by James H. Charlesworth. New Haven, CT: Yale University Press, 2010.

Chesnutt, Randall D. "Bread of Life in Joseph and Aseneth and in John 6," 1–16 in *Johannine Studies: Essays in Honor of Frank Pack*. Edited by James E. Priest. Malibu, LA: Pepperdine University Press, 1989.

—*From Death to Life: Conversion in Joseph and Aseneth*. Sheffield: Sheffield Academic, 1995.

—"Perceptions of Oil in Early Judaism and the Meal Formula in *Joseph and Aseneth*,"

Journal for the Study of the Pseudepigrapha 14.2 (2005): 113–32. https://doi.org/10.1177/0951820705051955

—"*Joseph and Aseneth*: Food as an Identity Marker," 357–65 in *The Historical Jesus in Context*. Edited by Amy-Jill Levine, Dale C. Allison, and John Dominic Crossan. Princeton, NJ: Princeton University Press, 2006.

Cohen, Shaye J. D. *The Beginnings of Jewishness: Boundaries, Varieties, Uncertainties*. Berkeley, CA: University of California Press, 1999.

Collins, John J. "Joseph and Aseneth: Jewish or Christian?," *Journal for the Study of the Pseudepigrapha* 14.2 (2005): 97–112. https://doi.org/10.1177/0951820705051954

—"The Transformation of Aseneth," 93–108 in *Bodies, Borders, Believers: Ancient Texts and Present Conversations; Essays in Honor of Turid Karlsen Seim on Her 70th Birthday*. Edited by Anne Hege Grung, Marianne Bjelland Kartzow, and Anna Rebecca Solevåg. Eugene, OR: Pickwick, 2015.

Davila. James R. *The Provenance of the Pseudepigrapha: Jewish, Christian, or Other?* Leiden: Brill, 2005.

Docherty, Susan. "*Joseph and Aseneth*: Rewritten Bible or Narrative Expansion?," *Journal for the Study of Judaism* 35.1 (2004): 27–48. https://doi.org/10.1163/157006304772913078

Fink, Uta Barbara. *Joseph und Aseneth: Revision des griechischen Textes und Edition der zweiten lateinischen Übersetzung*. Berlin: de Gruyter, 2008.

—"Textkritische Situation," 33–44 in *Joseph und Aseneth*. Edited by Eckart Reinmuth. Tübingen: Mohr Siebeck, 2009.

Gallagher, Eugene V. "Conversion and Community in Late Antiquity," *The Journal of Religion* 73.1 (1993): 1–15. https://doi.org/10.1086/489050

Hägg, Tomas. *The Novel in Antiquity*. Oxford: Blackwell, 1983.

Hartvigsen, Kirsten Marie. *Prepare the Way of the Lord: Towards a Cognitive Poetic Analysis of Audience Involvement with Characters and Events in the Markan World*. Berlin: de Gruyter, 2012. https://doi.org/10.1515/9783110253481

—"The Meal Formula, the Honeycomb, and Aseneth's Transformation," 1.223–51 in Hellholm and Sänger, eds., *The Eucharist—Its Origins and Contexts*, 2017.

—*Aseneth's Transformation*. Berlin: de Gruyter, 2018.

Hellholm, David, and Dieter Sänger, eds. *The Eucharist—Its Origins and Contexts: Sacred Meal, Communal Meal, Table Fellowship in Late Antiquity, Early Judaism, and Early Christianity. Vol. 1: Old Testament, Early Judaism, New Testament*. Edited by Tübingen: Mohr Siebeck, 2017.

Hill Collins, Patricia, and Valerie Chepp. "Intersectionality," 58–92 in *The Oxford Handbook of Gender and Politics*. Edited by Georgina Waylen, Karen Celis, Johanna Kantola, and Laurel Weldon. Oxford: Oxford University Press, 2013.

Kartzow, Marianne Bjelland. *Destabilizing the Margins: An Intersectional Approach to Early Christian Memory*. Eugene, OR: Pickwick, 2012.

Kee, Howard C. "The Socio-Cultural Setting of Joseph and Aseneth," *New Testament Studies* 29 (1983): 394–413. https://doi.org/10.1017/S002868850000607X

Kimber Buell, Denise. *Why This New Race: Ethnic Reasoning in Early Christianity*. New York: Columbia University Press, 2005. https://doi.org/10.7312/buel13334

Kraemer, Ross Shepard. "The Book of Aseneth," 859–88 in *Searching the Scriptures*. Edited by Elisabeth Schüssler Fiorenza. New York: Crossroad, 1993.

—"Aseneth as Wisdom," 218–39 in *Wisdom and Psalms*. Edited by Athalya Brenner and Carole Fontaine. Sheffield: Sheffield Academic Press, 1998.

—*When Aseneth Met Joseph: A Late Antique Tale of the Biblical Patriarch and His Egyptian Wife, Reconsidered.* New York: Oxford University Press, 1998.

—"When Aseneth Met Joseph: A Postscript," 128–35 in *For a Later Generation: The Transformation of Tradition in Israel, Early Judaism, and Early Christianity.* Edited by Randal A. Argall, Beverley A. Bow, and Rodney A. Werline. Harrisburg, PA: Trinity Press International, 2000.

Lieber, Andrea. "I Set a Table before You: The Jewish Eschatological Character of Aseneth's Conversion Meal," *Journal for the Study of Pseudepigrapha* 14.1 (2004): 63–77. https://doi.org/10.1177/095182070401400104

Lipsett, B. Diane. *Desiring Conversion: Hermas, Thecla, Aseneth.* Oxford: Oxford University Press, 2011. https://doi.org/10.1093/acprof:oso/9780199754519.001.0001

Mason, Steve. "Jews, Judaeans, Judaizing, Judaism: Problems of Categorization in Ancient History," *Journal for the Study of Judaism* 38 (2007): 457–512. https://doi.org/10.1163/156851507X193108

McEwan Humphrey, Edith. *The Ladies and the Cities: Transformation and Apocalyptic Identity in Joseph and Aseneth, 4 Ezra, the Apocalypse and The Shepherd of Hermas.* Sheffield: Sheffield Academic Press, 1995.

Nir, Rivka. *Joseph and Aseneth: A Christian Book.* Sheffield: Sheffield Phoenix Press, 2012.

Pervo, Richard I. "Joseph and Aseneth and the Greek Novel," 171–81 in *Society of Biblical Literature Seminar Papers* 1976. Edited by George MacRae. Missoula, MT: Scholars Press, 1976.

Portier-Young, Anathea E. "Sweet Mercy Metropolis: Interpreting Aseneth's Honeycomb," *Journal for the Study of the Pseudepigrapha* 14.2 (2005): 133–57. https://doi.org/10.1177/0951820705051956

Rambo, Lewis R., and Charles E. Farhadian. "Introduction," 1–22 in *The Oxford Handbook of Religious Conversion.* Edited by Lewis R. Rambo and Charles E. Farhadian. Oxford: Oxford University Press, 2014. https://doi.org/10.1093/oxfordhb/9780195338522.013.033

Raup Johnson, Sara. *Historical Fictions and Hellenistic Jewish Identity: Third Maccabees in Its Cultural Context.* Berkeley, CA: University of California Press, 2004. https://doi.org/10.1525/california/9780520233072.001.0001

Sänger, Dieter. *Antikes Judentum und die Mysterien.* Tübingen: J. C. B. Mohr, 1980.

—"'Brot des Lebens, Kelch der Unsterblichkeit': Vom Nutzen des Essens in 'Joseph und Aseneth'," 1.206–10 in Hellholm and Sänger, eds., *The Eucharist—Its Origins and Contexts,* 2017. https://doi.org/10.1628/978-3-16-153919-0

Schüssler Fiorenza, Elisabeth. "Introduction: Exploring the Intersections of Race, Gender, Status, and Ethnicity in Early Christian Studies," 1–23 in *Prejudice and Christian Beginnings: Investigating Race, Gender, and Ethnicity in Early Christian Studies.* Edited by Laura Nasrallah and Elisabeth Schüssler Fiorenza. Minneapolis, MN: Fortress, 2009.

Standhartinger, Angela. *Das Frauenbild im Judentum der hellenistischen Zeit: Ein Beitrag anhand von "Joseph und Aseneth."* Leiden: Brill, 1995. https://doi.org/10.1163/9789004332799

Stone, Ken. "Marriage and Sexual Relations in the World of the Hebrew Bible," 173–88 in *The Oxford Handbook of Theology, Sexuality, and Gender.* Edited by Adrian Thatcher. Oxford: Oxford University Press, 2014. https://doi.org/10.1093/oxfordhb/9780199664153.013.020

Vogel, Manuel. "Einführung in die Schrift," 3–31 in *Joseph und Aseneth*. Edited by Eckart Reinmuth. Tübingen: Mohr Siebeck, 2009.

Warren, Meredith J. C. "A Robe Like Lightning: Clothing Changes and Identification in Joseph and Aseneth," 137–53 in *Dressing Judeans and Christians in Antiquity*. Edited by Kristi Upson-Saia, Carly Daniel-Hughes, and Alicia J. Batten. Farnham: Ashgate Publishing, 2014.

West, Stephen L. "*Joseph and Asenath*: A Neglected Greek Romance," *The Classical Quarterly* 24.1 (1974): 70–81. https://doi.org/10.1017/S0009838800030251

Chapter Ten

Leaving the Traditions of the Fathers:
Perspectives on Conversion from a Christianity That Did Not Survive[*]

Kristine Toft Rosland

The fourth century is a turning point in Christian history. At the start of the century, the number of non-Christians far outweighs the number of Christians, but during the century, Christianity grows to become the majority religion.[1] The nature of the sources for this time period makes it difficult to give exact numbers for conversion. However, we can establish that the growth in the number of Christians must have been quite astonishing.[2] Because of

---

[*] This article has been written under the aegis of project NEWCONT (New Contexts for Old Texts: Unorthodox Texts and Monastic Manuscript Culture in Fourth- and Fifth-Century Egypt) at the University of Oslo, Faculty of Theology. The project is funded by the European Research Council (ERC) under the European Community's Seventh Framework Program (FP7/2007–2013) / ERC Grant Agreement no. 2837.

1. For the Roman Empire as a whole we will probably never have anything but "guestimates." In this article, I focus on Egypt and rely mainly on the numbers supplied by Mark Depauw and Willy Clarysse, "How Christian Was Fourth Century Egypt? Onomastic Perspectives on Conversion," *Vigiliae Christianae* 62 (2013): 407–35, the latest and most extensive contribution in a longer debate initiated by Roger Bagnall. In 1982, Bagnall estimated the number of Christians based on the occurrence of what he considered Christian names in selected texts in Roger Bagnall, "Religious Conversion and Onomastic Change," *The Bulletin of the American Society of Papyrologists* 19 (1982): 105–24. Later (in 1987), Bagnall modified the numbers and indicated a less rapid growth than he had initially suggested, in Roger Bagnall, "Conversion and Onomastics: A Reply," *Zeitschrift für Papyrologie und Epigraphik* 69 (1987): 243–50. The methods and results have been contested by Ewa Wipszycka, "La valeur de l'onomastique pour l'histoire de la christianisation de l'Égypte. À propos d'une étude de R. S. Bagnall," *Zeitschrift für Papyrologists und Epigraphik* 62 (1986): 173–81; Ewa Wipszycka, "La christianisation de l'Égypte aux 4ème–5ème siècles. Aspects sociaux et ethniques," *Aegyptus* 68 (1988): 117–65. While Depauw and Clarysse use the same method as Bagnall, they have the advantage of a much larger data set and their transparency on method and reasoning is admirable. They conclude (Abstract): "Our results are similar to the curve which can be distilled from Bagnall's adapted results in 1987, with 20-30% Christians around 313, a Christian majority around 350 and virtually complete Christianization around the middle of the fifth century" (407).

2. For an illustration of exponential curves and how a steady growth in percentage

this, a high number of Christians in this period were converts, many of them with strong ties of kinship to non-Christians. Being a convert is thus a very common Christian experience at the time.

The political shift in attitude towards Christianity during this century radically alters the nature of this experience. The beginning of the fourth century sees the start of "the great persecution."[3] Becoming a Christian, and consequently giving up the traditional and imperial cults,[4] could be an act of defiance and potentially expose the convert to considerable risks.[5] With the Constantinian turn, this changes. When Christianity becomes the state's official religion in 380, keeping to the old traditions constitutes disobedience to imperial power. With Christianity's new status, one also sees more uniformity in doctrine and liturgy established by an increasingly influential church hierarchy. But before and during this century of rapid religious change, Christianity is less homogenous than later descriptions of that era may lead us to believe.

It is in this century that a set of books now known as the Nag Hammadi Codices are copied and read. Among these is the *Apocryphon of John* (*Ap. John*),[6] a work portraying the creator god of Genesis as jealous, ignorant, and evil. Like many of the works from Nag Hammadi, *Ap. John*'s understanding of the creator god deviates from the orthodoxy that emerges from

---

will at some point give a seemingly explosive growth in absolute numbers: see Rodney Stark, *The Rise of Christianity: How the Obscure, Marginal Jesus Movement Became the Dominant Religious Force in the Western World in a Few Centuries* (New York: HarperCollins, 1997). Stark's model suggests 3.42% per year, not far from the growth rate of Mormonism in the last hundred years. See also Keith Hopkins, "Christian Number and Its Implications," *Journal of Early Christian Studies* 6.2 (1998): 185–226.

3. The persecution started in 303 CE and ended at different times in different parts of the empire, but in Egypt, the Syrian region, and Asia Minor, it lasted until 313. Timothy D. Barnes, *Early Christian Hagiography and Roman History* (Tübingen: Mohr Siebeck, 2010), 97–150, offers an interesting review of the evidence concerning the persecution of Christians in this period.

4. The fact that a lot of Christians did not see being Christian and participation in sacrifices as mutually exclusive is described in Éric Rebillard, *Christians and Their Many Identities in Late Antiquity, North Africa, 200–450 CE* (Ithaca, NY: Cornell University Press, 2012).

5. Although recent scholarship has questioned the portrayal of persecution found in Eusebius and Christian hagiography, as constant and massive, Christians were at times both prosecuted and executed. Barnes, *Early Christian Hagiography and Roman History*; Candida R. Moss, *Ancient Christian Martyrdom: Diverse Practices, Theologies, and Traditions* (New Haven, CT: Yale University Press, 2012); Rebillard, *Christians and Their Many Identities in Late Antiquity*.

6. *Ap. John* is found in three of the twelve codices from Nag Hammadi, and it is the opening text in all three.

the church councils and the writings of the most prominent theologians of that time. Yet, Christianity was diverse, and it has been argued that the manuscripts in which we find *Ap. John* are from a Christian monastic setting.[7]

The early Christians read the Bible, but also many other texts. Some have been transmitted to us within the Christian tradition as cherished works, but many others have been forgotten, some condemned, while others simply fell out of use. *Ap. John* is one of these forgotten books, rediscovered and made available to us in the last hundred years.[8] While *Ap. John* was never

---

7. See Hugo Lundhaug and Lance Jenott, *The Monastic Origins of the Nag Hammadi Codices* (Tübingen: Mohr Siebeck, 2015) for a comprehensive examinations of all the arguments used in the discussion of the monastic hypothesis. Nicola Denzey Lewis and Justine Ariel Blount have in "Rethinking the Origins of the Nag Hammadi Codices," *Journal of Biblical Literature* 133 (2014): 399–419 proposed an alternative hypothesis. Rather than being buried for safekeeping, the Nag Hammadi Codices were produced as Christian Books of the Dead and buried with a deceased. See also Nicola Denzey Lewis, "Death on the Nile: Egyptian Codices, Gnosticism, and Early Christian Books of the Dead," in April D. DeConick, Gregory Shaw, and John D. Turner, eds., *Practicing Gnosis: Ritual, Magic, Theurgy, and Liturgy in Nag Hammadi, Manichaean and Other Ancient Literature. Essays in Honor of Birger A. Pearson* (Leiden: Brill, 2013), 161–80. Together with Mark Goodacre's article "How Reliable Is the Story of the Nag Hammadi Discovery?," *Journal for the Study of the New Testament* 35 (2013): 303–22 Lewis and Blount's article reminds us that the Nag Hammadi Codices' provenance is reconstructed, and should be treated with caution regarding *all* details. Paula Tutty, "Books of the Dead or Books with the Dead? Interpreting Book Depositions in Late Antique Egypt," in Hugo Lundhaug and Lance Jenott, eds., *The Nag Hammadi Codices and Late Antique Egypt* (Tübingen: Mohr Siebeck, 2018), 287–328 holds that a Christian Book of the Dead tradition is unlikely. Brent Nongbri "Finding Early Christian Books at Nag Hammadi and Beyond," *Bulletin for the Study of Religion* 45 (2016): 11–9; goes through the evidence for books found with corpses. In many cases the discovery narratives' details about tombs, graves or bodies seem to be later additions to the stories. "The claim 'This manuscript was found in a graveyard with a corpse' might well be a trope used to pique the interest of potential European and American buyers and increase selling price" (17). The monastic hypothesis does not rest on the find spot or the discovery story, but rather on the codices themselves. Jenott and Lundhaug, *Monastic Origins*, consider cartonnage, colophons, decorations and contents, as well as what we know about monastic manuscript culture in late antique Egypt in their arguments favoring the hypothesis. The link to the general area, with its substantial Pachomian activity, can also be established through place names found in the cartonnage.

8. *Ap. John* is known from four different Coptic manuscripts. Three of these, Nag Hammadi Codices (NHC) II, III and IV, were found near the Egyptian town of Nag Hammadi in 1945. These are dated to the fourth to fifth century. The fourth manuscript, Codex Berolinensis 8502 (BG), is said to have been found near Achmim, but the history of the manuscript before its appearance on the antiquities market in Cairo is uncertain. The dating of this codex is clearly later than the Nag Hammadi Codices, quite possibly by a century or more. See Michael Waldstein and Frederik Wisse, "Introduction," in *The Apocryphon of John: Synopsis of Nag Hammadi Codices II,1, III,1, and IV,1 with*

recognized as canonical by the wider church, it was copied and read at least until the fifth century CE by people who considered themselves Christians.[9] The work is a revelatory dialogue set between the risen Christ and the apostle John, and it represents a form of Christianity that was labelled heretical and that eventually disappeared. It offers alternative views on God, creation, and humanity to those presented by the Christian leaders whom we have later come to interpret as representing orthodoxy. The distribution of *Ap. John* and the extent of its readership is unknown to us—but we do know that it was copied and read in the crucial period when Christianity went from being a minority to a majority religion. In this article, I will highlight how the themes of humanity's heavenly origin and struggles with the evil forces of this world may have helped converts make sense of their experiences of changing religious allegiance.

The Story Told by the Apocryphon of John

Ap. John is not an easy text to read. At several points, the storyline is confusing, the language is often obscure and ambiguous, and there are multiple variants between the manuscripts. The main part of the text, however, is a revelation from the Savior[10] to John, where John is told about a race of divine origin that must fight against the evil machinations of the rulers of this world.

The revelation has two main parts. The first describes the divine world, and the second is a commentary on the first chapters of Genesis, from creation to the flood. The description of the divine world starts with the original unity, the invisible Spirit, above and beyond everything. The invisible Spirit cannot be comprehended. It can, however, reflect on itself. This first thought, or image, of the Spirit becomes a separate entity, called Barbelo,

---

BG 8502,2 (Leiden: Brill, 1995), 3–8; Myriam Krutzsch and Günter Poethke, "Der Einband des Koptisch-Gnostischen Kodex Papyrus Berolinensis 8502," *Forschungen und Berichte* 24 (1984): 37–40; and Lundhaug and Jenott, *Monastic Origins*, 9–11.

9. This writing has for a long time been "trapped" in the category of Gnosticism and the search for Gnostic origins. For an overview of scholarship using the *Ap. John* in the quest for Gnostic origins, see David Creech, *The Use of Scripture in the Apocryphon of John* (Tübingen: Mohr Siebeck, 2017). For the discussion on Gnosticism, see Morton Smith, "The History of the Term Gnostikos," in Bentley Lanton, ed., *The Rediscovery of Gnosticism. Proceedings of the International Conference on Gnosticism at Yale New Haven, Connecticut, March 28-31, 1978.* Vol. 2: *Sethian Gnosticism, Studies in the History of Religions* (Leiden: Brill, 1981), 796–807; Karen L. King, *What Is Gnosticism?* (Cambridge, MA: Belknap Press–Harvard University Press, 2003), and Michael A. Williams, *Rethinking "Gnosticism": An Argument for Dismantling a Dubious Category* (Princeton, NJ: Princeton University Press, 1996).

10. In BG, "Christ" is used where the other versions have "the Savior."

who is also designated as the primal human. Subsequently, it is from Barbelo and the invisible Spirit that Christ comes into being.

In addition to the Spirit, Barbelo and Christ, long lists of divine entities, called eons, are brought forth in male-female pairs. With the last of these, Wisdom, a shift occurs. Wisdom wants to do what the invisible Spirit did; to create something from herself. This is a stark breach of order. Because she is divine, her thought becomes manifest. She is, however, acting outside the divine plan and place in the divine household. Because of this, the result of her thought, a son, is imperfect, ugly, and evil. He is called Yaldabaoth and he possesses divine power from his mother. He starts creating his own realms and minions, the rulers of this world, uttering the words: "I am a jealous god and there is no other except me."[11]

This statement signals the beginning of the second main part of the revelation, written as a commentary on Genesis. A complicated rescue mission is started to retrieve Yaldabaoth's power. As Yaldabaoth perceives his creation, a voice is heard and the image of the primal human is shown. Awed by this, the rulers decide to create a human after the image they have seen. At this point, man is made of only soul. However, the man they create remains lifeless. Yaldabaoth is tricked into breathing his power into Adam who then becomes alive and able to move about. Adam now has divine power, and his thinking is superior to that of the rulers. Angry and jealous of him, they throw him into matter.

The rest of the revelation represents a battle between good and evil forces, which try to gain control over the human mind. Divine emissaries are sent to Adam to awaken his thinking. The rulers strike back, creating a material body for him, thereby obscuring his thoughts, but Adam's thinking is awakened again when woman is created. A series of divine moves and evil countermoves occur, and Yaldabaoth introduces human beings to sexual desire, a further trap for them.

However, Christ assures John that all souls will be saved. The Holy Spirit will be sent and will join with the divine power in humanity. As a result,

---

11. NHC III 44.14–15. Yaldabaoth's statement is a paraphrase of related ideas found in the Hebrew Bible, a blend of several passages in which the creator demands exclusive worship and emphasizes his role in creation, and claims to be the only god. Isaiah 45 is one example of a text that combines these ideas, stating "I am the Lord, and there is no other" (45.18). The statement of jealousy and demand of exclusive worship are found repeatedly in Exodus 34.14, the ten commandments (Exod. 20.3-5 and Deut. 5.7-9), as well as Deut. 4.24 and Josh. 24.19.

All translations from Coptic are my own. I will follow the text from NHC III whenever it is possible, for the simple reason that this version is rarely presented. NHC III is quite fragmented, and when missing I will supply the text from BG, a version close to, but not identical with, NHC III.

human beings will be able to resist their flesh. In some people, the rulers have been able to place a counterfeit spirit to lead them astray. But even they will eventually be saved. Only apostates are truly lost. At the end of the revelation John is told to bring the message to his "fellow spirits." These fellow spirits are also mentioned in the introductory narrative frame, where they are said to be from the "immovable race."[12]

Narrative Frame

Ap. John opens with these words:

> It happened, one day, when John the brother of Jacob, these are the sons of Zebedee, came up to the temple, a Pharisee named Arimanias approached him. He said: "Where is your teacher, whom you used to follow?" He said to him: "He has returned to the place from which he came." The Pharisee said to him: "Deceitfully the Nazarene has deceived you (pl.), and he has filled your (pl.) ears with lies, and he has closed [your hearts]. He has turned you (pl.) away from the traditions of your (pl.) fathers! When I heard these things, I turned away from the temple, to a mountain, a desert place. And I was grieving greatly in my heart.[13]

It is in response to this grief and John's questions about his master's mission that Christ appears with a revelation.

Central to this confrontation is the Pharisee's allegation against Christ, "He has turned you from the traditions of your fathers." Similar complaints are made towards Jesus in the Gospels, often by Pharisees,[14] perhaps echoing allegations against Christ-believers at the time the Gospels were written. The words are certainly reminiscent of the complaints Christians met.

The Problem with Leaving the Traditions of the Fathers

Paula Fredriksen has highlighted the close relationship between family group and worship in the Roman Empire in Late Antiquity.[15] Gods protect family,

---

12. For a thorough study of this designation, see Michael A. Williams, *The Immovable Race: A Gnostic Designation and the Theme of Stability in Late Antiquity* (Leiden: Brill, 1985).

13. *Ap. John* BG 19.6–20.7 The narrative frame is very fragmented in both NHC III and NHC II, and most of the narrative frame is missing from NHC IV. The words "deception," "close," and "traditions," are also found in both NHC II and III, and we can therefore deduce that the allegations from the Pharisee are the same in these three versions.

14. Indirectly, through accusing his disciples of not observing the law, typically concerning the Sabbath (Matt. 15.1-2) and directly, leading people astray (Jn. 7.12 and 47).

15. Paula Fredriksen, "Mandatory Retirement: Ideas in the Study of Christian Origins Whose Time Has Come to Go," *Studies in Religion/Sciences Religieuses* 35.2

city, people, and empire. Cult assures the goodwill of the gods, thereby peace and prosperity are assured as well. The relationship with the gods is one of blood, and kinship ties are also ties to gods and cult. Belonging to a family includes cultic obligations. This is one reason behind resistance towards Christ-believers and later Christians in the first centuries CE.

> The problem, then, in the view of majority culture, was not that the Gentile Christians were "Christians." The problem was that, whatever religious practices these people chose to assume, the were still, nonetheless, "Gentiles," that is, members of their native *genos* or *natio*, with standing obligations to their own gods, who were the gods of the majority.[16]

Refusing to honor this obligation, as some Christians did, was perceived as endangering themselves and others. The problem did not result from the fact that people started worshiping a new god, but rather because many stopped serving the gods of their families and regions. According to Fredriksen, pagans who became Jews and thereby gave up their native cults were considered disrespectful or even traitors.[17] For the same reason, Christians were blamed for various misfortunes, like floods or droughts. Persecutions, when occurring,[18] were therefore not attempts at eradicating Christianity as a set of beliefs, but rather means to ensure that the relationship with

---

(2006): 231–46. While Fredriksen's article is mostly concerned with the time of Paul, she talks about the situation in Late Antiquity more generally with examples from different centuries, including references to the persecutions of Christians and the time of Augustine.

16. Fredriksen, "Mandatory Retirement," 239.
17. Fredriksen, "Mandatory Retirement," 236.
18. The available evidence does not support an understanding of persecution as a constant risk for Christians from the time of the apostles and onwards. Instead, it has been shown to be local, sporadic, and limited in time up until the year 250, and even between that date and the end of "the great persecution" there were long periods of time when Christians were not under direct threat. The portrayal of persecution in the Church Fathers and hagiographies serves the needs of later Christian times, in countering alleged heretics, schismatics, and people of other beliefs. Elizabeth A. Castelli, *Martyrdom and Memory: Early Christian Culture Making (New York: Columbia University Press, 2004);* Moss, *Ancient Christian Martyrdom;* Candida R. Moss, *The Myth of Persecution: How Early Christians Invented a Story of Martyrdom* (New York: HarperCollins, 2013). If the definition of persecution depends on a group being specifically targeted, persecution may not even be the right word for the cases where Christians were arrested, prosecuted, and sentenced. In the words of Candida Moss, Christians were subjected to "prosecution, not persecution." The works referenced also thematize how the idea of a constant persecution of Christians from Antiquity up until our own time functions rhetorically today. However, this rhetorical use in our time also illustrates that acts may be perceived as persecution by a group without that same group being intentionally targeted.

the traditional gods was also honored for the good of the empire, city, or region.[19] The Christian response to this varied.

Éric Rebillard's analysis of Christian identity regarding the "Decian persecution" in the middle of the third century is illuminating for an understanding of Christian responses to the required sacrifice.[20] Rebillard takes the fact that most Christians *did* sacrifice in response to the Decian edict as an indication that those who sacrificed did not see their identity as Christians as excluding participation in this ceremony, a participation expected on the basis of the person's other "memberships."[21] In other words, according to him, many Christians did not see participating in the required ceremony as being in conflict with their Christianity. In contrast to an idealized representation, Christians in Antiquity might have had many "memberships" that were not hierarchical, but interchangeable.

> Thus, when Decius ordered all inhabitants of the Roman Empire to sacrifice to the gods for the restoration of order and security, the majority of Christians complied, as it was a requirement of their membership in the imperial commonwealth. They did this either unaware that it might be contradictory to their Christian membership, or because they simply did not activate their Christian membership in this context, at least not until they were challenged to do so by Cyprian and his clergy.[22]

Rebillard supports this understanding by stating that most Christians expected to be able to return to their communities afterward. However, the many other solutions that made it possible for Christians not to sacrifice—bribery, sacrifice by proxy, and flight—indicate that many Christians did indeed see their Christianity as a hindrance to participation in the imperial cult.

It was not simply fear of prosecution that made "to sacrifice or not to sacrifice" a hard decision for Christians. A refusal was a direct challenge to ethnic identity and family ties. Stanley K. Stowers describes how sacrifice reenacted and reinforced kinship ties, gender roles, and political

---

19. Tertullian, at the very end of the second century, claims in the *Apology XL*, 1-2, "... they take the Christians to be the cause of every disaster to the State, of every misfortune of the people. If the Tiber reaches the walls, if the Nile does not rise to the fields, if the sky doesn't move or the earth does, if there is famine, if there is plague, the cry is at once: 'The Christians to the lion!'" Tertullian, *Apology; De Spectaculis* (Loeb Classical Library, 250; trans. T. R. Glover and Gerald H. Rendall; Cambridge, MA: Harvard University Press, 1931), 183. See also Moss, *Myth of Persecution,* ch. 5.

20. Rebillard, *Christians and Their Many Identities*, 50–5.

21. Rebillard, *Christians and Their Many Identities*, 51. Rebillard focuses the "analysis on identities based on category memberships such as ethnicity, religion, and occupation," 4.

22. Rebillard, *Christians and Their Many Identities*, 60.

hierarchies, and even contributed to their construction in a Greek context.[23] If cult both confirmed and constructed kinship, abandonment of cult could logically threaten the whole structure of family and people, both by relatives and civic authority.

The Solution: An Alternative and Truer Lineage

Allegations of having left the traditions of the fathers were related to allegations brought against the disciples of Jesus in the Gospels.[24] The early Christians had a particular problem when they needed to explain how they could appropriate the Scriptures and the god of the Jews without being Jews and/or without the Jews accepting their interpretation.[25] A new reading of the history of Israel solves this: the Jews are seen as disobedient and disbelieving and the Christians present themselves as the heirs to the patriarchs and prophets; the true people of God. This is just one of the many ways Christians use what Denise Kimber Buell refers to as "ethnic reasoning."[26] Based on the close connection between race/ethnicity and religious practices, Christians were able to present themselves as a race, separate from both Jews and other ethnic groups.

Clement of Alexandria provides an early Christian example of such ethnic reasoning. Clement recognizes the claim the traditions of the fathers have on people when he argues against a fictive audience, "the Greeks," who maintain that "it is not right for us to abandon the ways handed down

---

23. Stanley K. Stowers, "Greeks Who Sacrifice and Those Who Do Not: Toward an Anthropology of Greek Religion," in L. Michael White and O. Larry Yarbrough, eds., *The Social World of the First Christians: Essays in Honor of Wayne A. Meeks* (Minneapolis, MN: Fortress, 1995), 229–333. Stowers explains that he aims to "establish constant features of Greek sacrifice from the classical period into the early Roman Empire" (294). It is only with caution that his material can be applied to an Egyptian context in the third and fourth century. However, Stowers demonstrates how the development of new, larger, and more territorially based political units were also based on constructions of kinship established by sacrifice.

24. Matt. 15.2, Mk. 7.5, the disciples are accused of not living according to the tradition of the elders.

25. Rosemary R. Ruether, *Faith and Fratricide: The Theological Roots of Anti-Semitism* (New York: Seabury, 1974); Miriam S. Taylor, *Anti-Judaism and Early Christian Identity: A Critique of the Scholarly Consensus* (Leiden: Brill, 1995).

26. Denise Kimber Buell, *Why This New Race: Ethnic Reasoning in Early Christianity* (New York: Columbia University Press, 2005); *Making Christians: Clement of Alexandria and the Rhetoric of Legitimacy* (Princeton, NJ: Princeton University Press, 1999); "Race and Universalism in Early Christianity," *Journal of Early Christian Studies* 10 (2002): 429–68.

by our fathers."[27] His solution to "the Greek" question is to offer his readers an alternative lineage. It is not the fathers of the past generations they need to honor. The Christian god is the true Father, and the one towards whom they should be loyal.[28] Clement claims that Christians are a new race, made up of people from other races. Distinction between races or peoples are, among other things, dependent on cult and ancestral customs, but these should all be abolished, as humanity seeks to come together in the new race, unified in the only true worship. And even if this race of the Christians seems new, it is really the oldest of them all, true humanity.

> But we were before the foundation of the world, we who, because we were destined to be in Him, were begotten beforehand by God. We are the rational images formed by God's Word, or Reason, and we date from the beginning on account of our connection with Him, because "the Word was in the beginning."[29]

In depicting Christians as a race of their own, Clement acknowledges that religious loyalties are fundamental to membership in race or people, and at the same time, he refuses to accept that Christians should have obligations towards the gods of the peoples from whom they originated. Christianity is superior; it is the only true worship, and ultimately, the only true race.[30] Clement is not alone in representing Christians as a separate race. While the manner or ethnic reasoning and the uses it is put to vary among Christian leaders, the idea of Christians as a race is common.[31] This understanding accepts the traditional relationship between kin and cult at the same time as it redefines and expands the concept to accommodate for the situation of having joined a new and exclusive religion. Clement acknowledges the fact that cult is tied to family, so when the traditional cult is prohibited, a new family is constructed to legitimize the failure to uphold these commitments. *Ap. John* also engages in ethnic reasoning, by giving humanity a divine origin.

---

27. Clement of Alexandria, *The Exhortation to the Greeks*. This translation is by Denise Kimber Buell. See her discussion in Buell, *Making Christians*, 100–4. Ἀλλ' ἐκ πατέρων, φατέ, παραδεδομένον ἡμῖν ἔθος ἀνατρέπειν οὐκ εὔλογον: "But, you say, it is not reasonable to overthrow a way of life handed down to us from our forefathers." Clement of Alexandria, "The Exhortation to the Greeks [Protrepticus English & Greek]," in *The Exhortation to the Greeks; The Rich Man's Salvation; and the Fragment of an Address Entitled to the Newly Baptized* (Loeb Classical Library, 92; trans. G. W. Butterworth; Cambridge, MA: Harvard University Press, 1919).
28. Clement of Alexandria, *Exhortation to the Greeks*.
29. Clement, *Protr.* I.6. (Butterworth, LCL, 92).
30. Buell, "Race and Universalism."
31. For a discussion of uses and the complexity of ethnic reasoning, see Buell, *Why This New Race* and "Race and Universalism."

Humanity's Divine Origin

Ap. John is a revelation both to and about "the immovable race." The evil creator Yaldabaoth and his minions strive to conceal from human beings the fact that humanity is not entirely of this world. Even if human beings were formed by the rulers and clothed in matter by them, humans can trace their ancestry to the world above, to the power stolen from Wisdom, and to the primal human, the model after whom humanity was formed.

> [The] blessed one [revealed] his appearance to them, and the whole … of authority bent down and they <saw> [in the water] the form of the image. [They said] to each other, "Let [us create a man] according to the image of God and according to his likeness." And they created [from] themselves and [all] their powers. They molded a figure from themselves and one by one the authorities created a [soul] from their (own) power. Each created [from] its own [image], the one it saw, like the imitation [of the one who is from] the beginning, the [perfect human].[32]

The power from Wisdom brings the human being to life. This power is its soul,[33] and it is said plainly that all humans possess this power, otherwise "they would not be able to stand."[34]

Not only is the human being modeled after the image of God. The very part that makes it alive and able to think is divine. The power was never meant to leave the divine realms but it was transferred to the creator by the errors of Wisdom. The creation of the human being is part of a plan to bring this power back to its heavenly home. In this way, humanity is separated from the rest of creation. It is part of the world but does not belong to it. Since it is from heavenly origin, the foundation is laid for an ethnic reasoning that makes it possible to acknowledge the widespread claim that ethnicity determines cult, but, at the same time, that this is a different cult from those performed in the temples. While the interpretation of the Bible differs on crucial points between *Ap. John* and Clement of Alexandria, the logic behind their ethnic reasoning is similar. Yes, family ties determine religious allegiance, but the true family is not the family into which a person is born. *Ap. John* offers its readers an alternative genealogy than the one of their birth, which provides them with a valid reason to reject the traditional gods.

---

32. *Ap. John* NHC III 21.23–22.14.
33. *Ap. John* NHC III 34.13-14.
34. *Ap. John* NHC III 34.8-9.

The Immovable Race and the Mother's Seed

The theme of humanity's heavenly descent runs through *Ap. John*. In addition, a few terms occur that designate ethnicity and kinship. Common names of nations, like "Greek" or "Egyptian" are not used; instead, we hear about "the immovable race" and "the mother's seed." At the start of the revelation, Christ tells John to bring this revelation to his "[fel]low spirits, those who are [from] the im[mov]able race of the [per]fect man."[35] Ending the revelation, the Savior says, "And I am saying these things to you so that you may write them down and give them to your fellow spirits in secret, for this mystery is that of the immovable race."[36] The Savior's revelation is both for, and about, the immovable race of the perfect man. What race is this? John is clearly considered part of it, as are his "fellow spirits." Another clue to their identity is given in the eschatological part of the revelation: when John asks if all souls will be saved,[37] the Savior answers that it is difficult to reveal these matters to others "except for those only who are from the immovable race."[38] The members of this race are those who are not affected by the passions.

> For they do not [give them]selves to anything except the incorruptible con[gregation], attentive to it [from] now on without anger or envy, with[out ...or] desire or overindul[gence]. They are not restrained [by] any [of these ex]cept the state of being ...[39] while they use (it), waiting for [the time] when they will be received [by] the receivers [into] the dignity of the eternal life [and the] calling, enduring everything, [b]earing everything so that they might [complete] the contest and inherit eternal life.[40]

These people have been given the ability to resist passions and temptations by the "Spirit of Life." Ismo Dunderberg, who demonstrates *Ap. John*'s debt to ancient moral philosophy, highlights this passage. It "shows that *Secret John* subscribes to the Stoic ideal of *apatheia*."[41] This ideal also coincides with the ideals of the monastic life.[42] Those fulfilling these ideals are

---

35. *Ap. John* BG 22.14-16 NHC III is missing and NHC II (and IV) is very fragmented.
36. *Ap. John* BG 75.15–76.1.
37. The question as it is given in *Ap. John* is: "Will the [souls] of everyone be saved [into the pu]re light?" *Ap. John* NHC III 32.23-25.
38. *Ap. John* NHC III 32.25–33.3.
39. The parallel in NHC II 25.35 has "in the flesh".
40. *Ap. John* NHC III 33.9-23 See discussion in Williams, *The Immovable Race*, for the theme of stability in *Ap. John*, and in Late Antiquity more generally.
41. Ismo Dunderberg, *Gnostic Morality Revisited* (Tübingen: Mohr Siebeck, 2015), 33.
42. See for example Edward E. Malone, *The Monk and the Martyr: The Monk as the*

given an exclusive ethnic identity in *Ap. John*, and their salvation and passionlessness are attributed to the Spirit's assistance.

Humanity is the mother's "seed," and through different female revealers and helper figures she "assisted her seed," "takes form in her seed," and "set her seed upright." All these terms highlight the relationship between humanity and God, the lost and their Savior, as one of kinship. In *Ap. John*, Yaldabaoth, along with his minions, the powers of this world, hides this divine origin from human beings. These powers are evil and false gods, as well as demons.

True Gods and False Gods

One of the reasons why the claim of the traditional gods could feel challenging was the fact that transferring allegiance to the Christian god did not necessarily mean ceasing to believe in the existence of other gods.[43] For many, they were simply relocated in the hierarchy of powerful beings. The heavens were believed to be filled with angelic beings serving God, and the world was filled with other powers, recognized even in the Bible as lesser, or demonic, beings.[44] The traditional gods might be equated with demons[45] by those who had newly become Christians, but their existence was not called into question. Demons had powers Christians should fear, even if Christ was more powerful than demons.

Ap. John describes a whole host of gods, hierarchically arranged. On top and beyond all others is the invisible Spirit. Evil enters the story when Wisdom, the youngest of the divine beings (eons), imitates the act of the Father's self-reflection.

> Because of the lewdness within her, her reflection was not idle and her product came out imperfect, his shape was not in her shape, because she made him without her partner, his form was not in the mother's image ... She cast him away from her outside of those places so that none of the immortals might see him, since he was begotten in ignorance ... And she named him Yaldabaoth. He is the First Ruler ...[46]

Successor of the Martyr (Washington DC: The Catholic University of America Press, 1950), or William S. J. Harmeless, *Desert Christians: An Introduction to the Literature of Early Monasticism* (Oxford: Oxford University Press, 2004).

43. Fredriksen, "Mandatory Retirement."
44. 2 Cor. 4.4, Gal. 4.8-9 etc.
45. David Brakke, *Demons and the Making of the Monk: Spiritual Combat in Early Christianity* (Cambridge, MA: Harvard University Press, 2006).
46. *Ap. John* NHC III 15.3-9, 13-16 and 21-23.

After the birth of Yaldabaoth, we learn of all the powers of evil. These are the powers humanity encounters in the world. Yaldabaoth himself is identified with the creator god of Genesis. He rules the powers of the world. He sets up a hierarchy, like the one of the eternal, divine beings above him.

> He copulated with Ignorance, who is with him. He begat authorities who are under him, and the twelve angels, for each one of them an aeon according to the pattern of the imperishable ones ...[47]

> And he commanded seven to rule over the heavens and five over the chaos and the netherworld ....[48]

Among Yaldabaoth's minions are the astral powers, the demonic powers, fate, and all other forces that may influence people's lives.

> He made [a] plan and begot Fate. [He bound] the gods of heaven and angels and demons [and] human beings with measures and times and seasons so that everyone would [come to be] in [its] fetter, and so that it would be lo[rd over all.][49]

Read from the point of view of a person who has left the old gods behind, but still believes they exist, this message is powerful. The gods left behind are real and dangerous. But they are not true divinity, and they are not to be served. About this, many Christians would agree. Early Christian writers argued along such lines when they listed the reasons why these gods were not worthy of worship. They add that these gods and demons are the fallen angels and the offspring of the fallen angels from Genesis 6.2-4. Elaine Pagels argues that because of the connection between gods, cult, and imperial order, this was also a criticism of the Roman authorities.[50] Early Christian writers like Justin and Clement portray the Roman gods as demons, "active evil forces bent upon corrupting and destroying human beings."[51] These writers saw the gods as the offspring of the fallen angels in Genesis 6. According to Pagels, a refusal to sacrifice is therefore not just disobedience, but a stark criticism of the Roman authorities who claim their authority came from these gods.[52]

What separates the message of *Ap. John* from most strains of early Christianity is its strong condemnation of the creator god, the god most Christians would recognize as their god. He is malicious. He is ignorant. He is a

---

47. *Ap. John* NHC III 16.7-11.
48. *Ap. John* NHC III 17.17-20.
49. *Ap. John* NHC III 37.6-13.
50. Elaine Pagels, *Adam, Eve, and the Serpent* (New York: Vintage Books, 1989), ch. 2.
51. Pagels, *Adam, Eve, and the Serpent*, 39.
52. Pagels, *Adam, Eve, and the Serpent*, 32–56.

defective being produced by error. As the creator, he is responsible for the material world as well as the other gods and powers which human beings may know from experience. While many early Christian writers would use the moral shortcomings of the traditional gods, "arrogance, brutality, and licentiousness,"[53] as argument for their status as fallen angels and demons, *Ap. John* associates all these same traits with Yaldabaoth. In addition, the supernatural powers operating in the world are all made by him and serve him.

> Because of the glory of the light of the power of the mother within him, he called himself god over them, thus being disobedient to the source from which he had come into being.[54]

> He saw the creation which is below him and the multitude of angels which are below him, those who came into being by him. He said to them, "I am a jealous god; without me there is no one"—already indicating to the angels who are below him that there is another god. For if there were not another, of whom would he be jealous?[55]

Even if Yaldabaoth is a ridiculous figure, he is not without power. He is the ruler of this world, and he uses his power to imprison humanity.

Retribution by the Gods

If there is one thing *Ap. John* makes abundantly clear, it is that the gods populating this world are malicious beings. They are always ready to hurt those who turn away from them. *Ap. John*'s version of Genesis 3.8-24 states: "Yaldabaoth knew that they had withdrawn from him. He cursed them."[56] This is only one instance in a long line of similar events. Every time humans are revealed to be superior in their thinking to the creator god and his companions, their situation gets worse, and they become more material, "clothed in darkness," given sexual desire and a counterfeit spirit leading them astray. It should surprise no one that such deities will bring disaster to those who refuse to worship them. After all, their leader even boasts of being jealous. They are also shown to be able to give benefits to their human followers.

> And the Chief Ruler ... him and [placed] him in paradise, [of which] he said, "It belongs to his deli[ght]" but really deceiving him. For [their] delight is

---

53. Pagels, *Adam, Eve and the Serpent*, 43.
54. *Ap. John* NHC III 18.17-22.
55. One leaf is missing in NHC III, and I have therefore taken the quotation here from the parallel in BG 44.9-18.
56. *Ap. John* BG 61.7-10. NHC III 30.22-23 is almost identical in wording, but a lacuna occurs where we expect "cursed them".

bitter and their [beauty] is lawless and their foo[d] is deception and their trees [iniquity].[57]

Paradise does indeed appear as a paradise, filled with delight and beauty. But this is the deception of the false gods, and accepting it leads to nothing but death.

> [And I will] tell you what the [mystery] of their life is, namely their counterfeit [spirit] from each [other], their purpose is to turn him away [so] that he will not know his perfection. That tree is one of this kind: Its root (is) shame, and [its] branches are shadows of [death]. Its leaves are hate and deception. Its ointment is an ointment of evil. And its fruit is the desire for death. [And] its seed blossomed [from] darkness. The dwelling place of [those] who taste it is the netherworld.[58]

The ideal humans are those able to resist temptations and stay passionless. The delights found in this earthly "paradise" are those sought by the passions. By giving the human beings these options, the rulers try to keep them away from salvation. Satisfying such gods is not a good idea. Even if they come bringing gifts;

> They brought them gold [and] silver and gifts, and ... and iro[n] metal and everything of the sort. They [beguiled] them into distractions [so that] they would not remember their immovable Foreknowledge.[59]

This corresponds to the understanding of the relationship between gods and human beings described above. Gods will bring blessings if you serve them, bad things may happen if you do not. *Ap. John* does not deny the fact that the gods of this world may bless humans with worldly goods and good times, but it labels these as distractions. Rather than being true blessings, they are curses in disguise. For these distractions keep humankind from understanding what true divinity is, and likewise, understanding what true humanity is.

According to Karen King, *Ap. John* offers a strong social critique of the Roman Empire, through its portrayal of Yaldabaoth and his minions.[60] Only the higher realms of the divine world are harmonious, the mundane world and the powers that govern it are ignorant and malicious.

> Earthly rulers who claimed legitimacy by connecting themselves to the sovereignty of the gods were by implication complicit with Yaldabaoth and his false gods, and were mere tools in their malicious practices of domination,

---

57. *Ap. John* NHC III 27.4-12.
58. *Ap. John* NHC III 27.15–28.6.
59. *Ap. John* NHC III 38.25–39.4.
60. Karen L. King, *The Secret Revelation of John* (Cambridge, MA: Harvard University Press, 2006).

however ignorant of this fact these rulers might be. Wealth and power, which the elite claimed to exercise for the good of the whole populace, were revealed to be a mere simulacrum of the real article of divine generosity. The pious practices of civic and imperial worship, the sacred character and benefits of sacrifice, and the pleasures of reproduction, all were exposed as deceptions intended to keep people enslaved and to satisfy the power-hungry world rulers.[61]

Unlike much political theory of its time, that saw everything as hierarchically ordered, from the transcendental level down through states and cities, to households and individuals, *Ap. John* establishes a fundamental breach between the divine and the mundane world. In King's reading of *Ap. John*, the critique lies precisely in this contrast between the good and just world above and the faulty world below.[62] King's reading demonstrates the politically subversive potential of *Ap. John*.[63] In periods when Christians were facing or fearing prosecution worldly rulers would be considered hostile. At such times, a reading of *Ap. John* that involved critique of the political powers and their gods would not be surprising.

If *Ap. John* offers a critique of the political leadership of the Roman Empire, it is implicit. However, the critique of gods and powers is not. Like early Christian writers who saw the Roman gods as demons, *Ap. John* connects evil with the story of the sons of god and the daughters of men in Genesis 6. In *Ap. John*, this is only one of the acts intended to keep humanity enslaved.[64] The leader of the evil powers in *Ap. John* is a caricature of the creator god. The criticism against the rulers is therefore directed not only at the traditional gods and the political authorities, it is also an affront to the Christians who accepted this creator god as the only god. After the Constantinian turn, when the church venerating the creator as the only true God became associated with the political powers of this world, *Ap. John*'s criticism of this god would affect both political and Christian leaders. King

---

61. King, *Secret Revelation of John*, 63.
62. King, *Secret Revelation of John*, 155–62.
63. Williams, in *Rethinking "Gnosticism,"* written before King's *Secret Revelation of John*, argues that there is no certain way of going from myths to social reality. However, Williams is countering those who have read "Gnostic" texts as world-rejecting and therefore uninterested in worldly affairs. Instead, Williams argues that many so-called gnostic movements were formed in an effort to reduce tension with the surrounding society, 96–115.
64. On the the Myth of the Watchers in *Ap. John* see Christian H. Bull, "Women, Angels and Dangerous Knowledge: The Myth of the Watchers in the Apocryphon of John and Its Monastic Manuscript-Context," in Ulla Tervahauta, ed., *Women and Knowledge in Early Christianity* (Leiden: Brill, 2017), 75–107.

claims that a text with such utopian ideals[65] and strong condemnation of worldly powers would be too radical after the changes that took place in the fourth century, and suggests that this may be the reason why *Ap. John* (and similar texts) did not survive. However, the Berlin Codex, with a cover showing the inscription "Zacharias, Arch-presbyter, Abbot" is dated (at least) a century later than the Nag Hammadi Codices.[66] It shows that at least for a while there were monastic readers willing to engage with *Ap. John*.

Reading the Apocryphon of John *in a New Situation*

In *Ap. John*, a longer passage on the fate of souls is concluded by the following exchange,

> "Lord, those who did know and turned away, where are their souls, or where will they go to?" He said to me, "the place to which the angels of poverty will go, to whom repentance has not come. And they will be kept until that day in which everyone [who has blasphemed] the Holy Spirit with an eternal ... will be punished with eternal torture." [67]

In Egypt, "the great persecution" left a lasting memory. The Coptic church calendar starts with the beginning of emperor Diocletian's reign, "the era of the martyrs." The persecution, or rather, the issue whether, and how easily, Christians who lapsed during the persecution could be welcomed into the church again caused a major schism.[68] It is difficult to ascertain whether the "turning away" mentioned in *Ap. John* was originally intended as a reference to those who lapsed during the persecutions. Yet readers in the fourth century, or later, would likely associate the terms.

---

65. "The *Secret Revelation of John* lacks the vivid imagination of hellfire their opponents would suffer. It eschews all violent revenge bearing the false name of justice, and exposes it for naked arrogance and malice," King, *Secret Revelation of John*, 171. However, even if most souls will be saved, *Ap. John* makes an exception for apostates, see below.

66. Michael Waldstein and Frederik Wisse, *The Apocryphon of John: Synopsis of Nag Hammadi Codices II,1, III,1, and IV,1 with BG 8502,2* (Leiden: Brill, 1995). Krutzsch and Poethke, "Der Einband des Koptisch-Gnostischen Kodex Papyrus Berolinensis 8502."

67. *Ap. John*, NHC III 36.5-15.

68. Hans Hauben, "The Melitian 'Church of the Martyrs': Christian Dissenters in Ancient Egypt," in Tom W. Hillard, et al., eds., *Ancient History at a Modern University. Proceedings of a Conference Held at Macquarie University, 8–13 July 1993 to Mark Twenty-Five Years of the Teaching of Ancient History at Macquarie University and the Retirement from the Chair of Professor Edwin Judge* (Grand Rapids, MI: Macquarie University, 1998), 329–49.

With most of the population converted, and Christianity becoming the favored religion, the conflicting loyalties between the demands of kin and those of an exclusive Christian praxis abate. When martyrdom was no longer possible, monasticism emerged, and was considered a spiritual martyrdom. The struggles of the monastic, against desires and demons, were likened to the martyr's suffering in the arena.[69] Becoming a Christian was no longer a radical decision that demanded a break with society, but it was still possible to renounce the world by giving up family and the affairs of daily life and taking up the ascetic life, (at least ideally) located in the wilderness, separated from the busy world of cities, towns, and villages.

Although it is unlikely that the message of *Ap. John* appealed to every monk, its focus on asceticism and the continuous fight against evil forces would certainly be meaningful in a monastic context.[70] In the early years of the monastic movement, it is even possible that the double criticism of the creator and authorities of this world would not have been as problematic as King suggests. The first monastic leaders were not under the bishop's jurisdiction, and their authority, for a while, was independent from the church leaders.[71] This situation, however, soon changed. The image of Yaldabaoth and his minions may have worked as a very powerful critique of the new association of church and worldly powers, but not for very long—*Ap. John* is eventually buried and forgotten.

Conclusion: Of Divine Origin, Surrounded by Hostile Powers

Ap. John offers its readers an alternative "bloodline." It counters demands by kinship groups and family by offering membership in a more important and truer family. In this manner, it is possible to accept that kinship

---

69. Malone, *Monk and the Martyr*.

70. Frederik Wisse, "Gnosticism and Early Monasticism in Egypt," in Barbara Aland, ed., *Gnosis: Festschrift für Hans Jonas* (Göttingen: Vanderhoeck & Ruprecht, 1978), 431–40 suggests that it is the interest in asceticism that made monks read the Nag Hammadi Codices. Although concerned with only the works in Codex I, Lance Jenott and Elaine Pagels, "Anthony's Letters and Nag Hammadi Codex I: Sources of Religious Conflict in Fourth-Century Egypt," *Journal for Early Christian Studies* 18.4 (2010): 557–89, mentions many themes also relevant for a monastic reading of *Ap. John*. Brakke, *Demons and the Making of the Monk*, among many other things, shows how monastic authors consider the monk the successor of the martyr and how the demons he fought were identical to the traditional gods.

71. James E. Goehring, "New Frontiers in Pachomian Studies," in Birger A. Pearson and James E. Goehring, eds., *The Roots of Egyptian Christianity* (Philadelphia, PA: Fortress Press, 1986), 236–57.

requires loyalty, but to evaluate loyalty towards the birth family as crucially misinformed.

Ap. John speaks to these conflicting loyalties by confirming the reality of the traditional gods, but also by revealing to the reader that these are evil powers. When bad things happen to people who do not honor these gods, this is just to be expected. These gods are evil, and do not want humanity to succeed in returning to its origin in the divine world. It is not difficult to see that *Ap. John* may have had much to offer to those drawn between old and new traditions. Both these themes, a new, and more true family, and the danger of evil forces surrounding all human beings would also appeal in a new situation where martyrdom was no longer a possibility, but monasticism was.

The condemnation of apostasy found in it gives a most serious warning to those considering giving in to the pressures of family and civil authority. However, as times changed, this reading of *Ap. John* would become less and less relevant, and, with a more powerful church hierarchy, the portrayal of the god of Genesis would be increasingly problematic, leading to the gradual forgetting of *Ap. John*.

Biographical Note

Kristine Toft Rosland is Associate Professor of Religious Education at the University of South-Eastern Norway, and a PhD candidate at the faculty of theology at the University of Oslo. Her ongoing PhD project "Reading the *Apocryphon of John* in its Manuscript Context" is influenced by perspectives from New Philology and it explores the *Apocryphon of John* through the lens of the monastic hypothesis of the Nag Hammadi codices.

Bibliography

Bagnall, Roger. "Religious Conversion and Onomastic Change," *The Bulletin of the American Society of Papyrologists* 19 (1982): 105–24.

—"Conversion and Onomastics: A Reply," *Zeitschrift für Papyrologie und Epigraphik* 69 (1987): 243–50.

Barnes, Timothy D. *Early Christian Hagiography and Roman History*. Tübingen: Mohr Siebeck, 2010.

Brakke, David. *Demons and the Making of the Monk: Spiritual Combat in Early Christianity*. Cambridge, MA: Harvard University Press, 2006. https://doi.org/10.4159/9780674028654

Bull, Christian H. "Women, Angels and Dangerous Knowledge: The Myth of the Watchers in the Apocryphon of John and Its Monastic Manuscript-Context," 75–107 in *Women and Knowledge in Early Christianity*. Edited by Ulla Tervahauta. Leiden: Brill, 2017. https://doi.org/10.1163/9789004344938_006

Castelli, Elizabeth A. *Martyrdom and Memory: Early Christian Culture Making.* New York: Columbia University Press, 2004.

Clement of Alexandria, "The Exhortation to the Greeks [Protrepticus English & Greek]," in *The Exhortation to the Greeks; The Rich Man's Salvation; and the Fragment of an Address Entitled to the Newly Baptized.* Loeb Classical Library, 92. Trans. G. W. Butterworth; Cambridge, MA: Harvard University Press, 1919. https://doi.org/10.4159/DLCL.clement_alexandria-exhortation_greeks.1919

Creech, David. *The Use of Scripture in the Apocryphon of John.* Tübingen: Mohr Siebeck, 2017. https://doi.org/10.1628/978-3-16-153808-7

Denzey Lewis, Nicola. "Death on the Nile: Egyptian Codices, Gnosticism, and Early Christian Books of the Dead," 161–80 in *Practicing Gnosis: Ritual, Magic, Theurgy, and Liturgy in Nag Hammadi, Manichaean and Other Ancient Literature. Essays in Honor of Birger A. Pearson.* Edited by April D. DeConick, Gregory Shaw, and John D. Turner. Leiden: Brill, 2013. https://doi.org/10.1163/9789004248526_012

Denzey Lewis, Nicola, and Justine Ariel Blount. "Rethinking the Origins of the Nag Hammadi Codices," *Journal of Biblical Literature* 133 (2014): 399–419. https://doi.org/10.1353/jbl.2014.0017

Depauw, Mark, and Willy Clarysse. "How Christian Was Fourth Century Egypt? Onomastic Perspectives on Conversion," *Vigiliae Christianae* 62 (2013): 407–35. https://doi.org/10.1163/15700720-12341144

Dunderberg, Ismo. *Gnostic Morality Revisited.* Tübingen: Mohr Siebeck, 2015. https://doi.org/10.1628/978-3-16-153694-6

Fredriksen, Paula. "Mandatory Retirement: Ideas in the Study of Christian Origins Whose Time Has Come to Go," *Studies in Religion/Sciences Religieuses* 35.2 (2006): 231–46. https://doi.org/10.1177/000842980603500203

Goehring, James E. "New Frontiers in Pachomian Studies," 236–57 in *The Roots of Egyptian Christianity.* Edited by Birger A. Pearson and James E. Goehring. Philadelphia, PA: Fortress Press, 1986.

Goodacre, Mark. "How Reliable Is the Story of the Nag Hammadi Discovery?," *Journal for the Study of the New Testament* 35 (2013): 303–22. https://doi.org/10.1177/0142064X13482243

Harmless, William S. J. *Desert Christians: An Introduction to the Literature of Early Monasticism.* Oxford: Oxford University Press, 2004. https://doi.org/10.1093/0195162234.001.0001

Hauben, Hans. "The Melitian 'Church of the Martyrs': Christian Dissenters in Ancient Egypt," 329–49 in *Ancient History at a Modern University. Proceedings of a Conference Held at Macquarie University, 8–13 July 1993 to Mark Twenty-Five Years of the Teaching of Ancient History at Macquarie University and the Retirement from the Chair of Professor Edwin Judge.* Edited by Tom W. Hillard, Rosalinde A. Kearsley, Charles Edwin Vandervord Nixon, and Alanna M. Nobbs. Grand Rapids, MI: Macquarie University, 1998.

Hopkins, Keith. "Christian Number and Its Implications," *Journal of Early Christian Studies* 6.2 (1998): 185–226. https://doi.org/10.1353/earl.1998.0035

Jenott, Lance, and Elaine Pagels. "Anthony's Letters and Nag Hammadi Codex I: Sources of Religious Conflict in Fourth-Century Egypt," *Journal for Early Christian Studies* 18.4 (2010): 557–89.

Kimber Buell, Denise. *Making Christians.: Clement of Alexandria and the Rhetoric of Legitimacy.* Princeton, NJ: Princeton University Press, 1999. https://doi.org/10.1515/9780691221526

—"Race and Universalism in Early Christianity," *Journal of Early Christian Studies* 10 (2002): 429–68. https://doi.org/10.1353/earl.2002.0061

—*Why This New Race: Ethnic Reasoning in Early Christianity*. New York: Columbia University Press, 2005. https://doi.org/10.7312/buel13334

King, Karen L. *What is Gnosticism?* Cambridge, MA: Belknap Press–Harvard University Press, 2003.

—*The Secret Revelation of John*. Cambridge, MA: Harvard University Press, 2006. https://doi.org/10.4159/9780674039605

Krutzsch, Myriam, and Günter Poethke. "Der Einband des Koptisch-Gnostischen Kodex Papyrus Berolinensis 8502," *Forschungen und Berichte* 24 (1984): 37–40. https://doi.org/10.2307/3880920

Lundhaug, Hugo, and Lance Jenott, *The Monastic Origins of the Nag Hammadi Codices*. Tübingen: Mohr Siebeck, 2015. https://doi.org/10.1628/978-3-16-154173-5

Malone, Edward E. *The Monk and the Martyr: The Monk as the Successor of the Martyr*. Washington DC: The Catholic University of America Press, 1950.

Moss, Candida R. *Ancient Christian Martyrdom: Diverse Practices, Theologies, and Traditions*. New Haven, CT: Yale University Press, 2012.

—*The Myth of Persecution: How Early Christians Invented a Story of Martyrdom*. New York: HarperCollins, 2013.

Nongbri, Brent. "Finding Early Christian Books at Nag Hammadi and Beyond," *Bulletin for the Study of Religion* 45 (2016): 11–9. https://doi.org/10.1558/bsor.v45i2.28062

Pagels, Elaine. *Adam, Eve, and the Serpent*. New York: Vintage Books, 1989.

Rebillard, Éric. *Christians and Their Many Identities in Late Antiquity, North Africa, 200–450 CE*. Ithaca, NY: Cornell University Press, 2012. https://doi.org/10.7591/cornell/9780801451423.001.0001

Ruether, Rosemary R. *Faith and Fratricide: The Theological Roots of Anti-Semitism*. New York: Seabury, 1974.

Smith, Morton. "The History of the Term Gnostikos," 796–807 in *The Rediscovery of Gnosticism. Proceedings of the International Conference on Gnosticism at Yale New Haven, Connecticut, March 28—31, 1978*. Vol. 2: *Sethian Gnosticism, Studies in the History of Religions*. Edited by Bentley Lanton. Leiden: Brill, 1981. https://doi.org/10.1163/9789004378599_051

Stark, Rodney. *The Rise of Christianity: How the Obscure, Marginal Jesus Movement Became the Dominant Religious Force in the Western World in a Few Centuries*. New York: HarperCollins, 1997.

Stowers, Stanley K. "Greeks Who Sacrifice and Those Who Do Not: Toward an Anthropology of Greek Religion," 229–333 in *The Social World of the First Christians: Essays in Honor of Wayne A. Meeks*. Edited by L. Michael White and O. Larry Yarbrough. Minneapolis, MN: Fortress Press, 1995.

Taylor, Miriam S. *Anti-Judaism and Early Christian Identity: A Critique of the Scholarly Consensus*. Leiden: Brill, 1995.

Tertullian, *Apology; De Spectaculis*. Loeb Classical Library, 250. Trans. T. R. Glover and Gerald H. Rendall. Cambridge, MA: Harvard University Press, 1931. https://doi.org/10.4159/DLCL.tertullian-de_spectaculis.1931

Tutty, Paula. "Books of the Dead or Books with the Dead? Interpreting Book Depositions in Late Antique Egypt," 287–328 in *The Nag Hammadi Codices and Late Antique Egypt*. Edited by Hugo Lundhaug and Lance Jenott. Tübingen: Mohr Siebeck, 2018.

Waldstein, Michael, and Frederik Wisse, "Introduction," 3–8 in *The Apocryphon of*

John: *Synopsis of Nag Hammadi Codices II,1, III,1, and IV,1 with BG 8502,2*. Edited by Michael Waldstein and Frederic Wisse. Leiden: Brill, 1995.

—*The Apocryphon of John: Synopsis of Nag Hammadi Codices II,1, III,1, and IV,1 with BG 8502,2*. Leiden: Brill, 1995.

Williams, Michael A. *The Immovable Race: A Gnostic Designation and the Theme of Stability in Late Antiquity*. Leiden: Brill, 1985. https://doi.org/10.1163/9789004437326

—*Rethinking "Gnosticism": An Argument for Dismantling a Dubious Category*. Princeton, NJ: Princeton University Press, 1996.

Wipszycka, Ewa. "La valeur de l'onomastique pour l'histoire de la christianisation de l'Égypte: À propos d'une étude de R. S. Bagnall," *Zeitschrift für Papyrologists und Epigraphik* 62 (1986): 173–81.

—"La christianisation de l'Égypte aux 4ème-5ème siècles: Aspects sociaux et ethniques," *Aegyptus* 68 (1988): 117–65.

Wisse, Frederik. "Gnosticism and Early Monasticism in Egypt," 431–40 in *Gnosis: Festschrift für Hans Jonas*. Edited by Barbara Aland. Göttingen: Vanderhoeck & Ruprecht, 1978.

Chapter Eleven

Spatial Conversion and Christian Identity in Late Antiquity

Anna Lampadaridi

This article aims to shed light on the development of a particular form of conversion narrative in Late Antiquity and to explore the rhetoric of conversion in early Christian texts as well as the role of spatial categories in the construction of a Christian past. In other words, how could Christian writers describe spatial conversion? What kind of narrative could they produce to pass on their message? In this context, my article focuses on a late antique Greek text, the *Life of Porphyry of Gaza* by Mark the Deacon (*Bibliotheca Hagiographica Graeca* 1570),[1] and suggests a new reading of what is one of the most enigmatic late antique hagiographical narratives.[2] This text

---

1. In the frame of my PhD thesis, I have composed a new critical edition, a French translation, and a historical commentary of the *Life of Porphyry of Gaza*. References to the Greek text follow my new critical edition: Anna Lampadaridi, *La conversion de Gaza au christianisme. La Vie de S. Porphyre* (*Subsidia Hagiographica*, 95; Brussels: Société des Bollandistes, 2016) (hereafter Lampadaridi, *Vita Porphyrii*). The English text is a revised version of Hill's translation (Georges Francis Hill, *The Life of Porphyry, Bishop of Gaza, by Mark the Deacon* [Oxford: Clarendon Press, 1913]).

2. For a *status quaestionis*, see Henri Grégoire et Marc-Antoine Kugener, *Marc le Diacre: Vie de Porphyre, évêque de Gaza* (Paris: Les Belles Lettres, 1930), vii–xxix; Frank R. Trombley, *Hellenic Religion and Christianization c. 370-529* (Leiden: Brill, 1995), 1.187–272; Zeev Rubin, *Porphyrius of Gaza and the Conflict between Christianity and Paganism in Southern Palestine*, in Arieh Kofsky and Guy G. Stroumsa, eds., *Sharing the Sacred: Religious Contacts and Conflicts in the Holy Land* (Jerusalem: Yad Izhak Ben Zvi, 1998), 31–66, here 33–4; Ramón Teja, *Vida de Porfirio de Gaza: Marco el diácono. Introducción, Traducción y notas* (Madrid: Editorial Trotta, 2008), 15–8; Giulia Sfameni Gasparro, "Porfirio di Gaza, un 'uomo santo' fra pagani, eretici e maghi: modelli retorici di propaganda religiosa e realtà storica," in Mariangela Monaca, ed., *Problemi di Storia Religiosa del Mondo Tardo-Antico: Tra Mantica e Magia* (Cosenza: Giordano, 2009), 201–329; Timothy D. Barnes, *Early Christian Hagiography and Roman History* (Tübingen: Mohr Siebeck, 2010), 260–5; Adelheid Hübner, *Marcus Diaconus: Vita Sancti Porphyrii. Leben des Heiligen Porphyrius* (Freiburg: Herder, 2013), 7–96; Ramón Teja, "La *Vida de Porfirio de Gaza* de Marco el Diácono: ¿Hagiografía histórica o invención hagiográfica?," in Philippe Blaudeau and Peter Van Nuffelen, eds., *L'historiographie tardo-antique et la transmission des savoirs* (Berlin: De Gruyter, 2015), 145–52.

offers an interesting case study to consider the conversion of pagan space into Christian space, as an attempt to legitimate history.

The Text and Its Author

Porphyry, a rich citizen of Thessalonica, born around the middle of the fourth century, leaves his hometown to settle in the Egyptian desert and then spends five years living in a cave near the Jordan. Despite his impaired health, he regularly visits the Holy Places. In Jerusalem, he meets Mark who earns a living as a copyist and who will become his devout companion, remaining with him up to his death. In 392, Porphyry, still in Jerusalem, is ordained to the priesthood and the relic of the Holy Cross, kept in the church of the Anastasis, is also entrusted to him. Appointed bishop of Gaza (the Palestinian city in today's Gaza strip) in 395, Porphyry, from the first moment of his episcopate, experiences the hostile attitude of native polytheists towards Christians. In the context of his struggle against polytheist cults, he decides to seek imperial help. At first, he sends Mark to Constantinople, to obtain an imperial order which would allow the closure of the polytheist temples of Gaza. Thanks to John Chrysostom's intervention, Mark returns to Gaza carrying an edict for the destruction of the temples. However, the official responsible for the execution of the order is bribed with a large sum of money and, consequently, the Marneion, the most prominent of the eight polytheist temples of Gaza, remains open.

Porphyry then decides to organize a second embassy to the capital. This time, he himself goes to Constantinople, accompanied by Mark and John, the bishop of Caesarea. A large part of the *Vita* is located at the court of the emperor Arcadius and the prelates are present for the birth and the baptism of Theodosius II. Porphyry's prophecy for the birth of a son is accomplished, and thus the bishop manages to gain the support of the empress Eudoxia; by cleverly manipulating Arcadius, Eudoxia prevails upon him and manages to obtain an order for the closure and destruction of the temples of Gaza. Moreover, she orders the construction of a church on the foundations of the Marneion. The destruction of Gaza's main temple and the erection of the church on the site of the anterior temple are the main episodes of the *Vita*. Mark provides an extremely vivid account of the episode. The dedication of the church in honor of the empress takes place five years later and is followed by a sumptuous celebration. The *Vita* closes with Porphyry's death in 420.

The *Life of Porphyry of Gaza* is one of the most seductive and problematical pieces of Greek hagiography in the Early Byzantine period. Its author purports to be Mark the Deacon, a figure unknown from any other source.

He introduces himself early in the text as the saint's loyal disciple, narrating his master's life. He earns his daily bread working as a manuscript scribe and he is supposed to be almost the same age as Porphyry. Porphyry always calls him "my brother"[3] (and never my child) when he is addressing him. A careful reading of the text reveals that Mark is just the narrator and should not be confused with the author. As a narrator, Mark describes many scenes in which he is not supposed to be present: hiding behind the figure of Porphyry's faithful companion, there is an individual who knows much more than this devout servant to whom the *Vita* is attributed. This discrepancy functions as a signal to the reader, making him or her beware of what is told. The existence of such a narrator stems from a specific literary model, a *topos*, according to which disciples are often the writers of their master's life. This model offers a comfortable literary frame, a fiction, behind which the real writer can erase his traces: as we will see, this is quite important in the case of the *Vita*, as the text insists on the Christianization of the city of Gaza, an aspect of the city's history that late antique historians pass over.

The writer of the *Vita* thus remains anonymous, a problem complicated by the uncertain dating of the text. We know that the *Vita* is written after the saint's death in 420 (the only date clearly mentioned in the text),[4] probably shortly afterwards. On the one hand, the use of Theodoret of Cyrrhus' *Philotheos History* obliges us to establish another terminus *post quem*, the year 444.[5] On the other hand, the use of the *Vita* by a sixth-century byzantine writer, Cyrillus of Scythopolis, allows us to determine a *terminus ante quem* for its composition, the middle of the sixth century.[6] All in all, the *Vita* must have been composed after 444 and before the middle of the sixth century: the writer cannot be Porphyry's contemporary, so the figure of the devout biographer is tarnished.

An equivocal date of composition and a shady writer's figure are just two of the obscure points of the *Vita Porphyrii*. Furthermore, the text was at the heart of a controversial debate from the middle of the sixteenth century, when a Latin translation of the *Vita* was integrated in Lippomani's *Vitae sanctorum*.[7] Mark's narrative caused a lot of debate among scholars like Baronius, Blondel, and Le Nain de Tillemont, who pointed out various historical discrepancies which stain the *Vita*'s value as an historical

---

3. Lampadaridi, *Vita Porphyrii*, chs. 5 and 96, pp. 80 and 176.
4. Lampadaridi, *Vita Porphyrii*, chs. 103 and 186.
5. Grégoire and Kugener, *Marc le diacre*, xxxiii–xxxvii.
6. Lampadaridi, *Vita Porphyrii*, chs. 17–19. Concerning Cyrillus of Scythopolis and the dating of his writings, see Bernard Flusin, *Miracle et histoire dans l'œuvre de Cyrille de Scythopolis* (Paris: Études augustiniennes, 1983), especially 33.
7. Lippomani *Vitae Sanctorum*, V.590–605.

document.[8] Henri Grégoire and Marc-Antoine Kugener, the Belgian scholars to whom we owe the *Vita*'s last critical edition, dating back to the 1930s, even assumed that the current *Vita* is the result of a previous narrative's later revision[9]. The discovery of a Georgian version of the *Vita* in the 1940s by Paul Peeters[10] questioned the two editors' theory. The stakes are high, as the *Vita* presents itself in very historical garb and constitutes a major document for the process of Christianization in Late Antiquity.

Gaza at the End of the Fourth Century: A Polytheist City

Mark gives a unique picture of the level of Christianization in the city. Gaza was still largely polytheist at the end of the fourth century and the Christian congregation was only a scarce minority: Mark reports only 280 Christians, men, women, and children included,[11] at a time when the city's population was estimated at 20,000 habitants.[12] Buildings used for the Christian cult were also very few. One finds the ancient church founded by the bishop Asclepas[13] between 320 and 325, situated in the west of the city. Also, *extra muros*, there was a *martyrium*, the holy shrine of the martyr Timotheus, where the relics of two other local martyrs also reposed. Finally, the church named Irene, peace in Greek, was located into the agglomeration. Its

---

8. Louis Sébastien Le Nain de Tillemont, *Mémoires pour servir à l'histoire ecclésiastique des six premiers siècles justifiez par les citations des auteurs originaux* (Paris: Charles Robustel, 1705), 10.843–51. Concerning the debate on the historical value of the *Vita*, see Grégoire and Kugener, *Marc le diacre*, vii–xxix; Rubin, *Porphyrius of Gaza and the Conflict between Christianity and Paganism*, 33–4; Teja, *Vida de Porfirio de Gaza*, 15–8; Barnes, *Early Christian Hagiography*, 260–5; Lampadaridi, *Vita Porphyrii*, 15–7.

9. Grégoire and Kugener, *Marc le diacre*, lxxi. On the dating of the *Vita* see also Trombley, *Hellenic Religion and Christianization*, 278–9; Barnes, *Early Christian Hagiography*, 281–3; Lampadaridi, *Vita Porphyrii*, 15–9.

10. Paul Peeters, "La Vie géorgienne de Saint Porphyre de Gaza," *Analecta Bollandiana* 59 (1941): 65–216.

11. Lampadaridi, *Vita Porphyrii*, chs. 19 and 96.

12. On this subject, see Magen Broshi, "The Population of Western Palestine in the Roman-Byzantine Period," *Bulletin of the American Schools of Oriental Research* 236 (1979): 1–10, here 5; Trombley, *Hellenic Religion and Christianization*, 223; Joseph Geiger, "Aspects of Palestinian Paganism in Late Antiquity," in Kofsky and Stroumsa, eds., *Sharing the Sacred*, 3–18, here 10; Nicole Belayche, "Pagan Festivals in Fourth-Century Gaza," in Brouria Bitton-Ashkelony and Arieh Kofsky, eds., *Christian Gaza in Late Antiquity* (Leiden: Brill, 2004), 5–22, here 5.

13. Daniel Stiernon and Lucien Stiernon, "Gaza," *Dictionnaire d'histoire et de géographie ecclésiastique*, Vol. 20 (Turnhout: Brepols, 1984), 171–2.

construction, together with the bishop's palace, was attributed to the bishop Irenion,[14] between 360 and 380.

> ... the ancient church that is in the west of the city, which they say was founded by the most holy and blessed Asclepas, the bishop, who suffered many persecutions for the true faith (ch. 20)

> ... the holy shrine of the glorious martyr Timotheus, wherein are also laid other relics of Maiour the martyr and Thee the confessor ... (ch. 19)

> ... So we went to the bishop's house, which was founded by the forenamed saint Irenion, the bishop, together with the holy church that is called Irene (Peace). (ch. 18)

It is therefore important to point out that Gaza possesses only one Christian building *intra muros* until the end of the fourth century. This indicates that Christian presence in the city within the urban space was at the very least discreet, perhaps almost imperceptible.

On the other hand, Mark counts eight polytheist temples *intra muros*, among them the famous Marneion, dedicated to the God Marnas,[15] who has been identified with Zeus.

> Now there were in the city eight public temples of idols, of the Sun and of Aphrodite and of Apollo and of the Maiden and of Hecate and the temple called of the Hero, and the temple of the Fortune of the City, which they called the Tychaion, and the Marneion, which they said was the temple of the Cretanborn Zeus, which they accounted to be more famous than all the temples in the world. And there were also very many other idols in the houses and in the villages, whereof no man could reckon the number. (ch. 64)

Gaza's urban space was clearly dominated by polytheists, which explains the unfriendly welcome the natives offered to their new bishop at the very end of the fourth century.[16]

The Conversion of Sacred Space: From the Marneion to the Eudoxiana

After the destruction of the other polytheist temples of the city, the solution for the demolition of the Marneion is given through the intervention of a child who first speaks in Syriac, his mother tongue, and then miraculously repeats the same words in Greek, a language he is not supposed to have acquired by natural means.

---

14. Stiernon and Stiernon, "Gaza," 172.
15. On Marnas, see Gerard Mussies, "Marnas, God of Gaza," in Wolfgang Haase and Hildegard Temporini, eds., *Aufstieg und Niedergang der römischen Welt* II, 18.4 (Berlin: De Gruyter, 1990), 2412–57.
16. Lampadaridi, *Vita Porphyrii*, ch. 17, 92–5.

> At last, after we had all ceased, the boy opened his mouth and said in the Greek dialect: "Burn the inner temple unto the foundation; for many terrible things have been done in it, especially the sacrifices of human beings. And after this manner burn it: bring liquid pitch and sulphur and fat of swine, and mingle the three and anoint the brazen doors and set fire to them, and so shall all the temple be burned; for otherwise is it not possible. But the outer temple leave it with the court. And after the burning, having purified the place, found there a holy church. I swear unto you again before God, otherwise may it not be done. For it is not I who speaks, but Christ who is within me." And the most holy bishop Porphyry marveled, and all they that were with him, when they heard the bold saying of the boy, and how plainly he spoke; and calling his mother, the bishop asked her whether she or her son knew the Greek tongue; but she affirmed with oaths that neither she nor her child knew Greek. And when he heard it, again the most holy Porphyry glorified God, and bringing three coins gave them to the woman. But the boy beholding the coins in the hand of his mother cried out, saying in the Syriac tongue: "Take them not, Mother, do not sell the gift of God for gold." And we hearing it marveled again exceedingly. But the woman gave back the three coins saying to the bishop, "Pray for me and my child and commend us unto God." And the holy bishop sent them away in peace. (ch. 68)

The miraculous intervention of children is a literary *topos* in hagiographical literature[17] and the capacity to speak in a language previously unknown to the speaker, especially in Greek, is also considered as a sign of divine inspiration.[18] This episode plays a key role in the narrative as it provides an answer to the question concerning the demolition of the main polytheist temple and the construction of the Christian church in the same spot. The suggestion of the child, perceived as a divine sign, will be followed by the clergy, the Christians, and the army who take part in the campaign.

> But at dawn he called together the God-fearing clergy and the Christloving layfolk, and likewise the admirable Cynegius and the governors, and told them how the boy had spoken concerning the Marneion. And when they heard, they were astonished and with one mind said that according to the saying of the boy, even so it should be burned. Taking, therefore, the liquid pitch and the sulphur and the swine's fat and mingling the three they anointed the inner doors, and having made a prayer they kindled the fire, and straightway the entire temple took fire and was burned. And as many of the soldiers and of the strangers as were able seized out of the fire whatsoever they found, whether it was gold or silver or iron or lead. (chs. 68–9)

---

17. See for instance the *Life of Daniel the Stylite*: a child indicates to the saint the book which is meant to define his name. See Hippolyte Delehaye, ed., *Les saints stylites: Sancti Danielis stylitae Vita antiquior* (Brussels: Société des Bollandistes, 1923), 3.

18. See the *Dialogues* of Gregory the Great: Adalbert de Vogüé, ed. *Dialogues*, IV, 27, 11–12 (Paris: Cerf, 1980), 94–5.

The Christian conversion of the city of Gaza is narrated through spatial conversion, which leads to a kind of patriographical narrative composed to glorify a Christian monument. This provides a means to strengthen conversion to Christianity, to make the Christianization of the city more visible, more tangible and thus more comprehensible. The bishop Porphyry therefore organizes a sumptuous feast to celebrate the consecration of the new church.

> But after a period of five years the work of the great holy church was accomplished, and it was called Eudoxiana after the name of the Empress Eudoxia, most beloved of God. And the most holy Porphyry consecrated it on the day of the Resurrection of holy Easter very sumptuously, sparing no expense; but having gathered together all the monks, to the number of about a thousand persons, with other devout people, of the clergy and laymen and bishops, he made good cheer all the days of holy Easter. And there were to be seen angelic choirs not only in the office of the church, but also in the hours when they did eat their food. For their table was not only a visible, but also a spiritual table; for after the meat was said a psalm, and after the drink, a hymn. But when they of the idol-madness saw that which came to pass, their hearts were melted. For foreigners came from every quarter to see the beauty and greatness of the said holy church; for it was said to be greater than all the churches of that time. (ch. 92)

The construction of the church radically changed the urban landscape and the identity of the city, whose life was organized around its major sanctuary. A polytheist monument gives way to a Christian edifice, something that made an immediate, inevitable impact on the way inhabitants perceived the city in which they lived. The image of the foreigners flocking to the newly built monument suggests that the Christian building must now become the neuralgic center of the city, a point of interest and attraction. If the physical replacement of the building was not enough, the rhetorical impact of Porphyry's reconstruction aims to establish the Church as the new most important building of the area, not only by polytheist standards, but even by Christian standards.

However, the conversion of the local population to Christianity was not as radical as the transformation of the urban space: although Porphyry's miraculous activity leads to many conversions, which Mark carefully records,[19] we also read that the Eudoxiana church is considered too spacious in comparison with the number of Christians in the city:

> ... when he laid the foundations at the beginning he was accused by certain of the faithful, because he made it great, although the Christians in the city were few ... (ch. 93)

---

19. 162 polytheists become Christians in ch. 21 (See Lampadaridi, *Vita Porphyrii*, 98), 64 in ch. 31 (see p. 110), 39 in ch. 62 (p. 140), 300 in ch. 74 (p. 154).

In the *Vita Porphyrii*, the conversion of the city of Gaza into Christianity is basically perceived as a conversion of sacred space: the author pays less attention to the conversion of the local population itself, less spectacular and thus less able to create the image of a Christian city. The narrative offers another way to re-think the definition of Christianization. At the same time, the splendor and size of the Church themselves suggest that the conversion of people will automatically follow, to fill this newly-built structure.

Constructing a Conversion Narrative: Gaza and Its Harbor

Mark's narrative might now appear in the form of the *Vita* of a holy bishop but it was not initially written in order to promote Porphyry's cult. Many elements prevent us from considering this text as a typical hagiographical *Vita* narrating a saint's biography: the narrative reaches its end abruptly, relating the saint's death on 26 February in 420, but it does not include a death scene, which is one of the basic elements of a saint's *Vita*. Moreover, the periods of the life of Porphyry and his career are not equally treated: his stays in the desert and in Jerusalem are briefly summarized[20] and we know nothing about the last 13 years of his life, following the consecration of the Great church on the debris of the Marneion. On the other hand, the description of the Marneion's destruction and the edification of the Christian church on the same spot occupy the major part of the narrative: in fact, one third of the text is dedicated to this episode which represents a period no longer than five years at the very beginning of the fifth century.[21] Here we touch upon the heart of the text, its nucleus, in other words, its *raison d'être*: the demolition of Gaza's major polytheist sanctuary and the construction of a Christian church at the center of the city. The text is written in the memory of a monument. This point clearly differentiates it from typical hagiographical literature, which aims to describe the life of a saint, and not the life of a monument.

A glimpse into local history in Late Antiquity can clarify at least some of the reasons which led to the composition of such a narrative. Contrary to the city of Gaza, which remains, as we saw, a polytheist fortress, Maiouma, its harbor, proved more open and permeable to Christian influences and had an important Christian community at the time. The ecclesiastical historian Sozomenus (c.400–c.450) is our major source of information for this issue: Maiouma was Christianized very early, at the time of the emperor

---

20. Lampadaridi, *Vita Porphyrii*, chs. 4–10, 78–86.
21. Lampadaridi, *Vita Porphyrii*, chs. 66–93, 144–74, with many digressions which slow down the narrative.

Constantine, who raised it to the rank of a city and re-baptized it Constantia.[22] The harbor possessed a robust Christian community, a fact which generated tension between Gaza and Constantia. Thus, in Porphyry's time, Maiouma is Gaza's port again but it conserves its own episcopal see. This decision leads to a particularly strange situation, with one single city having two bishops: there was always an underlying conflict between these two sees, whose relations were far from being peaceful.[23]

To summarize, we have, next to Gaza—a largely polytheist city—a powerful Christian community with another bishop; this situation is a constant source of problems for the region.

Marks tells us very little about Maiouma's Christian congregation: the only information is that when Porphyry returns from his mission to Constantinople, there are, among the Christians who are welcoming him, also Christians from Maiouma. Those Christians from Maiouma, as Mark indicates, outnumber those of Gaza.

> And when we came ashore, the Christians there, when they heard of it, received us with psalm singing; and likewise also they of the city when they heard it came to meet us, having with them the sign of the precious Cross, themselves also singing psalms. And the people from the two places were mingled together, and there was no small number; those from the seaside were the more, because they had many Egyptians who were merchants of wines. (ch. 58)

Other than this mention, Maiouma is totally absent from Mark's narrative; he does not mention its bishop or the members of the community. The only local bishops mentioned in the text are Porphyry's predecessors. This silence makes sense in the context of the competition characteristic of the relations between the two sees: it makes up the context for Mark's narrative and is closely related to the nature of the text, its literary genre.

The edification of a Christian building at the heart of the city symbolizes the victory of the Christian religion, which finds its way to the very center of what is considered one of the major polytheist fortresses of the region. Moreover, beyond the construction of the church, the existence of the *Vita* proves that there was a need to produce a narrative of this transformation and thus to keep a record of it. The construction of the church seals the victory of Christianity and the composition of a narrative of this episode crystallizes this conversion by creating and entertaining a collective memory around this monument. Such a narrative provides, in a way, a counterweight

---

22. Joseph Bidez, ed., *Sozomenus, Ecclesiastical History* II, 5, 7–8 (Paris: Cerf, 1983), 254–5.

23. Sozomenus describes this situation: Joseph Bidez, ed. *Sozomenus, Ecclesiastical History* V, 3, 6–9 (Paris: Cerf, 2005), 104–5.

to the controversial character of the church: the *Vita* remains the only certain literary evidence on its existence, while the small tentative excavations in this area—Byzantine Gaza is covered by the still inhabited Old City—do not provide any supplementary clues. However, Porphyry's cult is well attested in the city of Gaza nowadays.[24]

Gaza has always been a polytheist city for Christian writers, who stressed the importance of the Christian community of Maiouma, its anchorage, without paying attention to the Christian presence in the city of Gaza itself. However, there was a need to demonstrate that Gaza, at the turn of the fourth to the fifth century, also had a Christian face, which official history erased. The *Life of Porphyry* aims to fill this gap by rewriting Gaza's history as a Christian city through the conversion of sacred space and thus to create a Christian past for what was considered a polytheist city. The conflict between the two bishop sees, Gaza and Maiouma, also sheds another light on such a text: it was not only about making a statement towards the polytheists in the city, but also about taking a stand inside the conflict between the two episcopal sees.

Biographical Note

Anna Lampadaridi is a researcher at the Centre National de la Recherche Scientifique (CNRS) in France. She holds a PhD in Hellenic Studies (Byzantine Literature) from Sorbonne University (Paris IV) (2011). In Paris, she takes part in various research programs (UMR 8167 Orient et Méditerranée / IRHT / Labex Resmed). She is a member of the Institut Français d'Études Byzantines (IFEB) and of the editorial board of the *Revue des Études Byzantines*. She teaches Ancient Greek at the Institut Protestant de Théologie (Paris) and the Institut Catholique (Paris). She was a Newton International Fellow (British Academy) at the University of Oxford (2018–2020). Her research focuses on Late Antique and Byzantine Hagiography. She won the 2019 Prix Marguerite and Charles Diehl (Académie des Inscriptions et Belles-Lettres) for her monograph: *La conversion de Gaza au christianisme. La Vie de S. Porphyre de Gaza par Marc le Diacre (BHG 1570). Édition critique–traduction–commentaire* (*Subsidia Hagiographica*, 95; Brussels: Société des Bollandistes, 2016).

---

24. Concerning this discussion, see Lampadaridi, *Vita Porphyrii*, 31–7, with previous literature.

Bibliography

Barnes, Timothy D. *Early Christian Hagiography and Roman History*. Tübingen: Mohr Siebeck, 2010.
Belayche, Nicole. "Pagan Festivals in Fourth-Century Gaza," 5–22 in *Christian Gaza in Late Antiquity*. Edited by Brouria Bitton-Ashkelony and Arieh Kofsky. Leiden: Brill, 2004.
Bidez, Joseph, ed. *Sozomenus, Ecclesiastical History* II. Introduction by Guy Sabbah and Bernard Grillet; translated by André-Jean Festugière; notes by Guy Sabbah. *Sources Chrétiennes*, 306. Paris: Cerf, 1983.
—*Sozomenus, Ecclesiastical History* V. Introduction and Notes by Guy Sabbah; translated by †André-Jean Festugière; reviewed by Bernard Grillet. *Sources Chrétiennes*, 495. Paris: Cerf, 2005.
Broshi, Magen. "The Population of Western Palestine in the Roman-Byzantine Period," *Bulletin of the American Schools of Oriental Research* 236 (1979): 1–10. https://doi.org/10.2307/1356664
Delehaye, Hippolyte, ed. *Sancti Danielis stylitae Vita antiquior. Subsidia Hagiographica*, 14. Brussels: Société des Bollandistes, 1923.
Flusin, Bernard. *Miracle et histoire dans l'œuvre de Cyrille de Scythopolis*. Paris: Études augustiniennes, 1983.
Geiger, Joseph. "Aspects of Palestinian Paganism in Late Antiquity," 3–18 in Kofsky and Stroumsa, eds., *Sharing the Sacred*, 1998.
Grégoire, Henri, et Marc-Antoine Kugener. *Marc le Diacre: Vie de Porphyre, évêque de Gaza*. Paris: Les Belles Lettres, 1930. https://doi.org/10.3406/bude.1930.6696
Hill, Georges Francis. *The Life of Porphyry, Bishop of Gaza, by Mark the Deacon*. Oxford: Clarendon Press, 1913.
Hübner, Adelheid. *Marcus Diaconus: Vita Sancti Porphyrii. Leben des Heiligen Porphyrius*. Freiburg: Herder, 2013.
Kofsky, Arieh, and Guy G. Stroumsa, eds. *Sharing the Sacred: Religious Contacts and Conflicts in the Holy Land*. Jerusalem: Yad Izhak Ben Zvi, 1998.
Mussies, Gerard. "Marnas, God of Gaza," 2412–57 in *Aufstieg und Niedergang der römischen Welt* II, 18.4. Edited by Wolfgang Haase and Hildegard Temporini. Berlin: De Gruyter, 1990. https://doi.org/10.1515/9783110877274-007
Lampadaridi, Anna. *La conversion de Gaza au christianisme: La Vie de S. Porphyre*. *Subsidia Hagiographica*, 95. Brussels: Société des Bollandistes, 2016.
Le Nain de Tillemont, Louis Sébastien. *Mémoires pour servir à l'histoire ecclésiastique des six premiers siècles justifiez par les citations des auteurs originaux*. Vol. 10. Venise: François Pitteri, 1732.
Peeters, Paul. "La Vie géorgienne de Saint Porphyre de Gaza," *Analecta Bollandiana* 59 (1941): 65–216. https://doi.org/10.1484/J.ABOL.4.00879
Rubin, Zeev. *Porphyrius of Gaza and the Conflict between Christianity and Paganism in Southern Palestine*, 31–66 in Kofsky and Stroumsa, eds., *Sharing the Sacred*, 1998.
Sfameni Gasparro, Giulia. "Porfirio di Gaza, un 'uomo santo' fra pagani, eretici e maghi: modelli retorici di propaganda religiosa e realtà storica," 201–329 in *Problemi di Storia Religiosa del Mondo Tardo-Antico: Tra Mantica e Magia*. Edited by Mariangela Monaca. Cosenza: Giordano, 2009.
Stiernon, Daniel, and Lucien Stiernon. "Gaza," 171–2 in *Dictionnaire d'histoire et de géographie ecclésiastique*, Vol. 20. Turnhout: Brepols, 1984.

Teja, Ramón. *Vida de Porfirio de Gaza: Marco el diácono. Introducción, Traducción y notas*. Madrid: Editorial Trotta, 2008.

—"La *Vida de Porfirio de Gaza* de Marco el Diácono: ¿Hagiografía histórica o invención hagiográfica?," 145–52 in *L'historiographie tardo-antique et la transmission des savoirs*. Edited by Philippe Blaudeau and Peter Van Nuffelen. Berlin: De Gruyter, 2015. https://doi.org/10.1515/9783110409239-009

Trombley, Frank R. *Hellenic Religion and Christianization c. 370-529*, Vol. 1. Leiden: Brill, 1995. https://doi.org/10.1163/9789004276772

Vogüé, Albert de, ed. *Dialogues de Grégoire le Grand*, IV. Translated by Paul Antin. *Sources Chrétiennes*, 265. Vol. 3. Paris: Cerf, 1980.

Chapter Twelve

Concluding Remarks

Valérie Nicolet

Did Conversion Exist in Antiquity?

Through our work in two conferences and through the essays in this edited volume, we attempted to bring out the "complexity" of conversion. At the close of this volume, it is time to reflect on what this complexity means and on the many ways the ten articles of this volume bring this complexity out. One obvious remark first: it is not that conversion did not happen in the ancient world. However, the articles in this volume have aimed to show that in the ways that conversion did happen in the ancient world, it might not be appropriate to label it as "conversion." Overall, the authors of this volume agree that, as Paula Fredriksen puts it, the term should go in "speedy retirement."[1] Talking about conversion for all the experiences explored in this volume reduces a complex reality to a single notion, which, in today's context, is not helpful to conceptualize ancient reality. The personal, individual, psychologizing definition of conversion elaborated by William James as well as by the study of Arthur D. Nock (both at the beginning of the twentieth century) do not match the realities which the articles in this volume explore. The present contributions delineate a broader understanding of conversion, and explore various terminologies, such as religious change, multiple belonging, or memberships. This discomfort around the term conversion and its psychologizing understanding crystallizes around several dimensions, to which I will return in these concluding remarks.

I choose to organize these remarks around five dimensions that allow us to broaden our understanding of conversion. First, several articles in the volume show that the notion of individual conversion is challenged when one includes a variety of persons, and does not simply focus on free, adult males. The question, who is affected/can be affected by conversion, is a first field of inquiry. Second, one can also reflect on how belonging is understood and whether one can talk about religious exclusivism for the ancient

---

1. Paula Fredriksen, "Mandatory Retirement: Ideas in the Study of Christian Origins Whose Time Has Come to Go," *Studies in Religion* 35.2 (2006): 231–46.

world. Third, the understanding of conversion is modified if one considers broader realities, such as a healing and physical transformation. Fourth, conversion, far from being individual in Antiquity, is affected and impacted by kinship and ethnic ties, that necessitate a different definition of the concept. The fifth dimension takes us back to the beginning of the book, which opens with two studies concerned with the contemporary world, and invites us to reflect on how we can talk about conversion today, if we keep in mind the variegated experiences of Antiquity. Not that the past would offer a response to our current questions, but it might allow us to de-familiarize ourselves from what we think we know, and allow us to ask new questions.[2] Finally, I will also reflect on the way this topic—conversion—opens different fields of inquiries, using the articles of the volume as inspiration.

Five Dimensions That Complicate Our Understanding of Conversion

One could easily summarize the five dimensions in five questions:

- Who could be converted/Who could convert?
- What did religious belonging mean?
- How did conversion manifest itself?
- How was conversion a communal phenomenon?
- How does conversion intersect with contemporary practices?

I will treat each question in turn.

Who Could Be Converted/Who Could Convert?

Kartzow specifically reflects on the fact that conversion, especially in the field of New Testament studies, is considered through male characters. For her, studies like those are simply blind to an entire population in the ancient world. Three articles in this volume bring to the fore this usually neglected population and show how conversion would have worked differently for different people. These marginalized people highlight that, in Antiquity, the question about conversion was indeed not only "who could convert?" but also "who could be converted?"

Heimola reflects on a famous story of conversion, contained in the book of Acts. Perhaps here we are closest to an individual, psychologizing

---

2. See Michel Foucault, "On the Genealogy of Ethics: An Overview of Work in Progress," in Paul Rabinow, ed., *The Foucault Reader* (New York: Pantheon Books, 1984), 340–72, here 343: "you can't find the solution of a problem in the solution of another problem raised at another moment by other people."

conversion, and yet, the fact that this immediate story of conversion is about an Ethiopian eunuch complicates matters. We encounter here a queer[3] character, in between genders, and further marginalized by his race and his status. Using some Church Fathers, Heimola can show that conversion, for the eunuch, does not mean only religious change, but also affects how his gender is perceived by various interpreters. His religious devotion, for some, augments his masculinity. Gender and religious orientation are closely connected in this story.

A similar phenomenon happens with the Corinthian women I chose to bring to life in my article. Indeed, I argue that for these women, the encounter with Paul's good news affected how they perceived and used their body. The controversy surrounding female prophesying without veiling (in 1 Cor. 11), when read with tools provided by Judith Butler, allows one to claim that the body manifested by the women prophets did not correspond to a proper physical embodiment of piety. In the case of these women, conversion allowed for new embodiment, perhaps even a new body, a new sex, that upset the traditional hierarchies of Antiquity. In this case, conversion is not only a religious change, but a new use of old norms to embody resistance. It has to do with agency as much as with piety.

Finally, Kartzow follows the step of Hagar, another marginalized character. Hagar asks questions about conversion that are usually masked if one considers only free, male converts. As a foreign slave in Abraham's household, she could be considered a convert, willing or not, to Judaism. Yet, her possible conversion is often ignored in analyses about conversion. With Hagar, again, conversion is not just about religious choice. While it is not impossible that Hagar might have changed her personal religious orientation when coming to Abraham and Sarah, her conversion could easily also have been imposed from outside, and been associated with her position in her master's household. For a slave (but also for a woman who married, as the case of Aseneth, also discussed in this volume, makes clear), every change of master or of household could have signified a change of religion. In this case, "religious switchings" might more appropriately reveal what is happening than the term conversion.

The fourth article which responds to the question "who could be converted?" adds yet another dimension to what conversion could be in Antiquity. Indeed, Lampadaridi, far from discussing people, studies the case of

---

3. "Queer" is here understood in its adjectival meaning, a term of identification or description. See for the various meanings of "queer": Joseph A. Marchal, "Queer Approaches: Improper Relations with Pauline Letters," in Marchal, ed., *Studying Paul's Letters: Contemporary Perspectives and Methods* (Minneapolis, MN: Fortress Press, 2012), 209–27.

the conversion of pagan space into Christian space, through her analysis of *The Life of Porphyry of Gaza*. Again, here conversion is less about an individualized, personal choice and more about a strategic use of space to establish the dominance of Christianity over a contested space. The narrative discussed by Lampadaridi uses divine intervention, through the intervention of an inspired child, to establish that polytheist space must be destroyed to make room for a Christian church. Using space, *The Life of Porphyry* strengthens the implantation of Christianity in Gaza and solidifies conversion to Christianity. No need for people converting in this story: if the space becomes Christian, then the nature and the identity of the city is deeply modified, and so are, one would guess, its inhabitants. Here we have moved to a completely depersonalized understanding of conversion, probably also reflecting the new more official status of Christianity in the fourth century. However, the text itself, though mostly hagiographic, notes a trace of resistance to this depersonalized conversion: the church is too big for the numbers of Christians in the city. Conversion, as Lampadaridi highlights, is more about creating a Christian identity and appearance for the city, than about individuals. Conversion functions as a strategy in a battle over a contested space, a city, traditionally perceived as pagan.

What Did Religious Belonging Mean?

Two articles in particular tie the notion of conversion with the question of religious belonging in Antiquity. Both van den Heever and Toft Rosland are able to show that multiple belongings to religious groups were possible in antiquity. Furthermore, memberships were not simply hierarchical (with one identity, or membership, trumping the other) but could be interchangeable. One activated various belongings depending on circumstances. Van den Heever demonstrates this for mystery cults, and Toft Rosland argues a similar point for Christians in the fourth century who chose to continue their participation in the emperor's cult through sacrifices.

What I find interesting in these reflections on religious belongings is the sense that conversion functioned in different ways for different people. In Antiquity, conversion to a specific religious group is not necessarily a case for exclusivism. Even for Christians in the fourth century, choosing Christianity did not necessarily mean renouncing all other practices. In the case of mystery cults, one got involved in various cults not because of individual emotions and convictions (even if they could play a role) but because participation in various cults was part of social and cultural life. Conversion is thus understood no longer in terms of Christian conversion only, as was the case with James and Nock, but rather can become something concerned with intelligence, experiences, rituals, affections, at the risk of having conversion as a concept disappear entirely. Perhaps this disappearance of (Christian) conversion can also teach us that we should be attentive to the diversity of religious experiences, and their connections with various aspects of the person.

How Did Conversion Manifest Itself?

In a further effort to vary our understanding of conversion, two articles approach the question of how conversion manifests itself. Hartvigsen's article is particularly intriguing in that regard because it considers the one text that might be most obviously considered as presenting a conversion in our survey of ancient texts (with *The Golden Ass*, discussed by van den Heever), namely *Joseph and Aseneth*. As is classic in ancient Hellenistic novels, the lovers have an obstacle to overcome before they can be united. Here that obstacle is Aseneth's religious belonging. Aseneth needs to abandon her Egyptian gods to become a bride worthy of Joseph. In *Joseph and Aseneth*, conversion allows the removal of the obstacle hindering Joseph and Aseneth's marriage. Here, too, however, conversion goes beyond religious choice. For Aseneth, to be able to marry Joseph involves a change that affects her religion but also her ethnicity, and perhaps her gender. For Aseneth, these changes are manifested in her physical appearance. Through her acceptance of the God of the Israelites, Aseneth is transformed physically: her beauty matches the one of the Hebrew matriarchs, but is also translated into a male face, which reflects her enlightenment and her access to superior truth. Conversion allows Aseneth to cross religious and ethnic boundaries, and perhaps even gender limits.

Solevåg's article explores yet another dimension of conversion, when she reads together healing narratives in the Gospel of Mark and conversion discourses in early Methodism. In her discussion of healing, she uncovers the specific link between healing from disability or illness and conversion. The miracle stories of the Gospels (here read in Mark) were a helpful resource for the Methodist interpretation of the affinities between healing and conversion. Here conversion manifests itself in the healing of body (and sometimes mind) and contributes to the wholeness of the person. Solevåg traces the roots of the contemporary understanding of conversion as a highly personal, religious experience, to Methodism, where personal narratives of conversion play an important role, often in relationship with healing. For Solevåg, one must be careful to not project the later, Methodist, understanding of conversion on ancient texts, and to see the difference between healing stories in the Gospels (where conversion is not mentioned) and the Methodist tradition, where healing becomes a symbol for conversion.

How Was Conversion Communal?

Starting with two very different ancient texts, both Toft Rosland and Hartvigsen help to see how conversion was connected to kinship and ethnicity in Antiquity. Again, we move away from a personalized, individual understanding of conversion to examine experiences that have to do with family belonging. In *Joseph and Aseneth*, one sees that Aseneth's transformation is perhaps more about ethnic belonging than about religious conviction: how can the daughter of the Egyptian priest find herself worthy of the Hebrew patriarch? Interestingly, along with her change of gods, Aseneth's physical beauty, which reminds one of the Hebrew matriarchs, as the narrator indicates, is the determining criterion to make her belong.

Toft Rosland shows how *Apocryphon of John*, with its complicated story of celestial beings of various grades, contributes to create an alternative sense of kinship for Christians, whose conversion might have isolated them from their family of origins. In the context of the fourth century, changing religious allegiance could mean losing important familial ties. Toft Rosland indicates that *Apocryphon of John*, with its story of humans' divine origin, permits converts to construct a new genealogy and a new lineage, that goes directly back to God. Conversion is constructed in terms of belonging to a new race, becoming the true heirs of the divine promise, which should make it easier for new Christians to distance themselves from the traditions of their ancestors. This is more about telling the story of a new kin, than about personal, individual change.

How Does Conversion Intersect with Contemporary Practices?

The complexity highlighted in response to the previous questions also comes to bear on contemporary discussions surrounding conversions. Grung's article, on contemporary conversion to Christianity from Islam in Norway, highlights the need for alternative understandings of conversion also in the contemporary context, making space for the social, political and cultural experiences associated with conversion. Her study insists on the legal aspects of conversion in today's context, and is an important reminder that, as much as conversion was a complicated notion in the ancient world, it is also today a contested notion. This is also seen, as Grung notes, in the religious communities' reactions to conversion: both Muslim and Christian faith communities indicate that conversion to one or the other group should include knowledge of the faith one wants to join. The need for such clarification demonstrates that conversion, now and in the past, is connected to a variety of reasons and implies various relationships (to the state, to family, to friends, to faith communities, and to a set of beliefs).

Like Grung, Neutel starts with a contemporary situation, namely a recent legal ruling around male circumcision in Germany. Here, we find an ancient practice, often connected to conversion, discussed in a contemporary setting which focuses on religious freedom and the right to convert. For the case in Cologne, male circumcision of infants or young children is presented as a form of bodily harm, that violates children's rights. The argument that interests Neutel here is the fact that circumcision (both for Jewish and Muslim boys) is seen as restricting freedom of religion for the male children. We notice, here, an evolution in the discourse around religion and conversion: explicitly here, freedom of religion, and thus the idea that conversion is a personal, individual choice, is presented as a key value. In this case, we have moved from an understanding of conversion as a social, cultural, political phenomenon towards an understanding that matches more closely the descriptions of James and Nock, assuming that each individual has the choice to move from one (dissatisfying) religious belonging to another, more satisfying choice. I think it is not surprising that this reappearance of conversion as an individual, personalized choice occurs in a context where "occidental" values can be pitched against "oriental" ones. In fact, ethnic, familial, cultural belonging (which are symbolized through circumcision) are opposed to an adult, free choice of one's religious belongings, implicitly (and unconsciously, perhaps) constructing religions that are not Judaism or Islam as more conscious and enlightened choices. This construction of conversion and of religious choices matches what van den Heever has identified in his article, following the insights of Børgh, namely that James and Nock's understanding of conversion is implicitly tied to conversion to Christianity.

Complexity Unlocked. Now What?

My concluding reflections about the essays in the present volume emphasize the complex dimensions attached to conversion. It is worth exploring it with an intersectional lens (as the authors have done in this volume) because it did not and does not mean the same thing depending on age, gender, social status, familial status, and race. All these dimensions should be considered to complicate our accounts of what conversion is/can be. I am convinced (and the two first articles of the volume highlight this) that the diversity of yesterday, described in the present volume, can make us aware of and attentive to the diversity of today. When one thinks of conversion, one needs to reflect on different modes of conversion for different groups and to keep in mind that one can participate in different religious memberships, without losing one's identity. This volume offers case studies to showcase this diversity of conversion.

While the essays in this volume all place themselves in an intersectional methodology, considering various dimensions affected by conversion, I would add that they are also intersectional because their discussion of conversion intersects with a variety of other topics, which are modified when considered in the light of conversion. I will briefly mention some themes here, not aiming to be exhaustive, but to underline how conversion as a topic can open venues for other discussions. Toft Rosland's analysis of conversion in the light of *Apocryphon of John* also offers pertinent remarks about the passage from martyrdom to monasticism once Christianity becomes the official religion of the empire. When martyrdom is no longer one of the possible consequences of converting to Christianity, the monastic life can be constructed in terms of sacrifice and struggle that builds on the same *topoi* as martyr narratives. Van den Heever's insistence on multiple religious belongings in Antiquity contributes to deconstruct a popular (but outdated) reconstruction of the rapid rise of Christianity as connected to a decline of pagan religion by the first century. The evidences presented by van den Heever show in contrast a flourishing of Greco-Roman religion in the centuries leading up to the establishment of Christianity, which could also partly explain some of the success of Christianity. Solevåg's reflections on the relationship between healing and conversion unmask the problematic construction of the disabled, sick body as a vehicle for sin, in need of forgiveness to become whole again. Both the Methodist narratives of conversion and the New Testament miracle stories mark a preference for able, healthy bodies, a preference one can question today, especially with the tools of disability studies. Hartvigsen's reading of *Joseph and Aseneth* exposes the need for further reflection on the relationship between ritual and conversion. Does Aseneth encounter an early ritual of conversion, and if so, is it a conversion from Egyptian religion to Judaism? Or from Judaism to Christianity? One needs to reflect on the link between narrated ritual and "real" life, and on the impact of a possibly made-up ritual on the construction of identity. The ritual of the story might facilitate the assimilation of change in real life, much as the literary genre of conversion story, such as the one alluded to in the introduction to the volume (the leader of the band Korn), permits to organize in a coherent whole an experience marked by ruptures and transitions.

Finally, when it comes to conversion, one consistent theme that unites the contributions in this volume is a reflection on inclusion/exclusion. Conversion is attached to mechanisms that contribute to create insiders and outsiders. It seemed important to the authors of this volume to show that these mechanisms, now and yesterday, are not dependent solely (and perhaps even mostly) on individual agency and personal choices, but are connected to complex realities, which involve cultural, social, political, and ethnic belongings.

Biographical Note

Since 2013, Valérie Nicolet has been "maîtresse de conférences" at the Institut protestant de théologie (faculté de Paris), where she teaches New Testament and Ancient Greek. In her research, she focuses on the Pauline letters. At the moment, she is working on the rhetorical construction of the law in Galatians. Her scholarship highlights interdisciplinary approaches, more prominently with philosophy, and recently, with queer theory. She has published a book on the construction of the self in Romans, *Constructing the Self: Thinking with Paul and Michel Foucault* (Tübingen: Mohr Siebeck, 2012).

Bibliography

Foucault, Michel, "On the Genealogy of Ethics: An Overview of Work in Progress," 340–72 in *The Foucault Reader*. Edited by Paul Rabinow. York: Pantheon Books, 1984.

Fredriksen, Paula. "Madatory Retirement: Ideas in the Study of Christian Origins Whose Time Has Come to Go," *Studies in Religion* 35.2 (2006): 231–46. https://doi.org/10.1177/000842980603500203

Marchal, Joseph A. "Queer Approaches: Improper Relations with Pauline Letters," 209–27 in *Studying Paul's Letters: Contemporary Perspectives and Methods*. Edited by Joseph A. Marchal. Minneapolis, MN: Fortress Press, 2012. https://doi.org/10.2307/j.ctt22nm6n1.17

Index of References

Hebrew Bible/Old Testament

Genesis		17.15	172	Leviticus	
3.8-24	226	17.20-21	172–3	22.24	127
6.2-4	225	17.23-27	172		
9.18–10.20		21	172	Deuteronomy	
	136	21.2	172	23.2	126
16	172	21.3	178		
16.3	172	21.4	178	Isaiah	
16.13	173	25.9	174	56.4-5	127
16.15	172, 178	41.45	185		
17.5	172	41.50	185	Jeremiah	
17.9-14	172	46.20	185	13.23	136
17.11-13	164				

New Testament

Matthew		Luke		16.27	141
5.30	104–5	14.15-24	105	16.30	141
9.12	104	16.1-9	134	16.31	141
Mark	99, 109–14	Romans		1 Corinthians	
1.1	112–3	9.8	178	1.11	151–2
1.15	109	13.14	157	7	150
1.23-26	109–10	16.1-2	152	7.4	147
1.30-31	109–10			11	149, 152
1.34-39	109	Acts of the Apostles		12.13	156, 157
1.40-44	109–10	8.23-40	123	16.19	152
1.45	110	8.26	125–6		
2.1-10	109, 112	8.27	126, 135	Galatians	
2.17	104, 113	8.28	126	3.27	157
5.1-20	111	8.36	127	3.28	138, 156, 178
5.25-34	110, 112	8.39	132	4.23	178
5.36	112	16	141	4.30	178
9.23-25	112	16.11-16	169		
10.46-52	110–2	16.14	141	2 Timothy	
				3.2	16

Other Ancient References

Josephus
Ant.
1.215-9   173–4
4.290-291 127

Philo of Alexandria
Deus Imm.
111   127

Spec. Leg.
2.344   127
3.40-42   127

Virtues
          192–3

Quran

Sura
2.257   44

Index of Modern Authors

Adamo, David Tuesday 137
Anrich, Gustav 75
Avalos, Hector 114

Baer, Marc David 91, 193
Bagnall, Roger 212 n.1
Bal, Mieke 5
Betcher, Sharon 117
Bøgh, Birgitte 66–9
Boyarin, Daniel 157–8
Bradley, Keith 82–3
Buell, Denise Kimber 192–3, 200, 220
Burchard, Christoph 186–7
Burke, Sean 125–6, 128, 132, 134
Butler, Judith 150–1, 154–8
Byron, Gay L. 136

Chaniotis, Angelos 76
Chesnutt, Randall D. 194
Clark, Elisabeth 178–9
Cliteur, Paul 24–5, 29, 31
Cohen, Shaye 142–3
Collins, John J. 14
Crook, Zeba A. 8–10

Davila, James R. 189
Descartes, René 10
Dibelius, Martin 64–5
Duba, Arlo 127
Dubuisson, Daniel 35
Dunderberg, Ismo 223

Earl, Riggins R. Jr 142–5
Eiesland, Nancy 105, 118

Fink, Uta B. 187
Fischbach, Rahel 48

Foucault, Michel 11, 11 n.38, 72
Fox, Marie 30
Frankfurter, David 84–5
Fredriksen, Paula 4, 111–2, 217, 247
Furey, Constance M. 146

Garber, Marjorie 125
Glancy, Jennifer 181
Gosman, Martin 70–1
Graf, Fritz 78
Grégoire, Henri 238
Gunn, Jeremy 32–3

Haddad, Yvonne Y. 48
Harland, Phil 77
Hassan, Riffat 180
Hill Fletcher, Jeannine 48
Hindmarsh, Bruce 103
Howarth, David J. 72 n.42

James, William 8
Johnson, Lee A. 148–9, 156

Kartzow, Marianne 124, 130–1, 134
Katz, Steven 73
King, Karen 227–9
Kling, David W. 6
Kraemer, Ross Shepard 147–8, 189
Kuefler, Mathew 130
Kugener, Marc-Antoine 238

Leirvik, Oddbjørn 48
Lieu, Judith 15
Lüderitz, Gert 168

MacMullen, Ramsey 13
Madden, Deborah 107–9
Maddox, Randy L. 106
Malina, Bruce 126

Marchal, Joseph 154–5
Martin, Clarice J. 135
Mason, Steve 191–2, 200
McCall, Leslie 124–5, 125 n.7
McClintock Fulkerson, Mary 148
McGuire, Meredith 85
McNeill, John 131
Melhuus, Marit 171
Merkel, Reinhard 25, 29, 31–2
Mitchell, David 104, 111, 113
Montgomery, Robert 101
Moss, Candida 218 n.18
Moxnes, Halvor 124

Nir, Rivka 189–90
Nock, Arthur D. 41, 60–8

Pagels, Elaine 225
Parsons, Mikeal 137
Peeters, Paul 238
Pilch, John 126
Pollack, Miriam 29
Proudfoot, Wayne 73
Pui-Lan, Kwok 56
Putzke, Holm 25, 29, 31–2

Rebillard, Éric 219
Reynolds, Joyce M. 168
Rudolph, Kurt 84

Sänger, Dieter 194
Sarajlic, Eldar 25–7, 29–30, 32
Schüssler Fiorenza, Elisabeth 150, 158, 195
Shauf, Scott 127–8
Singer, Margaret 69
Smith, Jonathan Z. 73 n.46, 74
Snyder, Sharon 104, 111, 113
Spittler, Janet 65–6
Stark, Rodney 114–5
Stavrakakis, Yannis 72 n.42
Stendahl, Krister 8–9
Sterling, Greg 65–6 n.20
Stowers, Stanley K. 219–20

Tambiah, Stanley 34
Terzic, Faruc 47–8
Thiessen, Matthew 163
Thomson, Michael 30
Thorbjørnsrud, Berit 41–2

Vogt, Kari 50

West, Mona 128, 131
Wire, Antoinette Clark 144, 146–7, 149–50
Woodhead, Linda 32–4

Index of Subjects

African theology 136–7
Aggadat Bereshit 176–7
Apocryphon of John, perspective
  of 212–31, 252, 254
  background context 212–21
  conclusion 230–1
  divine origin of humanity 222
  ethnicity and kinship in 223–4,
    252
  gods, hierarchy of 224–6
  gods, retribution by 226–9
  manuscripts 214–5 n.8
  in a monastic context 229–30, 254
  narrative 215–17
Apuleius, *Metamorphoses* 64–5,
  81–3
Arator 130, 135–6
Aristotle 129–30
Aseneth, conversion of 185–208,
  251–2, 254
  classification of
    transformation 190–4
  contexts of the work 188–90
  ethnicity 199–204, 207, 252
  gender role 198–201
  households, changing of 3, 170
  intersectional approach 195–7,
    206
  introduction 185–6
  personality 198–9
  physical change 204–6, 251
  plot 187–8
  texts 186–7
asylum seekers 1–2, 43, 45, 51–4
Augustine, saint 6–7, 36

baptism 2, 75, 135–6
Bede 129–30, 133–4, 136

black people, Christian attitudes
  towards 135–8
blindness 115
body, female *see* women, bodies of
body, modification of *see* castration;
  circumcision; disability in
  conversion

castration 131
  see also Ethiopian Eunuch,
    interpretations of
category crisis concept 125
charitable giving 118–9
children
  in hagiographical
    literature 239–40
  language used 29–30
  religious freedom of 23–6, 31
China 86
Christianity
  Arthur Darby Nock, view
    of 61–3
  black people, attitudes
    towards 135–8
  and circumcision 35–7
  concepts of religion 34–5
  conversion to 53
  conversion to from Islam 51–2
  conversion to Isis cult compared
    with 64–5
  as critical religion 90
  ethnicity and 192, 220–1
  eunuchs and 128–35
  growth in 212–3
  impact on traditional cult 88
  and intermarriage 45
  persecutions 218 n.18, 218–9
  see also Apocryphon of John,

Index of Subjects 261

perspective of; Church of
 Norway (Lutheran); Methodist
 movement; Pentecostal
 Appalachian churches; spatial
 conversion and Porphyry of
 Gaza
Church of Norway (Lutheran) 43–4,
 47, 49, 51, 54
church, temple converted to 239–42
circumcision 21–37, 253
 Christianity and 35–7
 gender and 27–31, 37, 163–4
 intersectional approaches 22,
  27–37, 253
 Judaism and 163–4
 religion, constructions of 31–7
 religious freedom of 23–7, 37,
  253
 slaves and 164, 171–2
classical conception 7–8
Clement of Alexandria 220–1
collective cultures 9
Cologne verdict on religious
 freedom 23–4, 29, 31
Confucianism 86
Constantia, harbor of Gaza 242–3
constructivism 73
conversion 1–17, 248–55
 anachronistic use of 111–2, 191
 communality of 252
 complexity of 1–3, 247–8
 contemporary 252–3
 definitions 4–5, 101–3, 191, 193
 individual vs. group
  membership 41–2, 52
 and mystery religions 61, 67–9,
  85 n.87, 89
 intersectional approach 11–3, 254
 manifestation of 251
 meaning of 3–4, 250–1
 patronage and reciprocity 9–10
 psychological approaches 8–9
 re-thinking religion 13–5
 social-scientific approaches 9
 sources 15–6

subject, understanding of 11
 traditional understandings 6–8
 who could convert 248–50
conversion careers 41–2, 70
critical religion 90
cults *see* mystery religions
culture
 collective cultures 9
 conversion and 71
 definition of 71 n.40
 movements between 56
 religion as 33–4, 86
 Roman 76

deafness 115
Decian persecution 219
depersonalized conversion 142–3
dialogical imagination 56
dialogue 47–9
diasporical consciousness 56
Dionysus, cult of 79 n.71, 79–80,
 147–8
disability in conversion 99–119,
 251, 254
 definitions used 100–2
 early Methodist
  movement 102–9, 119
 gender and disability 116
 health care in the early Christian
  movement 113–5, 251
 impairments, views of 115–6,
  116–9
 Mark, gospel of, healing
  in 109–4
disaspora settings 73–4 n.47
divided self 8

emotions 8
Encyclopedia Britannica 74
*Encyclopedia of the Bible and its
 Reception* 65
Ephraem of Syria 136
Ethiopian Eunuch, interpretations
 of 123–38, 248–9
 ethnic identity 135–8

262   *The Complexity of Conversion*

gender and sexual identity 128–32, 249
identities, ambivalence of 123–6
intersectional approaches 124–5
religious identity 126–8
social status 132–5
ethnicity
   and conversion 14, 191–3
   of the Ethiopian Eunuch 135–8
   ethnic reasoning by Christians 220–1
   Hebrew, of Aseneth 195–7, 199–204, 207
   and kinship 223–4
eunuchs *see* Ethiopian Eunuch, interpretations of
Eusebius 131

female bodies *see* women, bodies of
female genital mutilation (FGM) 28
food, consumption of 199, 202–4
forced converts 16
freedom, religious
   children and 31–2
   gender discrimination 27–9
   male circumcision and 23–7, 37
friends, influence of 50

Gaza 236, 238–44
gender
   in antiquity 129–30, 154
   circumcision and 27–31, 37, 163–4
   and disability 116
   discrimination on basis of 27–9
   early Christian views 129–32
   Ethiopian Eunuch, interpretations of 128–32, 249
   female body norms 150–1, 154–8
   language of 29–31, 37
   roles of Aseneth 198–201
   stereotypes 16
Genesis Rabbah 175, 177
glossolalic women 148–9
Gnosticism 215 n.9

gods and *Ap. John*
   hierarchy of gods 224–6
   relationships with humans 217–8
   retribution by gods 226–9
Gospel of Thomas 129
Great Dinner, parable of 105
Greco-Roman religions *see* mystery religions

Hagar, slave girl 162–81, 249
   circumcision, gender challenge of 163–4
   conclusion 179–81
   intersectional approaches 165–70, 179–80
   slaves, conversion of 164–5, 249
   texts on 171–9
hagiographical works *see* spatial conversion and Porphyry of Gaza
hair, covering of 152–3
healing and salvation 105–6
health care 101, 106–9, 113–9
Hebrew ethnicity 195–7, 201–4, 207
honeycomb of life 203–4
households, conversion of 3, 141–4, 158–9, 170
human rights 44
humanity, divine origin of 222
hymns 103–5

identity
   ambivalence of 123–6
   gender and 128–32, 249
   multiple religious identity 55
   performance of 71, 71 n.40
   religious 126–8
imperial cult 77, 79 n.71, 79–80
initiation rituals 75, 78, 82, 87–8, 194
   see also baptism; circumcision; purification rituals
initiations, multiple 86–9
inscriptions, monumental 86–9
intermarriage 45, 50–1, 55
intersectional approaches 11–3

to Aseneth 195–7, 206
to circumcision 22, 27–37, 253
to conversion 165–7, 169–70, 254
to disability 100–2, 115–6
to the Ethiopian Eunuch 124–5
to Hagar, slave girl 165–70, 179–80
intracategorical complexity 124–5, 125 n.7
introspection 8
Isis, cult of 64, 82–3
Islam 45, 50–3, 180–1
Islamic Council of Norway 43–4, 46–7, 49, 51

Jerome 136
Jesus Christ 104–5, 109–11, 117, 130
John Chrysostom 133
Joseph and Aseneth see Aseneth, conversion of
Judaism
  and circumcision 163–4
  conversion in 65–6 n.20
  of the Ethiopian Eunuch 126–7, 134
  eunuchs and 126–8
  in the Graeco-Roman world 191
  household conversion in 142
  leprosy in 115
  see also Hebrew ethnicity
Justin Martyr 36, 131

Lactantius 129
Life of Porphyry of Gaza see spatial conversion and Porphyry of Gaza
Livia, wife of Augustus 152–4 nn.43-44

madness 108
Maiouma, harbor of Gaza 242–3
Mark the Deacon *see* spatial conversion and Porphyry of Gaza
marriage 189, 197

see also intermarriage
medicine 106–9
Methodist movement 99, 102–9, 119
  healing as conversion metaphor 103–5
  medicine 106–9
  theology 105–6
midrash haggadah 174–7
missionary activity 43, 51
mystery religions 59–91, 254
  A. D. Nock, influence of 60–8
  conversion, definitions and description of 61, 67–70, 85 n.87, 89
  example of Apuleius, Lucius and *The Metamorphoses* 81–3
  multiple initiations 86–9
  mysteries, redescription of 74–80
  primal and critical religions 89–91
  religion, redescription of 70–4
  syncretism and conversion 84–6

Nag Hammadi Codices 214 n.7
  see also Apocryphon of John, perspective of
names, changing of 171–2
narrative prosthesis 104, 113
Norway, right to conversion in 40–57, 252
  asylum seekers 1–2, 43, 45, 51–4
  challenges of conversion 56
  church and state in Norway 54
  conversions in Norway 49–53, 252
  definitions of conversion 41–2, 52
  joint declaration, authority of 45–9
  joint declaration, Islamic and Christian 43–5
  multiple religious identity 55
  pluralism in Norway 53–6

Onesimus 164–5
oriental cults *see* mystery religions
Oxford Handbook of Gender and Politics 195
Oxford Handbook of Religious Conversion 4–5, 41–2, 191, 193

patronage 9–10
Paul, saint
    body, views of 117–8
    and circumcision 35–6
    conversion of 6–9
    on slave mothers 178
    and women 146, 149–52, 155–7
Pentecostal Appalachian churches 148–9
performance
    of identity 71, 71 n.40
    and mystery religions 76 n.56, 76–7, 79–80
persecutions 218 n.18, 218–9
Phrygianum, Rome 86–7
physician, Christ as 104–5
Pirqe d'Rabbi Eliezer, "Horeb," 29 176
politically motivated conversion 50–1
Porphyry of Gaza *see* spatial conversion and Porphyry of Gaza
primal religion 62, 89–90
prophetic religion 62
psychology 8–9
purification rituals 202

Queer Bible Commentary 131

Rabbinic texts 174–7
race *see* ethnicity
re-naming 171–2
reciprocity 9–10
religion
    concepts of 13–5, 70–1
    constructions of 31–7
    definitions of 32–4
    primal 62, 89–90
    as social discourse 71–3, 72 n.42
right to conversion *see* Norway, right to conversion in
Roman mystery cults 76–80, 77 n.61, 79 n.71
Rome, Italy 86–7

salvation, healing of 106
sin and disability 105, 115–6, 118
slave girls *see* Hagar, slave girl
slaves 16, 132–5, 142–3 n.5, 144–5, 164–5
social-scientific approaches 9
sociology of religion 69
Sozomenus 242
spatial conversion and Porphyry of Gaza 235–44, 249–50
    conversion of temple to church 239–42
    Gaza and the harbor of Maiouma 242–4
    Gaza, description of 238–9
    text and the author 236–8
supernatural characteristics 204–6
syncretism and conversion 84–6

temple, conversion to church 239–42
tongue-speaking women 148–9
tricksters 144–5

veiling of women 152–3
victimhood 30
virginity 157–8, 197
virtuous suffering 118
vocation 8–9

Wesley, John 102–4, 106–7
    Primitive Physic 107–8
women, bodies of 150–8
    ancient views of 129–30
    female genital mutilation (FGM) 28
    and gender norms 150–1, 154–5, 156–8

hair of 152–3
in missions of Paul 151–2, 155–7
new sex, creation of 154
social constructs 30
veiling of women 152–3
women, conversion of 141–59, 249
  bodies and power 150–8
  household conversions 141–4, 158–9
  power relationships 144–6
  speaking in tongues 148–9
  women in conversion 146–9, 249
    see also Aseneth, conversion of; Hagar, slave girl

Yalkut Shimoni 176

Studies in Ancient Religion and Culture

Series Editors:
Philip L. Tite, University of Washington
Michael Ng, Seattle University
https://www.equinoxpub.com/home/studies-in-ancient-religion-and-culture/

Published:
Death's Dominion: Power, Identity, and Memory at the Fourth-Century Martyr Shrine
Nathaniel J. Morehouse

Social and Cognitive Perspectives on the Sermon on the Mount
Edited by Rikard Roitto, Colleen Shantz, and Petri Luomanen

The Complexity of Conversion: Intersectional Perspectives on Religious Change in Antiquity and Beyond
Edited by Valérie Nicolet and Marianne Bjelland Kartzow

Theorizing "Religion" in Antiquity
Edited by Nickolas P. Roubekas

Forthcoming:
Critical Theory and Early Christianity
Edited by Matthew G. Whitlock

John Cassian and the Creation of Monastic Subjectivity
Joshua Schachterle

Re-Reading the Visions in *The Shepherd of Hermas*
Angela Kim Harkins

The Material of Christian Apocrypha
Edited by Janet E. Spittler

www.ingramcontent.com/pod-product-compliance
Lightning Source LLC
Chambersburg PA
CBHW050843230426
43667CB00012B/2126